Labour Relations:
The Unionized Workplace

Laurence M. Olivo and
Peter McKeracher

2005
EMOND MONTGOMERY PUBLICATIONS
TORONTO, CANADA

Emond Montgomery Publications Limited
60 Shaftesbury Avenue
Toronto ON M4T 1A3
http://www.emp.ca/highered

Printed in Canada.
Reprinted September 2014.

We acknowledge the financial support of the Government of Canada through the Canada Book Fund for our publishing activities.

The events and characters depicted in this book are fictitious. Any similarity to actual persons, living or dead, is purely coincidental.

Acquisitions editor: Bernard Sandler

Developmental editor: Sarah Gleadow

Marketing manager: Christine Davidson

Director, sales and marketing, higher education: Kevin Smulan

Production supervisor: Jim Lyons

Cover designer: John Vegter

Library and Archives Canada Cataloguing in Publication

Olivo, Laurence M., 1946-

    Labour relations : the unionized workplace / Larry Olivo, Peter McKeracher.

Includes index.
ISBN 978-1-55239-112-9

    1. Industrial relations—Canada—Textbooks.   I. McKeracher, Peter   II. Title.

KE3170.O44 2004   331'.0971   C2004-907474-1
KF3390.O44 2004

For Joyce, as always. — L.O.

Contents

Preface vii

CHAPTER 1
The Labour Movement 1

Introduction 1

Historical Development of
Labour Organizations 1

Labour Movement Theories
and Philosophies 20

The Structure and Function
of Trade Unions 31

Chapter Summary 40

Websites 40

Review Questions 41

Case Studies 41

CHAPTER 2
The Labour Relations System 43

Introduction 43

The Framework for Analysis 43

The Craig Model as a Tour of the
Labour Relations Landscape 47

The Constitutional and Legal
Environment of Labour Relations 56

Federal and Provincial Labour Legislation 61

Chapter Summary 64

Review Questions 64

Discussion Questions 65

CHAPTER 3
Organizing a Workplace 67

Introduction 67

Why Workers Organize 67

Organizing the Workplace 68

Eligibility To Be Organized 71

Rights and Responsibilities
During Organization 77

Unfair Labour Practices
During Organization 77

Determining an Appropriate
Bargaining Unit 82

Determining the Wishes of Employees 86

Certification Procedures 86

Voluntary Recognition 92

Bars to Certification 93

Terminating the
Bargaining Relationship 94

Succession Rights 96

Related Employers 97

Chapter Summary 99

Review Questions 99

Discussion Questions 100

Case Study 100

CHAPTER 4
Negotiating a Collective Agreement 103

Introduction 103

Theoretical Approaches to
Bargaining: An Overview 103

The Process of Negotiations 108

Good-Faith Bargaining and
Bad-Faith Bargaining 118

Third-Party Assistance 121

Third-Party Determination 124

Settlement Stages Data 131

Industrial Action 132

Chapter Summary 146

Review Questions 147

Discussion Questions 148

CHAPTER 5
Administering a Collective Agreement 149
Introduction 149
Structure and Provisions of a
    Collective Agreement 149
The Grievance Process 161
Commonly Grieved "Rights" Issues 170
Arbitration 182
Principal Features of the
    Arbitration Process in Canada 183
Dispute Resolution Options 193
Chapter Summary 195
Review Questions 195
Discussion Questions 196
Case Studies 196

CHAPTER 6
Federal Labour Relations 199
Introduction 199
Scope of Federal Regulation 199
Determination of Federal Versus
    Provincial Jurisdiction 202
Canada Labour Code 204
Canada Industrial Relations Board 204
Contrast with Ontario Law 205
Chapter Summary 208
Review Questions 208
Discussion Questions 208
Case Study 209

CHAPTER 7
Public Sector Bargaining 211
Introduction 211
Federal Public Sector 211
Provincial Public Sector 212
Chapter Summary 219
Review Questions 220
Discussion Questions 220

CHAPTER 8
Employment Standards 221
Introduction 221
Employment Standards and the Collective
    Bargaining Process: Then and Now 221
Union Obligation To Enforce
    Employment Standards 222
Union Agreements on Matters Covered
    by Employment Standards 223
The Employment Standards 224
Chapter Summary 231
Review Questions 232
Discussion Questions 233
Case Study 233

CHAPTER 9
Emerging Trends in Labour Relations 235
Introduction 235
Changes in the Workplace 235
Political Changes 236
Economic Changes 238
Social Changes 240
Technological Change 245
Effects of Workplace Changes on Unions 249
The Impact on Bargaining: An Overview 261
Chapter Summary 263
Review Questions 263
Discussion Questions 263

APPENDIX
**Case Study: Negotiating a
Collective Agreement** 265
Introduction 265
Background 265
Data 266
Procedure 267
Collective Agreement 268

GLOSSARY 291

INDEX 297

Preface

As teachers of labour relations subjects in human resources management programs and other labour-related programs at the college level, we had long felt that there was a need for a text that dealt with the legal aspects of labour relations in a practical way, taking into account current workplace practices and realities. Some texts currently in use we found overly simplistic; others, though interesting to us, were more academic than we thought would be useful for students with goals in the labour relations area.

So we have taken matters into our own hands, and this text is the result. We have aimed to be clear and succinct, while explaining what lies behind various practices and procedures in labour relations. We have also included many practical exercises and case studies, so that students can apply what they have learned and monitor their own understanding. As to the extent of our success, time will tell.

Laurence M. Olivo, Seneca College
Peter McKeracher, Durham College

CHAPTER 1

The Labour Movement

INTRODUCTION

This book is a practical guide to the labour relations system, which involves unions and their members on the one hand and employers and employers' organizations on the other.[1] Labour relations encompass union organizing, workplace certification, negotiation of collective agreements, strikes and lockouts, administration of collective agreements, and grievances, as well as more informal aspects of the relationship between union and management.

Those workers who are not unionized have a different relationship with the employer from unionized workers, both legally in terms of the employment contract, and in terms of other rights and responsibilities. Although there will be references to some of these differences from time to time, this text is primarily concerned with unionized employees and workplaces.

In this chapter we will examine the labour movement by first looking at how labour unions developed historically. We will then examine theories about why workers join unions and what factors affect how unions operate. Lastly, we will examine the structure and function of the labour movement in Canada.

HISTORICAL DEVELOPMENT OF LABOUR ORGANIZATIONS

In the Western world, unions can trace their origins back to the medieval craft guilds. The guilds were organizations of craftsmen who held a monopoly over the practice of their craft—for example, weaving. From this monopoly came the right to set working conditions, wages, and prices of the product, to admit or deny entry to the craft, and to control progress through its ranks. However, guilds were largely in the hands of masters, who were proprietors of their own businesses, and who employed journeymen and apprentices. It was this feature of ownership that distinguished guilds, where some workers were proprietors, from unions, where workers are all employees.

As modern capitalism developed, so did the ideas of competition, reinvestment of earnings, and risk protective devices such as limited liability corporations. This in turn allowed for greater capital accumulation and investment, which fostered economic growth, the development of national and international markets, and competition. In this context, many workers ceased to control and own the means of production; instead, they hired out their skills and labour to proprietors.

---

1   The term "industrial relations" is also used to describe this system, but it is an older term and less apt. It obscures the growing importance and impact of unionized workplaces in the service and public sectors, where union activity has increased.

By the late 18th century in Great Britain, and to a lesser extent in Europe, face-to-face relations between master and journeyman were being replaced by the more impersonal relationships of the factory system. As capitalism evolved, three conditions were in place that gave rise to modern trade unionism:

- workers ceased to own or control the resources they used in creating goods or services,

- wages and working conditions were determined solely by competitive market forces, and

- the state did not regulate or control any aspect of the workplace.[2]

In these circumstances, when wages fell and working conditions deteriorated, workers responded collectively. In Canada, there were sporadic attempts to organize local unions in the early to mid-19th century (between 1812 and 1850) in the most "industrialized" parts of Canada: the centres of the lumber, shipping, and ship-building trades in New Brunswick and Nova Scotia. Compared with other, smaller businesses in the rest of Canada, these industries employed relatively large workforces and were sensitive to competition and economic cycles, which resulted in wage and employment instability. Workers responded by trying to stabilize their situation and increase their economic security through collective bargaining.

As Canada's economy became wealthier, more complex, and more industrialized in the mid-19th century, more complicated and permanent forms of labour organization began to emerge, giving rise to modern Canadian unions.

Trade Unionism in Canada: Competing Visions

In the preceding section we identified some of the factors that gave rise to trade unionism as a worker response to changes in the economy and the workplace. However, there is no one trade union response or movement. Some employers and some of their political allies often speak of "the unions" as if they were a single, unified economic and political entity. They are not. Unions do value solidarity and often act collectively in pursuit of some goals (for example, they try to speak with one voice through a national labour federation such as the Canadian Labour Congress [CLC]). But the reality is that there is much diversity in the labour movement on a number of core issues and ideas, which we will examine below.

POLITICAL NEUTRALITY AND POLITICAL ACTIVISM

There has long been a debate in Canada and the United States about whether and to what extent labour organizations ought to be involved in politics. In Europe, by

---

2   These three economic factors were identified by the famous husband and wife team of Beatrice and Sidney Webb as essential preconditions for the formation of trade unions. Their observations and theories were set out in a variety of publications that advocated a politically conscious trade union movement. They were, not surprisingly, among the founders of the British Labour Party at the beginning of the 20th century. Their principal works, setting out an analysis of the forces that support the formation of trade unions and how these unions should operate, are *The History of Trade Unionism* (New York: Longmans, 1894) and *Industrial Democracy* (New York: Longmans, 1897).

contrast, there has long been a formal relationship between unions and political parties and movements.

In Europe, workers have defined themselves as working class and have identified with political parties that reflect their interests and aspirations, such as democratic socialist and communist parties; in some cases, the relationship has been with religious group, such as the Catholic worker parties in Germany and Italy. In Europe, a stratified, class-based society developed, and a conscious and intentional class-based politics emerged from the European scene.

But in the United States and Canada, the pattern has been different. In the United States, the Jeffersonian myth of the independent yeoman farmer, and the assumptions about individual liberty flowing from the American Revolution, formed the basis for a new ideology. This ideology advocated political, social, economic, and legal equality where individuals were not defined or constrained by a stratified class system.

These values have also affected Canada, though not as strongly. For example, Canada, having non-revolutionary origins, had a more conservative social and political order. As a result, working-class interests were more sharply defined. As well, in the late 19th century, as modern labour organizations were beginning to develop, the influence of British and working-class migrants, who had experience with unions that were overtly political, carried over into the Canadian labour movement to a greater extent than in the United States. That legacy can still be seen in the link between the New Democratic Party (NDP) and the Canadian Labour Congress, and a number of its union affiliates. In that relationship, unions have had official status within the party organization, and have been an important source of party financing. But this connection between unions and leftist parties is less robust than the one found in Europe, though more robust than anything currently found in the United States. There, a weaker relationship exists between some unions and the Democratic Party.

In Europe, the relationship between the unions and labour parties has begun to change. As Europe has grown more prosperous, the relationship appears to be weakening. The role of unions, for example, in the "New Labour" Party in Great Britain in the 21st century is much less prominent than it was in the 20th century, when unions formed an integral part of the structure of the Labour Party. Not surprisingly, the socialist and working-class ideology that once dominated the party's policies has declined in influence. It has been replaced by what Labour Party policymakers now refer to as "pragmatism."

Against this background, there has been a long-running debate between proponents of **business unionism** (also called "bread and butter unionism") and proponents of revolutionary unionism (more accurately called **political unionism**). Political unionism asserts that unions should be involved with political issues.

Business unionists have often come from the unionized skilled crafts, whose members are generally well paid. Business unionists have the bargaining power to negotiate good agreements: they are skilled workers and cannot easily be replaced if they strike. Their members tend to be inherently conservative and unconcerned with broader political issues or working-class solidarity. They are usually not connected to any political party, and their members may vote for conservative rather than leftist or centre-left parties. Their concerns are almost exclusively focused on negotiation and enforcement of their collective agreement in pursuit of their own, narrowly defined self-interest.

Political unionism, on the other hand, is more closely associated with **industrial unions**, which organize the less skilled on an industry-wide basis. In the early 20th century, some of these broad-based unions, particularly in western Canada, were Marxist and revolutionary in their politics. Later in the 20th century, and up to the present, some unions, such as the Canadian Auto Workers (CAW) and the Canadian Union of Public Employees (CUPE), separately and through labour federations have maintained a connection to national and provincial politics. This connection was first made through the Co-operative Commonwealth Federation (CCF) and later through the New Democratic Party. More recently, union political activity has bypassed political parties in favour of direct action and alliance with other, non-party organizations, as was the case for mobilization on issues having to do with free trade and globalization.

LOCAL, NATIONAL, AND INTERNATIONAL LABOUR ORGANIZATIONS

Early union organizations were local, often stand-alone organizations focused on one employer, or one industry in a city or town. In time, with industrialization and the development of a national economy, local unions expanded, setting up local offices, or "locals," to deal with employers in different towns or cities. For example, the Carpenters and Joiners Union established a head office and set up locals for the members of the union in several different cities. Truly local unions consisting of one group of workers with one collective agreement are very rare today, but were a feature of early unions in Canada.

Expansion of local unions took other forms. Because unionization was more advanced and mature in Great Britain, some British unions, such as the Amalgamated Engineers, established branches in Canada. These were founded by British migrants who brought with them the labour organizations they knew. But of greater significance was the expansion of American unions into Canada. The primary reason for this expansion was that American unions followed US employers when they established branch plants in Canada, as was the case with some of the railway, automotive, mining, and manufacturing unions. The secondary reason for the expansion was that wages were lower in Canada. This trend alarmed international unions, who feared that US jobs would be lost and so acted to retain and create jobs in the United States. These unions sought to organize Canadian workers, and included them in transborder negotiations in order to raise Canadian wage levels. Reducing the wage differential, they reasoned, would make branch plants in Canada less attractive.

Although internationals, such as the United Steel Workers of America (USWA) and the Service Employees International Union (SEIU), and **craft unions**, such as the International Brotherhood of Electrical Workers (IBEW), continue to be active on the Canadian labour scene, there is some ambivalence and hostility to them in Canada, particularly on the part of national unions. They complain that the internationals interfered with the activities of Canadian locals, and acted in ways that were not in the interests of Canadian members. Another problem involved Canadian national unions competing with internationals to organize workers at a particular plant or in a particular industry. Some of these "raids" have increased the friction between nationals and internationals, as when the IBEW tried to organize the postal workers when the postal bargaining unit was reorganized; similarly, the SEIU has suffered losses of members at the hands of raids by affiliates of the Canadian Auto Workers. The tensions between the international and national (often public sector) unions are muted but they do continue, with friction most evident in labour federations.

CRAFT AND INDUSTRIAL UNIONS

As noted earlier, craft unions are among the oldest in Canada. The members of the skilled trades already had a sense of camaraderie as tradesmen, and reached a stage where acting collectively as employees was a natural extension of that camaraderie. Many of these unions were well established by the start of the 20th century and were successful at advancing their members' interests. They were primarily interested in advancing the employment interests of their members and maintaining exclusive monopolies over their work and over membership. They were not overtly political, and to the extent that they engaged in politics, they were often conservative. Thus, they backed political parties that advanced the interests of their members, rather than the interests of labour as a whole, let alone the less fortunate members of society.

However, as workplaces became larger, complex, skilled work was broken down into jobs requiring fewer skills. Workforces became larger, and also less skilled, so that many plants and other workplaces increasingly employed largely unskilled or semi-skilled workers. In the face of these changes, the craft unions, representing skilled workers, were uninterested in organizing or assisting these workers. And these workers saw the craft unions as irrelevant, and responded by creating new employee organizations, the industrial unions. These unions organized all workers in one large industry or with one large employer. For example, unions such as the International Workers of the World (IWW) and One Big Union (OBU) were successful in the early years of the 20th century in organizing workers in forestry, mining, and heavy industry in western Canada and the western United States. The industrial unions also tended to have a Marxist and revolutionary view of politics.

By the 1930s, the craft unions in the American Federation of Labour (AFL) hesitantly provided some support for the new Committee for Industrial Organizations (CIO), which was assisting in organizing auto workers in the United States and Canada. Nonetheless, the industrial unions and the craft unions engaged in jurisdictional battles over which organization should represent workers in certain industries. For example, unions of skilled metal workers did not want to lose members who worked in an automobile plant to an industrial union.

Another issue involved politics. The craft unions were often apolitical, but industrial unions were often involved in politics and in alliances with other left-wing organizations. In the United States, after the 1930s, this meant an association with the Democratic Party, and in Canada, with the New Democrats. These different approaches to politics continued to divide industrial and craft unions within labour federations.

QUEBEC AND OTHER CANADIAN UNIONS

The Canadian labour environment is further complicated by the largely separate development of unions in Quebec. Industrialization came later to Quebec than to some other parts of Canada, so early unions in Quebec operated on a smaller scale, and in a more rural environment. Another factor was the early involvement of the Catholic Church in the trade union movement in Quebec. In part this was a response to a papal encyclical, *Rerum Novarum*, which recognized the right of workers to organize so as not to be treated as a commodity. It was also due in part to the desire of politicians to insulate Quebec from some of the forces of secularism and modernity, including outside labour unions, particularly Marxist-oriented ones. As a result, unions in Quebec developed on largely confessional lines, with many unions part of a Catholic union federation and a smaller group outside the federation. But the 1949 Asbestos Strike caused a re-examination of Quebec unionism by workers, resulting in a growing secularization, greater militancy, and stronger links with the rest of the Canadian union movement. However, Quebec unions remain largely separate from major Canadian unions and labour federations.

JURISDICTIONAL ISSUES

It is logically not possible for the same group of workers in a workplace to be represented by more than one union. In fact, labour legislation sets out rules for recognizing a union as an exclusive bargaining agent for a group of workers, and regulates the competition between unions to represent workers. The legislation is in part the result of the positions taken by the major labour federations: the American Federation of Labour, its ally, the Canadian Labour Congress, and the CLC's predecessors. These federations espoused the concept of **exclusive jurisdiction**, which in the context of craft union organization meant that one union would organize all workers in a particular craft or trade. Accordingly, these federations opposed the concept of **dual unionism**, in which one union might represent workers in several crafts. Dual unionism occurred more frequently with the advent of industrial unions, first in the West in the early part of the 20th century, and then in the industrial heartland in the 1930s and 1940s. Industrial unions organized all workers in an industry, but also sometimes sought to organize craft workers who were technically within the jurisdiction of another union.

Historically, there has been tension between international unions and domestic unions. Internationals have entered Canada and sought to represent workers who may have been represented by national or local unions. Domestic unions have returned the compliment by raiding groups represented by the internationals. Similarly, there has been tension between craft and industrial unions, where industrial unions have sought to represent all the workers in an industry or plant, including skilled workers represented by craft unions. Pacts and agreements have been made between unions or within labour federations to regulate these conflicts, often by requiring member unions to adhere to a policy of exclusive recognition. Under this policy, all unions promise not to raid the members of other unions at the expiry of their collective agreements. However, these agreements have often been more honoured in the breach than in the observance and have caused schisms within the labour movement.

Alphabet Soup: An Overview of Labour Organizations

Labour unions and their federations are often known by their acronyms. Table 1.1 lists the acronyms for the major Canadian and American federations and provides a few facts about each. Table 1.2 lists the acronyms for Quebec labour organizations, whose history has been largely separate from the rest of the country. It also provides a short summary.

TABLE 1.1 Canadian and American Labour Federations and Acronyms

ACCL   *All-Canadian Congress of Labour*
- founded in 1927, merged with Canadian Congress of Labour in 1940
- politically active, nationalist, and opposed to American influences through international unions
- favoured industrial unions

AFL   *American Federation of Labour*
- founded in 1886, merged with Congress of Industrial Organizations in 1955
- composed primarily of craft unions, with little control over affiliates;
- generally not active in politics and conservative in political orientation

AFL-CIO   *American Federation of Labour and Congress of Industrial Organizations*
- founded in 1955 as merger of AFL and CIO, the latter having been expelled by AFL in 1938
- agreements made not to raid other unions in federation
- composed of both craft and industrial unions, but has little control over affiliates
- conservative in politics, but generally supports Democratic Party

CCL   *Canadian Congress of Labour*
- founded in 1940, and composed of remnants of ACCL
- focused on organizing unskilled workers and on industrial unions
- nationalist in orientation and favoured government intervention in the economy
- had connections with American CIO, housing branches of international industrial unions, but favoured loosening US control over Canadian branches of international unions

CFL (no. 1)   *Canadian Federation of Labour*
- one of two labour federations of this name
- founded in 1908, was nationalist and regional in nature
- composed of Canadian unions and favoured Canadian control of the labour movement

CFL (no. 2)   *Canadian Federation of Labour*
- founded in 1982
- composed primarily of construction unions, which had sought more voting power in the Canadian Labour Congress
- closer relations with government of the day than had CLC
- generally non-partisan in politics

(The table is continued on the next page.)

TABLE 1.1   Continued

CIO   *Congress of Industrial Organizations*
- founded originally as Committee for Industrial Organization within AFL
- expelled from AFL in 1938
- favoured organizing unskilled workers and formation of industrial unions in the United States, as well as in Canada through internationals
- more active in politics than AFL and generally supported Democratic Party
- combined again with AFL in 1955

CLC   *Canadian Labour Congress*
- a merger of the conservative Trades and Labour Congress and the more politically active CCL in 1956
- members agreed not to raid affiliated unions
- like AFL-CIO, composed of craft and industrial unions, but less conservative than AFL-CIO
- has formal links to NDP
- strong supporter of local self-government for Canadian branches of international unions

IWW   *Industrial Workers of the World*
- founded in 1905
- also referred to as the "Wobblies"
- group of radical, industrial unions active in first quarter of the 20th century in western Canada and the United States

OBU   *One Big Union*
- founded in 1919 and absorbed into CLC in 1956
- composed of industrial workers, mainly in western Canada
- rejected conservative politics of TLC and craft unions, and embraced radical politics of IWW

TLC   *Trades and Labor Congress*
- founded in 1886, composed mainly of conservative craft unions and much influenced by AFL
- merged with CCL to form CLC in 1956

The Historical Development of Canadian Unions

As noted, there were some early local attempts at labour organization, primarily of craft workers as early as 1812 and mainly in the maritime provinces. These isolated groups formed where individual members saw themselves as a group with common interests, perhaps facing a common threat. But it was not until industrialization proceeded, with larger employers employing larger numbers of workers, that modern labour organizations began to develop. They took on recognizable forms in about the last quarter of the 19th century.

TABLE 1.2   Quebec Labour Federations and Acronyms

CCCL   *Canadian Catholic Confederation of Labour*
- founded in 1921
- focused on keeping member unions French speaking and Catholic
- dominated by the clergy until the 1940s, when it became more secular and more assertive
- reformed as Confederation of National Trade Unions in 1960

CDU   *Confederation of Democratic Unions*
- founded in 1972 as a breakaway of conservative unions not in agreement with the radicalism of CNTU
- conservative politically, not very active on Quebec labour scene

CNTU   *Confederation of National Trade Unions*
- founded in 1960 as a secular reformation of CCCL
- became radicalized in 1970s

QFL   *Quebec Federation of Labour*
- founded in 1956
- works in loose alliance with CNTU and is CLC Quebec affiliate

ORIGINS: 1872-1900

In pre-industrial Canada, unions developed slowly, beginning with craft unions in centres of industrialization. Among the earliest to organize were printers unions in Montreal, Toronto, and Hamilton, leading in 1872 to two local organizations joining a labour federation, the International Typographical Union. These unions and unions of other skilled craftsmen emerged to combat growing competitive pressures, which worked to lower wages and pit workers against other workers. The skilled crafts were the earliest to effectively unionize locally and link their locals in federated unions because they were literate, well informed, and had skills that facilitated labour organizing. And because they were skilled, they could use the strike weapon effectively, as they could not easily be replaced.

In a number of trades, federations of union locals began to develop, as did federations of unions in a city or region. For example, 15 craft union locals in Toronto formed the Toronto Trades Assembly (TTA) in the 1870s. The TTA campaigned for the 9-hour workday for labour, and also for the passage of the federal *Trades Union Act* and the *Criminal Law Amendment Act, 1872*. These two pieces of legislation helped to free unions from legal constraints. For example, before this new legislation, the common law criminalized union attempts to organize workers and negotiate collective agreements by characterizing these activities as criminal conspiracies in restraint of trade.

The Toronto Trades Assembly quickly expanded to form an association of all labour organizations in Ontario called the Central Labour Union, a first attempt at a homegrown regional federation. Unfortunately, the movement faltered as a result of a severe economic depression in the late 1870s.[3]

---

3   H.A. Logan, *Trade Unionism in Canada* (Toronto: Macmillan of Canada, 1949), 43-45.

International labour federations appeared in Canada in this period. Though American federations would later predominate, the earliest ones were British: the Amalgamated Society of Carpenters and Joiners, and the Amalgamated Society of Engineers. However, in the evolution of the union movement, the association with British unions was a dead end. Because the Canadian economy was closely linked to that of the United States, American unions saw Canadian workers as we today see workers in Mexico: a low-wage, competitive threat. American companies set up Canadian plants to jump the Canadian tariff barriers set up as part of the National Policy of John A. Macdonald's Conservative government and also to take advantage of lower Canadian wages. The response of some American unions was to follow the common employer northward and organize Canadian labour. This pattern emerged as early as the 1860s with the movement of shoemakers, and then iron moulders, into southern Ontario, which was emerging as Canada's industrial and manufacturing centre.

The largest of these federations in the early period was the Knights of Labor. This union was quite different from other international unions. It was the first American labour federation in the United States composed of locals in a variety of crafts and trades, and mixed locals, which included skilled and unskilled workers. In fact, it issued a general invitation to all workers, white collar and blue collar, to join locals, as if a local were a social organization like Kiwanis or the Masons. Prior to this, attempts at federation were made by forging links between locals in a particular craft or trade, to the exclusion of those in other crafts or trades. The Knights of Labour was among the earliest prototypes of the industrial unions that sought to organize unskilled workers by plant or by industry. However, at the time the Knights were setting up mixed, all-inclusive locals, they did not grasp that meeting the needs of a wide variety of workers in one local would be extremely difficult. Internal conflicts resulted and members came and went relatively quickly, leading to the demise of the Knights in both Canada and the United States by the beginning of the 20th century.

In Canada, the Knights of Labor established its first unit in Hamilton in 1875. A decade and a half later, it had about 250 local assemblies, organized into 7 district assemblies, with major strength in Ontario and Quebec. Its growth in Quebec was largely because it did not require workers to be members of a craft, nor did it focus only on industrial workers. Instead, by welcoming all workers, it was particularly suited to Quebec, which was more agricultural than industrial. It also gave up its insistence on secret initiation practices and oaths, making it more attractive to Quebec Catholic workers. This established a basis and laid the groundwork for the linking together of Quebec Catholic unions as the Canadian Catholic Confederation of Labour, which later evolved into a secular organization, Quebec's Confederation of National Trade Unions.[4] In fact, the Knights' greatest strength was in Quebec, and even after it faded away in the United States, it continued to operate in Quebec and other parts of Canada. The Knights went beyond bread and butter unionism, which focused on getting and enforcing a collective agreement, and embraced the general and moral welfare of its members, including their political interests. It finally died out in Canada after losing several strikes in the

---

4   A.W. Craig and N. Solomon, *The System of Industrial Relations in Canada*, 5th ed. (Scarborough, ON: Prentice Hall, 1996), 115.

first decade of the 20th century. But some of its characteristics—an interest in members' general well-being and a policy of inclusiveness—were to resurface later in the 20th century in other labour organizations.

While the Knights of Labor was an early form of an evolving labour movement, it was also a member, along with other unions, of Canada's first permanent national federation, the Trades and Labor Congress, established in 1886. Rather than being a combination of local unions in one trade or industry, it was an umbrella organization that included a wide variety of craft and industrial unions as well as "mixed" unions such as the Knights. The Trades and Labor Congress is the federation to which the modern Canadian Labour Congress can trace its roots.[5] Historically, the TLC and its successors were linked with and allied to the American Federation of Labor (AFL). They agreed with the AFL on two evolving issues that marked a search for organizational stability: a focus on exclusive jurisdiction as opposed to dual unionism to prevent intra-union conflict, and a pragmatic approach to politics.

International craft unions, which were members of the AFL, were also founders of the TLC. But they were not the only members. Various Knights of Labor assemblies were members, as were national Canadian unions. This mixed membership turned the TLC into a battlefield. Canadian directors from the Canadian branches of American internationals warred with the Knights and national Canadian unions, particularly on the issues of "foreign control" of the TLC and dual unionism. Gradually, the directors of the AFL-affiliated internationals gained control of the TLC and, in 1902, the TLC amended its constitution to bar dual unionism. The practical result was to expel the Knights of Labor, which endorsed and practised dual unionism, as well as national Canadian unions, which competed with American internationals for the same crafts or occupations. This tension would eventually lead to a split between craft and industrial unions in the United States and in Canada, the founding of competing federations, and continued tension between national and international unions operating in Canada.

GROWTH AND CONSOLIDATION: 1900-1920

The beginning of the 20th century was a period of growth and expansion for unions in Canada. While early unions such as the Knights of Labor were dying out, international unions, with their large memberships, ample funds, and ample resources, were expanding. They first focused on American branch plants but later expanded beyond that base to include Canadian industries. The economic environment supported this expansion in several ways. First, Canada's population was increasing rapidly, as the Prairies became settled. Second, there was tremendous industrial expansion in railway construction and resource extraction. Third, workplaces and workforces grew larger, making the organization of unions easier than it had been in preceding periods. Fourth, labour shortages made strikes a more potent weapon, and inflation caused a decrease in the real value of wages. This situation prevailed in the first decade of the 20th century and became acute during World War I, when significant labour shortages developed at a time of increased demand for industrial output to support the war effort.

---

5   Ibid., at 116ff.

During this period, industrial unionism gathered strength, particularly in the western provinces, where the international craft unions did not fit the needs of workers in the resource extraction industries of the West. Nor did these international unions speak to the political radicalism of the western frontier. In this environment, new and comprehensive industrial unions sought to organize all workers in an industry. The two most prominent were the Industrial Workers of the World and the One Big Union. The IWW had strength in the West in both the United States and Canada, and the OBU was strong in the prairies and on the West Coast. Both unions were politically militant and radical, seeing workers as involved not just in contract negotiations, but in a class struggle. And both were industrial unions that welcomed all workers and organized on an industry basis. These two unions participated in a series of hard-fought strikes in western Canada, but began to fade in the '20s and '30s. By the 1940s, the IWW had ceased to be a viable force and in the 1950s, the OBU was eventually absorbed by the CLC.

The radicalism and highly polarized labour relations of the first two decades of the 20th century, particularly in western Canada, culminated in the Winnipeg General Strike of 1919. The fuel for this labour conflagration included soaring inflation, diminishing purchasing power, and growing resentment toward employers who had made huge profits during the war. The strike started with a breakdown in negotiations between the metal workers unions and the employers over wage increases and recognition of a local labour council. What appeared to be a narrow contract issue became, in the charged and polarized atmosphere of postwar Winnipeg, an issue for workers generally, who were dissatisfied with Canada's postwar economic and social system. What had started as a local strike swiftly became a general strike, involving private and public sector unions, which came out in support of the metal workers. Joining them were others with economic grievances, such as war veterans. The strikers succeeded in bringing most economic activity in Winnipeg to a halt. Noting the recent triumph of Bolshevism in Russia, the government feared that the Winnipeg General Strike was the beginning of a communist revolution, and moved in troops and the RCMP to successfully crush the strike.

THE 1920s: REACTION AND RETRENCHMENT

The Winnipeg General Strike marked the high point in labour radicalism in Canada. The 1920s, a generally prosperous period, should have provided a positive environment for labour to organize and make gains. Instead, it was a period of slow growth for labour unions, particularly national and industrial unions. The TLC, dominated by the craft unions, most of which were international unions, suited the more conservative political atmosphere of this period. Reaction to the radicalism of the postwar period, particularly in the United States, led to an emphasis on individualism rather than collective action, which resulted on occasion in employer-dominated or -controlled unions, called **company unions**. Although this trend was more common in the United States, where employers aggressively pursued this agenda, it washed over into Canada as well. In addition, the international craft unions, though dominant in this period, grew slowly as the Canadian economy matured and became more industrialized. Increasingly large numbers of semi-skilled and unskilled employees found the craft unions irrelevant, particularly in western Canada, which was dominated by large bodies of workers in mining and resource extraction.

THE 1930s: THE DEPRESSION AND WORLD WAR II

Events in this period gave shape to labour organizations as we know them today. First, legislation established a stable legal regime of labour relations. Second, the internal conflict between industrial and craft unionism, and international and national unions, gradually subsided, which fostered greater unity within the labour movement.

Partly as a reaction to the volatile labour situation in the first decades of the 20th century, some provinces and the federal government began to legislate structures for settling and regulating labour disputes. These laws went beyond the initial legal steps of the 1870s, which had ended the definition of union activity as a criminal conspiracy. In 1900, the federal *Conciliation Act* was passed to allow the federal government to appoint conciliators to assist parties in reaching negotiated settlements. This was followed by the *Railway Disputes Act* of 1903, itself a reaction to a long railway strike. These acts were unsatisfactory as they allowed only voluntary agreements. They did not permit binding arbitration, nor did they set rules to govern strikes and lockouts. These defects were remedied in the *Industrial Disputes Investigation Act* of 1907.

This Act established a three-person conciliation and investigation board. The Act required that while an investigation of a labour–management dispute was under way, there could be no strike or lockout, and that the existing contract of employment remained in effect during this period. However, labour was critical of the legislation because it did not protect workers who joined a union from reprisals by the employer. Nor did it require the employer to bargain with the union chosen by the employees. In time, as a result of a constitutional challenge, the scope of the Act was restricted to industries under federal jurisdiction, such as interprovincial transportation and communications. But a number of provinces followed the federal lead and enacted legislation permitting the Act to apply within provincial jurisdiction.

The Depression initially resulted in a decrease in unionized workers. But by 1935, unions, particularly industrial unions, were rapidly expanding and asserting collective bargaining rights. These were vigorously resisted by some employers and led to a number of prolonged strikes. In this environment, starting in the United States with the *Wagner Act*, labour legislation went beyond mere regulation of ongoing industrial disputes, to embrace protection of the right of workers to organize and bargain a collective agreement. Under the *Wagner Act*, employers were no longer entitled to interfere with organization drives, discriminate against employees engaged in union activity, set up company-dominated unions, or refuse to bargain with or recognize a union chosen by employees. The Act also set up conciliation services similar to those legislated in Canada.

These reforms did not occur immediately in Canada. In 1937, for example, there was a lengthy, hard-fought strike in the auto sector in which the union sought recognition by the employer as bargaining agent. It was not until the beginning of World War II that Canada, seeking to create stable labour relations during wartime, enacted further labour legislation to create a completely new and modern system of labour relations, one similar to that of the United States.

In 1944, under Order in Council PC 1003, the old regime established under the *Industrial Disputes Investigation Act* was suspended and replaced by a labour relations regime that is with us today. Rules for the conciliation of disputes were kept, including those that limited strikes and lockouts to situations where negotiations had reached an impasse. But added to this system were principles similar to those embodied in the *Wagner Act*. They set out several important rights, rules, and obligations:

- the right of employees to choose a union,

- the duty of employers to recognize unions chosen by workers,

- the duty of employers to engage in collective bargaining where a union had been certified,

- protection against unfair labour practices by either party,

- provisions to define and certify bargaining units, and

- the limiting of strikes to a stage of contract negotiation where conciliation had been tried and had failed.

Eventually, a national labour relations board was established to administer this new labour relations regime. As well, during and following the war, the provinces established labour relations regimes that operated on the same principles as those underlying the federal system under PC 1003. This in turn provided for the system of labour relations we have today.

A second area of activity in this period, concerning internal struggles between industrial and craft unions, and international and national unions, also shaped labour organizations and federations in Canada. The late 19th and early 20th centuries were a period of industrial amalgamation. Large, often multinational, corporations developed. These companies engaged in large-scale, high-volume production using increasingly large numbers of semi-skilled and unskilled workers. In response, industrial unions formed. These unions recruited workers by industry or employer, rather than by membership in a skilled labour group, such as carpenters or electricians. The existing labour federations, founded largely by craft unions, were forced to adapt to the new reality of industrial unions, and international unions.

In the United States, in 1934, the AFL, after much debate, granted charters to **vertical unions**, which are unions that are organized in specific industries, such as the automobile industry. The AFL also began an organization drive in the steel industry. The industrial unions then set up their own Council of Industrial Organizations within the AFL. The AFL suspended these unions, which then departed in 1937 to form the Congress of Industrial Organizations (CIO). The CIO then proceeded throughout the '30s to engage in organization drives in a variety of industries. Employers resisted vigorously, and workers responded with violent and protracted strikes.

Because the industries that attracted CIO attention were often multinational, it was not long before the CIO and its international unions set their sights on the Canadian labour scene. The result was increased activity of industrial unions in Canada, and an increase in industrial strikes in the late 1930s, such as the strike led by the United Auto Workers against General Motors. Without the protections afforded by the *Wagner Act* to unions chosen by workers, the barriers were formidable for Canadian workers, who had to bargain union recognition along with wages, hours, and benefits. The Ontario government of the day, led by Mitch Hepburn's Liberals, joined General Motors in resisting the strike, leading to resignations by two of Hepburn's ministers and bloody confrontations between strikers and police in Oshawa. When the smoke cleared, the union had won a 44-hour week, overtime pay, recognition of shop stewards, seniority rights, and recognition as the bargaining agent. But it was a battle made more difficult by the absence of *Wagner Act*–like protections. For labour the gap would not begin to close until PC 1003 came into force in 1944, followed by the creation of a similar labour relations system in the provinces after the war.

The conflict between the AFL and the CIO in the United States carried over into Canada. The international industrial unions, as well as some national industrial unions, were expelled in 1939 from the then dominant Canadian federation, the Trades and Labor Congress. The Canadian branches of the international industrial unions, together with the national industrial unions, affiliated with the All-Canadian Congress of Labour to form a rival industrial union federation, the Canadian Congress of Labour. The two federations would continue to fight, mainly over issues involving raiding each other's members. These kinds of battles often led to an extra dimension of labour unrest beyond conflict between unions and employers. This involved disputes that developed when two or more unions competed for or claimed the same workers as members. In response, in the 1940s and 1950s the provinces and the federal government stepped in. They established rules about how and when one union could solicit employees in a workplace who were members of another union that had a contract with a specific employer. They also developed rules to determine which among several competing unions should be recognized or certified as representing workers who were previously unorganized. This issue was sorted out in the 1950s when the TLC and the CCL merged to form the Canadian Labour Congress, which is currently the dominant labour federation in Canada outside Quebec.

Quebec, meanwhile, had become largely isolated from the rest of the Canadian labour movement, organizing itself regionally on largely linguistic and religious lines. Its unions were perceived to be less militant than other unions in Canada and the United States. However, the advent of large multinationals in Quebec spurred the growth of local industrial unions, which, in response to deplorable working conditions in the textile industry, waged a hard-fought strike in 1937. Though it was eventually settled through mediation by the Catholic Church, this strike marked the beginnings of a more militant union movement in Quebec that would lead to secular trade unionism, but one that stayed largely separate from the rest of the Canadian trade union movement until after World War II.

In the 1940s, things changed for labour. The unemployment that had persisted through the 1930s evaporated as war industries began to increase production. As is often the case in wartime, prices and wages (and hence inflation) began to rise. To control this, the federal government introduced rationing of goods, and wage and price controls, which in effect froze wages and some expenses and limited consumer goods, and along with it demand. Because most unions had adhered to a no-strike policy out of patriotic motives from 1939 to 1945, few contract improvements were achieved during the war. Also, as part of wartime controls, the federal government took over control of labour relations at both the provincial and federal levels and created a labour relations regime under PC 1003 that provided the broad framework for modern labour relations in Canada. When the provinces had jurisdiction over labour relations returned to them after the war, they adopted the labour relations reforms that the federal government had introduced during the war.

When World War II ended in 1945, workers, expecting a brighter economic future, demanded better wages and working conditions. Unlike in the period after World War I, there was no recession following the end of World War II. Instead, heavy consumer demand kept employment and profits high. When employers resisted contract claims, a series of strikes followed in the late 1940s. Some of them involved basic issues such as union recognition and, notably, the issue of whether an employer should be collecting dues for the union from each employee's pay. This latter issue was settled in a uniquely Canadian way under a formula developed by Mr. Justice Ivan Rand in the course of mediating a strike in the auto industry. Rand proposed that the employer would collect and remit dues for all members of the bargaining unit, though no member would be compelled to join the union as a condition of employment. Under the Rand Formula, all workers who benefit from the union's negotiating and enforcing of a contract pay the expenses involved, whether they are members of the union or not.

THE POSTWAR PERIOD: 1945-1970

The 1950s and 1960s were characterized by economic growth and stability. During this time, union membership increased significantly. With continued growth, strikes were relatively infrequent as employers had the profits with which to buy labour peace; consequently, labour made advances in wages, working conditions, and benefits, particularly in the private sector and in manufacturing and resource extraction. During this period, the public sector remained as it had been: largely outside the union movement, due to legislative barriers to unionization and a blanket prohibition on strikes.

However, the friction between national and international unions and craft and industrial unions continued. Within the CCL considerable friction developed between the CIO-based internationals and the national industrial unions brought into the CCL from the ACCL. This tension was alleviated in part in 1948, when the CIO permitted its Canadian branches more autonomy. But the national unions were more radical and more politically engaged than the internationals. The ACCL and the CCL actively supported the Co-operative Commonwealth Federation. There were also a number of communist activists within the national unions, involved in organizing. All this led to factionalism and conflict within the CCL. In particular, the CCL never really developed a way of resolving jurisdictional conflicts between member unions. Nevertheless, generally, the CCL managed to operate as a Canadian house of labour that was independent of the US federation and was capable of organizing on an industrial basis.[6] In the early 1950s, the international unions gained control of the CCL, relegating the nationalists to a minority position within the federation.

---

6   Ibid., at 123.

By the mid-1950s, the conflict between the conservative craft union federations (the AFL and CIO in the United States, and the TLC and CCL in Canada) had been going on for 20 years. Three political changes brought the conflict to an end:

- In the United States, passage of the *Taft-Hartley Act*, which repealed and modified many of the advances of the *Wagner Act*, was recognized by both the AFL and CIO as an attack on labour, which enhanced unity and solidarity as goals for union activists.

- Both federations, which had differed on their approach to communists (the CIO being more welcoming), became strongly anti-communist.

- There was a turnover in leadership, with new, more flexible leaders coming to power in each federation.

Also of help was a structural change, a two-year no-raiding agreement, where unions in each federation promised not to raid other unions for members where other unions had already organized a group of workers.

The result was an agreement to merge the two federations into one: the AFL-CIO. The Canadian federations would soon follow suit. In 1953, the TLC and CCL began to explore a merger. The result, in 1956, was the creation of the Canadian Labour Congress, combining craft, industrial, national, and international unions in one federation. However, the tension between the more conservative craft unions, largely international, and the national industrial unions did not entirely disappear, and would lead later to a schism.

In Quebec, the close relationship between the Catholic Church and the Quebec labour movement under the Canadian Catholic Confederation of Labour was transformed by the 1949 Asbestos Strike. Although many clerics took the strikers' side, within progressive political circles and the labour movement as a whole there was a negative reaction to the paternalistic authoritarianism of the Church-supported Duplessis regime. The result was a more militant and secular CCCL. The CCCL also cemented ties with labour confederations in the rest of Canada, the TLC and CLC. In 1956, when the CLC was formed, the CCCL considered affiliation with it. However, there were some jurisdictional issues to sort out, as the old industrial union federation, the CLC, had affiliates who were members of the Quebec Federation of Labour, and inevitably this caused some conflicts, though the two Quebec federations managed to cooperate fairly well most of the time. But because of the conflict between the QFL, which was CLC-affiliated, and the CCCL, the latter stayed out of the CLC.

With modernization, industrialization, and the Quiet Revolution, Quebec society had become more urban, and more secular. These changes were reflected in the CCCL, which in 1960 formally severed its ties to the Church and became a secular organization, now called the Confederation of National Trade Unions.

THE 1970s TO THE 21st CENTURY

During the last quarter of the 20th century, several changes occurred that greatly affected unionized workers:

- The long period of economic growth that followed World War II came to an end in the early 1970s, in part as a result of fuel shortages arising from an embargo by oil producers in 1973. This resulted in a permanent increase in prices, which triggered inflation and recession.

- North American industries ceased to dominate world markets. European recovery was complete by the end of the 1960s, and industrialization in other parts of the world, notably in Asia, was creating strong competition. These market forces caused contraction of heavy industry and manufacturing, which had been the source of union strength in both Canada and the United States for nearly a century.

- The protective tariffs that had favoured domestic industry in Canada and the United States for over a century were replaced by a "free trade" regime. Trade regulation was liberalized to create a free flow of goods in a world economy and relatively few restrictions were imposed. Employers responded by setting up plants in low-wage, low-cost countries with few labour or environmental regulations. This in turn resulted in an export of good, high-paying industrial jobs to low-wage third world countries, in what critics have described as "a race to the bottom."

- Permanent, secure, relatively high-wage industrial jobs were replaced by lower-paying part-time jobs in the service sector.

- Public sector workers gained the right to organize public sector unions and, in many situations, gained the right to strike as part of the collective bargaining process.

During this period, membership in industrial unions fell as unionized jobs in manufacturing disappeared. Starting in the late 1960s and the 1970s, workers in the public sector became increasingly unionized, until by the century's end the membership in the public sector unions was greater than that in the private sector.

Many of the public sector unions formed their own federation, the National Union of Public and General Workers, but many were affiliated with the CLC as well. The CLC continued to develop its ties to the NDP, engage in confrontation with the federal government, particularly over wage and price controls in the 1970s, and encourage national unions at the expense of the internationals. The tension between the more conservative craft unions and industrial and public sector unions increased. In 1982, in a quasi reversal of the unity movement that created the CLC, some of the international craft unions in the building trade withdrew from the CLC to form the Canadian Federation of Labour.[7]

Also during this period, partly due to the growth of public sector unions, which were national and regional, a trend developed in favour of national unions. For example, the Canadian Paperworkers Union was established as a breakaway from the United Paperworkers International Union. Better known was the amicable parting of ways between the international United Auto Workers (UAW) and its Canadian locals, which formed the Canadian Auto Workers. Despite the departure of the unions joining the CFL, and the national splitoffs from some international unions, there was remarkably little raiding. One notable exception was the International Brotherhood of Electrical Workers' attempt in 1991 to raid the postal

---

7   The CFL of 1982 should not be confused with an earlier but by then extinct federation of the
     same name.

workers, represented by the Canadian Union of Postal Workers (CUPW), a CLC affiliate. This raid was not successful, but it demonstrated that the goal of labour unity and solidarity sought for over a century continued to elude the labour movement. Further raids at the century's end, sponsored by the CAW in the private service sector against the Service Employees International Union in Ontario, indicated that the conflict between national and international unions, and craft and industrial unions, continued as well.

In Quebec, the CNTU, now a secular union, became both more militant and more nationalist, and established strong roots among public sector unions. During the 1970s it also turned further to the left politically, cooperating with teachers' unions and the QFL to form the Common Front for public sector bargaining. The result was a series of massive strikes across Quebec—the closest thing to a national general strike seen in Canada to date.[8] A more fragmented labour scene emerged as some CNTU unions seceded from the federation to join the Federation of Democratic Unions, which had a more centrist, less ideological thrust. Meanwhile, the QFL maintained its ties to the CLC, although its affiliation, reflecting Quebec nationalism, is different from the arrangements for other affiliates—the QFL enjoys more control over dues paid to the CLC, local labour councils, and labour education. In effect, the QFL has achieved the "special status" that the province of Quebec has yet to achieve within the Canadian political confederation.

Currently, the QFL and the CNTU cooperate much of the time, and conflict between the two is generally muted. The CLC-affiliated QFL is the larger of the Quebec federations. The CNTU, rooted largely in the public sector, continues to be more politically radical than any other Quebec federation, but in its shadow is its less radical spinoff, the Confederation of Democratic Unions (CDU). In addition, the independent Quebec Teachers' Corporation competes with the CNTU and the CDU for members because it now organizes among all education workers. Further, there are breakaway construction unions. These fought with both the CNTU and the QFL to such an extent that the government intervened. It set up an employer's association, allowing employers to bargain with the federation with the most strength among the construction unions, which at the moment is the QFL. This mixture of nationalist, political, and ideological differences within Quebec, including the "special status" issues involved in links with other Canadian labour federations, has made Quebec a far more volatile and complex labour environment than is found in the rest of Canada.

FUTURE TRENDS

It is likely that the conflicts that have characterized organized labour in Canada for the past century will continue, although in other forms. The old industrial base of the union movement has shifted to the public sector and service sector. As well, changes in the workforce, particularly decreasing opportunities for unskilled workers and increasing numbers of women in the workplace, will probably change the way in which unions operate and relate to members. These matters are discussed in more detail in chapter 9, Emerging Trends in Labour Relations.

---

8   It differed from the Winnipeg General Strike in that it was regional rather than local, and
    involved a massive number of striking workers.

LABOUR MOVEMENT THEORIES AND PHILOSOPHIES

Improving labour relations and the interaction of unions with their environment is largely a practical undertaking, and has been the subject of relatively little abstract theoretical inquiry or speculation. But theories are important. They allow us to test hypotheses about how labour organizations operate and how workers and others view unions. The results often have practical value. For example, theories about how workers in particular settings view unions can be instrumental in planning more successful organizing drives, or in assisting managers in working with their unionized employees.

What does seem to be missing is an overarching general theory, a labour version of those theories in physics that grandly explain the origin of the universe. This lack of a grand theory is not surprising; after all, there is not much agreement on overarching theories of human behaviour, let alone overarching theories of how humans behave within institutions and social structures. In the labour movement, the theories tend to address the questions or issues that are foremost in the historical period in which they are developed. Hence, a theory from one period may be of limited use or interest in another—but together they still may help those engaged in practical tasks in industrial relations to order and interpret information. In this section, we will examine some of the major theories in a more or less chronological order in the context of the historical period in which they developed.

The Genesis of Workers' Organizations

As we have noted, labour unions took on a modern, recognizable form in the late 19th century. Key questions are, why then? and why in that form? The general theoretical answer is that economic conditions in the evolving capitalist system created conditions that produced worker responses to economic forces in the form of trade unions. But as the theories of Marx on the one hand and the Webbs on the other show, the prescriptions for what role these trade unions should play are different.

MARX AND LENIN: REVOLUTION

One of the earliest theorists to closely analyze the role of labour in capitalist production was Karl Marx, who described labour as simply one of the means of production, along with capital and natural resources. Marx argued that in the competitive market economy, where the goal was to maximize profits while minimizing cost, labour would be squeezed and dehumanized. The increasingly bleak conditions for labour would inevitably fuel a reaction by labour as a class, giving rise to a class struggle between workers and those who controlled capital. In the view of Marx and the Marxists, the historical forces of revolution would result in the demise of capitalism. Control of the means of production would pass to workers, who, freed from being merely producers, would be able to achieve their full potential as human beings.[9]

---

9   Marxist theory is of course far more complex. For a more detailed discussion see G. Sabine, *A History of Political Thought*, 3rd ed. (New York: Holt, Rinehart and Winston, 1965). For a sharper focus on the role of unions in Marxist and communist theory, see P. Taft, "Theories of the

Where do unions fit in this scheme? Like other theorists who look at the origin of trade unions, Marx saw unions as a class-conscious enterprise by workers who sought to fight exploitation by the employer and so improve their conditions. But here a problem emerges. Unions are, for Marx, an important tool in the struggle to overthrow capitalism and usher in an era of pure communism. If the revolutionary struggle is successful, unions, like the state, will wither away.

More important for Marxists, however, is another problem at the heart of a union's purpose. The union pursues the interests of its members. This may very well lead them off the long-term path of revolution to the short-term goals of improving working and living conditions—a combination of collective bargaining activities in the workplace and limited political activity focused on improving society. This means that if the union movement was successful, it could lose its role as a front-line tool of revolution and become a much more conservative force, with a bigger stake in the status quo. Lenin believed as much, and noted, "trade union politics are precisely working class bourgeois politics."[10]

What the Marxists did not foresee was that capital, faced with labour's demands, might compromise, rather than risk worker revolts. This is what happened in the industrial world of Europe and North America, and it is what appears to be happening in the advanced economies of Asia. The Marxist revolution became a victim of the success of unions in advancing the interests of their members. In a glaring example, conservative craft unions have satisfied their members' interests exclusively through collective bargaining. When they have engaged in politics, it has often been to take a politically conservative position. The rest of the union movement sits on the left side of the political spectrum, but it is focused on reform and progress rather than on revolution. While some European unions remain linked to the communists, their commitment to revolution is mainly rhetorical, if it is expressed at all.

In summary, some important ideas have emerged from Marxist-Leninist theory:

- The search for short-term relief from economic exploitation would create a sense of solidarity among the exploited that would express itself through unions as a means to improve conditions.

- If unions were not successful in improving conditions, they would turn to revolutionary struggle.

- If unions were successful in improving conditions, they would become part of the capitalist economic system, engaging in reformist politics rather than revolution.

Labour Movement" and J. Dunlop, "Development of Labour Organizations," in L.G. Reynolds et al., eds., *Readings in Labour Economics and Labour Relations*, 2nd ed. (Englewood Cliffs, NJ: Prentice Hall, 1978). For a more succinct analysis, see Craig and Solomon, supra note 4, at 98-99.

10 V.I. Lenin, *What Is To Be Done?* (New York: International Publishers, 1929), 90, quoted in Craig and Solomon, supra note 4, at 98.

THE WEBBS: EVOLUTION

Like Marx, Beatrice and Sidney Webb saw labour unions developing as a result of a capitalist, market economy in which workers no longer owned and controlled the means of production. Instead, as Marx noted, labour became a commodity in the production process, rather than the controller of the process. The loss of control of the process meant a loss of control over the profits, which allowed capital owners to suppress wages to maximize their own profits. For the Webbs, as for Marx, the recognition of the loss of control led workers to combine and organize to regain some control over their position as employees. They did so through collective action in an effort to regulate the effects of capitalist competition in the labour market.

At this point, the Webbs and Marx and Lenin part company. Marx saw capitalism as being prepared to use violence to repress workers, and unions as the vanguard of a violent revolutionary response. The Webbs, writing in the late 19th and early 20th centuries, thought that public ownership of the means of production through democratic socialism would bring about the necessary changes in the system and that unions would be centrally involved in bringing about these reforms as a kind of vanguard of an evolutionary response.[11]

The Webbs also did something Marx did not do: they studied how labour unions actually formed and operated and then identified problems and prescribed solutions. The Webbs saw unions arising locally when a group of workers became conscious of a common condition, which included the loss of control over production, the effect of competition on wages and working conditions and the need to regulate and control competition, and the lack of government protection.

The Webbs concluded that the success of trade unions depended on a local group of workers not simply focusing on its own community or workplace while ignoring others with similar problems. This scenario constituted a "local monopoly," according to the Webbs. In some respects, it describes the behaviour of some craft unions whose interest in working conditions does not extend beyond its own members. The Webbs optimistically noted that most unions managed to overcome local monopoly and commit to an idea of labour solidarity that saw local unions cooperating with others outside their community, achieving consensus on shared goals, and sharing activities to achieve those goals.

The Webbs' optimism about solidarity stemmed from their observations of the growing trade union movement in Britain at the end of the 19th century. There, local unions amalgamated with other local unions to form regional and then national federations. The tendency to amalgamate is readily observable in Canada, although the internal conflicts we identified earlier between national and international and craft and industrial unions have resulted in a more complicated path toward amalgamation than that envisaged by the Webbs.

The Webbs identified three mechanisms used by unions in the amalgamation process:

---

11 For their principal works, see note 2. This discussion of their theories is drawn from Craig and
    Solomon, supra note 4, at 76-80.

- *Mutual insurance.* Especially common in the early stages of the trade union movement, this mechanism involved unions amassing funds from members to be paid out for unemployment, illness, and death benefits. This system of mutual aid had roots in the pre-modern and pre-industrial period and often preceded collective bargaining as a union activity. Once unions were able to organize to bargain benefits, responsibility for benefits shifted to the employer or the state.

- *Collective bargaining.* The need to collectively bargain contracts gave rise to a permanent and ongoing union apparatus to serve as a repository of bargaining knowledge and information, and as a source of bargaining expertise.

- *The process of legal enactment.* This refers to activity that fosters amalgamation as a process, and solidarity as a value for labour. It involved the development of the workers' political agenda, often linked to a democratic socialist party, which required the development of a labour movement to provide resources and political pressure. In North America, this process has largely been divorced from a formal linkage to a "labour" party. But labour federations such as the CLC have been very active in promoting legislative activity. The federations have, for example, been involved in legal enactment campaigns to raise the minimum wage, obtain anti-scab legislation, oppose free trade, and advance human rights protections.

The Webbs thought legal enactment to be the most important part of trade union activity because it had the most direct impact on the improvement of social conditions. But to assume that rank and file union members share that interest may be naive, as may be the assumption that labour solidarity stretches much beyond the local workplace.

In summary, the Webbs made several notable contributions to theories about labour organization:

- They sought to develop a theory of labour organization that would promote the interests of labour without requiring political revolution or violence to achieve labour's goals.

- They demonstrated that unions began with a parochial or local focus, but tended to move beyond merely local concerns by engaging in amalgamation. The resulting large organizations created the basis for solidarity between different and diverse groups of workers.

- Closely connected to amalgamation was the process of legal enactment. The Webbs identified it as the most important purpose of trade unions, ensuring that certain minimum standards were legislated across the board for all workers.

The Early 20th Century: Explaining North American Unionism in Cultural Terms

The pioneering work of Marx and the Webbs did much to explain how trade unionism arose, and their theories also prescribed the role unions would and should play in Europe at the end of the 19th century. But their theories did not explain the behaviour of unions in North America, nor did they shed light on all of the issues that we have examined in looking at the history of the labour movement in North America.

By the beginning of the 20th century, the behaviour of organized labour had become a matter of interest to scholars, who examined unions' economic and social role in the North American setting. Hoxie, Commons, and Perlman were among the more important of these early commentators.

HOXIE

Robert Hoxie wrote extensively on the role of unions in the United States, providing lucid commentary on a number of issues that concern unionism both in the United States and Canada.[12]

Most theorists, as we have seen, explained the growth of unions as a reaction by workers to a common threat to wages and working conditions. But Hoxie, looking closer, saw something more. In his view, before workers would react to a common economic threat, they had to first see themselves as a social group—not a social class, as was the case for Marx and the Webbs, but a collectivity sharing values, views, and ideas. The mere perception of economic oppression by an employer was not sufficient to provoke a reaction. This sense of solidarity provides a basis for explaining the explosive growth of white-collar and professional unions, particularly in the public sector.

Hoxie analyzed unions in terms of their principal function in achieving the goal of improving workplace conditions. He recognized that some unions would emphasize some functions over others, and thus he developed a typology to classify them. Which functional type would be paramount depended on the values and perceptions of the group and how that group approached problem solving in the workplace. Hoxie described four major types of unionism in North America:

1. *Business unionism.* This type of union focuses almost exclusively on workplace conditions, negotiation, and enforcement of a collective agreement. It is workplace-centred and either has no interest in staking out positions on matters outside the workplace or takes a conservative view of politics. Solidarity extends no further than the members of the group, and members are either hostile or indifferent to the fates of workers outside the group, even those in the same workplace. This type of union is common among craft unions, but also describes the views of the rank and file of most unions.

---

12 Hoxie's main work is *Trade Unionism in the United States* (New York: Appleton, 1921). An edited, reissued version was published as R.F. Hoxie, *Trade Unionism in the United States* (New York: Russell & Russell, 1966). See also Craig and Solomon, supra note 4, at 83-90.

2. *Friendly/uplift unionism.* This type of unionism goes beyond the immediate contract concerns of members to include an interest in bettering conditions in society generally, and supporting progressive causes in alliance with other social and political groups. The social activism of the CAW is an example of this. This approach was emphasized, and is summed up, in the theme of the convention of the Ontario Public Service Employees Union (OPSEU) in the mid-1990s: "What we want for ourselves, we want for others."

3. *Revolutionary unionism.* This is the kind of unionism Marx had in mind, and which has been relatively uncommon in North America. For this type of unionism, the group is not just the workers in a local area, but workers in general as a social class, with class interests that can be expressed as a social movement combining trade unionism and politics. Hoxie identified two variants:

   a. The socialist version described and prescribed by the Webbs, where labour allies with a labour party and works within the democratic system for reform. The CLC with its connection to the NDP exemplifies this type of unionism at the federation level, though the attachment appears to be weaker when one looks at individual unions and their members within the federation. Witness the CAW's inability to deliver the vote to the NDP in Oshawa in the provincial elections of 1995, 1999, and 2003.

   b. The revolutionary version, which includes unions who see their primary purpose as engaging in a violent struggle with the capitalist class and their allies. Hoxie described this group as quasi anarchist, although that term may shed more heat than light on the issue. This type of union is far more interested in direct action against the employer and the state, including the following actions: sabotage in the workplace or to the employer's property; picket-line violence; and physical assaults on opponents, especially strike breakers. These kinds of activities take precedence over collective bargaining with the employer. An example is the IWW in its heyday in the early part of the 20th century, when it organized workers in mining and lumbering in the western United States and Canada.

4. *Predatory unionism.* This type of unionism is characterized by a union leadership concerned primarily with the use of power to gratify its own immediate goals, where the needs of the members are secondary. Hoxie described it as having two forms:

   a. *Guerrilla unionism.* There is an absence of a sense of ethics, and, at the least, tolerance for illegal activity to further the ends of the leadership. The leadership may use extortion or loot the union pension funds or other surpluses in its negotiations, but the members will still feel they are getting satisfactory contracts. As a Teamster member put it to one of the authors in referring to the Teamster leadership, "They get theirs, but we get ours."

b. *Hold-up unionism.* This type is similar to guerrilla unionism except that the leadership is in collusion with the employer, and negotiates **sweetheart deals** in which the workers' contract issues and interests are sacrificed in exchange for payoffs from the employer to the union leaders.

UP CLOSE

The Teamsters

The best example of predatory unionism is the Teamsters, an international union of the industrial type. The leadership often negotiated sweetheart deals, and were involved with organized crime in taking money from pension funds. The Teamsters were treated as pariahs by other unions, and were expelled from labour federations in both the United States and Canada. In the 1990s, union elections were supervised by the US government to prevent fraud, and a reform slate was elected, which proceeded to clean up the union to the extent that it was readmitted to labour federations in the United States and Canada.

To summarize, Hoxie's primary contributions to the understanding of the labour movement were as follows:

- A group consciousness, expressing values, ideas, and a group identity, was an important factor in workers joining a union and articulating goals and interests.

- Hoxie identified four different types of unions having certain primary functions: business unionism, friendly/uplift unionism, revolutionary unionism, and predatory unionism.

- While no union was purely one type or another, its general identity was closely connected to the group consciousness of its members.

THE WISCONSIN SCHOOL: COMMONS AND PERLMAN

Commons

Like Hoxie, Commons and Perlman sought to explain some of the distinct aspects of American unions. John R. Commons saw unions, as the Webbs did, as a continuous and permanent organization of workers. Commons saw a variety of variables as important in explaining how American unions worked, but he singled out two for particular attention: the availability of land, and the early granting of the universal right to vote without the requirement of voters having to own a minimal amount of property. Both factors, he asserted, would defuse any trends in American labour toward revolution and class consciousness.

For Commons, labour unions emerged as a result of growing competition and the division of labour that came with industrialization. His famous study, "American Shoemakers, 1648-1895,"[13] charted the separation of craftsmen from the own-ership and sale of the goods they made, with the conversion of craftsmen into wage earners. Commons noted further that the production and sale process was divided among many market players: manufacturers, wholesalers, distributors. With so many players seeking to profit from production, workers organized in order to ensure that competition would be based on product quality, not wage differences between union and non-union labour. In Commons's words, "wages would be taken out of competition." But to do this, workers had to do more than organize in one community; they had to reach out to help others to organize, building a chain of local unions, linked together in national unions, and then linked in federations. While such solidarity was an ideal in itself, it was also necessary to maintain both living standards for workers and product quality.

Commons's theory neatly explains the expansion of US unions into Canada. By establishing branches in Canada, these unions ensured that the salaries of lower-paid Canadian workers would increase so that US workers would not be competing with lower-paid workers in the same market. While Commons's theory accounts for the growth of unions in the early 20th-century North American economy, it does not explain well the operation of industrial unions. Nor is the hallmark of his theory—taking wages out of competition—likely to carry much weight in light of globalization and free trade. In the future, it is just as likely that wages will be a chief factor in competition in a race to the bottom where unions will face some serious challenges.

Commons, however, does make some major contributions by focusing on the peculiarities of the US experience. He has observed:

- Free land and universal suffrage defused class-conscious and revolutionary unionism.

- A complex production and distribution system would put pressure on price competition to reduce wages. Unions would focus competition on product quality, not wages.

- The key to preventing wage competition was to organize workers on a national scale, across a whole market.

Perlman

Selig Perlman began as a Marxist in his view of unions but in working with Commons and observing unions in the United States, he paid particular attention to how expressions of political ideas involved in unionism might undermine the goals of unions.[14] He noted that for unions to succeed in the United States they first had to be seen as legitimate social institutions. For this they would need the support of the middle class, and to get that support, they would have to demon-strate respect for private property and eschew any ideas of revolutionary unionism. Second, they would have to abandon their intellectual approach to trade unionism

---

13 J.R. Commons, "American Shoemakers, 1648-1895" (November 1909), *Quarterly Journal of Economics* 39-84. Commons's detailed study of American labour is set out in his major work, *History of Labor in the United States*, 2 vols. (New York: Macmillan, 1918).

14 Perlman's major work is *A Theory of the Labor Movement* (New York: A.M. Kelly, 1949).

and adherence to political theories such as socialism and intellectual idealism. The intellectual approach made unions less able to overcome what Perlman called the "resistance power of capital." Instead, unions must adopt a "manualist mentality." By this, Perlman meant that workers would be conscious of, and motivated by, the scarcity of job opportunities. This would lead to a conservative approach in the true sense of the word: an attempt to hold on to and conserve a resource—jobs.

Perlman noted that in the United States the perception of available land and opportunity had led workers to believe that there were abundant opportunities for them. It was only when they could be persuaded that scarcity rather than opportunity awaited them that they would take action to preserve and control job opportunities.

The idea of scarcity of job opportunity certainly applies to blue-collar workers and unions, but it can also be used to understand the reaction of white-collar workers in the service and public sectors to the impact of technology, where technological advances threaten jobs in all sectors.

Perlman's contribution, then was to focus on the psychology of workers as a factor in union formation:

- Unions could prosper when belief in the American myths of opportunity and abundance was replaced by consciousness of job scarcity in the face of the resistance power of capital.

- To survive, unions would have to have middle-class support, and endorse property rights. Revolutionary and class-conscious unionism did not speak to the North American condition.

- People joined unions in order to obtain job opportunities and job security.

The Mid-20th Century and Beyond: Modern Industrialism and Post-Industrialism

The discussion of labour unions and their place in the economy and society has been in the context of the "old economy," where the focus was on North American and European unions in the early phase of the industrial period, in democratic states. But the theories developed in this context do not necessarily fit the analysis of labour relations in other parts of the world as industrialization and democracy took hold. Nor do these theories adequately deal with the impact of globalization featuring large global corporations that can easily move from one location to another to seek yet greater competitive advantage and profit.

TANNENBAUM AND BAKKE: WHY DO PEOPLE JOIN UNIONS?

In *The Labor Movement* and *A Philosophy of Labor*, Tannenbaum examined why workers joined unions.[15] He found the reasons were not simply economic, but had much to do with attempts to create communities or re-create communities that had been damaged or had deteriorated as a result of the Industrial Revolution. The

---

15 F. Tannenbaum, *The Labor Movement: Its Conservative Functions and Social Consequences* (New York: G.P. Putnam and Sons, 1921); *A Philosophy of Labor* (New York: Knopf, 1951).

attempt to re-create a community originated in what Tannenbaum referred to as the "shop society" of the factory. Workers relied on each other for support and banded together socially and economically. Unions were an outgrowth of and gave a structure to the re-creation of community. He noted further that the creation of community caused unionization among professionals and within the civil service.

Bakke, in examining why people join unions, conducted surveys of workers to discover their reasons for joining or not joining unions.[16] He found that workers would join unions and hold positive attitudes about them if they felt that those unions would contribute to what Bakke called "successful living," which occurred if the worker experienced

- some assurance of respect of others,

- material well-being experienced by the most favoured of his or her peers,

- independence and control of his or her own life situation,

- understanding of outside forces affecting him or her, and

- a sense of wholeness, self-respect, and complacency with his or her situation in life.

THE FORD FOUNDATION STUDY: INDUSTRIALISM AND INDUSTRIAL MAN

Clark Kerr, John Dunlop, Frederick Harbison, and Charles Myers examined labour relations on a worldwide basis, not just in the context of the advanced industrial world of Europe and North America. Funded by the Ford Foundation, the authors gathered data from 1952 to 1975 and presented their findings in a variety of books and papers.[17]

The authors made a finding that was much at variance with the findings of previous studies we have touched on. They found that labour relations conflicts did not arise simply as a response of workers to the impact on them of the capitalist system. Instead, they argued, labour responded to the effects of industrialism on workers—management's search for efficiency colliding with the workers' desire for security. If the key is efficiency, then the form of ownership and the type of economic system are not all that important. In this context, the formal system of collective bargaining worked well in a democratic system, where contractual promises were understood by both sides. But it worked less well in a communist state such as China, where the state decided the form of labour policy outside of any workplace context and outside of any contractual agreement between workers and management.

In those states where industrialization was seen as a desirable economic goal by local elites, the International Monetary Fund (IMF), and the World Bank, workers responded by using whatever means was available: strikes, walkouts, sabotage, and

---

16 E.W. Bakke, "Why Workers Join Unions" (1945), vol. 22, no. 1 *Personnel.*

17 Much of their work has been consolidated in *Industrialism and Industrial Man* (New York: Oxford University Press, 1964). The authors, minus Clark Kerr, considered their original findings further in *Industrialism and Industrial Man Reconsidered: Some Perspectives on a Study over Two Decades of the Problems of Labour and Management in Economic Growth* (Princeton, NJ: Inter-University Study of Human Resources in National Development, 1975). For an overview, from which this is adapted, see Craig and Solomon, supra note 4, at 93-97.

political organization, including the organization of unions. It therefore followed for the authors that as industrialization proceeded, particularly under transnational corporations, the relationship between workers and managers would become similar from one place to another, despite political, economic, social, and cultural differences among nations.

What these trends may mean for unions is that union federations that have long shared information may become much more proactive in seeking uniform standards for labour. From the workers' perspective, this would result in something better than what one would otherwise expect to find at the end of a race to the bottom. In this connection, the International Labour Organization (ILO), established in 1919 after World War I as part of the League of Nations, and still in operation today, might emerge from the backwater it has long occupied. It may become a major player for international unions, which may become structurally and functionally similar to the transnational corporations with which they are in conflict. This kind of international union system, should it arise, will bear little similarity to what passes for international unions in North America.

KOCHAN, KATZ, AND McKERSIE: THE TRANSFORMATION OF INDUSTRIAL RELATIONS

In *The Transformation of American Industrial Relations*,[18] the authors argued that the standard systems models of labour relations, especially Dunlop's, are too static to explain how labour relations have actually worked since the 1960s. Since that time, what had been a stable labour relations environment, where each side accepted the other and the collective bargaining model, became far less stable, with a breakdown in the industrial relations consensus that had operated since the introduction of Roosevelt's New Deal in 1933. They note that labour relations have become much more fluid and unstable, citing several factors:

- a drop in union membership in the United States,
- increased foreign competition,
- strategic choices by senior managers to move away from the collective bargaining system, and
- a fall-off of communications between the top levels of national and international unions with the industry counterparts.

The result is, the authors note, a weakening of labour's influence on key workplace decisions, such as where and how to invest. At the same time, changes have been made at the level of the workplace to introduce more job flexibility, foster worker–manager cooperation, and in general make the relationships in the workplace much more fluid. However, the specifics of this analysis do not apply all that well to Canada, where unions remain stronger than in the United States, especially in the public sector. Still, many of the forces that the authors identify as creating a more fluid and less stable labour relations environment are observable in Canada, too.

---

18 T.A. Kochan, H.C. Katz, and R.B. McKersie, *The Transformation of American Industrial Relations* (New York: Basic Books, 1986).

A CANADIAN PERSPECTIVE ON THE TRANSFORMATION OF INDUSTRIAL RELATIONS: THOMPSON AND VERMA

Mark Thompson and Anil Verma examined the premises and conclusions in *The Transformation of American Industrial Relations* in the Canadian context.[19] They noted that the Canadian experience has been different from that of the United States, in part because of different cultural attitudes. They noted that Canadian managers were far less likely to abandon the collective bargaining model, and instead sought to use it in reacting to market forces. This had to do partly with the greater strength of unions in Canada, both in size and in determination to advance their own agendas. But this willingness of management to work within the industrial relations model created in Canada in the 1940s also appeared to exist on its own without reference to the strength of the union movement.

Summary

In this overview of theories about labour organization, we have focused on why workers join unions, and on how unions behave both in the workplace and outside in the larger world. The explanations have varied, often reflecting the biases of the authors and the periods in which they wrote. Marx, for example, who viewed the work world as the site of a class-conscious struggle, saw unions as part of a revolutionary force that would bring about the creation of a new economic and social order. Perlman, on the other hand, a former Marxist, rejected this approach and saw unions as participants in the maintenance of an economic system. The differences in their views of the world led them to different conclusions about how workers approached unions and how unions operated within the social and economic order. The important thing to recognize is that the variety of theories sketched here may provide information and analytic frameworks that can be useful, depending on the particular situation or question one faces. For example, Thompson and Verma's analysis of union–management relations in Canada can help explain how and why union leadership behaves differently here in some respects from the way it does in the United States.

THE STRUCTURE AND FUNCTION OF TRADE UNIONS

Having examined both how unions evolved historically and some of the theoretical explanations for the behaviour of unionized workers and their unions, we now turn to the structure and function of actual trade unions. We will base our discussion on the most common union structure in Canada, the union affiliated with the Canadian Labour Congress. Note, however, that not all Canadian-based unions are part of that structure. About 25 percent are unaffiliated with the CLC. Many of the construction craft unions, for example, belong to the CFL. Others are independent and unaffiliated, including some small unions confined to a particular region or

---

19 See A. Verma and M. Thompson, "Managerial Strategies in Canada and the United States in the 1980s," in *Proceedings of the Forty-First Annual Meeting of the Industrial Relations Research Association* (Madison, WI: Industrial Relations Research Association, 1988). See also Craig and Solomon, supra note 4, at 100-1.

FIGURE 1.1   Structural Components of a Typical National Union in Canada

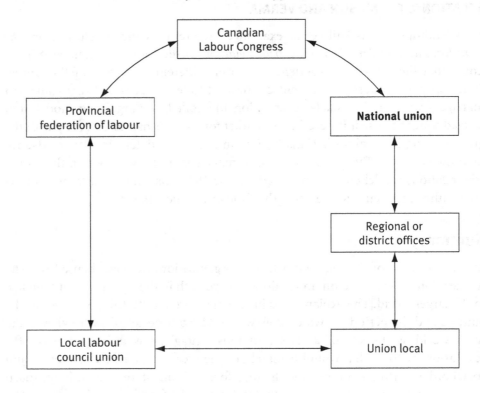

Source: Adapted from A.W. Craig and N. Solomon, *The System of Industrial Relations in Canada*, 5th ed. (Scarborough, ON: Prentice Hall, 1996), 151. Reprinted with permission by Pearson Education Canada Inc.

professional group. But the situation is changing. In particular, public sector unions, including teachers' unions and unionized professionals, which have long been outside the traditional labour movement, increasingly are joining the CLC.

There are a number of historical forces that have influenced the current structure of the labour movement, as we will see in the following discussion. The most influential of these are as follows:

- Unions began as local, community-based groupings—and it is the union local that remains the focus of the most important activity for most members.

- The notion of "labour solidarity," the idea that all unionized workers should support each other, has been the foundation on which larger union groupings—national and international unions, and labour federations—have been built.

- In the drive to organize workers, there have been numerous collisions between unions seeking to organize the same workers, and there have also been political and philosophical differences in approaches to trade unionism. Disputes within the labour movement have led to some structural complexities involving the formation of national/international unions and various federations. At the federation level, rules have evolved about jurisdiction and organizational ethics.

FIGURE 1.2   Structural Components of a Typical International Union in Canada

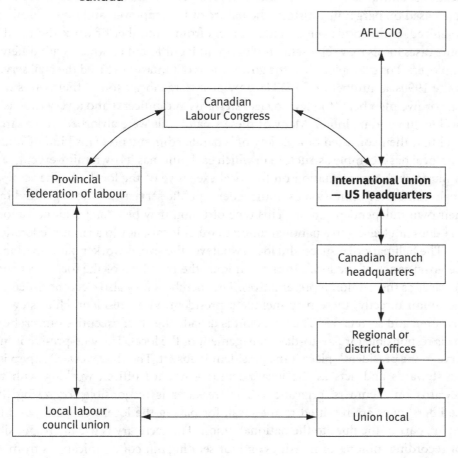

Source: Adapted from A.W. Craig and N. Solomon, *The System of Industrial Relations in Canada*, 5th ed. (Scarborough, ON: Prentice Hall, 1996), 151. Reprinted with permission by Pearson Education Canada Inc.

The structural components of a typical union in Canada include the local; the national or international union of which the local is a part; regional labour councils with which the local is likely to be affiliated; provincial federations; and national labour federations, such as the CLC, of which the national or international union is a member.

Figure 1.1 sets out the relationships for a national union. An international union operating in Canada has a slightly different organizational scheme, as shown in figure 1.2.

Union Locals

The union local is in many respects the most important structure of the union movement. For unionized workers, this is the part of the union they see and deal with on a day-to-day basis. Officers drawn from the local unit handle all grievances, contract negotiation, contract enforcement, contract ratifications, and strike action at the local level. Unionized workers rarely see union officials from the regional or national offices of the union, or even know who they are.

Generally, locals represent the members who work in specific jobs, in specific locations, and usually for a specific employer. However, there is much variation here based on bargaining history, the nature of the employer, and how a local was organized. Some locals will include workers from a number of work sites, and in some cases locals may represent employees under different contracts with different employers. For example, when the government of Ontario reduced the civil service in the 1990s, a number of OPSEU's previously large locals found themselves with four or five members (too few to elect stewards and officers) and a very expensive local to run and maintain. Many of these small locals were absorbed into a larger local that then consisted of a variety of separate components. This kind of multi-unit local has a complex structure in which each unit has its own mini-executive of stewards, with representation on the local executive of the local. In other cases, a small number of professionals in the federal public service may be organized into their own independent union. This type of union may be a "stand-alone," a local that does not belong to a national union of other locals, nor to a labour federation.

The hallmark of a successful local, whatever the size, is worker participation in the governance of the local. In most unions, the members of the local elect shop stewards as their union representatives. The members may also elect the officers of the union directly; these may include a president, vice-president, chief steward, treasurer, and secretary.[20] The president is usually the chief executive officer; he or she is responsible for day-to-day management of the local. The vice-president may serve in the president's place if the president is absent. The chief steward supervises the stewards and acts as the local's senior grievance officer, working with the stewards on members' grievances. The treasurer is responsible for seeing that members' dues are remitted to the local, for paying the local's expenses, and for paying part of the dues to the national union. The secretary is usually responsible for recording minutes of meetings and for sending out communications from the union to members. In addition, there may be other officers to deal with matters such as health and safety, employment equity, or other matters of concern to the members.

For these offices to be filled, the local requires a cadre of dedicated union activists drawn from the members of the bargaining unit. These volunteers are usually extroverted and articulate, and possess a strong sense of commitment to trade unionism or to the work group, or to both. They may also become active at the regional and national/international levels, and within the labour federations. In fact, senior union officials nearly all had their start at the local level, as local activists. Thus the local serves as a pool from which to select local leaders, and a source for national leaders.

Interestingly, the only training most union leaders receive is on-the-job training as activists. Most do not have formal organizational management training. And there is little leadership or management skill training available within the labour movement, although some unions and the CLC have developed what are essentially management training programs.

But advancement in union ranks is based less on management skills than on political wiles. In particular, the ability to persuade, motivate, and inspire ensures

---

20 In construction and craft unions, the person responsible for the day-to-day operations of the local is the business agent, combining the functions of president and chief steward.

that union leaders are elected to higher union positions. Contrast this with businesses, where there are many training opportunities for business managers, where managers do not usually work their way up from the shop floor, and where promotion is based on bureaucratic criteria rather than on elections by the rank and file.

The union activists serve another function at both the local and national level—they monitor the union leadership. They check on and question local and national officers and executive board members. If there are issues that worry them, they usually communicate their concerns to the rank and file, often informally through conversations on the shop floor. If leaders ignore the concerns, the activists provide the core of an opposition within the local.

The need for dedicated activists is underscored by the low participation rate of union members: a mere 10-15 percent of members attend union meetings, including meetings to elect officers. However, when it comes to strike or contract ratification votes, the vast majority will turn out to vote, and if a strike is called, most members will turn out for strike duty. Some have argued that the low participation rate indicates a low commitment to the union; but when one looks at strike and ratification votes, one sees evidence of strong commitment by the members.

How can this apparent contradiction be accounted for? One explanation may lie in the fact that members have busy lives, with a variety of family and other commitments. Members may feel that as long as other members are active in the union so that the routine operation is looked after, they are free to attend to their own business, content in the knowledge that their interests in the workplace are being promoted, even without their direct participation. But the real gauge of commitment is what the rank and file do when asked to vote on a contract or a motion to strike. These decisions concern their sense of well-being as a group and their future economic advancement and security. The obvious importance of the issues may explain the sudden increase in their interest and participation. More important, if the rank and file follow the advice of their leaders in casting their votes to strike or ratify, as the case may be, they are demonstrating, through their solidarity with the leadership and each other, a commitment to the union.

The rank and file may be uninterested in the day-to-day affairs of the local, particularly if they are satisfied that the union is being run properly. Low participation, coupled with member satisfaction, may explain why union officials, once elected, often continue in office for long periods. But the democratic constitutions and procedures of unions make it relatively easy for the rank and file to exert control when issues of concern to them arise and a consensus builds among a majority or even a large minority of members to support new policies or oppose the current leadership. Meetings and elections, run under procedurally fair rules, ensure that this will happen. And if the executive attempts to ignore the rules, there are other checks outside of the local; the national or international constitution may permit members to bring charges for constitutional breaches. These charges may result in severe penalties, including expulsion from the union. Further, the national/international office may intervene to direct a local that has run amok by putting it under trusteeship. In this case, the national or international union, as the case may be, rather than its elected officials, would run the local directly. If it is the national or international union that is problematic (for example, where the national leaders are misappropriating funds), the provincial and national federations to which a national or international union belongs may impose sanctions on the union. This was the case for the Teamsters in the 1980s, when the Canadian national and provincial federations, as well as the American labour federation, the AFL-CIO, imposed penalties.

It is important to note that the union local is the organization that is responsible for financing the labour movement as a whole. Unions do not own income-generating property, as a rule,[21] so the entire union movement, not just the local, is funded ultimately from the collection of dues from members. Some unions, particularly among the craft unions, have initiation fees as well as monthly dues. In most Canadian unions, dues are collected under the Rand Formula, where all members of the bargaining unit, whether they voluntarily joined the union or not, have their dues deducted by the employer from their salary and sent directly to the union. Note that, with some exceptions,[22] members of a bargaining unit are not required to be union members: joining a union remains a voluntary act. But all members covered by a collective agreement must pay dues because they are afforded the benefits of the contract negotiated by the union and are entitled to have the union process their grievances.[23]

Once dues are collected, the treasurer will use the funds for paying local expenses (perhaps purchasing partial time off for local officers so that they are able to spend time on union duties) or paying rent on an office. The balance of the dues will be turned over to the union head office. Often the share of dues sent to head office is based on a formula driven by membership numbers set out in the union's constitution or bylaws, or both.

Dues paid over to the national union may come back to the members in different ways. For example, if the local exercises its right to strike, a strike fund is usually funded by the national union, and the strike members are paid from that source while on strike.

Regional and District Labour Councils

In the early days of the labour movement, local unions often banded together within a community to deal with matters of common interest. Many district councils are older than the labour federations and many of the national unions. It was a Winnipeg labour council, for example, that provided the organizational

---

21 There are some exceptions where unions do own assets that can generate income, such as an office building in which some space is rented out commercially. In other cases, the union may have some control over a pension fund and be able to draw on it for revenue. However, this is unusual, especially because of the problems the Teamsters Union got into over misuse of members' pension funds in the United States.

22 Many construction unions negotiate into their contracts a requirement that the employer can only employ tradespersons who are members of the union.

23 In *Lavigne v. OPSEU*, [1991] 2 SCR 211, a member of OPSEU objected to his dues being used for political initiatives he did not support. The Supreme Court of Canada ruled that unions were not restricted to using dues simply for collective bargaining purposes, and that members' (and non-members') Charter rights were not unduly restricted or infringed if the union used the dues in part to pursue a political agenda. This, the court ruled, was a necessary and accepted part of trade union activity in Canada. A member of a union, or a non-member, had always had the option of union participation with the opportunity to persuade others to change union policy.

focus for the Winnipeg General Strike. The council represents the locals in a city or regional area of all of the national and international unions that are affiliated with the CLC. Councils are funded by a dues tax on each local, which makes the decision to join and send delegates. The councils perform the following functions:

- They promote labour solidarity: if there is a strike involving one local, they will rally other unions to support the strikers.

- They present the labour point of view on labour and non-labour issues in local matters.

- They provide labour representatives to local boards and agencies.

Provincial Labour Federations

Each province or territory has a provincial federation. The CLC constitution requires that all CLC-affiliated national and international unions, CLC-affiliated independent unions, CLC-affiliated local labour councils, and all other CLC-affiliated regional bodies belong to a provincial labour federation. The provincial federations are funded by a tax on each affiliated member body. The role of the provincial federation is to present labour's views on provincial issues of interest, and to organize political activities on behalf of labour within the province. Occasionally, a provincial federation may mediate jurisdictional disputes between unions in the province.

Nationals and Internationals

Locals, unless they are stand-alone independents, belong to either a national Canadian union, such as the CAW, or the Canadian branch of an international union, such as the Service Employees International Union. These head office operations are responsible for organizing workers in a particular workplace, and for chartering locals of workers they have organized. Head office will also assist the locals by providing expertise and assistance that the locals might not have in negotiating and administering contracts, handling grievances at arbitration, organizing non-unionized workers in an industry, and providing training programs for local activists. Head office, having deeper pockets than the locals, may also fund certain union activities at the local level, such as providing strike pay. For example, often a national or international union will have assets such as an office building that can be pledged as security to borrow the money necessary to support a strike if the dues base itself in insufficient.

Members of locals, through periodic union conventions (such as company annual meetings), held annually or every several years, govern the national and international unions. Representation at conventions is based on the size of the constituent locals: large locals generally send more delegates than small ones. To prevent small locals from having their interests overlooked, there is often a minimum number of delegates that all locals are entitled to. There also may be similar attempts to balance the interests of regions having many large locals with the interests of regions having a smaller number of relatively small locals.

At conventions, the delegates often elect officers and members of the executive board of the union. Although officers are usually elected by members at large, executive board members may be elected on the basis of geographical or occupational groupings or equity groups within the union to ensure that the board is broadly representative of the members. The conventions also serve as a forum for debate of policy options and policy decisions through resolutions. If the constitution or union bylaws are to be amended, the convention is the body that has the power to make those amendments.

Though most of the delegates will be union activists, few will be involved in running the union on a day-to-day basis. That job falls to the union's national executive, or, for internationals, the international executive. To maintain control, the constitution may permit the executive to use committees to screen resolutions, bylaws, and constitutional amendments, and to decide which of these come to the floor for debate by the delegates.

Committee members are usually appointed by the president or by the executive. This gives the executive a great deal of control over the flow of information and the formation of policy. And this control can be used to stifle initiatives from the convention floor, and derail internal opposition. To add to the delegates' difficulties, they are usually deluged with stacks of documents immediately prior to the convention. Unless there is an issue that activates delegates and the rank and file, delegates simply do not have the information or organizational resources to push an agenda that does not have executive support. However, when the rank and file do identify an issue of importance to them, as the Teamsters demonstrated in the 1980s, they can push those issues at convention and elect officers who support them.

Central or National Federations

Labour movements are organized in every country on a national basis, with a central national labour federation.[24] Canada follows this pattern, with the CLC as its principal national labour federation.[25] The CLC includes the Canadian branches of many internationals, national Canadian unions in both the public and private sectors, and some independent local unions that affiliate directly. Some district and regional labour councils and port councils are also directly affiliated to the CLC, particularly if, like some of the port councils, they were set up to solve jurisdictional problems between competing affiliated unions in a city or region.

The CLC performs a variety of functions at the national level that are also performed by the provincial federations at the provincial level. But some functions are unique to the national federation. These functions are as follows:

- *Formulating national policies for labour and formulating national political positions.* Although policies are made by the delegates, the officers and

---

24 The international unions, at first glance, appear to be exceptions to this pattern. But the internationals operating in Canada are really Canadian branches of American unions that are headquartered in the United States.

25 The CFL represents a handful of construction unions, and is not a national federation at the same level as the CLC.

CLC staff pursue the federation's policy agenda in a variety of ways. They may carry out advertising campaigns, as on free trade. They may lobby the government, as they did on wage and price controls in the 1970s. They may ask for standing and file briefs before royal commissions and in court proceedings involving issues of concern to labour. Finally, they may provide funding and support to the federal New Democratic Party. However, in the short run, they may not be very effective in carrying out their agenda, and it is certainly arguable that labour's voice is not much heeded by governments on major issues of concern to labour.

- *Adjudicating disputes between affiliated unions over jurisdictional issues.* As noted earlier, much of the internal conflict in the Canadian labour movement has resulted from jurisdictional disputes between unions trying to organize or represent the same group of workers. When the CLC was created in 1956 out of the CCL and TLC, the jurisdictions of affiliates were frozen. Subsequently, disputes were handled by an independent umpire to determine which union should represent a given group of workers. But the process proved inadequate to deal with some fierce disputes. A good example is the dispute involving the CAW, as it broke out of its industrial base in the auto industry and sought to organize in the service sector. After a hard-fought battle over a raid on a union representing fishery workers in the Maritimes in 1987, the executive council took over the task of deciding jurisdictional issues. Jurisdictional issues may also involve attempts to organize new groups of workers in sectors, such as financial services, that have historically been non-unionized. To avoid free-for-alls, the CLC acts to coordinate affiliates in industry-wide organizing drives, which may make the drive more efficient and effective, and also prevent internal conflict among affiliates.

- *Penalizing affiliates that fail to honour jurisdictional decisions.* When a jurisdictional issue involves a raid by one union on another at the end of a contract, the national federation's policy is to discourage raiding by penalizing the raider. This can mean barring the raiding union from using any of the services offered to affiliates by the CLC. If that fails, the raider can be ejected from the CLC, and from the provincial federations, putting it outside the labour movement.

- *Representing Canadian labour in the international arena.* The CLC has historically been active on the international labour scene, publicizing suppression of labour movements in other parts of the world, running training programs for third world trade unionists, and participating in international movements to oppose globalization. The CLC leaders have also been involved as labour representatives to the ILO.[26] The ILO, an international agency founded at the end of World War I, has representatives from government, labour, and industry and sets international labour standards. Long an administrative backwater, it is sometimes seen as a structure that can provide minimal labour standards

---

26 CLC president Shirley Carr, in 1992.

that will counter globalization trade pressures to constantly seek out cheap labour.

- *Developing a code of ethics.* The CLC is concerned about maintaining the image and reality of the labour movement as progressive and democratic. Its constitution contains a number of ethical practices, to which all affiliates must adhere. The code includes the following rights, rules, and obligations:

  - Union leaders are not to engage in corrupt practices, especially the misuse of union funds.

  - Members must have the right to run for office.

  - Unions must hold free and fair elections for officers.

  - Members have the right to the fair application of union rules, where, for example, a union runs a hiring hall.

  - Members have the right to have the union administered fairly.

When an affiliate breaches the code, the CLC executive first uses persuasion to correct the abuse. If that fails, the affiliate may be suspended from the CLC, and, ultimately, expelled, as was the case with the International Brotherhood of Teamsters in 1956.

CHAPTER SUMMARY

In this chapter, we examined the labour movement in Canada by examining three broad areas: the history of the labour movement, theories about labour organizations, and the structure and function of the labour movement. In examining the history of the labour movement, we noted its ad hoc beginnings, in part a response to the industrial system. We noted how, in the interest of maintaining labour strength, locals coalesced into national unions, which in turn affiliated with federations of many unions. The history of various organizations that have come and gone illustrates some of the key tensions in the labour movement between elite craft unions and later industrial unions, between politically active unions and those engaged in business unionism, and between national unions and international unions.

We also examined theories about labour organization, noting that theories that explain the nature and function of European unions do not explain North American unionism. Finally, we examined the work of leading American and Canadian theorists, whose theories help to explain attitudes toward unions, why workers join unions, and how those unions function.

WEBSITES

www.aflcio.org The website of the AFL-CIO, the US national labour federation. Contains links to other labour sites.

www.iamaw.ca Contains links to all of the provincial labour federations, as well as other labour information sites.

www.clc-ctc.ca The website of the CLC, with links to provincial federations.

REVIEW QUESTIONS

1. What factors gave rise to unionization?

2. Identify four core issues that have had a large impact on the historical development of Canadian unions, and explain how they have influenced organized labour in Canada.

3. What is the significance of PC 1003?

4. What forces led to the creation by merger of single, large federations in the United States and Canada?

5. Describe the contributions of the following people to labour movement theory:

   a. Marx and the Webbs

   b. Hoxie

   c. Perlman

   d. Kochan, Katz, and McKersie

   e. Thompson and Verma

6. What factors have led unions to coalesce into national federations such as the CLC?

7. Briefly describe the structure of a typical Canadian national union.

8. Does poor union participation by the rank and file at 10-15 percent indicate that unions do not have strong membership support?

9. Is the CLC more than just a voice for labour? Are there necessary, concrete functions that it performs?

CASE STUDIES

1. Ali Kamina is an organizer for the Amalgamated Service Workers. He has been assigned the task of organizing the customer service representatives who work for the Caring Bank, a major financial institution. Ali is in the process of preparing some promotional materials to hand to the customer service representatives. Ali says labour theorizing is all very well for academics but it has no practical use. Explain to Ali how some of the theories covered in this chapter might be useful to him in his task.

2. Stella Adamant is the president of Local 4 of the Glass Workers Union. Les Lavalle is the president of the Glass Workers Union of Canada, which is a member of the regional labour council, the provincial federation, and the CLC. Stella has discovered that Les is apparently appropriating union funds for his personal use. She seeks your advice, as an expert on union structure, on what steps might be taken to put a stop to it.

The Labour Relations System

INTRODUCTION

In this chapter, we will begin by briefly examining the labour relations system and models that assist us in analyzing how the system works. Then we will examine the legal foundations that underlie the system, including the effects of the constitutional division of powers between the federal and provincial governments, and the impact of the *Canadian Charter of Rights and Freedoms*. We will also highlight key legislation that governs or affects the system.

THE FRAMEWORK FOR ANALYSIS

Labour relations theorists and practitioners assume that labour relations form a system. A system is a regularly interacting or interdependent group of items forming a unified whole.[1] In the context of labour relations, this means that

- labour relations activity consists of a variety of variables or factors that are all interrelated,

- these variables or factors exist within system boundaries, and

- changes in one variable or factor will cause changes in others.

The variable or factor that causes the change is the **independent variable**; the variable that is changed or affected is called the **dependent variable**. For example, salary is a dependent variable affected by the independent variables of experience, qualifications, and market demand. Factors outside the system are considered to be largely irrelevant. Though components may change, the system itself persists over time.

Systems theory is based on the social science adaptation of systems theory, which was originally developed in the hard sciences to analyze and predict "outputs" from processes and events. The outputs are the effects produced by these processes and events. Processes and events are often referred to as "inputs." Inputs, such as an increase in the cost of borrowing money and management goals of cutting costs, may lead to use of the negotiation process, resulting in the output of changes in wages and working conditions. Figure 2.1 shows the relationship of inputs to outputs in a system, according to systems theory. The key to systems

---

1   Merriam-Webster Online, available at http://www.m-w.com.

theory is that it identified a system—in effect, a closed universe—where changes in one factor or variable necessarily produce changes in other variables within the system. For the purpose of scientific or social experimentation, it enables the observer to identify key variables and make statements about causation. It also lends itself to quantitative analysis, rather than intuitive or descriptive analysis.

FIGURE 2.1   A System, According to Systems Theory

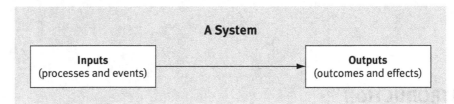

Systems theory is not without its critics, particularly in the social sciences. Critics in that field have charged that it has a conservative bias, that it focuses too heavily on the control of change, and that it wrongly assumes that the system as it has been defined is immutable, inherently stable, and therefore legitimate. In brief, systems theorists believe that if you discover a system, it must have always been there; and if it functions, it must work and be beneficial. The critics also say that by focusing on the operations of the system, theorists may miss the impact of factors that lie outside the system as it has been defined. (The area outside the system is called the external environment.) And as we will see, there is also plenty of room for argument about what factors need to be considered in studying a labour relations system, and what factors may be omitted because they are irrelevant.

In labour relations, there are two classic systems theories that academics and practitioners often draw on: the classic Dunlop model, and an expanded, Canadian model developed by Craig.

Dunlop: Industrial Relations Systems

Following the chaotic and conflict-ridden labour relations scene of the 1930s and 1940s in the United States, J.T. Dunlop published his now classic systems model of US labour relations in 1958.[2] His theory contained four basic elements, each of which has a number of subcategories. Events or activities involving one element, called system inputs, would affect the other three in determining system output. Dunlop's four basic elements are as follows:

1. *Actors.* These consist of three groups:

    a. employees, unions, and union representatives;

    b. employers, employer organizations, and employer representatives; and

    c. government agencies such as labour boards, labour regulators, arbitrators, the courts, the legislature, and the executive branch of government.

---

2   J.T. Dunlop, *Industrial Relations Systems* (New York: Holt, 1958). There is also a revised edition published in 1993 by the Harvard Business School. The latter edition updates the analysis, and answers some of the system's critics.

2. *Environmental factors.* These include the nature of the market for goods and services, production techniques, the power of the parties, and the influence of government, the press, and the public.

3. *The ideology held by the parties.* This requires some consensus and agreement on values if the system is to work.

4. *The rule system, or "web of rules."* This system contains ordinary legislation as well as specialized rules and regulations that govern labour relations, including the provisions of the collective agreement.

Critics noticed some biases in Dunlop's approach. His model assumed a consensus among the actors and labour relations harmony as a natural state. This was not far off the reality of labour relations in the United States in the prosperous 1950s. But where there is systemic labour conflict, Dunlop's systems approach is not a particularly effective tool for analyzing or predicting outcomes.

Craig: A Systems Framework for Analysis of Industrial Relations

In the 1960s, Alton Craig developed a model of the Canadian labour relations system that is better suited than Dunlop's model to the Canadian environment. In particular, it can be used effectively to study a system where there is a lack of consensus and considerable conflict. The Canadian system was the focus of considerable examination in the 1960s due to labour unrest, prompting Craig to develop and refine his approach to assist the research for the Task Force on Labour Relations in 1966.[3] It has been further refined over the years.[4]

Craig's model is an open system—it focuses not only on the variables within the boundaries of the system, but also on related factors and variables in the external environment. In the Craig labour relations model, there are two sites of activity: the labour relations system and the external environment. Together, they form a feedback loop. Activity within the labour relations system feeds into the external environment. In turn, activity in the external environment feeds into the labour relations system (see figure 2.2). More specifically, internal inputs (refer again to figure 2.2) are converted into organizational and worker-oriented outputs within the labour relations system. These outputs then move into the external environment, where they become external inputs. They are "external" because they are in the external environment and "inputs" because they feed back into the labour relations system.

The main components of the framework are:[5]

- internal inputs, expressed as goals, values, and power of the participants in the system, mediated by external inputs from the external environment;

- the interrelated private and public processes for converting the inputs into outputs;

---

3 *Report of the Task Force on Industrial Relations* (Ottawa: Privy Council Office, 1968).

4 It is set out in detail in chapter 1 of A.W. Craig and N. Solomon, *The System of Industrial Relations in Canada* (Scarborough, ON: Prentice Hall, 1996).

5 Ibid., at 3-4.

FIGURE 2.2   The Craig Labour Relations Model

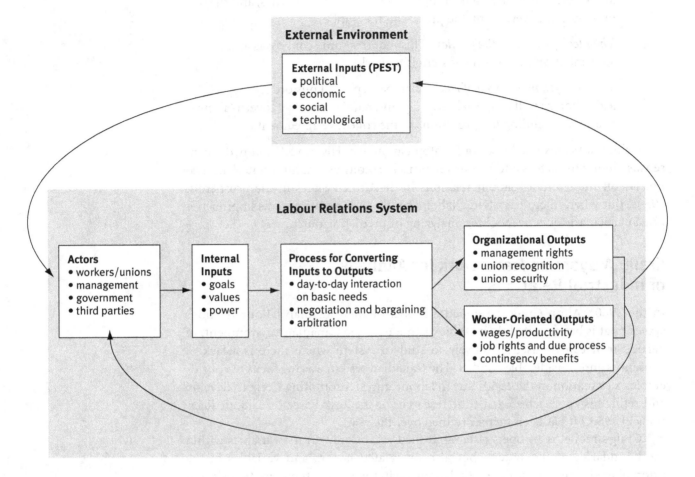

Source: Adapted from A.W. Craig and N. Solomon, *The System of Industrial Relations in Canada*, 5th ed. (Scarborough, ON: Prentice Hall, 1996), 4. Reprinted with permission by Pearson Education Canada Inc.

- the outputs, consisting of the material, social, and psychological rewards workers receive in exchange for their services; and

- a feedback loop, through which the outputs affect both the labour relations system and the external environment.

The feedback loop provides a dynamism that allows the system to persist and adapt over time. As a result of feedback, outputs (for example, an economic downturn) shape subsequent goals, values, and power (for example, job security) of actors in the industrial system and in the external environment. As Craig notes, the model also assumes that goals, values, and the use of power are problematic rather than consensual or harmonious—that is, they will be sources of conflict and stress for the system. The model also emphasizes that the actors are goal-oriented, which in turn emphasizes the necessity of making choices to achieve goals and the means to achieve those goals.[6]

_____

6 Ibid.

THE CRAIG MODEL AS A TOUR OF THE LABOUR RELATIONS LANDSCAPE

To someone new to labour relations, the Craig model can provide a useful introduction to the variables that affect labour relations, as well as to the way in which they influence each other within the industrial system and in the external environment.[7]

Labour Relations System Actors

The main actors in the labour relations system are the unions, including their individual workers; the employers; and third parties.

UNIONS

Unions are voluntary associations of workers combined to negotiate employment contracts, called collective agreements, with employers. But unions in Canada, through their affiliations, have taken on a broader role, taking action on various public policy issues outside the workplace. Unions may seem like a monolith to their opponents, but they vary considerably one from another. Some are more politically active than others. Some restrict themselves to workers in certain occupations, while others will organize almost any group of workers. And within any individual union, independent variables such as sex, age, experience, training, ethnicity, or political and ideological views may be the source of dissension and conflict within the group.

Although unions developed in the context of for-profit businesses, many unions now operate in the public and not-for-profit sectors. These sectors focus on efficiency and effectiveness rather than simply profit. Measuring effectiveness can be more difficult than determining "the bottom line," and this may result in less clarity about issues in bargaining collective agreements.

EMPLOYERS

Employers fall into various categories. The chief vehicle used by employers is the corporation, where ownership is often divorced from management. Management has become the subject of professionalization and specialization. Often there are managers in large corporations who are responsible for, and who specialize in, the field of labour relations. Like unions, management is not a monolith. Management attitudes toward unions may vary considerably, as may their views on interaction with the external world.

THIRD PARTIES

Public sector industrial relations also may draw in third parties, on the assumption that when important public services are at stake, the legislature may step in to end a strike, usually by referring some or all of the strike issues to arbitration by an appointed arbitrator.

---

7   Ibid., chapter 1. The description of the Craig model is with some modifications adapted from the discussion in chapter 1.

Industrial Relations Systems Internal Inputs

In the Craig model there are two types of industrial relations system inputs:

- internal inputs, consisting of the goals, values, and power of the system actors; and

- external inputs, consisting of the environmental effects on the goals, values, and power of the actors.

INTERNAL INPUTS: GOALS

Goals are the objectives that actors wish to achieve or meet. This is true for both individual actors and for groups. The discussion of goals is often framed in terms of a hierarchy of needs to be met. Basic needs, such as safety, minimum wages, and job security, are first addressed. Once basic needs are satisfied, the next higher needs in the hierarchy become the motivating focus. In a developed society like Canada, most basic needs in the industrial system are satisfied, so actors focus on higher needs such as workplace satisfaction and other psychosocial needs.

INTERNAL INPUTS: VALUES

Values are the norms or ideas that actors adhere to in determining a view of the world. They provide guides to deciding what is right or wrong, desirable or undesirable. Depending on system outputs, they may change over time. Workers may have different values from those expressed by their unions: workers may, for example, be less willing to provide generous welfare benefits to others than their unions would support.

As well, management and unions often focus on very different values, and the extent of these differences will determine whether there is conflict or harmony in the system. Marked differences can bring about changes in the system. For example, the hostility of US managers to unions after the 1970s may have been responsible for the decrease in the number of unionized workers in the United States. In Canada, the relative absence of such hostility may be responsible for the greater strength of the union movement. Other forces may be at work, too, such as the greater willingness of workers to participate in collective action to achieve goals.

INTERNAL INPUTS: POWER

Power can be defined as the ability of actors to achieve goals in the face of resistance from other actors. According to Craig, power has two elements: a strong attachment to a particular goal or object, and an ability to impose sanctions to achieve the goal. Sanctions may mean violence or physical coercion, as in the 1930s when automobile manufacturers and their employees resorted to violence in the pursuit of goals, such as getting the union recognized or keeping the union out. Unions and management may also use more restrained and legal forms of coercion, such as strikes or lockouts. Or they may use moral suasion, often to move public opinion.

GOALS, VALUES, AND POWER OF THE ACTORS: EXAMPLES

Goals and values are notoriously hard to identify and measure with any precision or accuracy. Power is more straightforward because the results of its exercise often can be measured—the success of a strike or lockout, for example. But even with power, although its result may be observable, the reasons for its use, in terms of motivating goals or objects, may be less discernible. For example, the tenacity of a union during a strike may be due to an ostensible desire for higher wages, but other, more important goals may lurk beneath the surface: the union's need to prove its effectiveness to its members, or a personal conflict between union and management actors.

In the strike by community college teachers in Ontario in 1984, the teachers were concerned about increases in workload. Though they shared many goals and values with management and with the public, the teachers were at odds with management on this issue. Management was more interested in keeping costs down by increasing class size without increasing the size of faculty, thus maximizing the provincial grant per student enrolled. Conflict lay ahead. Through demand setting, teachers made it very clear to union officers that this was a unifying issue, cutting across subgroups within the union. Management would have little success in any direct appeal to teachers over the heads of the union bargaining team. For the teachers, workplace satisfaction, quality education, and student well-being were important motivating factors, as were workload and larger class sizes.

The teachers understood collective action as being the only way to achieve control over workload that would support their values, because neither local nor provincial management identified the issue as a serious problem. They also understood the importance of quality education to students and their families, and appealed directly to those groups for support. The teachers, holding strongly to the objective of workload control and motivated by a desire for workplace satisfaction and quality education, voted in large numbers to strike. They maintained strike solidarity until the strike was ended by legislation.

From management's perspective, concessions on workload meant less efficiency and the transfer of the power to manage and "control production" to the faculty. Management's goal was to maintain control of the workplace on this important issue, and this led to resistance to union demands, and to the ensuing strike. Management appealed to the public, suggesting that students could lose their school year if the strike went on. By doing this, management passed responsibility for ending the strike to a third party, the Ontario legislature, which did end it. The teachers, however, continued to press the issue for the next round of bargaining. Fear of further conflict and another strike, and recognition that a compromise could be reached, brought about a resolution of the issue. As this example has shown, the Craig model demonstrates how conflict can develop, but it also shows that conflict may result in harmony or at least stability.

External factors may also influence the actors. For example, a government deficit and funding shortfalls could indicate to a union that there is no money to fund contract demands, and union militancy may fall off in consequence.

External Inputs: A PEST Analysis of Environmental Effects

In Craig's model, external inputs consist of environmental effects on the goals, values, and power of the actors, and he sets out a list of these external inputs, or factors. The format used here to examine these factors is a PEST analysis. The acronym PEST stands for political, economic, social, and technological. A PEST analysis is a scan or study of external macro-environmental factors that influence labour relations.

EXTERNAL INPUTS: POLITICAL FACTORS

Political factors can vary according to what is being analyzed. They may include the legislated process for organization, which will include the labour relations legislation and regulations, which govern the organizing and incorporation of trade unions. More important, the legislation and regulations set out the rules governing who may be organized into unions, and how the process is to take place. Usually the legislation will set out the rules for certification. During this process the bargaining unit is defined, the wishes of the members of the bargaining unit are determined, and the union is given official status as sole representative of the members of the bargaining unit. In Canada, the consequences for management of certification are that it must recognize the union and bargain a collective agreement with it.

The political system will also determine a framework for collective agreement enforcement. Labour relations legislation does this by insisting on a mandatory arbitration clause in every collective agreement. The clause states that contract disputes that the parties cannot resolve themselves must be referred to an independent adjudicator, whose ruling will be binding and will settle the matter.

Legislation will also provide general workplace regulation in the form of minimum employment standards for wages, hours of work, and (in some cases) working conditions. The minimum standards will apply to all workers, but unionized workers will usually be able to go beyond the minimum by negotiating a collective agreement that sets higher standards. The ability to do this is a measure of success or failure for a union.

The political system may also provide for mandatory benefits such as education, universal health care, employment insurance, and old age pensions. This may provide a floor that unions try to get above with training rights, supplemental health benefits, supplemental parental leave, and an employer pension plan.

The presence of a labour-backed political party may be an indicator of how strong and well organized unions are, and how sophisticated they are in their approach to politics. It may also demonstrate labour's ideology in actively pursuing a labour agenda on behalf of workers in general. The absence or weak presence of a labour-backed party may indicate a union movement more concerned with business unionism and bargaining than with a broader public agenda.

Is there union security legislation or the presence of **right to work laws**? In Canada, a union, once certified, has a right to bargain for its workers, and the law generally does not restrict the rights of unions. In the United States, the situation is different. Some laws make it difficult to organize workers and obtain certification. In many cases, laws also guarantee that individual workers have the right not to join or be compelled to join a union. In Canada, union membership is generally voluntary, but once the union is certified, it has the right to collect dues from members and non-members who are in the bargaining unit in exchange for negotiating and administering the collective agreement on behalf of all members.

Finally, what is the level of state regulation? Generally the higher the level of state regulation, the greater the stability of labour relations, and the greater the security for unions and their workers. In North America there has been since the mid-20th century a regulatory scheme to recognize unions chosen by workers as exclusive bargaining agents. It also oversees labour conflict that goes beyond contract negotiation—for example, unfair labour practices by any party, certification, and decertification of unions.

EXTERNAL INPUTS: ECONOMIC FACTORS

External Inputs: Labour Costs

How do labour costs affect labour relations? Generally management will seek to keep labour costs down through technological advances to eliminate workers, and through the use of casual and part-time workers, who get lower wages and fewer benefits than unionized workers and are often not included in collective agreements. Unions will try to increase wages, which will raise labour costs, and often a trade-off results in which workers secure a higher salary but must work harder and be more productive.

Until the 1970s, technological innovation and lack of competition ensured a high-wage North American economy. Since that time, increased competition from Asia and Europe and the advent of globalized free trade have undermined the high-wage economy and have increased pressure on workers to accept lower wages. But there are exceptions: the highly skilled workers in efficient industries in automotives and aerospace are able to command high wages. In these sectors, high labour costs alone do not necessarily indicate what will happen during contract negotiations. This point should remind you that in a systems analysis, the findings on one variable cannot be used to accurately predict outcomes. The process is more complex, involving a scan of all of the relevant variables, and the exercise of informed and experienced judgment.

External Inputs: Unemployment Rate

The unemployment rate generally will set the tone for bargaining. If unemployment is generally high, there will be pressure on unions to trade job security for lower wages, greater productivity, or some other concession. However, general unemployment may not affect bargaining where skilled trades or professions are involved and demand remains steady. But if a high employment rate is tied to economic recession, pressure on workers and their unions is likely to be felt eventually.

External Inputs: Inflation Rate

A rising rate of inflation generally triggers price increases to cover increased costs of production, and prompts increased demands for wages to cover increased costs of living. A drop in the inflation rate can indicate a downturn in the economy, as was the case in the 1930s, when an economic depression seriously harmed both workers and their employers. A moderate drop to a stable, low inflationary level is generally regarded as a prescription for economic growth, which generally favours workers' demands. Because inflation is ever-present, many unions will bargain for **escalator clauses** in collective agreements. These clauses allow for increases in wages during the life of an agreement that will keep pace with the rate of inflation. They are also called **cost of living clauses**. Escalator clauses are often separate and distinct from bargained wage increases over and above the rate of inflation.

External Inputs: Economic Growth Rate

The economic growth rate is a matter of debate for economists, but it is generally deemed to measure and describe "real growth"—that is, true economic expansion with inflationary effects factored out. The inflationary effects are deemed to be price or cost increases not associated with economic growth. Usually, a growing economy favours unions, because it tends to be accompanied by low rates of unemployment and greater productivity and profits from which to pay the cost of labour. If the economic growth rate falls or stagnates, that may indicate recession or a depression. In such times of economic downturn, management is often able to put pressure on labour for concession bargaining. During the depression in the 1990s, there was a fall in real wages, job losses, and a reduction in the number of unionized workers.

External Inputs: Stage in Business Cycle

Economic growth can be erratic, and it is mediated by outside forces such as changes in demand, competition, available resources, and production. Generally governments through their financial institutions, such as the US Federal Reserve System or the Bank of Canada, try to regulate the money supply and interest rates. By controlling these factors, they keep growth from spiralling into inflation in an "overheated" economy, or from deflating too rapidly into recession or depression. This strategy recognizes the existence of a business cycle that follows a dynamic process of expansion and contraction, where governments and businesses try to balance the process to produce steady growth.

Economists have spilled plenty of ink in developing theories and models to predict where we are in the business cycle at any one time. If we are on a predicted upswing to expansion, this will favour unions. If the opposite is true, this will favour contraction and concessions to management. Thus, a big problem in bargaining is achieving consensus on where the economy is in the cycle at the time of negotiations. This in turn depends on which economic forecast is cited, particularly if there is disagreement among the experts.

EXTERNAL INPUTS: SOCIAL FACTORS

Social factors include the makeup of the general population, and the values and attitudes held by the populace or by subsectors of it.

External Inputs: Demographics

Demographics refers to factors and indicators of the makeup of the population. For labour relations, relevant factors include sex, general skill levels, skill deficits, the size and characteristics of various **age cohorts**, the rate of immigration and emigration, the size of the working-age population, the number of workers at or near retirement age, and the age of workforce entry.

Demographics can have an impact on bargaining in many ways. A lack of workers with a particular skill can drive up wage costs. A large influx of immigrants with needed skills may be perceived to drive down wage costs, which in the past has often put labour unions on the side of those who wish to restrict immigration. The size of an age cohort may also have an impact. For example, the baby boomer generation, a very large cohort compared with those both older and younger, is on the verge of retirement. Many labour analysts see a looming labour shortage resulting, which puts pressure on employers to increase hiring. Unions favour this, and can be expected to fight to ensure that new hires are not deflected to part-time or contract positions. As this age cohort moves through the life cycle, it can be expected to create growth in some industries such as health care, which will also have an impact on labour relations.

External Inputs: Education Levels

Education levels affect the labour relations system in various ways. The better educated the workforce is, the more sophisticated the workers are in their responses to management, both in bargaining and in the workplace. Union members are also more sophisticated in dealing with their own union officials, being both more critical of and more active in union affairs. Higher levels of education also mean higher wages and greater specialization, making such workers harder to replace during a strike.

External Inputs: Attitude Toward Acceptance of Unions

The attitude toward acceptance of unions has three aspects: acceptance by workers, acceptance by management, and acceptance by the general public. The chief issue for workers is whether or not they see unionization as an answer to workplace issues, or whether they prefer to approach issues individually. Workers' willingness to see unions as useful will be a key to certification, and also to their participation in the union.

The management attitude turns on whether it sees unions as an unwarranted interference with its freedom of action, or as cooperative players in the system. When there is harmony and consensus about the labour relations system, managers see unions as legitimate. When there is disharmony, management will fight hard in bargaining and try to get rid of the union altogether, if possible.

The attitudes of workers and management toward unions will be greatly affected by the political values of the society. In the United States, where individualism and free markets are often tied together, unions are often seen as interfering, and a drag on production. Where political values are more supportive of group action, as is probably the case in Canada, unions may be regarded more favourably. Certainly, the more negative attitudes toward unions in the United States than in Canada are reflected in the proportionally smaller share of the US workforce that is unionized.

EXTERNAL INPUTS: TECHNOLOGICAL FACTORS

The extent to which a workplace is technologically intensive can influence the labour relations system in several ways. New technology in production has the effect of increasing individual worker productivity, which gives a competitive advantage over less technologically advanced workplaces. The increased productivity creates greater profit, which allows for a high-wage industry that can compete with less advanced workplaces that use more labour but pay workers less. The other side of this coin is that those workers who fear that technology will be used to displace them will view technology negatively. Unions have attempted to address this concern. For example, the Canadian Auto Workers union, noting an increased use of robotics in automobile manufacturing, has tried with some success to negotiate retraining programs for displaced workers. However, technologically advanced industries in Asia, with lower wages, may serve to cancel out the advantages North American industry enjoyed up to the 1970s and 1980s.

External Inputs: A Labour- or Capital-Intensive Workplace

Capital-intensive workplaces are those in which investments in machinery and technology can be used to offset the need for labour, or where few workers are required. Computer and software development companies fall into this category, as do, increasingly, financial services. Industries that are labour-intensive tend to fall into the service and public sectors, such as the hospitality industry and education, health care, and public security. Enterprises that are by nature labour-intensive, particularly in the service sectors, are either unionized or targets for unionization. Those that are capital-intensive often have fewer workers, and may be difficult to unionize because of resistance by workers who are not union-oriented, and because work units may be too small to effectively organize.

External Inputs: Rate of Technological Change

The rate of technological change can have effects on the stability of a unionized workplace. Rapid technological change can make whole industries obsolete, particularly if they do not react quickly enough to changes. Ship building in North America, once a large established industry, has for the most part disappeared in the face of Asian competition. Technologically advanced production, combined with intensive capital investment, gave Asian shipyards a crucial edge in efficiency and productivity.

Rapid technological change can also cause jobs to disappear, and skills to become quickly outmoded. Most unions in these circumstances will be looking for retraining opportunities for these displaced workers. Management, on the other hand, often prefers to avoid the costs of retraining by jettisoning obsolete workers and hiring those who already have the requisite skills. Management may also be looking for greater flexibility in job classification so that people can be moved around from task to task in a reorganized workplace. If the pace of technological change is slower, there are greater opportunities for both sides to adjust to changes, at lower financial and human cost.

Conversion of Inputs to Outputs

Recall that internal inputs consist of goals, values, and power, and that external inputs consist of political, economic, social, and technological effects. A scan of the inputs, both internal and external, gives us a useful introduction to the labour relations landscape. But it is a static landscape like a photograph. To turn the photograph into a movie, we need to have a way of conceptualizing and talking about the processes that result in internal inputs becoming outputs. Craig identifies three of the more relevant processes: unilateral decisions, bipartite negotiations, and third-party assistance.[8]

UNILATERAL DECISIONS

Some input conversions into outputs are the result of one party or one individual deciding and acting. In a non-unionized setting, the employer makes most decisions about whom to hire, what to pay, what work is done, and how it is to be done. Although the employer might be affected by a variety of environmental inputs— for example, new technology in the workplace—he or she need not share the decision making. In a unionized setting, each side has some opportunities for independent action. The union decides which grievances to take forward and when sanctions should be invoked. The employer maintains the freedom to manage the business subject only to limits imposed by the collective agreement.

BIPARTITE NEGOTIATIONS

One of the features of a unionized labour relations setting is the conversion of inputs into outputs through negotiation between the parties. If the relationship is harmonious, a broader range of outputs are likely to be determined after negotiation. Relevant bipartite negotiations include negotiation between groups within the union to determine goals. For example, there may be matters primarily of interest to female workers, such as subsidized day care, that are of less interest to male workers. Similarly, there may be internal negotiations within the ranks of management, because different managers have different agendas. The human resources manager will be concerned with employee morale, while the chief financial officer may be more interested in lowering labour costs. The third set of bipartite negotiations usually follows from the first two sets, negotiations between labour and management. This includes not just contract negotiations, but also more informal types of bipartite negotiations over grievances, workplace irritants that are not grievable, and other matters.

THIRD-PARTY ASSISTANCE

Bipartite negotiations do not always end in a mutually satisfactory settlement. They can stall, turn into angry confrontations where one party or the other or both stalk off, or continue at great length without any resolution. In Canada, contract negotiations cannot go directly to a strike or lockout unless a conciliator has tried

---

8   Ibid., at 22-23.

and failed to bring about a settlement. The parties may also use mediators to try to work out a settlement, or agree to arbitration, although only conciliation is required. Where strikes are prohibited, as in the case of essential public services, the parties are required to resort to compulsory arbitration. From these efforts will come the output in the form of a collective agreement.

If bipartite negotiations fail to resolve workplace grievances, the issues must be sent by the grievor to be arbitrated by an independent arbitrator or a panel of arbitrators. Other workplace issues may also arise that are not arbitrable, and here many contracts will provide for, at minimum, a forum where union and management can discuss these issues.

Where third-party assistance fails to resolve issues, particularly in the context of contract negotiations, then the parties turn to coercive outputs: strikes and lockouts. The parties hope these will lead to a settlement down the road as a final output that will produce system stability (unless the settlement leaves key issues unresolved).

THE CONSTITUTIONAL AND LEGAL ENVIRONMENT OF LABOUR RELATIONS

Labour relations in Canada originated in a process where workers voluntarily joined together to found and shape organizations to speak on their behalf in the workplace. It was after that happened that the state found it necessary to become involved in labour relations, largely to regulate and channel conflict. When the state steps in, it must do so within the constraints on state power. In Canada, a federal state, the chief constraint is the constitutional division of powers that gives the federal government and Parliament power over some aspects of labour relations, while other powers fall to the provinces. Another constraint is the *Canadian Charter of Rights and Freedoms*.[9] The Charter defines rights and freedoms of individuals that the state cannot interfere with. This can raise interesting conflicts in which the rights of individuals clash with the rights of unions, which act on behalf of members as a whole. These disputes may involve federal and provincial labour legislation that elevates the rights of collectivities over the rights of individuals.

The Constitution Act, 1867

The *Constitution Act, 1867*[10] sets out the structure of Canadian government, creating the Canadian state, and dividing its powers between the federal and provincial governments. The powers of the provinces are set out in s. 92, and were designed to permit provinces to deal with matters that fell primarily within their boundaries, matters that were of a "private or local nature." Section 92.13 is particularly important as it empowers the provinces to pass laws governing "property and civil rights in the province." The courts have interpreted this section as giving the provinces the power to pass labour legislation regulating minimum wages, hours of work,

---

9   Part I of the *Constitution Act, 1982*, RSC 1985, app. II, no. 44.

10 30 & 31 Vict., c. 3 (UK).

overtime, occupational health and safety, and labour relations in unionized workplaces.

The federal government has the power to regulate labour relations and pass laws under powers granted by the *Constitution Act, 1867*, but the rights are specific rather than general. These include

- s. 91.2, "the regulation of trade and commerce,"

- s. 91.10, "navigation and shipping,"

- federally funded undertakings,

- works declared to be for the primary advantage of Canada (rather than a province),

- activities undertaken during a national emergency, and

- activity undertaken directly by the federal government.

In practice this means that labour legislation governing certain industries will come under federal jurisdiction in the following cases: when the industries are primarily involved in interprovincial or international activity; when the industries are involved in transportation or shipping or both; or when the federal government is directly or indirectly involved in the enterprise.

SORTING OUT JURISDICTIONAL CONFLICT: TORONTO ELECTRIC COMMISSIONERS v. SNIDER

Until 1872, unions had been considered to be a conspiracy in restraint of trade, and were technically illegal. In 1872, the *Trades Union Act* passed by the federal Parliament gave unions legal status. At the beginning of the 20th century following several lengthy strikes, particularly on the railways, the federal government passed the *Industrial Disputes Investigation Act*, a first venture in regulating labour relations. Until the end of World War I, initial attempts to regulate labour unions were left to the federal government. The provinces took no part in regulating unionized workplaces. In 1925, the legality of the *Industrial Disputes Investigation Act* was challenged in *Toronto Electric Commissioners v. Snider*.[11] The case went all the way to the Judicial Committee of the Privy Council in Britain, which ruled that Parliament had exceeded its jurisdiction, and declared the Act *ultra vires*, or outside the authority of the federal government. The court also ruled that labour relations fell within provincial jurisdiction under s. 92.13, property and civil rights in the province. This left the federal government to govern labour relations within its own sphere.

Initially, the provinces took advantage of the constitutional right to delegate by, in most cases, simply adopting the federal labour legislation as its own. However, during the wartime emergency in the 1940s, the federal government, using the emergency doctrines developed under the constitution, took control over all labour relations in Canada under a wartime regulation, Order in Council PC 1003. This regulation also modernized labour relations, requiring unions to be certified as bargaining agents, and requiring employers to recognize and bargain with unions

---

11 [1925] AC 396 (PC).

that had been certified. This became the basis for the current labour relations regime in Canada, and the model for provincial legislation enacted after the war.

The Charter of Rights and Freedoms

Until 1982, constitutional law involving labour relations was mostly concerned with disputes about the division of powers: which level of government had jurisdiction to legislate on labour relations matters. In 1982, with the passage of the *Constitution Act, 1982*,[12] which includes the Charter, further constitutional issues were added. Under the Charter, enumerated individual rights are protected from government action and legislation, at both the provincial and federal level, according to s. 31(2) of the Act. The Charter is declared to be the supreme law of Canada, overriding ordinary legislation under s. 52 of the Act, so that laws, including labour relations laws, that are inconsistent with it are of no force and effect.

The legal basis for the labour relations regime we now have was assembled during the 1940s, at first by the federal government and later by the provinces. It is a regime that recognizes collective or group rights, sometimes at the expense of individual rights. Some examples follow:

- Once a union is certified, the employer is compelled to deal with or associate with the union in many instances, rather than with the individual employee.

- Once a union is certified, individual workers' rights to deal directly with the employer or to act independently are subordinated to the union's right to deal with the employer on behalf of all employees and to act on behalf of all members collectively.

- In some instances, the rights of an individual in a bargaining unit will be subordinated to the rights of the union membership as a whole.

- All members of bargaining units are required to pay union dues, whether they are members of the union or not. In some cases, they must be union members in order to work for a specific employer, as is the case in the construction industry.

How the tension between balancing collective rights and individual rights under the Charter is to be resolved is not altogether clear. Certainly, the Charter is not self-explanatory or self-applying. Under s. 24 of the Act, the rights in the Charter are broadly and generally stated, and the interpretation of how those rights are applied has been left to the courts, and by inference to tribunals, such as labour boards and boards of arbitration. The rights in the Charter are not absolute but are subject to limitations set out in s. 1, which guarantees rights subject to "such reasonable limits prescribed by law as can be demonstrably justified in a free and democratic society." The courts have developed a scheme for analyzing Charter problems in the context of s. 1, starting in the case of *R v. Oakes*:[13]

---

12 RSC 1985, app. II, no. 44.

13 [1986] 1 SCR 103.

- Does the impugned state action or legislation have an objective of pressing and substantial concern?

- If so, is this objective proportional to the impugned measure?

- Is it rationally connected to the objective?

- Does it impair the right or freedom as little as possible?

- Is there a proportionality between the objective and the effects of the measure which limits the right or freedom?

Failure at any stage of this step-by-step analysis will mean that the impugned government action cannot be upheld as a reasonable limit on a Charter right.

The impact of the Charter on labour relations has been the subject of some commentary by labour relations practitioners and academics. The gist of the problem has been summed up as follows:

> [I]t is very difficult to defend the solidaristic and collectivist principles of trade unionism when faced with the existence of constitutionally entrenched individual rights. ... [I]t is still possible that traditional union rights will be seen to be of second class nature insofar as they are political-legal rights without constitutional bases.[14]

CHARTER ISSUE: GRIEVANCE ARBITRATION

A number of Charter issues have arisen in grievance arbitration. The respected arbitrator and academic Donald Carter[15] has noted that grievance arbitrations operate with external values derived from labour legislation that makes arbitration mandatory. Because the Charter applies to government-directed activity, it could apply to the arbitration process, importing Charter-protected external values such as freedom of speech or religion into the arbitration process. In the arbitration process, these external values might override interpretations reflecting internal values of collective agreements that reflect the views of private parties to those agreements. For example, the internal value of seniority in determining work assignments, which is set out in the terms of a contract and which an arbitrator would normally follow, may be overridden by Charter-protected freedom of religion. Thus, the external value of freedom of religion becomes a factor in determining a work assignment so as to conform to a worker's religious-observance requirements, despite his or her low seniority. In one sense, grievance arbitration is a private dispute settlement activity that should fall outside the Charter. But the structure for it is established by legislation, and imports a public dimension.

Will that public dimension provide a point of entry where the Charter will be used to disrupt and destroy the arbitral process, and challenge the conventions of contract interpretation developed over decades? The courts have already decided that individuals affected by an arbitration, other than the parties, must be given

---

14 D. Carter and T. McIntosh, "Collective Bargaining and the Charter: Assessing the Impact of American Judicial Doctrines" (1991), vol. 46, no. 4 *Relations Industrielles* 745, cited in Craig and Solomon, supra note 4, at 453.

15 Ibid., at 352-54. Carter's observations were originally set out in D.D. Carter, "Grievance Arbitration and the Charter: The Emerging Issues" (1989), vol. 44, no. 2 *Relations Industrielles* 338.

notice of the proceedings. Courts have also held that the members of the board of arbitration must not be too closely associated with either party.[16] Carter notes that some arbitrators initially ruled that the Charter applies to arbitrations, while others ruled that it did not, on the grounds that arbitrations are concerned primarily with private matters. It is now clear, at least in Ontario, that under s. 54 of the Ontario *Labour Relations Act, 1995*[17] a collective agreement cannot discriminate against someone if that discrimination would violate the Charter or the *Canadian Human Rights Act*.[18] Arguably this means that the arbitration process, which is mandatory in every collective agreement, must conform to the Charter.

CHARTER ISSUE: THE RIGHT TO STRIKE AND BARGAIN COLLECTIVELY

Some argue that if freedom of association in s. 2(d) of the Charter creates a right for individuals to join trade unions, then this section also creates a right for those acting in association to do what they joined to do, including conducting strikes and bargaining collectively. However, the courts have ruled that freedom of association confers the right on individuals to join organizations, but that that right does not create a Charter licence to engage in strikes or to bargain collectively.[19] Constitutionally valid legislation at the provincial and federal levels continues to bar strikes by workers performing essential services. Picketing is still restricted by the courts in an attempt to balance, on the one hand, strikers' rights to communicate with the public and pressure the employer and, on the other, the right of the public to come and go freely. Although limitations on striking and picketing have been found to violate the Charter, so far the courts have ruled that limitations on these activities can be justified under s. 1 of the Charter.

CHARTER ISSUE: FREEDOM NOT TO ASSOCIATE

While s. 2(d) of the Charter clearly creates a right to join a trade union, does it also create a right not to be associated with a trade union? This was the issue raised in *Lavigne v. OPSEU*.[20] In this case, Mervyn Lavigne was a college teacher and a member of the bargaining unit represented by the Ontario Public Service Employees Union (OPSEU). Because there was a compulsory dues check-off, he had to pay dues. Lavigne objected to being associated with the union by being forced to pay dues for things he did not agree with. The lower court recognized the legitimacy of the labour relations scheme in place, saying that some degree of association was unavoidable. But the court also held that Lavigne, although obliged to pay dues to support core functions connected to bargaining, should not have to pay for union

---

16 The common three-person arbitration board consists of one nominee chosen by each party, and a neutral chair chosen by the nominees or selected by lot. The court's concern was with the nominees.

17 SO 1995, c. 1, sched. A.

18 RSC 1985, c. H-6.

19 *Reference re: Public Service Employee Relations Act (Alberta)*, [1987] 1 SCR 313; and *Professional Institute of the Public Service of Canada v. Northwest Territories (Commissioner)*, [1990] 2 SCR 367.

20 [1991] 2 SCR 211.

political initiatives he disagreed with. However, the Court of Appeal and the Supreme Court of Canada ruled that he was obliged to pay dues for legitimate union activities. Legitimate union activities, in the courts' view, included not only collective bargaining and contract administration but also political activity in the greater community. The union had a right to collect dues from Lavigne for all of the things a union does. This case was extremely important for the labour movement, because it recognized for Charter purposes the right of a union to fund itself from those who benefit from its services, and to subordinate individual rights in some circumstances to the interest of the union in acting collectively.

In another case, *Arlington Crane Service et al. v. Ontario Ministry of Labour*,[21] the court held that a union in the construction industry was entitled to maintain a closed shop—that is, a job applicant could be denied a position if he or she was not a member of the union. In this case the owners of the crane company were prevented from hiring their grandson, a non-union member, because of a closed-shop agreement. The court held that the matter did not attract Charter intervention because the legislation merely authorized but did not require a closed shop. Since this was something the parties had agreed to as a private matter, the courts would not intervene under the Charter, because it only applied to government acts and legislation.

FEDERAL AND PROVINCIAL LABOUR LEGISLATION

Canada's modern regime governing labour relations began to develop in the 1940s as the federal and provincial governments recognized that a legal framework was necessary to support a stable and predictable labour relations system in the public interest. Important aspects of that legislation are briefly described here.

Federal Labour Relations Legislation

As we know from *Toronto Electric Commissioners v. Snider*, labour relations at the federal level are restricted to activities and legislation that come within the federal jurisdiction. This includes federal public sector labour relations involving the federal public service and a handful of industries and enterprises that are within the federal sphere.

THE CANADA LABOUR CODE

Since 1970, labour relations at the federal level have come under division V of part I of the *Canada Labour Code*.[22] This part applies to workers in enterprises that fall within the federal jurisdiction under the *Constitution Act, 1867*. These enterprises include:

- air transportation;
- interprovincial or international communications, transportation, shipping, and connections such as bridges, tunnels, pipelines and ferries;

---

21 (1989), 89 CLLC 12.

22 RSC 1985, c. L-2.

- banks and other federally chartered financial institutions;

- federal Crown corporations; and

- specific undertakings that have been "declared ... to be for the general Advantage of Canada"[23] (they include, for example, the processing, storage, and shipping of grain, and the uranium mining industry).

Under division V of part I of the Code, employees have the right to organize and join unions and to bargain with employers. The code sets out minimum contract requirements, including a clause to arbitrate all contract disputes during the life of the agreement. Unfair labour practices by both unions and employers are prohibited. The Code lays down procedures for conciliation during negotiation. The administration of labour relations at the federal level falls to the Canada Labour Relations Board.

THE FEDERAL PUBLIC SECTOR: THE PUBLIC SERVICE STAFF RELATIONS ACT

The rights of public service employees in the federal government to unionization rights came with the passage in 1967 of the *Public Service Staff Relations Act*.[24] It set up a scheme where employees could organize and join unions and bargain with the Treasury Board as the body responsible for public service labour relations. The Act provides somewhat different rules for negotiations for public sector workers from those for private sector workers, partly because the right of public service workers to strike is much more limited. Unions have to choose either (1) negotiations with conciliation, followed by the right to strike, or (2) compulsory arbitration, without the right to strike, where if there is an impasse, the arbitrator determines the contents of the collective agreement.

Provincial Labour Relations Legislation

After the federal government set up the basic framework of the labour relations regulatory scheme during World War II, the provinces followed suit with similar labour relations legislation. As a result, every province now has its own labour relations legislation to govern labour activities within the province. Some legislation covers all workers, and some covers only workers in specific sectors, such as the public service. Described here is the legislative framework in Ontario.

THE ONTARIO LABOUR RELATIONS ACT, 1995

This Act applies to all unionized workplaces except where more specific legislation overrides it, as is the case for provincial employees who are wholly or partly governed by different legislation. Like its federal counterpart, this Act sets up a process for certifying unions after an organization drive, with mandatory bargaining of collective agreements. The agreements all must contain certain basic provisions, such as an arbitration clause to deal with contract disputes during the life of the contract. Bargaining in good faith is required, and the Ontario Labour Rela-

---

23 *Constitution Act, 1867*, s. 92(10).

24 RSC 1985, c. P-35.

tions Board has jurisdiction over complaints of any party that alleges unfair labour practices. Compulsory conciliation is required during negotiations before the parties can resort to strikes or lockouts. The legislation may also set up special procedures for some sectors, such as the construction industry.

THE CROWN EMPLOYEES COLLECTIVE BARGAINING ACT, 1993

All provinces have an act like Ontario's *Crown Employees Collective Bargaining Act, 1993*[25] to govern labour relations with the civil service. The Act sets up a grievance settlement board to arbitrate all complaints arising under collective agreements. The legislation also deals with other complaints, such as unfair labour practices that are heard by the labour board under the Ontario *Labour Relations Act, 1995*. Unlike with the legislation in other provinces, as a result of changes in the early 1990s the right to bargain collectively and to strike has been extended to nearly all public servants in Ontario. However, in 1995, the government of then premier Mike Harris exempted new employers from having to deal with successor rights where public services with previously unionized employees are privatized. Other changes eliminated bargaining rights for a variety of specialized workers and professionals in the public service, and limited the powers of the grievance settlement board to fashion remedies to complaints.

Workers in the broader public sector, such as teachers, police, firefighters, and hospital workers, are covered under different contracts and different specialized legislation. For example, college teachers are governed by the *Colleges Collective Bargaining Act* rather than by the *Labour Relations Act, 1995*.

EMPLOYMENT STANDARDS ACT, 2000

The *Employment Standards Act, 2000*[26] sets minimum standards for wages, hours, and working conditions for employees who are not unionized. Collective agreements will usually contain provisions that go well beyond the minimum. The legislation provides the machinery for processing complaints by workers, and for enforcing the standards in the legislation. Other provinces have similar legislation. Note that some employment rights are left to the courts and the common law. For example, a non-unionized employee who is wrongfully dismissed may refuse to take pay in lieu of notice at the level outlined in employment standards legislation, and sue for more in the civil courts. A unionized employee, however, must use the grievance arbitration provisions in the collective agreement.

OCCUPATIONAL HEALTH AND SAFETY ACT

The *Occupational Health and Safety Act*[27] is general legislation that applies to unionized and non-unionized workplaces in the province. It sets out minimum health and safety standards for various types of workplaces. It also sets up a scheme where workers and employers, through joint workplace committees, oversee safety

---

25 SO 1993, c. 38.

26 SO 2000, c. 41.

27 RSO 1990, c. O.1.

standards and issues, and attempt to resolve problems. If they cannot be resolved, the Ministry of Labour may step in. The Act also sets standards and a procedure allowing a worker to refuse unsafe work. If the standards are violated, any party to the violation may be prosecuted.

WORKPLACE SAFETY AND INSURANCE ACT, 1997

The *Workplace Safety and Insurance Act, 1997*,[28] like similar legislation in other provinces, sets up an insurance scheme to compensate workers who are injured in the course of employment. It applies to unionized and non-unionized employees. It generally prohibits an injured worker from suing the employer for negligence, and does not require fault to be proven, because it is a no-fault system, funded through the payment of premiums by employers.

CHAPTER SUMMARY

This chapter introduced some of the basic elements of the labour relations system in Canada involving unionized workplaces. It began with an overview of systems theory, with references to both its utility and some of its shortcomings. It then examined two of the classic systems models for analyzing labour relations: the Dunlop model and the Craig model. The Dunlop model, developed in the United States in the 1950s, systematically describes the variables that affect outcomes in the labour relations system. Dunlop focused on four key factors: actors, environmental factors, ideology of the parties, and rule systems. His model presumed harmony and consensus, which is not always characteristic of labour relations. Discussion then turned to the Craig model, noting that it was better suited to the Canadian environment than Dunlop's because it took levels of conflict into account as part of its system analysis. The main components of the Craig analytic framework are internal inputs from the participants, external inputs from the general environment, a way of showing internal inputs creating outputs, and a feedback loop demonstrating how outputs influenced future inputs and future system behaviour. Internal inputs, external inputs, and outputs were then examined in more detail, providing a panoramic view of the labour relations system. Finally, the chapter examined the legal and constitutional foundations that underlie labour relations, noting the effect of the division of powers and the impact of the Charter.

REVIEW QUESTIONS

1. How does a systems model of labour relations help us to understand labour relations?

2. What are the negative aspects of the systems analysis of labour relations?

3. What are the principal features of the Dunlop model?

---

28 SO 1997, c. 16, sched. A.

4. What are the principal features of the Craig model?

5. What is the significance of the *Toronto Electric Commissioners v. Snider* case?

6. Identify three areas where the Charter might be of concern to labour relations professionals.

7. What are the key pieces of legislation governing labour relations at the federal level?

8. What are the key pieces of legislation governing labour relations in Ontario?

DISCUSSION QUESTIONS

1. You are the business agent for a union local that represents machinists and other workers in a factory that manufactures industrial machinery. You have received some questions from area shop stewards that require some answers:

   a. One of the workers has been dismissed for sending nasty, anonymous emails to management. She has denied doing this, and grieved her dismissal. At arbitration, one of the witnesses gave evidence that implicated another employee, who is not a member of the union or of the bargaining unit. Can the grievance continue without notice being given to the employee who was implicated, if the employee is not a member of the bargaining unit?

   b. A steward has heard grumbling from one or two members about paying dues when they disagree with what the union is doing in current negotiations. As well, apparently at a convention for the national union, the delegates approved a motion giving funds to a terrorist group that is trying to liberate its homeland from foreign control. Can the members withhold payment of union dues if they disagree with union policies?

CHAPTER 3

Organizing a Workplace

INTRODUCTION

In this chapter, we will examine the process that a union must use to be authorized to represent a group of employees. We will also outline the steps that an employer may legally take to respond to a union's activities. We will describe the right of the workers to take part in a union and their right to remove a union if they become disenchanted with that union.

Initially the legal system treated unionization as an illegal restraint of trade, and organizers of unions were punished.[1] The law was changed to make unions legal, but this did not make unions the automatic representatives of the workers. The only mechanisms for a union to be made the representative for workers were either the exercise of force through a strike or, less commonly, a voluntary agreement by the employer to accept the union. This issue of recognition led to work stoppages, some of which became acrimonious. To reduce instances of industrial conflict, the labour legislation was again amended. It replaced a system of recognition based on labour power with a system of determining representative rights through a legal process based on membership evidence and workplace votes. Labour boards were invested with the power to supervise this legal system, including the power to award unions with representation rights and to authorize sanctions against parties who violated the rules.

Under the present system for organization in Ontario, the union solicits workers to sign membership cards. When the union has signed up enough members, it applies to the Ontario Labour Relations Board (OLRB). The board will conduct a vote. If the union wins the vote, the board will issue a certificate stating that the union now represents a specified group of workers and that the employer must now bargain with those workers. The board will also have to deal with disputes over technical issues with respect to the process and alleged violations of the rules.

WHY WORKERS ORGANIZE

In general, workers organize in unions to obtain greater bargaining power and to use this power to obtain better terms and conditions of employment from their employer—usually, better salary, benefits, and job security.

In the absence of a union, workers who wish to improve their terms and conditions of employment must either request improvements, and threaten to quit

---

1   For a history of this subject, see L. Panitch and D. Swartz, *The Attack on Trade Union Freedoms* (Toronto: Garamond Press, 1993), 2.

if these improvements are not given, or simply quit and go to another employer offering better terms. The employer may grant improvements if a worker has special skills that the employer needs and if that worker is hard to replace. Or, the employer may refuse the request and replace that worker if he or she quits. The worker may then find better conditions elsewhere or, if not, may have to remain under the existing conditions.

In a unionized work environment, workers can use collective action to obtain improvements. All the workers collectively decide on what improvements should be requested and withdraw services in concert if the employer does not offer adequate improvements. Ideally, this collective action will give workers greater power and result in enhanced working conditions.[2]

Unions engaged in organizing a workplace will try to persuade workers to join the union by selling workers on the benefits of the union. They will often argue that a union will improve their conditions of employment through

- job security based on length of service;

- increased salary and benefits;

- a grievance system to solve workplace disputes;

- the assistance of union representatives both within the workplace and with external agencies such as the Workplace Safety and Insurance Appeals Tribunal, employment insurance information, pension information, etc.;

- a collective agreement that spells out their rights and benefits; and

- collective bargaining, which will give them more power.[3]

ORGANIZING THE WORKPLACE

Who Can Organize?

To make an application to be recognized as a union, an applicant must show that it qualifies as a "trade union" under s. 1 of the Ontario *Labour Relations Act, 1995* (OLRA or "the Act").[4] To qualify as a **trade union**, the applicant must show the following characteristics:

- it is an organization of employees; and

- it bargains to improve working conditions.

There must also be an operating organization that includes officers who are responsible for the actions of the organization and some form of constitution or founding document to govern the operation of the organization. The union must

---

2 On the impact of a union, see R. Freeman and J. Medoff, *What Do Unions Do?* (New York: Basic Books, 1984).

3 Two of the largest Canadian unions outline these reasons publicly on their websites. The Steelworkers give reasons why workers should organize at http://www.uswa.ca/eng/who_we_are/swgendis_2.htm and the Canadian Auto Workers at http://www.caw.ca/jointheCAW/index.asp.

4 SO 1995, c. 1, sched. A. See also D. Randazzo, *The 2003 Annotated Labour Relations Act* (Toronto: Carswell, 2002).

also be an organization of "employees" as defined under the Act. (See below for a detailed discussion of the definition of employees.) Finally, the union must be set up at the time an application to the OLRB is made.

A trade union must have as one of its objectives "the regulation of relations between employees and employers." This means that the purpose of the union must include negotiating to improve wages, benefits, and other aspects of its members' work lives. This objective is often expressly contained in the constitution that created the union. For example, the Ontario Public Service Employees Union (OPSEU) includes in its constitution the following aim:[5]

> (a) To regulate labour relations between the Members and their employers and managers, said labour relations to include the scope of negotiation, collective bargaining, the enforcement of collective agreements and health and safety standards, and the safeguarding of human rights.

The first time a new union appears before the OLRB, it will have to show these characteristics. For a new union, this means it must have had a meeting of its members to adopt its founding document and elect its officers, such as a president, vice-president, and treasurer. The labour board, in the case of *Local 199 UAW Building Corp.*,[6] suggested that the ideal process a new union should follow includes the following five steps:

1. Drafting a constitution for the organization. The constitution should set out the purposes of the organization. One of the purposes must be the regulation of labour relations. The constitution should also set out procedures for electing officers and calling meetings.

2. Calling a meeting of the employees to approve the constitution and to elect officers.

3. Admitting the employees at the meeting to membership.

4. Voting by the members at the meeting to adopt the constitution.

5. Electing officers according to the newly adopted constitution.

In most cases, the unions appearing before the board are established and over time have made numerous applications. Their status as trade unions will be accepted without argument. Section 113 of the Act provides that once an organization has been determined to be a trade union, then that finding will apply in subsequent cases unless evidence to the contrary is provided.

How Do Unions Organize a Workplace?

Unions organize a workplace by initiating an **organizing drive**. Many unions employ professional organizers who sign up members and prepare the applications for the labour board.

In other cases, dissatisfied employees at the workplace approach a union to initiate an organizing drive, or the union's organizers may approach employees,

---

5   Available online at http://www.opseu.org/constitution/main.htm, section 2.

6   [1977] OLRB Rep. July 472.

who then agree to join the union. Bob White, former president of the Canadian Auto Workers (CAW) and the Canadian Labour Congress (CLC), describes a common union organizing process in his autobiography:[7]

> Jack Pawson came over the next morning. Pawson was a little guy who talked a mile a minute. We went to a doughnut shop for breakfast while he filled me in on what had to be done and what Barrie was like. We were on our own. What we did, and how we did it, was up to us. According to Ontario labour legislation, the union had to get 55 percent of employees to sign membership cards before the UAW would be recognized as the official bargaining agent.[8]
>
> Our first task was to figure out how many people worked in the plants. That wasn't as easy as it sounds because employees are always being hired and laid off, shifts come and go, and there are part-time workers. Once we knew the numbers, we had to go out and get the requisite cards signed.
>
> Neither of us knew a soul in Barrie so we started from scratch. We stood outside the plants at quitting time looking at the workers coming out, trying to pick out a likely one. Then we'd follow that person home, hoping we weren't too obvious about it, and make a note of the address. After giving the worker time to have dinner, we would go back at night and knock on the door. We said we were from the UAW and we'd like to talk for a few minutes, if it was convenient. Once inside, we'd make our pitch. Talking enthusiastically about the UAW wasn't difficult for me. I loved the union and it showed.
>
> Then we'd do the same thing for the night shift—follow workers home when they left the gates at dawn, give them time to sleep, and knock on doors in the afternoons. Saturdays and Sundays, we worked like hell.

The methods used to get members to join the union will depend on an assessment of how best to reach the employees without alerting the employer until the drive is well on its way. The union hopes that the employer does not become aware of the organizing drive until the organizers give the employer a copy of the application that it has already submitted to the board. If the employer learns of the organizing drive, it may attempt to block it.

In the case where a dissatisfied worker approaches a union, the union will have to ensure that this worker is an employee under the Act. Then it will have to assess the reasons this employee, and perhaps other employees, may be dissatisfied and develop a campaign to show that the union will satisfy those needs. It will then have to approach the workers. The initial contact may be able to provide the union with the names and addresses of other dissatisfied employees. These workers could be approached at home, and the professional organizer could be accompanied by the initial contact if the organizer assesses that the contact has sufficient credibility with other employees. If the workplace is large enough, the union may recruit some of the early enthusiastic members to enlist subsequent members. However, the union must ensure that these volunteers understand the rules regarding organizing; otherwise, the labour board may exclude the memberships solicited by these persons for violation of the rules. The union will also want to contact employees who may have access to lists of addresses of employees. These may be workers who facilitate social groups such as a bowling league or events such as a golf tournament.

---

7   B. White, *Hard Bargains: My Life on the Line* (Toronto: McClelland & Stewart, 1987), 59.

8   The OLRA has been changed to eliminate the automatic certification provision.

As the organizing drive proceeds, the union may switch tactics. For example, the union may use visible plant gating, an activity where organizers show up at the workplace when employees are entering for their shift in order to give them information on the union and encourage them to join. The drawback of this tactic is that it immediately alerts the employer. Alternatively, the union may invite workers to a mass meeting at a union hall to listen to union speeches and then ask the workers to sign up. This tactic, too, has its pitfalls, including alerting the employer. Worse, if the meeting is poorly attended, it will be a disaster for the momentum of the drive.

If the union does not have a contact at a particular workplace, it may have to resort to following workers home at the end of the day, as described by Bob White. Or they may try to meet workers at a location near the plant, such as a transit stop or restaurant, in order to start the drive. Unions now operate websites, which include a section where a worker can contact the organizing department in confidence to discuss joining the union.

What Is the Goal of the Organizing Drive?

A trade union must get a sufficient number of employees to sign a membership card in order to trigger a **certification** vote at the workplace. Then the union must win this vote. Sections 8(2) and 10(1) of the Act require that at least 40 percent of the employees sign up as union members and that over 50 percent of the votes in a certification vote be in favour of the union. If these conditions are met, the union will be certified as the bargaining agent for a group of workers and the employer will be required by law to deal with that union.

Ideally, a union will persuade all the employees to become members, but that is seldom a realistic objective. Moreover, seeking a higher number of registered members may prolong the organizing drive and allow the employer time to dissuade workers from voting. If the union is able to sign up only the bare minimum of 40 percent that is required to trigger a vote, it is unlikely to succeed in the vote. Thus, organizers have to assess when they have signed up enough members to achieve a successful vote.

ELIGIBILITY TO BE ORGANIZED

Who Is Eligible?

A trade union is certified to represent a group of employees, and the Ontario Labour Relations Board sets out who are **employees** for the purposes of the Act. Some workers are deemed to be employees under common law for the purposes of other legislation but not the Ontario *Labour Relations Act, 1995*. These workers are excluded from the protections of and mechanisms for certification in the OLRB. In addition, an organization that admits as members workers who are not employees as defined by the Act would not be an "organization of employees" and thus would not be a valid trade union under the OLRA. Workers who are not employees under the OLRA often do organize, but in a form different from that of a certified union, and some do have considerable bargaining power based on their specialized skills.

Below is a list of the most significant groups of workers that are excluded from the definition of employees under s. 1(3) of the OLRA. A discussion of each group follows the list.

- Managers: persons who direct the organization.

- Confidentials: persons who have access to sensitive material on labour relations matters.

- Professionals: specific employment groups who have been historically excluded from collective bargaining.

MANAGERS

A manager is not an employee for the purposes of the OLRA. An organization that includes managers as members cannot be a trade union for the purposes of recognition under the Act. The scheme of the Act recognizes that there is an inherent conflict if the persons who make the workplace rules are part of the trade union that is asking for changes to those rules.

Note that the title of a person is not crucial to determining whether he or she is or is not a manager—it is the actual functions performed by that person. In general terms, a **manager** is a person who makes decisions that affect the economic lives of other workers. A manager's activities include

- hiring,

- firing,

- promoting,

- demoting,

- disciplining,

- determining wages,

- determining work schedules,

- determining vacation schedules and other benefits, and

- making policy decisions for the organization, including decisions regarding budget development.

It is not necessary that a manager perform all these tasks to be classified as a manager. Further, a person may still be a manager even though he or she does not make the final decision on the treatment of an employee—for example, if his or her recommendation is subject in practice to automatic approval ("rubber stamping") by a superior. This is called the ability to make **effective recommendations** and is a characteristic of a manager.

However, merely directing the work of other employees does not make a person a manager. For example, many workplaces have persons with the title of **lead hand** who direct the work of other employees but do not discipline them. When an issue emerges, such as poor performance, they report the matter to a superior, who then takes action. These lead hands are not managers under the Act and can properly be part of the union.

Whichever party wants to argue that certain employees are managers has the burden or onus of showing that these employees are managers and should be excluded. Note that the board will not permit the employer to defeat the possibility of unionization by assigning a management function to virtually all the employees. The board will expect to see a relationship between the number of supervisors and the number of employees that is consistent with industry norms and practices.

If the trade union signs up members who are later determined to be managers, the membership evidence for these workers will not be counted for the purpose of determining whether the union has sufficient support to trigger a vote. In addition, the votes of these workers will not be counted in any vote.

CONFIDENTIALS

A **confidential** is a person employed in a confidential capacity in labour relations matters and is not an employee under the OLRA. This provision is based on the view that these workers would be in a tremendous conflict of interest. For example, workers in human resources departments are privy to confidential information that is used by employers to form proposals or responses in collective bargaining or grievance negotiations. If such workers were granted union membership, the Act argues, they could reveal this information to the union to enhance its bargaining power. As employees entrusted with confidential matters, they would risk breaching their employment contract if they revealed matters to the union. To avoid this conflict, they are excluded from collective bargaining.

Note, though, that in the case of human resources workers, they must have a regular and important involvement in collective bargaining matters. If they were limited to answering the phone and directing calls within the human resources department, they would not be confidentials. In the board's terminology, they would not have a material involvement in collective bargaining. Similarly, if they were called in on an emergency basis to deal with a grievance matter on only one occasion in the past year, they would not be confidential employees.

Any membership cards signed by confidentials will be excluded both for the purpose of obtaining a vote and for the recognition vote itself.

PROFESSIONALS

Some professionals are not employees for the purposes of the OLRA. Architects, lawyers, land surveyors, doctors, and dentists entitled to practise their profession in Ontario and employed in a professional capacity are not covered by the OLRA. The exclusion of the professions is historical; there is no logical inconsistency with the process of collective bargaining if these groups of professionals engaged in collective bargaining with their employers. Even though many of these professionals work in partnerships or as sole proprietors and are not employees, there is nothing in the Act that should prevent professionals who act as employees from exercising collective bargaining rights. Most of these professions have their own professional associations that can improve working conditions by controlling access to the profession (for example, the Law Society of Upper Canada for lawyers) or engage in a form of collective negotiations with the government to deal with their terms and conditions of employment (as the Ontario Medical Association does with the Ontario government).

If the member of a profession is acting outside their professional capacity, they can be included in a **bargaining unit**. Thus professionals employed by educational institutions to train new members of the profession will be part of a bargaining unit that represents the teaching staff of the educational institution. Likewise, lawyers hired by universities to teach law students have been included in the bargaining unit covering professors at the university. However, a lawyer hired on a full-time or part-time basis by a university to perform legal work would be excluded from any unionization efforts by a union organizing the university workforce. In such a case, the lawyer would be acting in a professional capacity and therefore would not be eligible to be included in a bargaining unit.

Workplaces Not Covered by the OLRA

The OLRA does not apply to workplaces regulated by the federal government under the constitution. (See the section "The Ontario Labour Relations Act, 1995" in chapter 2 for details.) Also, s. 4 of the OLRA states that employees of the provincial government are covered by specific legislation regulating public servants.

In addition, s. 3 of the Act states that the Act does not apply to work settings in which the following employees are found:

- labour mediators or labour conciliators,

- police officers, including both the Ontario Provincial Police and municipal police officers,

- firefighters,

- teachers,

- employees of community colleges,

- provincial judges,

- agricultural workers,

- domestics employed in a private home,

- hunters and trappers, and

- horticultural workers employed by an employer whose primary business is horticulture or agriculture, but not horticultural workers who are employed in forestry.

Labour mediators and conciliators and provincial judges are excluded from unionization because they must act as neutrals in dealing with disputes between unions and employers. That neutrality would be compromised in the eyes of an employer if they were made members of a union. But police officers, firefighters, teachers, and some community college employees are allowed to organize under specific legislation governing their professions. Part-time and occasional workers in community colleges, however, are excluded from the collective bargaining scheme covering the community colleges. Thus they are excluded from collective bargaining.

Agricultural workers are covered by a legislative scheme that does not provide them the full set of rights to bargain collectively. One of the stated objectives of the exclusion of agricultural workers from the scheme of collective bargaining in the OLRB was to preserve the traditional "family farm." The board argued that if employees of farmers could organize, this could threaten the survival of the traditional farming arrangement.

This exclusion is clearly too broad if its objective is to protect only small sole proprietorship family farms. The exclusion of all agricultural workers meant that operations that looked more like factories than traditional farms would be insulated from collective bargaining because their output was agricultural. Consider "mushroom farms," which operate entirely in production buildings where forklifts move slabs of mushrooms in and out of growing rooms. Shifts of workers are engaged in operating the forklifts and other machinery, but because the output is mushrooms and not car parts, it was held in the case of *Wellington Mushroom Farm*[9] that the workers were excluded from the OLRB. Chicken cultivation also often operates entirely in a setting resembling a factory. It is highly mechanized and technologically sophisticated, with work shifts and year-round operations. Nevertheless, because the output is agricultural, the Supreme Court of Canada in the case of *Cuddy Chicks*[10] held that the workers could not unionize.

The exclusion of agricultural workers came under the scrutiny of the Supreme Court again in the case of *Dunmore v. Ontario (Attorney General)*.[11] In this case, the union argued that the exclusion of agricultural workers from collective bargaining violated the workers' freedom of association, which is protected under s. 2(d) of the *Canadian Charter of Rights and Freedoms* ("the Charter").[12] The Supreme Court held that the exclusion did violate the Charter and that the stated justification for the exclusion, protection of the family farm, could not be sustained as a reasonable limit in a free and democratic society.

The court went further to say that the government had to provide a legislative scheme that would allow agricultural workers to effectively exercise their right to association. In the absence of such legislation, it argued, there was no effective protection from unfair labour practices and no real mechanism to organize. However, the court did not mandate that the government include agricultural workers in the OLRA, so the government has responded by creating a special piece of labour legislation that does not give agricultural workers many of the rights normally associated with unionization. For example, agricultural workers have neither the right to strike nor the right to arbitration or other forms of adjudicated settlement if they cannot reach agreement with their employer on a contract. If this legislation is not amended, the courts in a subsequent case will probably be called upon to determine whether this new legislative structure is an adequate protection for the agricultural workers' right to freedom of association.

Domestic workers, hunters, trappers, and horticultural workers are completely excluded from any scheme that protects employees' rights to collectively bargain. Many of these workers operate their own business or work as a single employee

---

9   [1980] OLRB Rep. 813.

10 *Cuddy Chicks Ltd. v. Ontario (Labour Relations Board)*, [1991] 2 SCR 5.

11 *Dunmore v. Ontario (Attorney General)*, [2001] 3 SCR 1016.

12 *Canadian Charter of Rights and Freedoms*, part I of the *Constitution Act, 1982*, RSC 1985, app. II, no. 44.

and thus a collective bargaining regime would not apply to them. In light of the *Dunmore* case, there is arguably no reasonable justification that the government could raise for continuing to exclude these workers from their right to associate with other workers in a collective bargaining regime.

DEPENDENT CONTRACTORS

Sections 1 and 9 of the Act specifically provide that workers who can be described as dependent contractors are considered to be employees. Dependent contractors may not be considered to be employees in other contexts, but they are considered employees for the purpose of collective bargaining. The legal system makes a distinction between employees and independent contractors for the purposes of employment standards rules, notice for termination, taxation, employment insurance, and other matters. An employer has more responsibilities for its employees than it has for independent contractors. The distinction between independent contractors and employees is sometimes difficult to discern but it turns on such issues as how much control is exercised by the employer over the worker, who owns the tools, and how integral the worker is to the operation. Specifically, the Act protects the rights of workers who may not legally fit the strict definition of employee and may be classified as independent contractors under general legal principles but who, because they rely on one particular source of work, are deemed eligible to organize and bargain collectively.

The Act provides that workers are dependent contractors whether or not they supply tools or whether or not they have an employment contract if (1) they perform work for another person for compensation in circumstances where they are in a position of economic dependence and (2) they are obliged to perform duties for that person in a relationship that more closely resembles employment than an independent contract. This provision has been used in the case of truck drivers who may own their own trucks but haul materials for one company only.

Dependent contractors are deemed to be an appropriate bargaining unit on their own but they can be added to another bargaining unit if a majority of the dependent contractors involved agree to this. This could be shown either by membership evidence or a vote of this group.

EMPLOYMENT STATUS ISSUES AFTER CERTIFICATION

Sometimes a new classification of worker is created after a union is certified or the duties of an employee are altered. In this case, the employer and the union may be able to agree on whether that worker is or continues to be covered by the certification and is or is not represented by the union. If they cannot reach agreement on this issue, then s. 114(2) of the Act gives the OLRB the power to make a final and binding determination as to whether that worker is an employee. This matter may also be resolved by way of grievance arbitration. In 2001-2 the labour board dealt with 19 applications under this section: 10 of these were settled, 2 were granted, 2 were dismissed, and 5 were pending.[13]

---

13 OLRB Annual Report, available online at http://www.gov.on.ca/lab/olrb/eng/arnot.htm.

RIGHTS AND RESPONSIBILITIES DURING ORGANIZATION

Employer Rights

Section 70 of the Act states that the employer has the freedom to express its views but cannot use coercion, intimidation, threats, promises, or undue influence in its communications with workers. The law would consider such tactics unfair labour practice.

Employee and Union Rights

Under s. 5 of the OLRA, employees are free to join a trade union of their own choice and are free to participate in the lawful activities of the union. We will see that the Act provides for specific prohibited unfair labour practices in order to protect these freedoms.

Under s. 119 of the Act, workers are also entitled to have information as to whether or not they have joined a trade union kept confidential. Membership evidence filed with the OLRB by a union must be kept confidential, as must any petitions or statements by workers objecting to the certification of a union. A union must get the permission of a member before it discloses in its communications that this person has joined the union. Unions must also get the permission of an employee if they wish to use his or her name in campaign materials during the organizing drive. Showing that a well-respected employee has joined the union may encourage other employees to join up as well.

The general rule is that the union must conduct an organizing campaign outside the workplace. There is an exception where the employees live on premises owned or controlled by the employer. In this case, the union has a right of access to the employer's property, or to property that the employer controls, if the employees live on that property. This right sometimes applies in the case of mining and logging operations in remote areas where the workers live in a mining or logging camp while employed.

UNFAIR LABOUR PRACTICES DURING ORGANIZATION

Unfair Labour Practices by the Union

Section 76 of the Act says that it would be an unfair labour practice for a union to use intimidation or coercion to get workers to sign union cards. The union organizers often work in groups of two when approaching a member at his or her home after work. If the union were to send a larger group of people to the employee's home, this could be seen as intimidation. The OLRB would have the power to exclude membership evidence obtained by intimidation when it determines if the union has sufficient support to trigger a certification vote. Finally, a union is not permitted by the Act to organize during working hours. Under s. 77 of the Act, an employer could get the board to order that such activity cease.

Unfair Labour Practices by the Employer

The provisions of the Act dealing with employer unfair labour practices are designed to give effect to the employees' right to freely organize and join a union of their choice. The board, in interpreting employer prohibitions, keeps in mind that the employee is in a vulnerable position relative to the employer. The employer can, for example, terminate the employment relationship. Although the board has the power to rectify illegal terminations, this cannot be done immediately.

In addition, it is difficult for a union to show that any particular action taken by the employer is taken solely for reasons related to defeating the union. As long as the board can conclude that the employer's actions are taken at least in part for anti-union reasons, this is enough to support a claim of unfair labour practices. The employer must show that its actions are in no part due to **anti-union animus** (ill feeling). Instead, it must show it would have taken these actions whether or not a union was organizing the workplace. Another item to be noted is that there is significant overlap between the prohibited activities, and a single action of an employer may conflict with several provisions at the same time. For example, firing a union organizer will be both intimidation of the employees in general and a particular violation of the individual employee's right to join a union.

INTERFERING WITH THE FORMATION OF THE UNION

The employer or persons acting on its behalf are prohibited from interfering with the formation of a trade union, according to s. 70 of the Act. Thus, the employer cannot contribute resources to a particular union to help its organizing efforts. Further, the employer or persons acting on its behalf are prohibited from interfering with the selection of a trade union. If two unions are attempting to organize the same workplace, the employer must take care not to favour one union. The employer may have decided that one of the unions would be preferable because its workers are less militant or because the contracts they have negotiated with other employers result in lower costs. Even if the employer was correct in its conclusions, it would commit an unfair labour practice if it allowed one union access to company bulletin boards and denied the other union the same access.

THREATS, COERCION, AND OTHER UNFAIR EMPLOYER LABOUR PRACTICES

As stated earlier, it is an unfair labour practice for the employer to use threats, coercion, intimidation, promises, or undue influence when communicating with employees. An illustration of each prohibited practice is provided below:

- *Coercion.* Employers may run afoul of this prohibition if they call workers into one-on-one meetings to talk about the union drive.

- *Intimidation.* Firing the suspected union organizers would be intimidation.

- *Threats.* A statement that the employer will close the plant if the workers join the union would be a clear violation of this prohibition.

- *Promises.* A promise to raise wages if the workers vote against the union would be improper.

- *Undue influence.* A captive meeting called at work to discuss the union activities can easily run afoul of these prohibitions if there is any hint that pressure is being applied to encourage the workers to reject the union.

If the employer wants to communicate with the employees about the union drive, the safest technique is a letter sent to the employee. And an employer planning to send such a letter will be wise to get professional advice on the content of the letter. The OLRB operates on the premise that workers are aware that the employer will not be happy about the union organizing drive and that there is no real need for the employer to communicate this obvious statement, although the employer is entitled to do so. An employer should be careful about multiple communications (letters) on this topic. Each single communication may not by itself violate the prohibitions in the Act, but when taken as a group they may create an atmosphere of intimidation.

REFUSAL TO EMPLOY

Under s. 72(a) of the Act, an employer cannot refuse to hire a person because he or she might join, or is a member of, a union. Nor can an employer terminate an employee who is or may become a member of a union. An employer cannot ask a job applicant if he or she has ever been in a union or would join a union, nor can the employer keep or circulate lists of people who have been involved in unions in order to avoid hiring those people.

ILLEGAL CONTRACTUAL PROVISIONS

According to s. 72(b) of the Act, an employer cannot put in a contract of employment a clause that the employee will not join a union. In the 1800s such clauses were put in contracts of employment tendered to the most vulnerable set of employees, who were often new immigrants. In particular, in Canada, these clauses were required of immigrants from China who wanted to work on the railways; hence, they were given the racially motivated name "yellow dog contracts."

THREATENING AND FIRING

Section 72(c) of the Act states that an employer cannot threaten a person with firing or make any other threat or impose any other penalty to keep a person out of a union or get a person to quit the union.

STATUTORY FREEZE

Once the union has applied for certification and the employer has been given notice of the application, a statutory freeze on terms and conditions of employment goes into effect under s. 86(2) of the Act. The employer cannot alter the "rates of wages or any other term or condition of employment or any right, privilege or duty of the employer or the employees." The employer is not to alter the terms and conditions of employment unless or until

- the employer gets permission of the union;

- the application for certification is dismissed, terminated, or withdrawn; or

- the union is certified and gives notice to bargain, in which case a new statutory freeze comes into effect.

This does not mean that no changes to employment conditions can be made. For example, failure to award a year-end bonus that is always given by the employer would not amount to an alteration of terms of employment if the employer could show that business had been bad that year and the bonus would not have been paid in the normal course of business. The employer is to carry on business as usual as if there had been no application for certification. In addition, the employees are entitled to employment conditions that they reasonably expected would exist or occur in the absence of an organizing drive, such as the distribution of a Christmas bonus by the employer in the years prior to the drive.

Note that the intention of the employer is irrelevant in an allegation that an employer has violated this provision. It is not necessary that the OLRB find anti-union animus on the part of the employer; the board need only find that the employer would not have taken the offending action in the course of business as usual.

Avoiding Unfair Labour Practice Complaints

Where an employer decides to respond to employee concerns only at the stage where it becomes aware of a union organizing drive, the union will likely argue that these changes are a violation of the statutory freeze on the terms and conditions of employment and thus an unfair labour practice. Clearly the message to employers is to respond to employee concerns prior to an organizing drive. Following are the legitimate actions that employers may take well in advance of an organizing drive to make a drive less likely to succeed or never occur at all:

- Providing terms and conditions of employment, including wages and benefits, that mirror conditions in unionized plants. The employer would not have a cost advantage over a unionized plant but may decide that the benefits of not having to adhere to a collective agreement outweigh the loss of the non-union cost advantage.

- Creating an internal complaint procedure for employees who have complaints. This move would be intended to negate the union's selling point during the organizing drive that a collective agreement would include a grievance procedure. This procedure would have to be seen by employees as legitimate and perhaps involve an independent ombudsman for employees to take complaints to for resolution. This action, however, may result in the employer losing some control over decision making.

- Providing training for and investment in employees and exhibiting fairness in the distribution of opportunities for advancement.

- Creating a culture where the workers clearly feel valued by the organization.

Procedures and Remedies for Unfair Labour Practices[14]

The party alleging that an unfair labour practice has occurred (for example, the union) will file a complaint with the OLRB and deliver a copy of the complaint to the other party (for example, the employer). The complaint will set out the events

---

14 OLRA, s. 96.

that are alleged to amount to an unfair labour practice. The complainant must be sure to include all the items that they allege are unfair labour practices, and do so within a reasonable time of the events occurring. Otherwise, the complaint may be dismissed.

The OLRB will appoint a **labour relations officer**, who will investigate the complaint and attempt to get a settlement. A settlement is often reached, because the parties are sometimes simply unaware of their rights and obligations under the Act.

If the labour relations officer is unsuccessful, a hearing is scheduled at the labour board. A hearing at the OLRB is conducted in much the same way as a court hearing, with the parties calling witnesses and presenting evidence.

The general rule in the complaint process is that the party that makes the allegation has the onus or burden of proof to show that its allegation is more likely than not to be true. If, however, the union alleges that the employer refused to employ, fired, threatened, discriminated, coerced, intimidated or engaged in any other prohibited activity, then the burden is on the employer to show that it did not violate the Act. This means that the employer must show that its actions were in no way motivated by anti-union reasons. This is referred to as **reverse onus**.

In the case of a person who was fired and is asking for compensation for lost wages and benefits, that person will have to show that he or she tried to minimize his or her damages after being fired. This attempt to limit damages is referred to as **mitigation of damages** and is usually satisfied by showing that the person made a reasonable job search for other employment after being fired.

The OLRB has broad powers to construct a remedy to correct an unfair labour practice, including the power to

- order a party to cease and desist an activity;

- reinstate a terminated employee with compensation;

- order damages to be paid (for example, award extra costs for the union drive or compensation for lost work time);

- order that notices be posted in the workplace (these notices will state that the employer violated the Act and outline the steps that the employer must take to remedy the violation);

- give the union the power to hold a meeting at the workplace during work time;

- require that an apology be given;

- give the union access to the workplace;

- require that the board decision be read to the employees or mailed to them by the employer;

- give the union an office at the work site;

- make the employer give the union information about the workers, including names, dates, and addresses of newly hired employees; and

- order another certification vote.

However, there are limitations on the OLRB's powers. The board cannot order that the union be certified without a vote. The board is limited to ordering an additional vote if the employer's unfair labour relations practices tainted the first vote. In addition, the board will not order a remedy if it concludes that no labour relations purposes are served in doing so. Such a situation arises when a union has won its certification vote in the face of the unfair labour practices but still requests a second vote in its application in order to increase its vote total and thereby enhance the perception of its success in the organizing drive.

In other cases, the OLRB may have the power to impose a penalty but choose not to do so in the interest of providing harmony between the union and the employer. For example, s. 104 of the Act gives the board the power to authorize a prosecution for a breach of the Act, which could result in a fine of $2,000 to an individual or $25,000 to a union or employer for each breach of the Act. Permission to prosecute is almost never given because the board takes the view that fining a party would not contribute to healthy long-term labour relations. Permission would probably be authorized by the board only if there was a continuing, flagrant, and blatant ignoring of lawful procedure. In 2001-2 only four applications were received for consent to prosecute and none was granted.[15]

DETERMINING AN APPROPRIATE BARGAINING UNIT

A union is certified to represent a "bargaining unit." In a circular and unhelpful definition, s. 1(1) of the Act provides that a bargaining unit is "a unit of employees appropriate for collective bargaining, whether it is an employer unit or a plant unit or a subdivision of either of them." Thus, the OLRB has been left to determine what it means to be a "unit of employees appropriate for collective bargaining." In practice, the union will initially decide what group of employees, or unit, it wishes to represent. Then the employer will file an objection arguing that the unit the union has proposed is either too limited or too large to be appropriate. The employer and the union will often base their choice of unit on tactical reasons. The union will propose a unit for which they have sufficient membership to trigger a vote and for which they believe they have sufficient support to win the vote. The employer may propose a different bargaining unit, either to dilute the union's support to the point where it cannot obtain a vote, or to increase the possibility that the union will lose the vote.

The following simplified example illustrates the tactics involved. The employer Falstaff Metals Inc. operates a metal fabrication plant and a warehouse in Lindsay, Ontario. The fabrication plant has 1 plant manager, 3 shift supervisors, 2 office workers, and 50 fabrication workers. The warehouse has 1 supervisor and 16 warehouse workers. If the union has signed up only 26 workers in the fabrication plant and none in the warehouse, it will propose that the bargaining unit not include the warehouse. The management is likely to ask for the warehouse to be included because this would result in the union's application being defeated. If the union has signed up all the fabrication workers but none in the warehouse, it may ask for the inclusion of the warehouse. Its reasoning is that it is likely to win the

---

15 OLRB Annual Report.

vote and have a larger number of dues payers without the necessity of another organizing drive.

The board is not required to determine what is the best unit for collective bargaining. It only has to decide whether the union's proposed bargaining unit is appropriate. One specific rule is that a bargaining unit must consist of more than one person. It would be logically incompatible with "collective" negotiations to have one employee in a bargaining unit. The board has developed a set of indicators to help it determine what constitutes an appropriate bargaining unit. It considers several questions in its determination. These questions are set out below, along with a discussion of each.

1. Do the employees in the particular proposed bargaining unit have a "community of interest"?

    The principle is that the group of workers must have sufficient interests in common so that the union can effectively engage in bargaining for those employees. If the working conditions are too dissimilar, there will be no effective way of deciding which issue to pursue without totally ignoring one portion of the workforce.

    In determining community of interest, the board considers

    a. the nature of the work performed: is it similar?

    b. the conditions of employment: do the employees in the proposed unit work under similar conditions?

    c. the skills of employees: do the employees in the proposed unit have similar skills and training?

    d. administration: for example, is there a single benefits package covering the proposed unit?

    e. geographic circumstances, including if multiple locations are in the proposed unit: are the locations close or distant?

    f. functional coherence and interdependence: for example, do transfers of employees to other work sites occur within the proposed unit?[16]

2. Will the grouping that is suggested fragment the workplace into small bargaining units resulting in a potential for too much industrial conflict?

    If the workplace is divided into numerous small bargaining units and the collective agreements for those units expire at different times, the employer may be continually engaged in conflict and thus unable to effectively manage the organization. In addition, each small unit in a larger workplace may be able to exercise inordinate bargaining power if they can effectively shut operations down. It may be necessary for an employer to settle a dispute with a small number of employees quickly— and in the employees' favour—to get the larger group back to work.

    To complicate matters, the board will often have to balance competing principles: avoiding fragmentation may require putting together groups that have a very limited community of interest.

---

16 See *Usarco Limited*, [1967] OLRB Rep. Sept. 526.

3. Will this grouping interfere with the administrative structure of the employer?

    If the employer engages in significant transfers of employees between two work sites, there could be considerable dislocation of the employer's operation if these work locations were made separate bargaining units. To transfer bargaining unit members out of the unit or non-bargaining members into the unit would likely be a violation of any collective agreement that would emerge.

4. What are the wishes of the employees?

    The board, while attempting to avoid fragmentation and keeping together reasonable communities of interest, must also consider whom the employees wish to associate with in a union.

5. Will the proposed unit leave some employees without a reasonable prospect of ever forming a union?

    The board will try to avoid leaving "tag-end" groups or individuals out of a bargaining unit if this effectively means they could never join a union. For example, a proposed unit that includes all employees except one truck driver would effectively mean that truck driver could never unionize since there would be only one person in that tag-end unit.

Once the board has determined the scope of the appropriate bargaining unit, it will able to describe that unit. The description may take the following form:

> All the employees of Acme Manufacturing Company below the rank of supervisor located at 2000 Gormwood Road in the City of Peterborough excluding those who work less than 24 hours per week on a regular basis.

In recent years, bargaining units have tended to be small. In 2001-2 the average unit certified by the board comprised 53 members.

Skill and Craft Unions

The principle of avoiding fragmentation in determining the appropriate bargaining unit posed a significant threat to the existence of skill and craft unions. Their members include carpenters, electricians, bricklayers, and millwrights. Certification of craft unions will often tend to fragment the workplace. By contrast, industrial unions, which organize all the workers in a particular workplace, by their very nature satisfy the principle of avoiding fragmentation. To preserve the existence of craft unions, s. 9(3) of the OLRA provides that:

> [a]ny group of employees who exercise technical skills or who are members of a craft by reason of which they are distinguishable from the other employees and commonly bargain separately and apart from other employees through a trade union that according to established trade union practice pertains to such skills or crafts shall be deemed by the Board to be a unit appropriate for collective bargaining if the application is made by a trade union pertaining to the skills or craft, and the Board may include in the unit persons who according to established trade union practice are commonly associated in their work and bargaining with the group, but the Board shall not be required to apply this subsection where the group of employees is included in a bargaining unit represented by another bargaining agent at the time the application is made.

This provision is intended to protect existing historical craft unions. No new craft unions can be created and use this section to carve themselves out of a larger bargaining unit.

Security Guards

Historically, security guards could not be in the same union with other employees in their workplace, even if the union had applied to keep the security guards in a separate bargaining unit. This provision in the Act was based on an assumption that there was an inherent conflict of interest if unionized security guards were called upon to deal with employees who were members of any union. Perhaps unionized security guards would look the other way if striking workers were, for example, damaging the employer's property.

Section 14 of the Act now provides that if it can be shown that no real conflict of interest exists, then security guards can be part of a union with other workers. In fact, they can also be included in the same bargaining unit with other employees.

If the employer makes a request to deny the certification, it will object to either

- a union admitting guards and non-guards to membership where the guards are in a separate bargaining unit; or

- a union including both guards and non-guards in a single bargaining unit.

Once the employer objects, it is up to the union to show that there is no conflict of interest. The board is required to consider the following factors in its decision:

- The extent of the guards' duty in monitoring other employees or protecting the employer's property from other employees. There should be no conflict if the sole role of the guards is to guard the employer's property with respect to the public. For example, guards who protect armoured vehicles should not be in any conflict of interest with respect to their union's dealings with the employer and there would be no conflict if they were included in a bargaining unit with other employees. But where the task of the guards is to protect the property of the employer from both the public and other employees, then the issue of a conflict of interest may arise. Also, guards may be called upon to protect the employer's property during a strike of other employees at the workplace. Here, there would be a strong argument to put the guards into a separate bargaining unit.

- Any other duties that may give rise to a conflict of interest.

- Other factors the board considers relevant.

Professional Engineers

Section 9(4) of the Act provides that groups of professional engineers are deemed to be an appropriate bargaining unit, thus expressly overriding the principle against fragmenting the workplace. Some professional groups are entirely excluded from the operation of the OLRA. Professional engineers were not excluded from the Act, but as a concession to their professional status they are allowed to bargain in a separate unit as a matter of right.

DETERMINING THE WISHES OF EMPLOYEES

The board determines the wishes of employees by taking a vote or votes at the workplace under the supervision of the board at times that afford all the workers in the proposed bargaining unit the option to vote. One difficulty that the board has had to address is the possibility that protracted legal issues on the questions of what unit is appropriate and which workers are in fact managers could lead to a lengthy delay before a vote would be taken. The union would be concerned that during the delay management would exert pressure on employees to vote against the union. The union would also worry that the composition of the workforce might change over time, thus requiring essentially continual organizing drives. To address these problems, the board has developed procedures to allow for an early vote, which can be counted after all legal issues are determined.

These procedures include the segregation of ballots where there is some dispute as to whether the voter is in the unit or not. The voter marks a ballot, which is then sealed in an unmarked envelope. That envelope is sealed in a second envelope, which is marked with information on the voter. If it is subsequently determined that the voter is not a member of the unit, then the material is destroyed. If the voter is a member of the unit, then the outer envelope is removed and the ballot is counted without revealing the identity of the voter.

CERTIFICATION PROCEDURES

Timeliness

Section 7 of the OLRA states that applications for certification may be brought only at appropriate times, referred to as **open periods**. The principle is that an employer should not be subject to potentially continual applications for certification but should enjoy periods of labour relations peace. Conversely, a union should have some periods in which a relationship with the employer can be developed and not be subject to disruptive displacement or termination applications. The rules governing open periods are as follows:

1. If there is no certified union and there is no collective agreement in place, then an application for certification is timely at any time.

2. If a trade union is certified but there is no collective agreement in place, then an application can be brought one year after the certification has been granted. Thus, the union has one year to get an agreement before another union can bring a new certification application and attempt to displace the first union.

3. If a trade union is certified and there is a collective agreement in place that lasts one, two, or three years, then the open period is the last three months of the agreement. That is, for a one-year deal, the open period is the 10th, 11th, and 12th months; for a two-year deal, the 22nd, 23rd, and 24th months; and for a three-year deal, the 34th, 35th, and 36th months.

4. If the agreement is for more than three years, the open period is the last three months of the third year and the last three months of every year after that. This provision is designed to prevent a union or management

from entering into a very long agreement simply as a means of eliminating the open period.

5. If the agreement provides that it continues in operation as long as no party gives notice to bargain, then the open period is the last three months of the agreement and the last three months of any additional year of operation. Again, this provision is designed to prevent a union or management from avoiding the open period simply by letting an agreement continue in operation.

The Application[17]

As we have noted, if the union can show that 40 percent of the members of the bargaining unit have signed union cards, then the OLRB will authorize and supervise a certification vote. The procedures are designed so that this certification vote will take place very soon after the application is made. Over 90 percent of the votes take place five to seven days after the union has filed its application for certification. If there is a dispute, a hearing into the dispute takes place after the vote so that legal interventions cannot be used to delay a vote. If the vote is successful, the union will be certified and the employer will have to deal with the union as the exclusive bargaining agent of the employees.

The Act requires documents to be prepared by the parties, delivered to the other parties, and filed with the board, all within a specified number of days. The rules of the board provide that only weekdays count, excluding statutory holidays and any other day the OLRB is closed. A document is deemed delivered when it is hand-delivered, couriered, faxed, or delivered in a manner agreed upon by the parties. A document is considered filed with the board when it is hand-delivered, couriered, or in some cases faxed to the board. The document is to be filed during normal business hours, 8:30 a.m. to 5:00 p.m. Late documents are deemed to be received on the next day. Copies of the documents can be obtained from the OLRB or downloaded from its website.

Certification Package

When the union is satisfied that it has signed up enough members to be successful in its application, it must deliver a certification package consisting of the following documents to the employer:

- a notice to the employer that it is applying for certification,
- the application for certification,

---

17 OLRA, ss. 7, 8, 9, and 10. In addition, this section is based on the OLRB rules, information bulletins, and forms. The relevant information bulletins are as follows: Bulletin 1, Certification of a Trade Union, available online at http://www.gov.on.ca/lab/olrb/eng/infbul/infbull.htm; Bulletin 3, Vote Arrangements, available online at http://www.gov.on.ca/lab/olrb/eng/infbul/infbul3.htm; and Bulletin 4, Status Disputes in Certification Applications, available online at http://www.gov.on.ca/lab/olrb/eng/infbul/infbul4.htm.

The rules of the board are available online at http://www.gov.on.ca/lab/olrb/eng/rules.htm. The required forms are available online at http://www.gov.on.ca/lab/olrb/eng/forms/formsnot.htm.

- a blank employer's response form, including a blank document for providing lists of employees in the bargaining unit, and

- copies of the OLRB information bulletins on certification and the board's rules of procedure on certification.

If the union is aware that it is applying to displace another union, it must provide a similar set of documents to that other union. This set would include the application for certification, a blank form that the other union may use to apply to intervene at the OLRB, and the board's information bulletins and rules of procedure.

Documents Filed

The union, within two days of serving the employer, must then, by a means other than fax, file with the OLRB

- five copies of the application for certification,

- membership evidence (often union membership cards) in writing, signed by the members and dated,

- lists of union members in the proposed bargaining unit, and

- a declaration that the membership evidence is accurate.

If the union does not deliver these documents within two days of notifying the employer, the application is deemed to be terminated. The union must not disclose its membership evidence to the employer or to other unions. This information is confidential.

Information Provided

The union must provide certain information in its application form. On its application, the union will

- set out its proposal for a bargaining unit;

- give the board the name and information of the union and a contact person with the union;

- give information on the identity of the employer, the nature of the business, and the location of the affected workplaces;

- estimate the number of employees in the bargaining unit at each of the work locations and indicate whether it has 40 percent of the employees in the proposed unit signed up;

- indicate whether it is aware of any other unions with bargaining rights to all or part of the bargaining unit that it is proposing;

- set out proposals for conduct of the vote, including times and locations for the vote; and

- indicate whether security guards are included in the unit.

Employer Response

The employer must file a response to the union's application with the board and deliver this response to the union. These documents may be delivered and filed by fax. In the response, the employer will

- correct any errors in the union's address information on the employer;

- name a contact person;

- set out the general nature of the business;

- challenge the union's estimate of numbers in the bargaining unit that the union proposed if it disagrees with the union's estimate;

- provide a different description of the bargaining unit if it disagrees with the union's description of the bargaining unit;

- estimate the number of employees in the bargaining unit it proposes;

- disagree with the details of the union's unit or allege that the unit proposed by the union is not an appropriate unit for collective bargaining purposes;

- object to the inclusion of security guards in the bargaining unit;

- either agree to the union's proposals for voting procedures or suggest its own variation;

- argue that the matters in issue should be determined before the counting of ballots; and

- indicate whether there is another affected union that the applicant union failed to mention; state the date that the affected union was certified or voluntarily recognized; and if there is a collective agreement in force, state the date of the agreement and the agreement's expiry date.

The employer must also provide a list of all the employees included in the bargaining unit proposed by the applicant union. All employees who are part of the bargaining unit and who have an ongoing relationship with the employer on the application date should be included on this list. This covers employees on vacation or on parental leave, sick leave, or other forms of leave. It also includes those off work and receiving Workplace Safety and Insurance Board benefits and those on layoff, provided that in all these cases there is a reasonable chance the person will return to work. The employer must give the person's name and job classification and, if he or she is not at work on the date the application was received, the last day that that employee worked, the reason for the absence, and the expected date that this employee will return to work.

The employer is required to first list full-time employees in alphabetical order. Full-time employees are those who are employed for more than 24 hours per week. Then the employer lists part-time employees in the proposed bargaining unit— that is, those workers who do not work more than 24 hours on a regular basis. Finally, the employer lists any students who work more than 24 hours per week during the vacation period.

If the employer objects to the union's inclusion of a particular employee in the bargaining unit, it must note its objection in the list by placing an asterisk next to that person's name. For example, the union may want to include the clerical employees in the human resources department in the bargaining unit. The employer may argue that these employees are confidentials, so the employer will indicate this by placing an asterisk next to the name of every employee with this job classification.

If the employer proposes a different bargaining unit from that proposed by the union, the employer must provide the same employee list covering the employees in its proposed bargaining unit.

If the employer fails to file its response with the board within two days of the union's application, the employer may be deemed to have accepted all the information in the union's application. The board may then proceed to set up the vote without further discussion with the employer.

Any other affected union has the right to intervene in the process. As noted earlier, the affected union should have been notified by the applicant union at the same time the employer was notified. If the applicant union did not do this, the information will still emerge from the employer's response. In this case, the board will ensure that the affected union is given notice and has time to respond before a vote is taken. If the affected union responds and has bargaining rights for the existing employees, then the vote will take place between the two unions as long as it is in an open period as defined by the Act.

Pre-Voting Procedures

Upon receiving an application, the board will send out a notice to both the employer and the applicant union, and to affected unions that have received an application. The board will also contact the employer to make sure it has received the required documents from the union.

The employer is required to post a notice of the application and a notice to the employees from the OLRB. The notice from the board describes the process and the rights that employees have under the Act. The employer must notify the board that it has posted these documents, and the union must confirm that this notice has been posted.

A labour relations officer employed by the board will contact the parties and discuss the issues that emerge from the application and the response. The officer will attempt to get an agreement from the parties that will resolve the disputes. If the parties make an agreement with the officer, they are bound by this agreement.

The board will determine the voting constituency. If there are disputes about whether a person should be included or not included, the board will allow the person to vote, then segregate the ballot and make the determination after the vote. The board will then either count the ballot or destroy the ballot.

The Vote

The board will examine the application, response, and intervention (if any), and determine the voting times and places. The board will usually accept and accommodate the procedures suggested by the parties. It will overrule the parties if the suggested procedure either is too costly or does not adequately accommodate the rights of the employees and ensure that they have a chance to vote. The board will notify the parties of the voting procedures and will discuss the matter with them, but the final determination of voting times and places will be done by the board and there is no hearing into these decisions.

The board will set up the ballots for the vote. It will either ask the voter whether he or she wishes to be represented by the applicant union or, in the case of a raid, ask the voter which union he or she wishes to be represented by.

A labour relations officer will supervise the vote. The parties may appoint scrutineers to observe the taking of the vote and an agent to observe the vote counting. As noted earlier, if there is an objection to a person voting, then the vote is taken, the ballot segregated, and the eligibility of that person to vote determined later.

The vote will usually take place five to seven days after the union files its application.[18] It will be a secret ballot vote. No advance polls or proxy votes are permitted. Proxy votes occur when a person cannot attend on the vote date and authorizes another person to vote for him or her. Similarly, if an employee is on vacation outside the country, he or she cannot authorize another person to vote for him or her. The board will in rare instances allow mail-in votes: they will not enable absent employees to vote but may permit employees in a remote location with few voters to vote. In the absence of a mail-in vote, the board officer would be required to travel to the remote location to collect the votes.

Various other rules apply to the voting process. A 60-minute period must be allocated to 60 voters. Turnout for certification votes averaged 86 percent in 2001-2.[19] The vote takes place on the employer's premises during working hours. They use lunchrooms, cafeterias, and empty offices for the voting locations. Whichever location is chosen, it will ideally be a quiet one. The board will supply ballot boxes and private voting screens. If there are multiple voting locations, the voting must be scheduled to allow adequate travelling time for one board officer to supervise all the locations.

The employees who show up to vote must be identified. They will be given a ballot, which they will mark in private. The votes may be counted on the date of the vote or the votes may be counted later if there are unresolved issues such as the description of the bargaining unit, which must be determined before counting can begin. After the vote is counted, the board officer will provide the results of the vote to the parties. The employer is then required to post the results of the vote. The parties have five days to object to the vote.

Post-Voting Procedures

Employees at the workplace have a right to make objections, called representations, to the board. The board must consider and deal with these representations if they are relevant. A board officer will often contact the person who makes the representation to assess the relevance. An employee who objects that he or she did not like the result of the vote or was on vacation when the vote was taken is not making a relevant representation. A relevant representation is one that objects to conduct that would bring into question the fairness of the vote.

---

18 According to recent board figures, 94 percent of votes took five to seven days and 97 percent of votes less than 10 days. See OLRB Annual Report.

19 OLRB Annual Report, at 8.

If there are no outstanding issues in dispute between the parties and there are no relevant representations, the board can issue a final decision. If the union received more than 50 percent of the votes, it will be certified. If it did not, the certification application will be dismissed.

Where there are outstanding issues, the labour relations officer will contact the parties to try to get agreement. There will then be a meeting of the parties on the Wednesday of the third week after the vote has taken place. This is called a regional certification meeting; in it, the board officer will try to get agreement to resolve the issues or to narrow the issues. The board will hear any final matters in dispute one week after the regional meeting.

There is an exception to this procedure, where the dispute is about the status of employees. The dispute may arise because a party is objecting to a particular person being on the list of voters or there may be a disagreement about the union's estimate of the number of employees in the bargaining unit. A hearing into a status dispute takes place five weeks after a vote. The parties will be asked to provide written submissions stating the reasons for their objection and the material facts on which they rely in support of their application. The parties must also indicate the witnesses that they intend to call at the hearing.

OLRB Activity

The board dealt with 624 new applications for certification in 2001-2, with 198 carried over from the previous year. It disposed of 686 applications and left 136 pending. In 307 cases, the union was certified; in 198 cases, the application was dismissed; 180 cases were settled; and in 1 case, the application was terminated. The board conducted 514 representation votes—that is, votes where a union has applied for certification in order to represent a group of employees. In 444 cases, there was only one union involved and in 70 cases, there was more than one union involved. The applicant union won 315 votes and lost 199 votes.[20] The median time to complete a file from application to ruling was 24 days. In 2001-2 the total number of employees newly covered by unionization was 16,255.

VOLUNTARY RECOGNITION

There is no prohibition in the Act against an employer simply recognizing a union and attempting to negotiate an agreement with it. The employer may assess the situation, determine that a union will eventually be successful in organizing the employees in a particular workplace, and so choose this option to avoid expensive, time-consuming, and futile litigation before the board. This is referred to as **voluntary recognition** and although it is permissible, it cannot be used by the employer as a mechanism for choosing a union that the employer prefers.

In order to protect the employees' right to choose a union, s. 66 of the Act provides that the representation rights of a union acquired by way of voluntary recognition are more vulnerable to challenge for a period of a year. If the selection of the union did not reflect the wishes of the employees and was merely a collusion

---

20 Ibid.

between the union and the employer, the workers will be able to bring an application for decertification.

BARS TO CERTIFICATION

The Act provides an absolute bar to certification for a trade union if an employer or employer's organization

- participated in the formation of the union,
- participated in the administration of the union, and/or
- contributed financially or otherwise to the support of the union.

The union is, by law, an organization of employees that the employer must not interfere with. Further, the employer must not favour any particular union. In the event that there are two unions battling for representation rights at a particular workplace, the employer must be careful not to favour one union by allowing only one of the unions access to photocopiers or other facilities. The employers also should not indicate to the employees that it prefers the settlements negotiated by one of the competing unions.

Section 15 of the Act states that a union will also be barred from certification if it discriminates against any person on grounds prohibited by the Ontario *Human Rights Code*[21] or the Charter.

Section 5(2) of the *Human Rights Code* lists the following prohibited grounds of discrimination:

Every person who is an employee has a right to freedom from harassment in the workplace by the employer or agent of the employer or by another employee because of race, ancestry, place of origin, colour, ethnic origin, citizenship, creed, age, record of offences, marital status, same-sex partnership status, family status or handicap.

Section 15(1) of the Charter contains the following prohibited grounds of discrimination:

Every individual is equal before and under the law and has the right to the equal protection and equal benefit of the law without discrimination and, in particular, without discrimination based on race, national or ethnic origin, colour, religion, sex, age or mental or physical disability.

In addition, if the union has conducted an organizing drive, applied for certification, and lost the vote, any subsequent application will be banned for one year from the date the board dismissed the application. This provision is designed to give employers some labour peace between certification applications. Note that this bar applies to all trade unions, not just the union that lost the application. The board also may impose a certification ban for one year if the union withdraws an application before a representation vote is taken. Under ss. 7(9) and (9.1) of the Act, this ban becomes automatic if the union has taken the same action within the previous six months.

---

21 RSO 1990, c. H.19.

TERMINATING THE BARGAINING RELATIONSHIP

There are several reasons in the Act why a certification will be terminated:

- the union's "sleeping on its rights,"
- fraud on the part of the union in getting certification,
- decertification by the employees, or
- raiding.

Sleeping on Its Rights

A union's right to represent a workplace will be terminated in the following case. If another union subsequently organizes the workplace by signing up sufficient members and then applies during an open period and is certified to represent all or part of that workplace, the new certification will automatically replace all or part of the existing certification. This will also end the operation of any collective agreement that had been in force. It is not obligatory that the new certificate cover the identical bargaining unit covered by the existing certificate. The board, however, is resistant to applications that would carve out parts of an existing bargaining unit because of its principle of attempting to avoid fragmenting the workplace.

According to s. 65 of the Act, if the new union fails to give notice to bargain within 60 days of being certified, or if it gives notice but fails to bargain within 60 days, or if it starts to bargain but has a gap of 60 days in trying to bargain, the employer or the employees in the unit may apply to have the union decertified. Under s. 132 of the Act, if a union fails to get a collective agreement with the employer within six months of being certified, then any employee in the workplace may apply to the board to have the union certificate terminated. The union is not permitted to **sleep on its rights** by not seriously engaging in attempts to get a collective agreement. If the union were engaged in activities such as conciliation to get an agreement, then an application to terminate the union would be premature. As part of its defence of the application, the union may be able to explain to the board why there had been gaps and satisfy the board that it had reasons for its period of inactivity.

Fraud

If a trade union committed a fraud in order to obtain certification, the OLRB may at any time terminate the certification under s. 64 of the Act. Such a fraud could be committed by deliberately understating the number of employees in the unit to get a vote or by submitting falsified membership records. A termination order will terminate any collective agreement between the union and the employer. The key to this section is that it must be shown that the union engaged in some form of misrepresentation to the board. Whether the union misrepresented itself to the employer is not the issue.

Decertification

Employees have a right to form and join a union. Under ss. 63 and 67 of the Act, they also have a right to remove a union if they are not satisfied. The process of removing an unwanted union is called **decertification** and it mirrors the certification process in the Act.

Section 63.1 of the Act provides that the employer is required to post in a unionized workplace a decertification document prepared by the Ministry of Labour. This document must describe the process involved in decertifying a union, and the ministry must annually provide this information to employees. When this provision was added to the Act in 2000, there was no corresponding obligation on non-unionized employers to post information on certification.

The open periods for decertification are the same as the open periods for certification:

1. If there is no collective agreement in place, an application can be brought one year after the certification has been granted. Thus, the union has one year to get an agreement before another union can bring a new certification application and attempt to displace the first union.

2. If there is a collective agreement in place that lasts one, two, or three years, the open period is the last three months of the agreement: for a one-year deal, the 10th, 11th, and 12th months; for a two-year deal, the 22nd, 23rd, and 24th months; and for a three-year deal, the 34th, 35th, and 36th months.

3. If the agreement is for more than three years, the open period is the last three months of the third year and the last three months of every year after that. This provision is designed to prevent a union or management from entering into a very long agreement simply as a method of trying to eliminate the open period.

4. If the agreement provides that it continues in operation as long as no party gives notice to bargain, the open period is the last three months of the agreement and the last three months of any additional year of operation. Again, this provision is designed to prevent a union or management from avoiding the open period simply by letting an agreement continue in operation.

Opponents of the union must be able to provide evidence to the OLRB that at least 40 percent of the employees covered by the certification are in favour of decertification. This may be done by way of a petition in opposition to the union. If that is the case, then the board will hold a decertification vote. If more than 50 percent of the employees vote in favour of decertification, then the union's representation rights will be cancelled along with any existing collective agreement.

In 2001-2 there were 180 new applications for termination of certification rights and 47 carried over from the previous year. In 86 cases, certification rights were terminated; in 46 cases, applications were dismissed; 36 cases were settled; and in 53 cases, applications were pending. The board conducted 103 votes on decertification.

In some cases of decertification, a vote will not be necessary, because the union may have clearly ceased to operate in this workplace and would indicate to the board that it was abandoning its bargaining rights.

Raiding

Raiding occurs where a union applies to be certified for a group of employees who are already represented by another trade union. The Act provides that when a new union is certified to represent the employees, the incumbent union is displaced and its bargaining rights terminated.

The union movement has frowned on raiding activities. Unions are expected to organize the unorganized, not expend their efforts and limited resources fighting over already unionized workers. Section 3 of the constitution of the Canadian Labour Congress provides that

> [n]o affiliate shall organize or attempt to represent employees as to whom an established collective bargaining relationship exists with any other affiliate, or otherwise seek to disrupt or disturb such relationship except as hereafter provided in this Article. The integrity of each affiliate of this Congress shall be maintained and preserved and each affiliate shall respect the established collective bargaining relationship of every other affiliate.[22]

The difficulty faced by the CLC is that it has no effective mechanism to enforce this prohibition. In the event that a member of the CLC decides to ignore this provision, the only action the CLC can take is to expel the offending union.

An employer may be concerned that unions engaged in organizing drives might continuously disrupt their operation. In order to provide for periods of labour relations peace, the Act provides that raiding applications can only be done during open periods.

SUCCESSION RIGHTS

Sale of a Workplace

If an employer could sell a workplace free of the obligation to recognize a union, there would be an economic incentive to do so and this would be a prevalent way to avoid union contracts. To prevent this from occurring, s. 69 of the OLRA provides that if a business is being sold, the union contract goes with the business as part of the sale. At the other extreme, a union should not expect to gain bargaining rights when an asset of the employer is sold. For example, an employer may sell some of its older manufacturing equipment after it has purchased a new machine and the union contract will not follow the machinery. The general rule is that a party who purchases all or part of a business that is bound by a collective agreement takes over that business subject to the collective agreement. The test is whether there is a sale of a business as a going concern or merely the sale of an asset. If the business is sold as a going concern, the union contract goes with the business.

Sometimes, workplaces are merged as a result of the sale of a business, and one or both of the workplaces are unionized. In such cases, the OLRB can conduct votes to determine the wishes of the employees. For example, a car parts manufacturer whose plant has been organized by the CAW may purchase a plant organized by the Steelworkers. If there is no change in operations, the existing certification

---

22 Constitution of the Canadian Labour Congress, available online at http://www.clc-ctc.ca/web/menu/english/en_index.htm.

rights would continue, with each bargaining unit limited to one of the plants. However, if the purchaser chooses to completely amalgamate the operations, a vote would be conducted to determine which union would represent the employees.

Change of the Union

The legal system recognizes that unions change, as well as employers. Two unions may merge to create a new union, or a single union may change names, split into smaller groups, or be absorbed into another union. The Act recognizes that a change in the status of the union should not terminate the bargaining rights of the workers. The bargaining rights do continue and if there is a challenge about the wishes of the employees, the board is empowered to conduct a vote.[23]

RELATED EMPLOYERS

According to s. 1(4) of the Act, the OLRB has the power to look behind the legal structure of an organization to determine the employer for labour relations purposes. A corporation is legally a separate person from the shareholders who own the corporation. Creative use could be made of this legal distinction to avoid the collective bargaining obligations created under the labour relations scheme. In order to prevent this, the OLRB is given the power to "pierce the corporate veil" and look behind the legal structure to see who is the real controlling mind of an organization. If the real controller of the organization is subject to obligations under the Act to recognize a union, the board will make a related-employer declaration and force the real employer to live up to its obligations.

The OLRB dealt with 294 applications concerning related employers and successor rights in 2001-2. The vast majority of these were dealt with by settlement discussions with labour relations officers. In 2001-2, 124 cases were settled, 23 applications were granted, 15 applications were dismissed, and 132 cases were pending.[24]

---

23 OLRA, s. 68. Forty-seven applications were dealt with by the board in 2001-2. Of these cases, 41 were successful, 1 was settled, 2 were dismissed, and 3 are pending. OLRB Annual Report, at 10.

24 Ibid., at 10-11.

UP TO THE MINUTE

Labour Law Reform and Organizing a Workplace

On November 3, 2004, the Ontario government introduced a bill for changes to labour laws primarily affecting the area of union organizing. Some of this legislation would have the effect of reversing changes made by the previous government, which, the unions argued, had tipped the balance of power too far in favour of the employer. Bill 144, the *Labour Relations Statute Law Amendment Act, 2004*, was at first reading at the time of writing and may be subject to future amendments. The bill includes the following changes to the law:

- Employers in unionized workplaces would no longer be required to post and distribute information describing the process of decertifying a unionized workplace. This requirement was introduced by the previous government. The unions had complained that it was unbalanced because there was no corresponding obligation to post certification information in non-unionized workplaces.

- The OLRB would have the power to certify a union without a vote in circumstances where the employer engaged in unfair labour practices. Those unfair labour practices must have either made the union lose a representation vote or prevented the union from obtaining the level of support necessary to trigger a vote. This power had been removed from the labour board by the previous government.

- The OLRB would have the power to dismiss a union's application for certification and bar that union from making a subsequent application for a year if the union engages in unfair labour practices that make it impossible to determine the true wishes of the employees through a vote. This is a new power but it is intended to balance the power given to the OLRB to certify without a vote in the case of employer unfair labour practices.

- The OLRB's power to make interim awards would be increased. Interim awards are made during a hearing prior to a final determination in order to preserve the parties' rights and make sure that delays in process do not advantage one of the parties. These interim orders could include reinstating an employee who was fired during an organizing drive where it appears that the employee was terminated for anti-union reasons. Also, interim orders could be issued about the terms and conditions of employment of a worker if it appears that during an organizing drive the employer altered these terms and conditions for anti-union reasons. This would include situations where the employee had been disciplined or was subject to reprisals or penalties.

- In the construction sector, a union would be automatically certified without a vote if the union can demonstrate by way of signed membership cards that it represents more than 55 percent of the employees in the bargaining unit. This rule used to apply in all workplaces but was changed by the previous government to require a vote in all cases. The government has restored card-based certification only in the construction industry.

CHAPTER SUMMARY

Our labour relations system has replaced a method whereby a union would be recognized only if it could force the employer through job action with a system based on votes and litigation. In an organizing drive, the union persuades workers to sign membership cards. It does this by contacting workers and explaining the benefits of unionization to encourage them to sign up. Contact could be made at the plant gate, at the worker's home, through the Internet, or at a public meeting. Unions often employ professional organizers to conduct the organizing drive. The right of workers to join the union of their choice is protected by a set of rules to prevent unfair labour practices. These rules are designed to prevent the employer from abusing its power over the worker and to make sure the membership acquired by the union is legitimate. A union is limited to groups of employees and does not include managers and labour relations confidentials. In addition, it must be structured into a group called a bargaining unit. That is, the union must combine workers who can get together and agree on a common bargaining agenda. Further, the workplace should not be divided into such small units that there is a potential for constant labour disruption.

When the union has at least 40 percent of the workers signed up and the timing is appropriate, then an application is made to the Ontario Labour Relations Board. The board will conduct a vote and if the union is successful, it will be certified. The employer will then be required to bargain with the union. The Ontario *Labour Relations Act, 1995* includes provisions to prevent the employer from trying to eliminate the union by creating a complex legal structure or simply selling the business. If the employees become disenchanted with the union, there is a mirror process to certification that the employees can take to decertify the union and revert to negotiating with the employer as individuals.

REVIEW QUESTIONS

1. Why do workers join unions?

2. How do union organizers persuade workers to sign cards?

3. What groups of workers are not employees under the Ontario *Labour Relations Act, 1995*?

4. What factors does the Ontario Labour Relations Board consider in determining an appropriate bargaining unit?

5. In what circumstances will the OLRB terminate a union's bargaining rights?

6. Describe the steps a union must take to apply for certification at the OLRB.

7. List and describe actions that an employer should not take in its response to a union organizing drive.

8. What actions can the OLRB take to remedy unfair labour practices?

9. In what circumstances will the OLRB bar a union from being certified?

10. How do the rules that provide that the collective agreement is transferred on the sale of a business and that allow the OLRB to declare separate companies to be related employers protect the workers' right to be free to join a union of their choice?

DISCUSSION QUESTIONS

1. Consider the rules governing unfair labour practice, which limit the employer's ability to fully comment on the organizing drive and place limits on meetings with the employees. Are these rules a violation of the employer's right to free speech guaranteed in the *Charter of Rights and Freedoms*?

2. The OLRA used to include provisions that gave the board the power to award automatic certification if the union had substantial support from the members but had lost a certification vote, and if the union could show that the employer engaged in unfair labour practices to a degree that the true wishes of the employees could not be determined. Should that power be restored to the board?

3. If the union shows that it has significant support from the workers, is a vote at the workplace unnecessary and can the union be certified without a vote?

CASE STUDY

Freeman's Famous Furniture was a furniture manufacturer operating in Peterborough and Oshawa, Ontario. Two worksites were located in Peterborough: a manufacturing plant and a warehouse. A second manufacturing site was situated in Oshawa. A total of 179 people worked at the Peterborough plant: the president, Mr. Freeman; a vice-president; 2 production managers; 1 director of human resources; 5 clerical and accounting staff in the main office; 2 clerical staff in the human resources office; 6 shift supervisors; 12 lead hands; 116 full-time production workers; 3 security guards; and 30 part-time production workers. The 12 shift supervisors had no power to fire employees, but if they said a worker should be let go, the production managers always agreed.

The warehouse in Peterborough employed 25: 1 supervisor, 1 office person, 16 full-time and 4 part-time warehouse workers, and 3 truck drivers who owned their own trucks but worked exclusively for Freeman's. If the warehouse became busy, workers would be transferred from the other facility to Peterborough to cover the work.

The Oshawa facility was smaller. It had 22 employees: 1 supervisor, 2 lead hands, 14 production workers, and 4 licensed electricians who worked on the specialized machinery at the plant.

James Jones, a worker at the Peterborough manufacturing plant, saw a website for a union online. He contacted a union organizer and they started signing up workers. He enlisted his friend Mark Smith in the warehouse. Jones had some minor notes on his work record for being late. Smith had once been caught drinking at work but was only suspended.

The union signed up the following workers at the three sites.

Peterborough manufacturing plant:

- 2 clerical staff

- 1 clerk in human resources

- 4 shift supervisors

- 9 lead hands

- 78 full-time production workers

- 13 part-time production workers

- 3 security guards

Peterborough warehouse:

- 1 office worker

- 12 full-time workers (4 of whom were signed up by Smith during work hours)

- 3 part-time workers

- 3 truck drivers

Oshawa manufacturing plant:

- 4 production workers

The International Brotherhood of Electrical Workers signed up the four electricians at the Oshawa plant and made an application to represent those employees.

When Mr. Freeman, the company president, found out about the union organizing drive, he was angry and took the following steps:

- he fired Jones and Smith (Smith had also missed a day of work without an excuse, but no decision on what punishment would be imposed had been determined);

- he called the employees to a meeting to say that if the union came in, they would be looking for another job;

- he started calling in employees one by one to tell each of them why the union was not to their advantage;

- he sent a letter to the employees saying that the union could not guarantee better conditions and that they would be spending union dues money for nothing; and

- he cancelled a Christmas bonus.

Some employees who opposed the union offered to set up an employees association as an alternative to the union. Freeman promised to help them set up. He pledged to pay for office costs, provide free office space, and allow them to meet on work time.

You are the human resources director. You were on holidays when all these activities occurred and have just returned. Review the facts of this case and then help Mr. Freeman answer the following questions:

1. What is the appropriate bargaining unit?

2. Who would be included as employees in the bargaining unit?

3. How will the board deal with Mr. Freeman's actions?

4. What will be the process at the OLRB?

5. What will happen to Smith and Jones?

6. How will the electricians situation be resolved?

7. What should Mr. Freeman do about the employees' association?

CHAPTER 4

Negotiating a Collective Agreement

INTRODUCTION

Once a union is certified, it will turn its attention to getting an agreement with management to improve the terms and conditions of work for the employees in the bargaining unit. It will meet management and enter into discussions in order to obtain an agreement. This process is called negotiations.

This chapter will start with a brief theoretical background on negotiations theory. It will then turn to the legal framework for negotiations—that is, the set of ground rules for the discussions between union and management. If the union and management cannot reach an agreement, then the law requires that the parties ask for assistance in negotiations from professionals. In some cases the law provides that these outside professionals will resolve the dispute. Where the law does not, the parties will be entitled to engage in activities to persuade the other party to change its position, including strikes and lockouts. This chapter will examine the rules governing the legal use of the strike and lockout weapons. It will then turn to the issue of how an employer gets workers on an illegal strike back to work. The operation of picketing and the legal rules surrounding it are examined. The chapter will conclude by examining how employers may use a superior court's power to issue injunctions to control union activity.

THEORETICAL APPROACHES TO BARGAINING: AN OVERVIEW

This chapter contains a brief introduction to several of the leading models of labour negotiations theory: the economic model, contract zone model, bargaining power models, behavioural models, prescriptive models, and strategic models.

Economic Model

The economic model suggests that the interaction between supply and demand will determine the price of labour in terms of wages and benefits and the quantity of labour—that is, the number of workers required.[1] At the intersection of supply

---

1   See general texts on economics such as P.A. Samuelson and W.D. Nordhaus, *Economics*, 16th ed.
    (New York: McGraw-Hill, 1998) and R. Lipsey and A. Chrystal, *Economics*, 10th ed. (Oxford:

and demand in a competitive marketplace there is a unique single point of wage levels and number of workers required.

According to this model, the union will not be able to raise wages without creating economic inefficiencies and putting the employer out of business, unless the union is able to cut back the supply of workers or increase the demand for a particular product. The union may, for example, engage in a "buy union" campaign with consumers. Or it may try to limit the supply of workers through a closed shop or union hiring hall, which restricts the entry of new workers. It may also limit supply by using work rules, which force an artificial limit on the speed at which work is done. Critics of this model question the reality of the assumptions on which it is based, namely, competitive markets, easy access to information on available jobs, and mobility of labour.

Contract Zone Model

In order to illustrate this theory of negotiations, we will examine a simple, one-dimensional bargaining situation.[2] The only issue under discussion will be an hourly wage increase.

The union goes to the table hoping for a $3 per hour wage increase. It is willing to negotiate something lower but it will not go below a $1 per hour increase or it will conclude that its best alternative is to strike. (The best alternative to a negotiated agreement is sometimes abbreviated BATNA.) Because the union knows it will have to modify its demand during bargaining, it will start off with a demand above $3 but not with a demand so outrageous that it will damage its relationship with the other party, its own members, or the public. So, the union presents a $4 per hour demand. It also takes into account the fact that it cannot increase its demand once the demand has been made, unless circumstances change significantly. Thus, it is careful not to make an initial demand that is too low or management may agree immediately. Management, for its part, would like to go no higher than a $2 per hour increase and would rather take a strike than go above $2.50. So, it may start with an offer of $1 per hour.

After the initial positions of a $4 union demand and $1 management offer are presented, or tabled, there will be discussions back and forth between the union and management. If the parties are able to communicate, then in the example given there should be a settlement in the range between the union's strike point of $1 per hour and management's strike point of $2.50 per hour. This is the **contract zone** in this round of negotiations. Where the parties end up will depend on the skill of the negotiators and the bargaining power of the parties.

Let us change the example. The parties still start with an initial union demand of $4 and a management offer of $1, but now management will take a strike rather

---

Oxford University Press, 2003). Information specific to labour matters may be found in A.W. Craig and N. Solomon, *The System of Industrial Relations in Canada*, 5th ed. (Scarborough, ON: Prentice Hall, 1996); F. Kehoe and M. Archer, *Canadian Industrial Relations*, 10th ed. (Oakville, ON: Century Labour Publications, 2002); C. Adams, *Canadian Labour Law*, 2nd ed. (Aurora, ON: Canada Law Book, 1995); and D. Randazzo, *The 2003 Annotated Labour Relations Act* (Toronto: Carswell, 2002).

2   J. Manwaring, "Negotiation," in J. McFarlane, ed., *Dispute Resolution: Readings and Case Studies*, 2nd ed. (Toronto: Emond Montgomery, 2002), 118-28.

than offer more than a $2 per hour increase and the union will take a strike rather than accept less than a $3 per hour increase. In this case, there is no contract zone. The parties will not agree to a settlement until one or both parties change their strike points to create a contract zone, and the resulting strike may cause a loss of production and loss of income until such a change takes place.

Bargaining Power Models

Under the bargaining power models, whether a negotiated settlement falls closer to the union's or the management's end of the contract zone will depend on both parties' perception of their relative bargaining power and the willingness of the party with greater bargaining power to use its advantage.

Bargaining power may be created by external factors or by the parties themselves, who may take actions that will enhance or weaken their bargaining power. External factors include the legal regime and how the web of legal rules shifts the balance of power. If the legal system restricts the use of picket lines, this would shift the balance to the employer. If the legal system prohibits replacement workers, this should enhance the union's power. The bargaining unit structure within a workplace will also have an effect on bargaining power. A small unit of skilled workers in a large workplace should have greater leverage than a larger unit of unskilled workers in the same workplace. The small unit may be able to effectively shut down the whole plant, and the total wage costs of satisfying their demands may be small compared with the entire budget of the organization. Finally, an economic depression will affect bargaining power. The depression will put many workers out of work, giving the employer a larger potential pool of replacement workers and thus weakening union power.

Any action that a party takes to enhance bargaining power will affect the other party. The action will either

- make it harder for the other side to say no, or

- make it easier for the other side to say yes.

Examples of actions a union can take to make it harder for management to say no include

- striking,

- setting up effective picket lines that few workers cross,

- providing strike pay out of a large strike fund, and

- getting money from other unions to supplement its strike fund.

Examples of actions a union can take to make it easier for an employer to say yes include

- extending wage and other demands across industry so that the employer will not lose competitiveness (see pattern bargaining below), and

- lowering demands in response to management's offers.

Examples of actions an employer can take to make it harder for a union to say no include

- stockpiling its products prior to the strike,

- continuing production during the strike,

- hiring replacement workers,

- having the agreement end when demand for the product is at a cyclical low, and

- transferring production to other plants, possibly to sites outside the country.

There is only one action an employer can take to make it easier for the union to say yes:

- improving its offer in response to the union's demands.

Behavioural Models

A behavioural model of negotiations emphasizes that negotiations take place between people and focuses on the human aspect of the interaction.

Walton and McKersie, in their analysis of negotiations entitled *A Behavioral Theory of Negotiations*,[3] divide the negotiation process into four subsets:

- distributive bargaining,

- integrative bargaining,

- intra-organizational bargaining, and

- attitudinal structuring.

DISTRIBUTIVE BARGAINING

Distributive bargaining is what most people think of when they think of negotiations. It is the process by which one party attempts to get the other party to agree to its demands or at least a position closer to its demands. For example, the union demands a 5 percent increase, management offers 2 percent, and the parties work to achieve a settlement closer to their own position. If the final settlement is closer to a 5 percent increase in wages, the union is seen to have won and management to have lost. The opposite is true if the final increase is closer to 2 percent. Distributive bargaining emphasizes that there is a limited pot of money and that the negotiation process is about dividing this limited resource.

INTEGRATIVE BARGAINING

Integrative bargaining refers to situations where both parties benefit from the result of the negotiated settlement. For example, a settlement of a particular labour dispute may signal to investors that the industry may be a good investment and prompt them to invest. The resulting increase in production may both improve the employer's profits and enhance the workers' job security, as well as increase the size of the union. Thus, both parties may benefit because of this agreement.

---

3   R. Walton and R. McKersie, *A Behavioral Theory of Labor Relations* (New York: McGraw-Hill, 1965).

INTRA-ORGANIZATIONAL BARGAINING

Intra-organizational bargaining occurs within the management and union structure. For example, the union may have to decide whether to negotiate to increase pensions or to increase wages. It may not be possible to achieve both goals simultaneously. Pensions tend to be an issue that is given more priority by long-term employees, and wage gains tend to be more important to newer employees. The union will have to structure a process to settle which demand will be given priority and also achieve agreement within its own group. Management may face a conflict between financial departments wishing to reduce costs, thus tempering wage demands, and human resources departments wanting substantial increases to create a more satisfied workforce.

ATTITUDINAL STRUCTURING

Attitudinal structuring looks at the relationship between the parties. For example, it may be in the best long-term interests of both the union and management to foster a relationship that promotes settlement of disputes. One party may drop a demand in a particular round of negotiations to signal to the other side that it is willing to work with the other party on a long-term relationship.

Prescriptive Models

Prescriptive models of negotiation provide a method or remedy to improve the process and results of bargaining. One such model is the interest-based bargaining model advocated in the book *Getting to Yes* by Roger Fisher and William Ury.[4] This model prescribes that negotiators move away from advocating for positions and instead advocate for the interests that underlie the positions. An example of a position is: "the union members want a 5 percent wage increase." The interest underlying the position is: union members want a higher income. Therefore, an employer that uses the interest-based bargaining model will attempt to satisfy this interest, not the position, of the union members. The employer may do so through a number of mechanisms, including an increase in benefits. Some of these options may be more preferable to the employer than a straight wage increase and still satisfy the union members' interest—a higher income. The argument is that the results of the negotiation may be achieved with less conflict and still provide potential benefits to each side.

The interest-based bargaining model prescribes the following steps for constructive negotiations:

1. Separate the people from the problem. Allowing personal conflict to enter into the negotiations will only make finding a mutually acceptable solution more difficult, and may cause negotiations to break down.

2. Focus on interests, not positions. Focusing on positions often leads to conflict and makes it difficult for negotiators to see alternative solutions.

---

4   R. Fisher and W. Ury, *Getting to Yes: Negotiating Agreement Without Giving In* (Boston: Houghton Mifflin, 1981).

If the parties delve into the interests behind their positions, they may be able to design creative solutions that will satisfy both parties' needs.

3. Invent options for mutual gain. In this step, the negotiators brainstorm solutions that will benefit both parties. That is, they put aside judgments and generate as many possible solutions to a problem as they can.

4. Insist on objective criteria. Last, the parties agree to criteria for assessing the options for mutual gain. These criteria should be based on reason and not power.

Strategic Models

Strategic models of negotiation provide a framework for understanding the strategic trends in labour negotiations, not a prescription for the conduct of the parties.[5] The strategies of employers could be characterized as fostering change, forcing change, or escaping the unionized work environment.

Fostering change is taking actions to promote cooperation between the union and management and to encourage commitment to the workplace among employees. Practical activities include openly exchanging information, including union representatives on management committees, and building trust with the other side.

Forcing change is taking actions to enhance bargaining power in order to compel the other party to accept your position. This strategy includes developing a stronger "us versus them" mentality, heightening the differences in positions with the other side, and distorting information to win the debate.

Escaping the unionized work environment is a management strategy that takes many forms. It includes relocating work to areas where the legal rules make unionization difficult, contracting out work, and increasing investment in non-union plants. It may also involve taking a long strike, which will effectively replace the striking workers permanently, and setting up conditions at the workplace that may result in the workers starting a decertification application.

THE PROCESS OF NEGOTIATIONS

This section will describe the selection of bargaining teams and choosing of demands. It will then examine the typical processes that tend to be followed in labour negotiations, including some of the strategic and tactical actions that parties often take to advance their positions.

Role of Human Resources Managers and Union Negotiating Teams

During the negotiating process, the human resources manager is expected to advise the organization on trends in negotiated settlements, issues emerging from

---

5   R. Walton, J. Cutcher-Gershenfeld, and R. McKersie, *Strategic Negotiations: A Theory of Change in Labor-Management Relations* (Ithaca, NY: IRL Press, 2000). The authors focus on the strategy that employers have employed in recent rounds of negotiations. They studied 13 recent rounds of negotiations in three industries to form their conclusions.

new and amended statutes that will have to be addressed in bargaining, and recent arbitration awards relevant to the negotiations. The manager must also assess the human resources implications of the union demands and brief legal counsel on the issues if a lawyer has been hired to advise the parties.

The union negotiating teams will have to advocate demands passed by the members and proposed by the union, communicate with the membership, assess and respond to management's proposals and management's responses, and determine the strategic direction of the union during negotiations.

Notice To Bargain

Section 16 of the Ontario *Labour Relations Act, 1995* (OLRA or "the Act")[6] provides that once the union is certified or voluntarily recognized, it must give notice to the employer to bargain. Section 65(1) of the Act says that if the union fails to do so within 60 days, it risks being decertified because it is "sleeping on its rights" (see chapter 3).

Section 59 of the Act also provides that in cases where there is an agreement in force, the parties may give notice to bargain either within 90 days of the end of the agreement or in accordance with a provision on renewal in the agreement itself. The parties may have agreed in a previous round of negotiations that 30 days is adequate notice of a desire to bargain or they may agree to the need for a longer notice period. The parties may also agree that if neither party gives notice to bargain, the contract will be automatically renewed. Under s. 65(1) of the Act, if the union fails to give notice to bargain for renewal in accordance with the OLRA or the collective agreement, the employer may apply to terminate the union's bargaining rights because it has abandoned this workplace.

Structure of Negotiations

The vast majority of negotiations in Canada take place between a single employer and a single union and yield a single collective agreement. Each set of negotiations is independent of other sets of negotiations. However, there are exceptions. These are discussed below.

In some cases, the union uses negotiations with a particular employer as a template for negotiations with other employers. This practice of **pattern bargaining** was used for many years in the auto industry by the United Auto Workers (UAW) and its successor, the Canadian Auto Workers (CAW).[7] The union represented virtually all the production workers at the three largest automakers in Canada: General Motors, Ford, and Chrysler. The collective agreements were generally of three years in length. The union would select one of the three manufacturers as a target, based on an assessment that the union's bargaining power was greatest relative to that company. It would then negotiate an agreement with that

6   SO 1995, c. 1, sched. A.

7   S. Gindin, *The Canadian Auto Workers: The Birth and Transformation of a Union* (Toronto: Lorimer, 1995), 112; and P. Kumar, "In Search of Competitive Efficiency: The General Motors Experience with Restructuring," in A. Verma and R. Chaykowski, eds., *Contract and Commitment Employment Relations in the New Economy* (Kingston, ON: IRC Press, 1999), 142.

manufacturer. As one union historian noted, "Striking only one company at a time, and threatening it with a loss in market share to the others, put competitive pressures on the target."[8] The union would then demand the same agreement from each of the other two automakers. Despite its use by the auto unions, pattern bargaining never became the negotiation norm and its use has declined due to plant closures, foreign competition, concession bargaining, and the entrance of non-unionized competitors. Pattern bargaining works best when all industry competitors are unionized and the imposition of a pattern does not create competitive disadvantages.

In other cases, a single union will negotiate an agreement with a single employer to cover several bargaining units. Again, the auto industry provides a good example. The CAW negotiates a master agreement with an automobile manufacturer that covers all the bargaining units in that company. The master agreement covers issues such as basic rights and responsibilities of union and management, hours of work, layoff and promotions, overtime, grievances, leaves, holidays, wage increases, and benefits. The CAW then negotiates local agreements for each of the bargaining units. Each bargaining unit represents the workers at one plant in one municipality. For example, CAW Local 222 covers the workers at General Motors in Oshawa, Ontario. The local agreement deals with matters such as wages scales, job classifications, transfer of workers, seniority, and distribution of overtime.[9]

In the industrial, commercial, and institutional sector of the construction industry, a single agreement is negotiated between a single union and many employers across the province.

The multiple union and multiple employer negotiation structure is rare in Canada. One example of this occurrence was the social contract negotiations where the province of Ontario determined that, before imposing wage reductions on public sector employees in Ontario, it would have public sector employers and public sector unions negotiate how these reductions would take place. The negotiations primarily took place at sector tables. The college/university sector included the Ontario Public Service Employees Union (OPSEU), the Canadian Union of Public Employees (CUPE), and university faculty associations on the union side and colleges and universities on the employer's side.

Bargaining Committees: Their Composition and Selection

It is rare that the entire membership of the union is involved in the negotiations. Instead, a process is set up to select a few of the members to represent the union. A special election may be held to determine the negotiating team, or the executive of the union may negotiate on behalf of the members. There may be provisions in the union's constitution or bylaws to specify that a certain number of members on the committee come from a particular geographic area, or there may be a requirement to have a certain number of members from a particular job classification on the committee. If the local union ("local") is part of a larger union, that larger union will often have professional negotiators on staff to assist the local with negotiations. A labour lawyer may also be hired by the union to provide advice.

---

8   Gindin, supra note 7, at 112.

9   Kumar, supra note 7, at 142.

Management, too, must set up a team to represent them in negotiations. Depending on the size of the organization, the human resources department may have professional negotiators on staff. It is also possible to hire management labour lawyers to assist the management team in negotiations.

It is usually advisable not to have the chief executive of the organization on the bargaining committee. Instead, the chief executive can act as a sounding board for the management bargaining team, which is not directly involved in the negotiations, and can operate as a final ratifier of the agreement. The union has to take the tentative agreement back to the membership for ratification. Management, similarly, needs the opportunity to have a senior person who is not at the table review the progress of negotiations. The reviewer can also act as a sounding board if the team reaches a point in negotiations where they need the opinion of someone who is outside the process. The employer's team will often include a person who understands the financial implications of the proposals as well as the human resources professional and a shop-floor supervisor, who can advise on the implications of the agreement for the day-to-day operations of the workplace. Often both parties will have the same size committee, even though this is not required by legislation.

Demands (or Proposals)

The parties will have to determine what their demands (sometimes called proposals to be less confrontational in tone) will be in this round of negotiations. The local union will often have a demand-setting meeting where demands are debated and voted on by the members. Sometimes, the larger national or international union will set some goals for bargaining that are pursued by all their locals as a matter of policy. The union may also seek the advice of professional negotiators or labour lawyers as to what they should demand. Some unions conduct surveys of all their members to put their demands together.

The employer, in choosing its demands, should consult with the shop-floor supervisors, although in many cases the employer will be content to react to the union's demands.

Research

Both parties will have to determine their "research needs" to aid them in negotiations. Some common areas of research are listed below:

- wage comparisons
- general wage trends
- inflation rates
- employment law
- contract language
- arbitration awards that interpret contract language in general
- arbitration awards from interpreting their collective agreement
- employer's financial position
- benefit costs
- pension costs.

In the case of many of these areas, the parties will hire experts to provide the answers. The parties will also inquire of health insurance companies about the cost of particular types of insurance.

In conducting their research, the parties draw on three main sources of data: settlement information, contract clauses, and inflation statistics.

SETTLEMENT INFORMATION

The Ontario Ministry of Labour, Labour Management Services, Office of Collective Bargaining Information regularly publishes statistics based on recent settlements in the province involving bargaining units of more than 200 people. The ministry publishes both a monthly set of highlights and a quarterly summary.

The monthly highlights include the following:

- *A negotiations update.* A notification of major negotiations under way, including the union, the location, the number of employees involved, and the expiry date of the collective agreement, which the parties can use to monitor developments in related workplaces.

- *Selected settlements.* Summaries of the full agreement are given for selected settlements. A union local in a casino that is negotiating or preparing to negotiate would be interested in the summary of the Windsor Casino settlement contained in the May 2004 highlights.

  > Windsor Casino Ltd. and National Automobile, Aerospace, Transportation and General Workers' Union of Canada (CAW-Canada), Local 444 (3,500 full-time and part-time employees)
  > - a four-year renewal agreement effective April 1, 2004, expiring April 3, 2008
  > - wage settlement includes lump sum payments of $75 to $1,500 for eligible employees and wage increases of $0.50 in the first year, $0.40 in each of the second, third, and fourth years; additional adjustments for certain classifications
  > - improvements to health and welfare benefits, bereavement leave, and child care provisions
  > - increases in safety shoe, tuition fee, and jury duty allowances, as well as an additional floating holiday in each year
  > - modifications to job security and technological change provisions and the creation of a new Social Justice fund[10]

- *Wage settlements by industry.* Included here are the total number of settlements that month plus the number of employees and the annual wage increase. These data are broken down by public sector or private sector, then by industry group. The industry groups are as follows: Primary, Manufacturing, Construction, Trade and Finance, Transportation, Communications & Utilities, Public Administration, Education & Related Services, Health & Social Services, and Other Services.

- *Monthly settlements.* Each settlement that month is summarized. The summary lists the employer; the union; the average annual wage increase,

---

10 Available online at http://www.gov.on.ca/LAB/english/lr/pubs_type.html.

including cost of living adjustments; the increase in the first year of the agreement; the number of employees involved; and the duration of both the agreement and the wage increases.

The quarterly summary includes the following:

- *Major settlements.* The full agreements for major settlements are summarized. Major settlements are selected based on size of unit, significant bargaining issues, and public interest.

- *Quarterly wage data.* Wage increases over the three months of that quarter plus the information for previous quarters in that year are given.

- *Negotiations information.* Negotiations data are given, such as the length of negotiations and the stage at which settlements occurred.

- *Work stoppages.* Information on strikes and lockouts, including person-days lost, is given.

CONTRACT CLAUSES

Sample contract clauses may be produced by the union representing the workers or by the industry association. The Canadian Association of University Teachers (CAUT), a federation of unions in the postsecondary education sector, publishes model language on their website for use by its member unions. Model contract language may also be found in texts such as *Contract Clauses.*[11]

INFLATION STATISTICS

Statistics Canada publishes data on the consumer price index (CPI). The CPI is the standard measure of inflation used in most negotiations. The Ontario Ministry of Labour, Labour Management Services, Office of Collective Bargaining Information publishes the Statistics Canada data in its monthly collective bargaining highlights bulletin.

Costing of Proposals

The parties will need to do at least an approximate costing of the proposals they are negotiating. The employer will calculate costs to determine whether it can afford to agree to any of the union's demands. The union will usually want to verify management's cost estimates and will often use costing to assess the reasonability of its demands.

When the parties calculate the costs of a proposal, they must be careful not to omit **impacted costs**. Let us assume that an employer has 100 employees and they earn an average of $20.00 per hour. This hourly amount is sometimes called the base rate. Assume that each worker's regular work week is 40 hours and the worker is at work for 48 weeks per year. On average each worker will work 1,920 hours per year. If the parties agree to increase wages by $1.00 an hour on average, the cost to the employer of the straight hourly increase would be $1.00 per hour × 1,920 hours

---

11 J. Sack and E. Poskanzer, *Contract Clauses*, 3rd ed. (Toronto: Lancaster House, 1996).

per employee per year × 100 employees = $192,000. But that would not be the end of the costing. There may be benefits and tax costs that depend on the hourly rate of the employees and these would have to be factored in. Also, if the employer pays a premium rate for overtime, then that cost, too, will increase. Because the employer is unlikely to know the exact amount of overtime that will be worked in the next year, an assumption has to be made. The best assumption is usually just to follow historical precedent, unless there is some new factor that clearly indicates that more overtime will be worked in the future. In our simplified example, if we assume that each employee averages 60 hours of overtime per year and the premium payment is 1½ times salary, then, factoring in the $1.00 hourly increase, the premium rate has increased from $30.00 per hour ($20.00 × 1.5) to $31.50 per hour ($21.00 × 1.5). The total impact on overtime costs due to the wage increase is $1.50 per hour × 60 hours per employee × 100 employees = $9,000.

The parties should be aware of the different impact on workers of percentage increases versus constant-dollar increases. Let us assume a workplace with two classifications of workers. One classification earns $18.00 per hour and the other earns $40.00 per hour. If a 5 percent across the board increase is negotiated, then the person earning $18.00 per hour will see an increase of $0.90 per hour and the person earning $40.00 per hour will receive a $2.00 per hour increase. Note also that the gap between those wage rates will increase by $1.10 per hour. If, instead, the parties negotiated a $1.10 per hour increase to each classification, then the $18.00 per hour worker will see a 6 percent increase and the $40.00 per hour worker will receive a 2.75 percent increase. In this scenario, the gap will stay the same. Sometimes, the parties will negotiate a lump-sum increase. A lump-sum increase is a sum of money that is usually not included in the base rate. If the lump sum is not rolled into the base rate, it will not be the subject of compounding in future rounds of negotiations. For example, if the base rate is $18.00 per hour and, instead of increasing the base rate, the workers are given a $2,000 lump sum, the parties will start the next round of negotiations at $18.00 per hour. If the lump sum is rolled in at the end of the contract, the $18.00 base rate would be increased prior to the start of negotiations to reflect the $2,000 lump sum.

Meetings

Under s. 17 of the OLRA, the parties must meet within 15 days after the notice to bargain has been given or they must agree on a later meeting time. In most cases, the representatives of the parties will exchange a series of dates on which they are available and they will agree to mutually acceptable times. In some cases, meetings take place away from the worksite in hotel meeting rooms or other meeting spaces. Meetings may also take place at the worksite, but after hours. If meetings take place at the worksite during work hours, there is the possibility of considerable interruptions and disruptions as interested employees speculate and focus on the ongoing negotiations. In some cases, the union negotiating team may be released from some of its work duties in order to attend the meetings.

Typically, each side will need a room to meet and discuss its proposals before these proposals are presented to the other side. These rooms are often called caucus rooms. It is common to refer to these meetings as a caucus meetings. There is also a need for a room for joint meetings of the parties. This room will contain a long table so that the management team can sit on one side of the table and the union on the other.

In many situations, the parties will discuss matters for hours in caucus and then present essentially a scripted and rehearsed speech to the other side. That side may ask a few questions about the presentation and then retire to their caucus room to decide on their response. It may take a long time to formulate a response, in which case the response will be delivered in another joint session. Thus, the parties may spend considerably more time in caucus than in face-to-face negotiations.

In some cases, it may be beneficial for a small subcommittee of both negotiating teams to meet and try to resolve a single issue. In the later stages of bargaining, it may be productive for the chairs of the two bargaining committees to meet and talk about options.

A variation of this typical process, called single-team bargaining, is sometimes used. In this variation, separate caucuses are discouraged and the representatives are mingled in around the table, sometimes alternating around a circular table. This is done to facilitate joint problem solving.

Procedure

In most negotiations, the union will ask for improvements to the agreement. The union will tend to outline its demands and give the rationale for each demand, perhaps with supporting research. This is most often referred to as "tabling the demands." If management is tabling demands, it will most likely call for a reduction or weakening in the language previously negotiated by the parties. The union will label these as concessions and will tend to resist them quite strongly.

In order to proceed, the parties will often separate the demands into monetary demands and non-monetary demands. Monetary demands are clearly identifiable added costs to the employer, such as wage or benefit increases. With non-monetary demands, the cost is less clear. A non-monetary demand would include the name of an arbitrator who will hear disputes during the term of the agreement. The logic of starting with non-monetary demands is that it will be easier to reach agreement on these items, and the act of solving these items may give some momentum to the bargaining process on the more difficult issues.

In some circumstances, management may want to negotiate the monetary part of the agreement by getting an agreement on the total cost of the package and then letting the union decide where the money will be spent. Management may not care whether the union puts it all into a wage increase or divides it between wages and benefits, as long as the total cost does not exceed a given limit.

A party will sometimes put together a set of proposals and tell the other side that these are a package and that one proposal cannot be accepted without the others. For example, the employer may propose a larger salary increase if the union agrees to weaken its seniority language on promotions. If this proposal is presented as part of a package, the union cannot accept the salary increase, reject the seniority change, and then argue that management had agreed to the salary.

In some cases, a party may want to make a proposal that is off the record or "without prejudice." A party usually makes this kind of a proposal in an attempt to settle all the issues. If the parties do not reach a settlement, the party making the proposal does not want its willingness to settle used against it publicly, including before an arbitrator. For example, management could make an off-the-record proposal to increase its wage offer in return for weaker seniority language, provided that the union is willing to drop the rest of its demands. If the union does not agree to this proposal, it cannot publish to its members the wage increase that management had offered, saying, "this is the kind of wage increase we will get in the end." This would violate the rules of good-faith bargaining and would permanently damage the bargaining relationship with the employer's bargaining team. Equally, if the union makes an off-the-record proposal to the employer in which it offers to drop some demands and the proposal is rejected, the employer cannot then go to the union members to say, "see what the union bargaining team is willing to drop? They are not representing you."

Tactics

The parties will want to support and advocate for the positions taken at the bargaining table, and this advocacy will be addressed to the public and the other side. The union will try to convince the employer that the union's position is justified while maintaining the support of its members. It may also try to elicit the support of the public.

Often the negotiations process will go right to the last minute. In fact, settlements are most likely to take place "at the 11th hour" or right at the strike deadline. One of the reasons for this tendency is the problem the negotiators face with their own group if they do not work up to the last minute. If the union settles an agreement early, some of the members may believe that if the union had held out for a little longer, it would have gotten a better deal. And if this sentiment is widespread, the members might reject the tentative agreement in the ratification vote and send the union back to the bargaining table to seek a better deal. Knowing this, management may be reluctant to put its best offer on the table until the last minute.

Supervised Final-Offer Vote

Section 42 of the OLRA provides that if the employer believes that the union negotiating team is not reflecting the views of the workers when it rejects the employer's offer the employer has the right to force a **final-offer vote** on the employer's final offer. The final offer being voted on by the workers must conclusively deal with all matters in dispute between the parties. An application for a final-offer vote is made to the minister of labour. This option may be taken before or after a strike or lockout has taken place. A final-offer vote is only available if there is a right to strike, so it is not available in sectors such as hospitals, where strikes are not permitted. Also, if a first-contract arbitration is directed, and management can no longer apply for a final-offer vote, a strike is prohibited.

In the case of the construction industry, the minister of labour has the discretion to refuse a final-offer vote. The application for a final-offer vote will not extend other time limits under the Act so it will not delay a possible strike. Where a final-offer vote is taken and the workers vote to accept the offer, it is considered an unfair labour practice on the part of the union not to sign an agreement corresponding to the final offer that was voted on and accepted by its members. Even though this option is available, it is seldom used, because in most cases the union does reflect the views of the members. If the employer forces the vote and loses, its credibility with both the union and the employees will be damaged.

In 2001-2, the Ontario Labour Relations Board (OLRB) received 36 new applications to hold final-offer votes: 25 votes were ordered, 7 matters were settled, and 4 were pending. Of the 25 votes that were held, in 11 cases the workers voted to accept the offer and in 14 cases they rejected the offer.[12]

EXPIRY DATE OF CONTRACT

The parties will sometimes try to select an end date for the collective agreement that corresponds to a time of enhanced power for that party. This is especially true when the demand for the product has an annual cycle. The employer will try to select a date when demand for the product is low. When demand is low, there are often stockpiles of product, which the employer can continue to sell during a potential strike. The union will try to select a period of high demand when the employer can least afford to lose sales.

Ratification

If the negotiating teams reach an agreement, it becomes a tentative agreement and is subject to **ratification** by the bargaining unit and the employer. As part of the tentative settlement, the negotiating teams will agree to recommend "acceptance to their principles." That is, the union will communicate to its members that the agreement should be accepted, as will the management negotiating team with senior managers. The teams will usually sign a document containing the amendments to the agreement. This document is called either a **memorandum of settlement** or a **tentative agreement** or a **memorandum of understanding**.

The union negotiating team will often hold membership meetings at which they will explain the terms of the deal to the members and explain why they believe the agreement should be accepted. Then, under ss. 44, 79, and 79.1 of the Act, a ratification vote must be held on the tentative agreement. The collective agreement will have no effect until the vote is held and more than 50 percent of those voting indicate that they are in favour of the tentative agreement. The vote is conducted by the union and is not supervised by the labour board. However, in order for the vote to be valid, the union must conduct the vote in accordance with the following set of conditions:

- the vote must be by secret ballot;
- all the employees in the bargaining unit covered by the tentative agreement must be allowed to vote, even if they have not joined the union;
- the voters must have ample opportunity to vote;
- the time and place of the vote must be reasonably convenient;
- the ballot used in the vote must give only the options of ratifying or not ratifying the agreement; and

---

12 Ontario Labour Relations Board Annual Report 2001-2002 (herein referred to as OLRB 2001-2 Annual Report), available online at http://www.olrb.gov.on.ca/english/annrep0102.pdf.

- the option to use mail-in ballots must be made available.

It is very seldom that the members reject the recommendation of the negotiating team. If they do, then the team is left with the options of either resigning and letting a new team try to get a better deal or going back to the employer and trying to get a better agreement themselves. The employer would be reluctant to offer a better deal because the employees might reject this new tentative agreement to get more improvements and the process would continue.

The management negotiating team will take the proposed deal back to senior management for approval. In most cases this is a mere formality since senior management has usually been kept in the loop over the course of negotiations. In the event that management rejects the agreement, the union bargaining team is likely to move to a strike rather than cut back on the agreed terms and conditions. The union also will be reluctant to enter into negotiations with the management negotiating team, since it would view these negotiations as a waste of time. It will want instead to talk to representatives of management who have the real authority to bargain.

GOOD-FAITH BARGAINING AND BAD-FAITH BARGAINING

Both the union and the employer are required by law to engage in "good-faith bargaining," in which representatives of the employer meet with the union's representatives. Both sides must present their proposals; listen to the other party's proposals; articulate arguments supporting their position and refuting the other side's positions; and search for common ground in a serious attempt to reach an agreement.

The OLRB in the case of *DeVilbiss (Canada) Limited*[13] described the reason for the duty to bargain in good faith as follows:

> [R]ational discussion is likely to minimize the number of problems the parties are unable to resolve without the use of economic weapons thereby focusing the parties' attention in the eleventh hour on the "true" differences between them.

Bargaining in good faith does not mean that the parties cannot engage in "hard bargaining." The employer may take a strong stand that it needs concessions to deal with financial difficulties. Concessions consist of reductions in or limitations on the provisions in the collective agreement negotiated by the union in prior rounds of negotiation. For example, management may want to reduce labour costs by demanding a reduction in salaries or a limitation on certain benefits. What management must be prepared to do is justify its position and consider alternatives suggested by the union as a means of reducing costs. The Manitoba Labour Board in the *Buhler Versatile Inc.* case[14] described hard bargaining as

> [a] situation where one party insists on onerous terms the other refuses to accept. A resulting impasse in bargaining will not be found to stem from a breach of the duty of good faith if it can be said that the proponent is merely using its economic position to negotiate terms which favour its legitimate interests. In effect, where the board finds a party's bargaining position to be a violation of the

13 [1976] OLRB Rep. Mar. 49.

14 [2001] MLRB no. 9.

duty it is not so much assessing the inherent reasonableness of a proposal as it is using the proposal, in the wider context, as an indicator of the party's unwillingness to conclude any agreement.

The line between hard bargaining and **bad-faith bargaining** is sometimes a difficult one to draw. Is the party unwilling to conclude any agreement, or is it simply willing to use its power to force the agreement that it wants on the other party? Labour boards and courts have articulated several principles to guide parties in avoiding charges of bad-faith bargaining. Section 17 of the OLRA requires that the parties

> meet within 15 days from the giving of the notice or within such further period as the parties agree upon and they shall bargain in good faith and make every reasonable effort to make a collective agreement.

Engaging in the following activities may lead a labour board to decide that a party has engaged in a failure to bargain in good faith:[15]

- refusing to meet
- refusing to recognize the union
- not giving the negotiating team any power to bargain
- surface bargaining
- deception
- concealing important information
- deliberate provocation
- refusing to justify a position
- refusing to make every reasonable effort to enter into a collective agreement.

Refusing to meet. Simply refusing to meet with the other party would be a clear instance of bad faith. It would also be bad faith to never be available or to constantly cancel all agreed bargaining sessions.

Refusing to recognize the union. The employer cannot ignore the fact that the union is now the authorized representative of the employees. The union is the bargaining agent for the workers covered by the certification or voluntary recognition. The employer must not take actions that show it is not taking the representation rights of the union seriously. This would include attempts to bargain directly with the employees, perhaps by disclosing bargaining positions to the employees before releasing them to the union negotiating team.

Not giving the negotiating team any power to bargain. The parties must have the true decision maker at the table. That is, the negotiating team must have some authority to make decisions that further bargaining. Negotiation may reach a stage where the team has to consult its principals on how to proceed, but it cannot do so with respect to every item and every discussion.

---

15 See *Buhler Versatile Inc.*, [2001] MLRB Rep. no. 9; *DeVilbiss (Canada) Limited*, [1976] OLRB Rep. Mar. 49; *Radio Shack*, [1979] OLRB Rep. Dec. 1220.

Surface bargaining. The parties must avoid **surface bargaining**, a delaying tactic in which a party bargains without any intention of concluding negotiations. The party may agree to meet and discuss the issues but does not make any real attempt to reach an agreement. Parties must act with the intent of concluding, revising, or renewing a collective agreement; the intention cannot be to delay until the other party launches an unnecessary strike.

Deception. The parties must avoid deception in their statements to each other. Statements must be both accurate and honest. If a statement is made by a party, the party should check that the statement is accurate. The employer is legally required to respond honestly when asked if it is thinking about taking actions that may significantly affect the bargaining unit.

Concealing important information. The employer is expected to disclose information that the union needs to conduct effective bargaining, such as the number of employees, the wage rate, or the salary levels of employees. The union must request this information and it must be relevant to the issues involved in the negotiations. The employer is not required to disclose private financial information or trade secrets.

The employer is also expected to disclose bargaining data that would affect the union's bargaining positions. This is considered in the same light as misrepresentation. In the case of *Buhler*,[16] the Manitoba Labour Board observed that

> [it] is "tantamount to a misrepresentation" for an employer not to reveal during bargaining a decision it has already made which will have a significant impact on terms and conditions of employment, such as a plant closing, and which the union could not have anticipated.

The employer is not required to reveal all its decisions and data to the union. What the employer must disclose is any intention to take actions that might change the bargaining position of the union. If, for example, the employer informs the union of a pending plant closure, the union might want to alter its position to emphasize job security, severance, or retraining, rather than wage and benefit issues. The board also observed in *Buhler* that

> an employer is under [a legal] obligation to reveal to the union on his own initiative those decisions already made which may have a major impact on the bargaining unit. Without this information a trade union is effectively put in the dark. The union cannot realistically assess its priorities or formulate a meaningful bargaining response to matters of fundamental importance to the employees it represents. Failure to inform in these circumstances may properly be characterized as an attempt to secure the agreement of the trade union for a fixed term on the basis of a misrepresentation in respect of matters which could fundamentally alter the content of the bargain.

Unjustifiable changes in bargaining positions. Once a party takes a position in bargaining, it should not be able to change that position without valid reason. The reason may be a response to the other party's request or advocacy. For example, an employer could increase its wage offer to respond to the union's demand. Or a union could decrease its wage demand in response to management's financial

---

16 Supra note 15.

hardship. Once the union has tabled a wage proposal, it is difficult for the union to increase that demand without being accused of bargaining in bad faith. The argument is that management will not be able to assess these demands and determine how to respond if the target changes upward. Equally difficult would be a party that makes sudden and unexplained changes in position. A labour board might conclude that such a party has no intention of reaching any agreement. A change in bargaining motivated by an amendment in the law, however, would be justifiable.

Deliberate provocation. This would include tabling positions that are not only disliked by the opposing party but also intended to deliberately provoke a breakdown in negotiations. A proposal that would effectively require the union to give up its rights to file grievances, thus ending its effectiveness, would be a deliberate provocation.

Refusal to justify position. The parties must engage in full, rational, informed discussion about the issues. A party cannot merely take a position: it must be willing to justify its position.

Refusal to make every reasonable effort to enter into a collective agreement. Refusing to assist the other party with costing its proposals or refusing to hear the other side's proposals about new options to solve an impasse would fall into this category of bad faith.

Again, the *Buhler* case provides examples of several of the above activities. The employer made constant threats of closure and sale, did not provide supporting material to justify its demands, switched positions in the middle of bargaining, lowered its offer as time went on, failed to disclose information, and did not attempt to reach any common ground. The labour board found the employer's actions to be in bad faith.

THIRD-PARTY ASSISTANCE

Before the parties can take part in actions such as strikes or lockouts, a third-party professional must be employed to try to assist the parties in resolving their differences. These professionals may be involved in the process at any time before, during, or after a strike or lockout right up to the settlement. The types of assistance available are as follows:

- conciliation
- mediation
- fact finding
- conciliation boards.

Conciliation

According to s. 18 of the OLRA, at any time after notice to bargain is given, either party may apply to the minister of labour to appoint a conciliation officer for **conciliation**. The minister is obligated to appoint the conciliation officer. In this case, the Act does not require that any bargaining have taken place. In another case, the parties may not have given notice but they may have started to bargain. In this case, the minister of labour may appoint a conciliator if either party requests that one be appointed.

The conciliation officer is an employee of the Ministry of Labour and is usually referred to as a conciliator. The conciliator will meet with the parties and try to assist them in reaching an agreement. Section 20 of the Act states that the conciliator has 14 days to meet with the parties and help them to reach an agreement. The time limit can be extended if the parties agree or if the minister extends the limit at the request of the conciliation officer. The conciliation officer may ask for an extension only if he or she believes that a settlement is possible soon after the expiry of the 14 days.

Conciliation is mandatory prior to a scheduled strike or lockout. A union that wants to start a strike on a particular date will have to make sure that conciliation is completed prior to that date. In the case of a sophisticated bargaining relationship, the conciliator may not be able to offer the parties any assistance. So, the appointment becomes a mere formality on the way to either an agreement or a strike or lockout.

Once the conciliator is finished, he or she will report to the minister that an agreement was or was not reached. If no agreement was reached, the minister has the option to set up a conciliation board to examine the dispute, or the minister will inform the parties that a conciliation board will not be appointed. A conciliation board has not been appointed in Ontario in many years, so the minister will inform the parties that no conciliation board will be appointed. This is called a **no-board report** and it starts the countdown for a possible strike or lockout.

The key disadvantage to conciliation in reaching an agreement is that by law a conciliator must finish before the last minute of negotiations. This is to allow a cooling-off period between the end of conciliation and the start of a legal strike or lockout. Because of the tendency for negotiations to go to the last minute, the conciliator will be finished prior to that crucial time and often will not be able to help avert the strike or lockout.

Mediation

Mediation is another type of third-party assistance that is used to reach an agreement. The differences between conciliation and mediation are that mediation is not mandatory and it can occur at any time in the negotiation process, including just before, during, or after a strike or lockout. The parties first agree to the person who will act as mediator. The mediator does not have to be an employee of the Ministry of Labour. The mediator then meets with the parties and assists them in trying to reach an agreement. The mediator has two key advantages over the conciliator in completing this task. One, the mediator is usually chosen by the parties, not appointed by the minister. Thus, both parties will have some confidence in this person prior to the start of mediation. Two, the mediator operates right up to and past the start of a strike or lockout. Thus, the mediator is able to work at the last moment when the pressure to settle is greatest.

The Practice of Mediation and Conciliation

The objective in the case of both conciliation and mediation is to assist the parties in reaching an agreement. It is the result that is important and thus each mediator or conciliator will use his or her own techniques of assisting the parties and will vary those techniques depending on the circumstances. It must be clearly noted that a mediator or conciliator has no power to impose any kind of agreement on the parties. The mediator or conciliator is limited to tools of persuasion to encourage the parties to settle their problems. One of the important skills for a mediator or conciliator is to know when a deal is possible. If there is the potential for an agreement, the conciliator or mediator should try to press the parties to get that agreement and be prepared for lengthy, sometimes round-the-clock negotiation sessions. If no agreement is possible, it is usually best to put off the talks for a period of time, perhaps until some new action in the negotiating process intervenes, to place more pressure on the parties to settle. This may include a strike vote or an actual strike or lockout.

In most cases, a variation of the following pattern takes place:

1. The mediator or conciliator meets with the parties together to hear from the parties what the issues are that they cannot resolve. In most cases, the parties will explain their positions to the mediator or conciliator. The mediator or conciliator often imposes a media blackout during these talks.

2. The mediator or conciliator will then meet with each party separately to get more information on each party's position and try to assess whether there is any possibility for a settlement. This will include trying to determine the real and most important priorities of each negotiating team.

3. The mediator or conciliator sometimes suggests to the parties possible solutions to their issues. Or he or she may offer to carry messages between the parties that the parties will not deliver publicly to each other. The message will have come from the mediator, so the parties can deny that they made the suggestion if the negotiations fall apart.

4. The mediator or conciliator may suggest that negotiations between smaller subcommittees of the negotiating teams take place, or that without-prejudice positions be used to advance negotiations. Without-prejudice positions in the context of labour negotiations are positions that a party can take but withdraw if agreement is not reached. The other side cannot report or use these positions if the negotiations break off.

5. If the mediator or conciliator senses that a settlement is possible, he or she will pressure the parties to modify their positions just that little bit more to achieve a settlement. The mediator or conciliator may, for example, emphasize the costs of a strike or lockout, or the precarious financial position of the employer or the strong support that the union has for a particular proposal.

Fact Finding

The fact-finding process is sometimes used to facilitate negotiations. A third party is called in to objectively report on the facts surrounding a particular negotiation prior to a strike or lockout.[17] The report of the fact finder is designed to assist the parties in negotiations and embarrass a party that is making outrageous demands. In the report, the fact finder generally describes the issues separating the parties, and looks at settlements in comparable bargaining situations. A fact finder sometimes assesses the range in which a settlement should take place. It is seldom that the proposals of the parties are significantly outside this settlement range.

Conciliation Board

Conciliation boards are provided for under ss. 21 to 34 of the Act but are in practice never appointed. A conciliation board would consist of a representative of the employer, a representative of the union, and a neutral chairperson selected by the minister on the recommendations of the parties. The board would hold hearings, investigate the dispute, hear witnesses, and conduct an investigation. It would then file a report to the minister with recommendations on how the dispute should be solved. The report would then be given to the parties. The logic is that the report, especially the recommendations of the conciliation board, would be so compelling that the parties would settle. If they did not settle, the report would be made public. Public pressure would be brought to bear on the parties, especially if one party was being unreasonable. In practice, this did not occur. Reports of conciliation boards seldom resulted in a strike or lockout being averted. The only impact of a conciliation board was added cost to the public and the parties and a delay in the resolution of a dispute. Thus, the conciliation board route is never used anymore.

THIRD-PARTY DETERMINATION

Third-party determination of the terms of a collective agreement is called **interest arbitration** to distinguish it from rights arbitration, which takes place during the term of a collective agreement. In third-party determination, the third party will decide on the terms and conditions of employment and impose them on the parties. Thus, the collective agreement will be imposed by the third party. This differs from conciliation/mediation, where the third party will try to persuade the parties to accept certain terms and conditions of employment.

Voluntary Interest Arbitration

The parties can always agree to send their dispute to voluntary interest arbitration, usually called binding interest arbitration. Section 40 of the OLRA provides that at any time after giving notice to bargain, the parties may

---

17 This process is sometimes used in the education sector. See *Colleges Collective Bargaining Act*, RSO 1990, c. C.15.

irrevocably agree in writing to refer all matters remaining in dispute between them to an arbitrator or a board of arbitration for final and binding determination.

An arbitrator is a single person selected to decide on the terms and conditions in a new collective agreement. The parties create an arbitration board by each selecting a person to sit on the board. These two representatives then agree on a neutral third party who will chair the arbitration tribunal. The decision of the arbitrator or arbitration board is binding on the parties.

The party in the negotiations that has a more powerful bargaining position will always be reluctant to send the dispute to voluntary interest arbitration because this party will believe that the exercise of bargaining power through a strike or lockout will result in a better outcome. Thus, voluntary interest arbitration is seldom agreed to.

Compulsory Interest Arbitration

In some cases, the government determines that the impact of a strike or lockout would be intolerably damaging to society. It intervenes and removes the right to strike, either on a permanent basis or on an ad hoc basis, and sends the dispute to interest arbitration for resolution. Workers in hospitals, police officers, and firefighters are denied the right to strike because their absence from work could do substantial harm to the health, safety, and property of people in society. Their right to strike is replaced by third-party interest arbitration on a permanent basis.

In some situations, where the government decides that an ongoing dispute is having a significant impact on the public, the government will end the strike and send the dispute to interest arbitration for resolution. Public school teachers have the right to strike in Ontario. However, when the government believes that the continuation of a strike may threaten the completion of a school year, it will order that the dispute be settled by interest arbitration.

First-Contract Arbitration

The legal system in Ontario recognizes that the bargaining power of a newly certified union may be weak and particularly vulnerable to management resistance. The certification process may have been difficult and management may not have accepted the existence of the union and may have improperly exercised its superior bargaining power. If the union is given some assistance to get through its first contract negotiations, then a long-term, healthy bargaining relationship may develop.[18] The Ontario Labour Relations Board outlines these principles in the following passage:

> It is clear from these provisions that the legislature has acknowledged the significance to the collective bargaining relationship of the first contract, and has given statutory recognition to the potential difficulties that may be encountered in achieving it. This remedy does not supplant the primacy of the free bargaining

---

18 On first-contract arbitration, see J. Sack and M. Mitchell, *Ontario Labour Relations Board Law and Practice* (Toronto: Butterworths, 1985), chapter 12.

process; rather, it recognizes that the negotiation of the first agreement may sometimes be thwarted by unjustified intransigence.[19]

GROUNDS FOR FIRST-CONTRACT ARBITRATION

Section 43(1) of the Act provides that to have a first collective agreement imposed, the union must first give notice to bargain and attempt to reach mutual agreement, including taking part in the conciliation process. The union must also wait until the no-board report is issued. That is the earliest time at which the union could apply to the OLRB for an imposed first collective agreement. However, the union might try to continue to get an agreement through a strike and apply later.

To be eligible for first-contract arbitration, the union must show more than the fact that it has been unable to get a collective agreement. However, it is not necessary for the union to show that management has violated the duty to bargain in good faith. Management's actions may not be due to bad faith but may be a result of inexperience or carelessness. The union will have to demonstrate to the board the reason that negotiations have failed. Under s. 43(2) of the Act, the union must show that the employer either

- failed to recognize the union,

- took an uncompromising position without reasonable justification,

- did not make reasonable or effective efforts to get an agreement (in other words, stalled), or

- engaged in any other practice that the OLRB concludes caused the negotiations to fail.

Failure to recognize. Failure to recognize the union includes refusing to meet with the union's negotiating team or trying to individually bargain with employees; openly stating that it would never accept a union; refusing to give the union information that it needs in order to bargain;[20] demanding changes to the composition of the certified bargaining unit; or refusing to include in the agreement employment practices that management intended to continue doing.[21]

Uncompromising and unreasonable position. An uncompromising and unreasonable position in bargaining would include holding to a position that asks the union to, in effect, render itself ineffective. For example, in one case an employer demanded that a union agree to the following condition. The employer stated that if workers were reinstated by the arbitration process, it would exercise a right to give notice of termination to those employees. The OLRB held that the employer was holding an unreasonable position and that the union would be totally ineffective if the employer could simply terminate employees assisted by the union. The test applied by the OLRB is not to look at whether or not a particular employer has its own reason for taking a certain position, but instead whether a reasonable employer

---

19 *Nepean Roof Truss Ltd.*, [1986] OLRB Rep. Aug. 1071.

20 *Co-Fo Concrete Forming Construction Limited*, [1987] OLRB Rep. Sept. 1213.

21 Sack and Mitchell, *supra* note 18, at 12.5

would take the same position.[22] Another example of an unreasonable position was an employer's refusal to implement the Rand Formula for union dues deduction,[23] because the OLRA provides that the union can have the Rand Formula just by asking for it.

Stalling. Examples of stalling tactics that would trigger the third ground for ordering first-contract arbitration include the following: not meeting with the union;[24] stopping the negotiations; not reading and responding to union proposals;[25] refusing to discuss certain items; engaging in surface bargaining; proposing terms that are less than what the employees already have; sending unprepared negotiators who have no authority and who contribute nothing to the process;[26] failing to provide information; and tabling numerous proposals, many of which have no logical purpose. These actions may be taken in the hope that the delay would cause the union to collapse.

Other unfair labour practices. Other reasons that cause negotiations to fail have included a strong pattern of unfair labour practices on the part of the employer.[27]

PROCEDURE FOR FIRST-CONTRACT ARBITRATION

The union applies for first-contract arbitration by filing a form and documents with both the OLRB and the employer. The form will contain

- the date of certification or voluntary recognition
- a description of the bargaining unit
- the number of employees in the unit
- a contact person for the union
- the date of the no-board report
- the dates of scheduled negotiations
- a statement of all the facts and allegations that the union intends to rely on
- a list and copy of documents that the union intends to use in its application
- a list of agreed items, if any
- a list of items in dispute
- a proposed agreement that the union is willing to sign.[28]

---

22 Ibid., at 12.7.

23 *Fort William Clinic,* [1997] OLRB Rep. 406.

24 In one case, the employer would meet only in the evening for four hours at maximum. See *Fort William Clinic,* ibid.

25 *Mansour Rockbolting Ltd.,* [1986] OLRB Rep. 1346.

26 Sack and Mitchell, supra note 18, at 12.9.2.

27 Ibid., at 12.11.

28 Rules of Procedure of the Ontario Labour Relations Board, rule 78 and form A-19.

The employer has eight days to file a response and give it to the union. The response will contain

- a description of the bargaining unit

- the number of employees in the unit

- a contact person for the employer

- a description of the business

- the dates of scheduled negotiations

- a statement of agreement or disagreement with each fact or allegation in the union's document

- a statement of all the facts and allegations that the employer intends to rely on

- a list and copy of documents that the employer intends to use in its application

- a list of agreed items, if any

- a list of items in dispute

- a proposed agreement that the employer is willing to sign.[29]

If the parties omit some fact or allegation from their documents, the board may refuse to hear evidence about the matter.

Sections 43(4) and (5) of the Act instruct the following. If the board determines that the employer has completed at least one of the categories of prohibited actions and that this course of conduct caused the failure to complete the agreement, then the OLRB will direct the settlement of the first contract by arbitration. An arbitration board will have to be set up, unless the parties agree to have the OLRB adjudicate the agreement.

According to ss. 43(14) to (16) of the Act, the order will have the following additional consequences:

- There is to be no strike or lockout.

- Any strike or lockout that is in progress is over.

- The employer has to reinstate the striking or locked out workers all at once or in order of seniority, unless it has permanently discontinued the operations these workers were involved in.

- The terms and conditions of employment are frozen as of the date of notice to bargain.[30]

- If the terms and conditions have been changed since the date of notice to bargain, then they must go back to the state they were in on the date of notice.

- The cost of the arbitration will be shared by the employer and the union.

Section 43(19) of the Act provides that collective agreement established by first-contract arbitration will be two years in duration. After this first contract expires, the

---

29 Ibid., rule 79 and form A-20.

30 In *Fort William Clinic*, supra note 23, the employer violated this duty by failing to pay the regular Christmas bonus, although the cancellation of the Christmas party did not violate the freeze.

union will have to use its bargaining power to get a second and subsequent agreement. Under s. 43(18) of the Act, the agreement must include any items the parties had already agreed to in writing. The parties can add new items to the demands when they argue before the arbitration board. They can also bring back matters they had already withdrawn. The imposed collective agreement will not achieve major breakthroughs for the union.[31] Instead, it will include the terms the parties would have had if bargaining had not broken down. It should also reflect the general view of what should be in a collective agreement in that industry and in that geographic area adapted to that specific workplace. The imposed collective agreement will not reflect the dominant bargaining position of the employer. Section 43(19) provides that it can be made retroactive but only back to the date of notice to bargain.

In 2001-2 the OLRB dealt with 16 applications for first-contract arbitrations.[32] The OLRB granted 2 orders for arbitration, 1 case was dismissed, and 1 case was pending. In the other 12 cases, the matter was settled after intervention by labour relations officers from the OLRB. In these cases, the parties were able to negotiate their own agreement voluntarily prior to the need for arbitration.

Interest Arbitration Practice

An interest arbitrator will usually hold an oral hearing. At the hearing, the parties will present their proposals, provide arguments to justify the proposals, refute the arguments made by the opposing party, and answer any questions posed by the arbitrator. The parties will also often present written briefs, which contain the background to their arguments, including economic data such as the inflation rate, general wage increases, and the results of contract negotiations at comparable workplaces (for example, an interest arbitration involving nurses at one hospital will be influenced by the result of negotiations at other hospitals).

One of the controversial issues in the interest arbitration process for public service employees is the concept of ability to pay. In the private sector an employer can demonstrate, by revealing accurate accounting data, that it cannot afford to pay salary increases without becoming unprofitable. The employer will further argue that it cannot simply get more money from its customers. In the public sector, there are no such objective data. A government may not currently have the revenue to pay a salary increase to its employees, but it could raise taxes to generate it. Thus, a limit on salary increases is really a decision by society that it is unwilling to pay more, not that it is unable to pay more.

Problems with Interest Arbitration and Modifications of the Traditional Model

The optimistic view that interest arbitration offers a simple alternative that would eliminate the need for strikes or lockouts is tempered by the following considerations:

- the interest arbitrator is an outsider who does not know the real circumstances of the issues,

---

31 *Egan Visual Inc.*, [1986] OLRB Rep. 1687.

32 OLRB 2001-2 Annual Report, at 13.

- interest arbitration inhibits bargaining between the parties (that is, creates an arbitration freeze), and

- interest arbitration removes any incentive to make internal compromises.

Each of these difficulties is discussed below.

ARBITRATOR AS OUTSIDER

A general problem with the arbitration model of settling contract disputes is described by an eminent legal scholar in this fashion:

> But, we are asked, why not use that model for negotiation strikes? Why not sub-
> stitute the rational, judicial-type system of interest-dispute arbitration? If the
> parties cannot mutually agree on acceptable terms of employment, let them go to
> an arbitration board which will issue a legally binding award. The problem with
> that solution should be apparent. Although it does preserve the collective ability
> of employees to challenge the unilateral prerogative of their employer, it does so
> at the expense of free collective bargaining. The analogy with grievance arbitra-
> tion does not really hold. The latter applies standards which the parties have al-
> ready freely negotiated in their contract, in order to resolve concrete and largely
> marginal disputes about their application. By contrast the job of the interest ar-
> bitrator is to create those contract standards, not to apply them. By and large the
> interest arbitrator creates them out of whole cloth, out of his own sense of fair-
> ness and economic reasonability, or, conceivably and occasionally, by applying
> general standards for collective agreements laid down in a statute. But in either
> case we sacrifice the right of the parties to agree on the terms of a contract which
> is satisfactory to their particular needs. We replace that with the power of the
> government or one of its legal agents to impose a contract, which ideally, will
> avoid a work stoppage.[33]

ARBITRATION FREEZE

The disincentive to bargain created when the parties know that the dispute will be settled by arbitration is called an "arbitration freeze." It is expected by all parties that the arbitrator will, by and large, select a settlement that is close to the mid-point between the parties' positions. If, for example, the union demands a 5 percent increase and management offers 3 percent, the arbitrator will choose some point close to 4 percent as the wage increase. Now consider the problem of the parties as they enter into negotiations. The union is demanding a 7 percent increase and management is offering 1 percent. If the parties know that the dispute will go to arbitration and they assume that the arbitrator will split the difference, then any attempt to modify a position to get an agreement could result in the settlement being closer to the other party's demand. If there is no movement, the wage increase in the end would be about 4 percent. But, if the union, in an attempt to reach an agreement, reduces its demand to 5 percent and fails to get an agreement and management does not change its 1 percent offer, splitting the difference would result in only a 3 percent wage increase. Thus, neither party has an incentive to modify its position if the dispute is going to arbitration.

---

33 P. Weiler, *Reconcilable Differences* (Toronto: Carswell, 1980), 67.

NO INTERNAL COMPROMISE

In addition, there will be no incentive for the parties to seek compromises within their own groups. If they were to drop a popular position, they could potentially alienate some of their members. Thus, they will be inclined to let the arbitrator weed out the demands for which there is limited support. By doing so, they will avoid the difficult political task of justifying to some of their members why their favourite proposal was dropped. One of the problems for unions is that because the arbitrator is an outsider, he or she will not be able to accurately assess which demands are important and which are not important. The same problem exists on the management side of negotiations.

Modified Interest Arbitration: Final-Offer Selection and Med-Arb

In an attempt to correct for the arbitration freeze phenomenon, a form of arbitration called final-offer selection was created. In final-offer selection, the arbitrator is given the final positions of both parties and selects either the union's or management's offer. There is no opportunity to split the difference. If one opponent's final offer is outrageous but the other's is even more outrageous, then the first opponent will get what it wants. So, there is an incentive for both parties to make their offers more reasonable. If one party does so, so will its opponent. This will go on until both parties have reasonable final offers and they will possibly settle or at least make tough decisions on limiting their positions. In a modified form of final-offer selection, the arbitrator does not choose between two complete packages but between final positions on each item in dispute.

Another modification of the traditional arbitration model is to have the arbitrator attempt to mediate the dispute prior to entering into arbitration. This method is commonly called med-arb. In that way, the arbitrator will glean information through mediation about the true nature of the parties' positions and the internal compromises they are willing to make.

SETTLEMENT STAGES DATA

In the first quarter of 2004 there were 82 collective agreements negotiated in Ontario that involved bargaining units of more than 200 employees. These agreements were settled at the following stages in the process:[34]

Stage of the process	Number of agreements
Direct negotiations (that is, no third-party assistance)	35
Conciliation	12
Post-conciliation negotiations	11
Mediation	15
Interest arbitration	4 (3 public sector, 1 private sector)
Work stoppage	5

---

34 Ontario, Ministry of Labour, Collective Bargaining Information Services (CBIS), *Quarterly Review of Collective Bargaining Developments in Ontario—First Quarter.*

INDUSTRIAL ACTION

In the event that the parties are unable to agree to the terms of a new collective agreement, each side will want to put pressure on the other side to accept its terms. Pressure tactics include strikes and lockouts, and other forms of industrial action.

Strikes

The traditional method unions use to pressure management is to call on all its members in the workplace to collectively stop working. The collective action of workers ceasing to work is called a **strike**. A strike is effective if enough workers cease to report to work so that production is halted or significantly reduced. If there were no legal regulations governing this action, strikes could take place any time that the union and management had a disagreement. Management could then immediately terminate the striking workers and try to replace them. If the strike was effective, management would sign a collective agreement and the strikers would return to work. If management was successful, the union would be either eliminated or significantly reduced in power.

To limit the frequency of strikes and to minimize the conflict involved during strikes, a legal regime was imposed to set up rules to govern this collective action. Section 1(1) of the OLRA defines "strike" in a broad manner, stating that it includes

> a cessation of work, a refusal to work or to continue to work by employees in combination or in concert or in accordance with a common understanding, or a slow-down or other concerted activity on the part of employees designed to restrict or limit output.

The two indicators of a strike are that

- the action is a "concerted one," in other words, an advertently taken group action; and

- it results in a reduction of production and thus some economic loss to the employer.

Any concerted or agreed action that results in a loss of production will be considered a strike. The purpose of the activity does not have to relate to collective bargaining. So, if workers decide to take off a day of work to take part in protests against the government, this is a strike.

Even an action that could legally be taken by an individual may be deemed a strike if done by a group. In the case of *Cambridge (City)*[35] the workers all agreed to refuse to do voluntary overtime. This was ruled a strike because of the union's decision to act as a group and the cost to the employer of lost overtime production. The OLRB applied the same principle when workers in a plant decided to all take a discretionary break at the same time. In the usual circumstances, the breaks were taken by individual workers at different times and there was no impact on production. But when the breaks were all taken together, the plant was forced to shut down for a short period. Thus, there was a group action that limited production. In

---

35 *Cambridge (City)*, [1989] OLRB Rep. Nov. 1095.

another case, the workers all decided to take their lunch period and picket the establishment to hand out leaflets to the public. This action was not deemed a strike because there was no consequent loss of production.[36]

It is not possible for a union to use the collective agreement to contract out of the prohibitions against unlawful strikes. In the *Empress Graphics* case,[37] the union had negotiated a special provision in the collective agreement. The provision provided that the workers could refuse to handle materials coming from any plant where another local of the union was on strike. The workers relied on this clause and refused to handle material coming from a plant where another local of the union was on strike. The OLRB held that this was an illegal strike and the workers were ordered to work with material from the struck plant. This type of collective agreement provision that the workers tried to rely on in *Empress Graphics* is called a **hot-cargo clause** and it is unenforceable in Ontario.

In the case of *Hickeson-Langs Supply Co.*,[38] the collective agreement contained a provision stating that it was not a violation of the agreement for a worker to refuse to cross a legal picket line. The workers refused to cross a picket line set up by the same local of the union but against a different employer. Workers who had a valid collective agreement in force with a different employer refused to cross the picket line and argued that it was not an illegal strike because the collective agreement allowed them to cross. The OLRB said, however, that the Act overrode the agreement, that it was an illegal strike, and that they would have to cross the line and report to work. Note that in both these cases, the employer agreed to the provision and later used the OLRA to overturn its own agreement. Even though the employer has the ability to take such actions, it may choose not to do so because of the negative long-term labour relations they may create with the union at its own workplace.

Lockouts

For the employer, the traditional parallel action to a strike is a **lockout**. In a lockout, the employer refuses to let the workers come in to work. Section 1(1) of the OLRA defines lockout as including

> the closing of a place of employment, a suspension of work or a refusal by an employer to continue to employ a number of employees, with a view to compel or induce the employees, or to aid another employer to compel or induce that employer's employees, to refrain from exercising any rights or privileges under this Act or to agree to provisions or changes in provisions respecting terms or conditions of employment or the rights, privileges or duties of the employer, an employers' organization, the trade union, or the employees.

A lockout is indicated by a refusal to let workers do work, where the purpose of the work refusal is related to collective bargaining. In contrast to a strike, a lockout has to be related to a collective bargaining purpose. The legal definition of a lockout includes a refusal to employ in order to advance collective bargaining

---

36 *Art Gallery of Ontario*, [1989] OLRB Rep. 537.

37 [1989] OLRB Rep. 587.

38 [1991] OLRB Rep. 625.

purposes. A lockout is used to get the union to agree to the employer's proposals. Thus, an employer, in order to protest government action, could legally refuse to allow the workers to come to work.

An employer may lock out the bargaining unit to try to force concessions from the union. The employer may also engage in this activity if the union or the workers are taking part in activities that limit production, such as a work-to-rule campaign. For a lockout to be legal, the contract must not be in force, a no-board report must have been issued, and the cooling-off period must have expired.

Because the union is usually the party driving for improvements to the agreement and the employer would be satisfied with the status quo, the employer is not often interested in locking out the workforce. An employer is likely to order a lockout only if

- it is trying to force concessions from the union; or

- the disruption and uncertainty created by protracted negotiations are harming profitability; or

- the union tactics, such as a work-to-rule, are seriously harming productivity; or

- the employer has such a glut of product that it would be more profitable to shut down production and just sell out of its stockpile.

Legality of Strike/Lockout

For a strike or lockout to be legal, a sequence of activities must have taken place before the strike or lockout.

1. The collective agreement must have expired. No strikes or lockouts are permitted during the term of a collective agreement. While the agreement is in force, the parties are to use the grievance/arbitration process to settle disputes.

2. Conciliation must have taken place and not resulted in a new agreement.

3. The minister of labour must have issued a decision that a conciliation board will not be appointed (a no-board report). Because no conciliation boards are ever appointed, it is issued as a formality after conciliation fails.

4. Fourteen days must have passed after the no-board report was issued. Recall that this cooling-off period was created as a time during which the parties could reconsider their decision to engage in a strike or lockout.

5. In the case of a strike, under s. 79(3) of the Act the union must have conducted a strike vote. If there is a collective agreement, the earliest a strike vote can be taken is 30 days prior to the expiry of the agreement. If there is no agreement, the earliest the vote can be taken is when the conciliation officer is appointed.

6. Under ss. 79(7), 79(8), 79(9), and 79.1 of the Act, more than 50 percent of those voting must have indicated that they are in favour of a strike. The

vote is conducted by the union and is not supervised by the labour board. However, for the vote to be valid, it must be conducted in accordance with the following set of conditions. The vote must be by secret ballot. All the employees in the bargaining unit covered by the tentative agreement must be allowed to vote, even if they have not joined the union. The voters must have an opportunity to vote. The time and place of the vote must be reasonably convenient. The ballot used in the vote must only give the options of authorizing the calling of a strike or not authorizing the calling of a strike. Mail-in ballots are permitted.

In the event that the union engages in a strike without completing the prerequisite conditions, the strike is referred to as a "wildcat strike." Such action is illegal and potentially the subject of sanctions.

Other Forms of Industrial Action

There are actions other than a traditional strike that a union may take to advance its demands in bargaining. They include working to rule, organizing a boycott of both the employer's products and the workplace, and occupying the workplace to stop production.

WORK-TO-RULE

The definition of a strike in Ontario is any group action by the workers to limit production. This includes stopping work and leaving the plant or remaining at the work site and refusing to work. It includes any group activities to slow down production, such as a work-to-rule. In a work-to-rule, the workers agree to follow the work rules to the letter in order to reduce their production output. Thus, they will not volunteer for extra duties or they may ask for direction from supervisors in every circumstance where they do not have specific instructions at work and take no initiative.

BOYCOTT

If the union cannot effectively shut down production, it may turn to the public and ask that the public not buy any products from the struck employer. The union will advertise this through union media such as newsletters, bulletins, and e-mails. It may also extend the request to the public by way of advertisements and leaflet campaigns at the sites where the customers buy the product. Leafleting at these sites in support of a boycott has been held by the Supreme Court of Canada to be an exercise of free speech protected by the *Charter of Rights and Freedoms* as long as the leafleting is peaceful and does not block entrances.[39]

SIT-DOWN STRIKE

In some cases, the employees do not leave the plant; instead, they stay at their work stations and refuse both to work and to leave. This technique has been used to

---

39 *UFCW, Local 1518 v. KMart Canada Ltd.*, [1999] 2 SCR 1083.

prevent replacement workers from entering the workplace and continuing production. Once the workers cease to respond to direction and stop working, management will ask them to leave. If they refuse to leave, the workers become trespassers subject to ejection and legal action.

NOTICE TO JOB APPLICANTS

Unions have been known to publish information to prospective job applicants urging them not to apply for a job with a particular employer until that employer has settled contract issues with its existing employees. Because this does not involve the withdrawal of services by existing employees, this has been held not to be a strike.[40]

Duration of a Strike

The conventional wisdom is that unions win short strikes and lose long strikes. Unions suffer during long strikes because it is difficult to make up the wage losses that result from a long strike. In addition, there are legal and practical difficulties that a union faces in the event of a long strike. As a strike goes on, the strikers will be receiving only strike pay and will likely have to take on other work to pay the bills. They are not eligible for employment insurance, either. Some will take other jobs and the picket lines will often shrink. As time goes on, the employer may decide that this is an opportunity to eliminate the union.

Section 1(2) of the OLRA provides that an employee does not lose employment status as the result of simply going on a strike or being locked out. This provision does not protect an employee who, while on strike, engages in conduct against the employer that would justify dismissal, such as destruction of the employer's property or violence on the picket line.[41] Also, under ss. 72 and 76 of the Act, it would be interference with a right to strike if an employer was to discipline a worker for engaging in a lawful strike.

These provisions in the OLRA protect the workers' employment status but they do not get the workers back to work. They are able to return to work if they reach a collective agreement because a return-to-work protocol, including a schedule of return dates, is usually part of the negotiated settlement. Section 80 of the Act states that if no collective agreement is reached, workers on a lawful strike have a right to go back to work and be reinstated to their former job if they make an unconditional application within six months of going on strike. In other words, they earn this right if they surrender within six months of starting the strike. If a worker does apply to return to work, the employer is obligated to give the worker his or her job back as long as the work is still being done. In such a case, the employer is obligated to terminate replacement workers if necessary. If the workers stay out on strike past six months, they will have to get an agreement in order to guarantee a return to work. This legal provision makes the six-month anniversary date of the start of the strike a crucial one during the course of a strike. If the employees continue on strike past six months, they will have a right to return to work

---

40 *Niagara Catholic District School Board*, [1998] OLRB Rep. 995.

41 *Pre Fab Cushioning Products Ltd.*, [1986] OLRB Rep. 273.

only if a collective agreement is negotiated. Fear of losing this right may cause strikers to return to work prior to the expiry of this deadline and the strike may collapse.

Professional Strike Breakers

Section 78 of the OLRA specifically makes it an unfair labour practice for an employer to engage in strike-related misconduct. Strike-related misconduct is conduct intended to interfere with, obstruct, restrain, or disrupt a union's lawful right to strike. Specifically, the OLRA prohibits incitement, intimidation, coercion, undue influence, provocation, infiltration, or surveillance or any similar conduct if this conduct has the improper purpose of damaging the union's lawful right to strike. An employer can conduct surveillance of a union picket line in order to prevent destruction to its property or to prevent injury to people entering the struck workplace, but it must not conduct surveillance of the union's strike headquarters to learn about the union's plans. This prohibition operates both before and during the strike.

It is also an unfair labour practice for an employer to hire a company or individuals to act as strike breakers or for a person or company to offer services as a professional strike breaker. Specifically, the OLRA prohibits employing any person not involved in the dispute for the primary purpose of interfering with, obstructing, preventing, restraining, or disrupting the union's lawful right to strike. This prohibition applies both before and during a strike. It was added to the OLRA after lobbying by the union movement. The union movement was upset by a situation where employers hired private security companies that in addition to providing the customary security for a strike also provided undercover agents for the employer. These agents would pose as regular workers and would be hired by the employer into the bargaining unit. Further, they would provoke violence on the picket line and disrupt the union meetings. The employers' motivation was to prolong the strike until the union collapsed. In the *Securicor* case, the OLRB ordered that the security company pay the union damages for the expenses related to the increased length of the strike, such as increased strike pay.[42]

The OLRA makes it a parallel unfair labour practice for a union to engage in strike-related misconduct. Strike-related misconduct is conduct intended to interfere with, obstruct, restrain, or disrupt an employer's lawful right to lockout. Specifically, the Act prohibits incitement, intimidation, coercion, undue influence, provocation, infiltration, or surveillance or nay like conduct if this conduct has the improper purpose of damaging the employer's lawful right to lockout. This prohibition operates both before and during the lockout. The union is also prohibited from hiring a professional strike breaker to interfere with the employer's right to lockout.

Replacement Workers

An employer in Ontario is entitled to continue to operate its business during a strike. It is entitled to do so with the employees who are not part of the bargaining unit, including managers and confidentials. The employer is also permitted to either use bargaining unit members who do not support the strike but still show

---

42 *Securicor Investigation and Security Ltd.*, [1983] OLRB Rep. 720.

up for work or hire new workers to replace the striking employees. These latter replacement workers are called "scabs" in the union movement. In the event that the employer hires replacement workers, the union is likely to increase the size of its picket lines to convince these workers not to cross. It is in those circumstances that picket line violence is prevalent.

The union's bargaining power is enhanced if it is difficult for the employer to hire replacement workers. The employer may have trouble finding replacement workers when the striking workers possess special skills that cannot easily be found in the unemployed and when training for replacement is not practical. In other cases, there may simply be too many workers for the employer to replace in a large workplace.

Remedy for an Illegal Strike or Lockout

There are a number of possible remedies that an employer can take in the event of an unlawful strike. Before an employer undertakes a legal option against its own employees or union, it should contact the union and request that the union get its members back to work. The union is under an obligation both from the collective agreement and the OLRA not to be involved in an illegal strike. The union risks being subject to claims for damages if it does not act to get its members back to work.

It is an unfair labour practice for a union to call or authorize an illegal strike. It is also an unlawful labour practice for a union to threaten an illegal strike. Union officials are specifically prohibited from ordering workers to go on an illegal strike, working to bring about an unlawful strike, or supporting or encouraging an unlawful strike. If management believes that any of these prohibited practices have been employed, it may seek a remedy by

- applying for a declaration of unlawful strike,

- filing a grievance for breach of the collective agreement,

- filing a complaint under s. 103 of the OLRA if no collective agreement is in place,

- filing a damages claim alleging unfair labour practice under s. 96 of the Act,

- disciplining the workers on illegal strike, or

- applying for consent to prosecute for a breach of the OLRA.

Each of these remedies is discussed below.

Declaration. Section 100 of the OLRA gives the labour board the power to declare that an unlawful strike has taken place or that the union is threatening an unlawful strike. In either case, the board will direct the trade union to stop the illegal strike or to stop threatening an illegal strike.

Grievance. Every collective agreement must contain a clause stating that it is a breach of the agreement to conduct a strike or lockout while the agreement is in force. An employer faced with an illegal strike could file a grievance and claim damages for the lost production time. The problems with this option are that the grievance process tends to be slow and if the employer wants to be awarded damages, it will have to show that the lost production time led to lost profit. Further, even if the employer shows that it is losing considerable sums of money, the union will use these data in the next round of negotiations to justify a significant wage increase.

Damage claim if no collective agreement in place. The OLRA sets up an arbitration process that is similar to the one found in many collective agreements. The process covers the situations where the board declares that an unlawful strike has taken place and where there is no collective agreement in operation. The employer would use this arbitration route to claim damages caused by the illegal strike.

Damages claim under s. 96 of the Act. Section 96 of the OLRA gives the labour board the power, in the event that it determines that an unlawful strike has occurred, to determine

> what, if anything, the ... trade union, council of trade unions, person or employee shall do or refrain from doing with respect thereto ... and ... may include ... (a) on order directing the ... trade union council of trade unions, employee or other person to cease doing the act or acts complained of; (b) an order directing the ... trade union, council of trade unions, employee or other person to rectify the act or acts complained of.

This may include an order to stop the illegal strike and pay the employer for the damages associated with the illegal strike. The employer faces the problem that if it wants damages, it has to reveal its financial position, which may be used to its disadvantage in subsequent bargaining.

Disciplining of workers. It is improper for a worker to fail to show up for work without a valid excuse, and being on an illegal strike is not a valid excuse. The employer is justified in imposing discipline in these circumstances. The problem with this remedy is that the workers are already off work without pay, so imposing a suspension may not get them back in the plant. And imposing discipline may prolong the wildcat strike because the workers will not return until the discipline is removed.

Application for consent to prosecute. Taking part in an illegal strike is a breach of the OLRA. In the event of a breach of the Act, a fine of $2,000 per day can be imposed on an individual and $25,000 per day can be imposed on a trade union. The problem with this remedy is that the employer has to ask the OLRB for consent to take the matter to a provincial offences court for prosecution, and the board almost never gives permission. In addition, the fine goes to the government, not to the employer. The action of getting the union fined would be certain to worsen the relationship between the parties. This is why the OLRB seldom believes that granting a consent to prosecute is in the interests of improving collective bargaining.

Usually, if an illegal strike is in progress, the primary interest of management is getting production back in operation as soon as possible. There are a number of remedies open to management in the face of an illegal strike, as discussed above, but the most effective in getting production started again is the application to the labour board for a declaration that the strike is illegal.

If the workers are conducting an illegal strike because of the actions of another person, then the labour board has the power to order a stop to the actions that are causing the illegal strike. For example, the entrance to the work site may be shared by several employers. The employees of one of the employers may engage in an illegal strike and set up peaceful picket lines at the shared entrance. The employees of one of the other employers may refuse to cross the picket line. The employer of the striking workers, however, may be content to let the illegal job action go on: the employer may be willing to supply customers out of stockpiles or simply unwilling to enter into conflict with the union. Section 83 of the Act states that no person shall "do any act if the person knows or ought to know that, as a probable and reasonable consequence of the act, another person or persons will engage in an unlawful strike." The injured employer could take action under that section to have the illegal picket lines removed." Note that this section of the OLRA cannot be used to limit picket lines set up as part of a legal strike for situations where picketing as part of a legal strike may be limited. See the sections on picketing and injunctions below.

During 2001-2 the OLRB dealt with 28 applications alleging an illegal strike. Of these applications, 6 were granted ordering an end to the activity, 1 was dismissed, and 3 were still pending. In the remaining 18 cases, settlements were obtained primarily through labour relations officers persuading workers to return to work if they had a valid collective agreement in force.[43]

During 2001-2 the OLRB dealt with two applications alleging an unlawful lockout. One application was granted ordering an end to the action and the other was pending.[44]

Picketing

The union will want to enhance its bargaining power by conducting a strike that effectively shuts down the employer's productive capability. The union will want all the workers to refuse to work and no replacement workers to take on the struck work. The usual tool for effecting this purpose is the picket line. The purpose of picketing and the conflict related to picket lines are described by a leading union activist writing about the 1996 Ontario public service strike:

> The union's ability to control entry and exit at work sites was a main battle-ground. OPSEU [the Ontario Public Service Employees Union] used any means to picket and control every entrance to every workplace in order to disrupt the regular business of the government. Meanwhile, the government's strategy was to pretend that everything was normal. This meant minimizing the number and effectiveness of our picket lines. The government tried to extend the essential services agreements to as many places as possible, especially in the jails, the highways, and abattoirs. It applied for more than eighty injunctions to contain or ban picket lines, and it filed more than thirty "illegal strike" applications against OPSEU at the Labour Board. Meanwhile, it encouraged and publicized strike-breaking in order to demoralize the picket lines. At first, it refused to negotiate picket line protocols, because that would have been a recognition of the legiti-

---

43 OLRB 2001-2 Annual Report, at 11.

44 Ibid.

macy of the picket lines. It tried to keep open the Queen's Park tunnel so that managers and strikebreakers could bypass the picket lines on their way to work, and it called the police every time the union pushed the envelope just a little bit farther. And while the government bargained in public, it distorted negotiating issues, trying to make the union leadership look unreasonable. The entire strategy was aimed at wearing down the determination of picketers.[45]

PURPOSE AND LIMITS OF PICKETING

When workers go on strike, they intend to inflict some economic harm on their employer to force the employer to revise its bargaining position until it is acceptable to the union. To do this, the workers withdraw their services. By itself, this may not be sufficient to cause the employer to change its offer, so the union will almost always set up a picket. A picket line will usually consist of a group of striking workers walking across the entrances to a work site and carrying signs to indicate that the union is on strike. The signs may also carry a short statement describing the nature of the labour dispute. Customers, suppliers, and especially workers attempting to enter the workplace are stopped and asked to support the strike and to not cross the picket lines. The workers on the picket line are not permitted to blockade the entrance. Nor, generally, are they entitled to be on private property. Hence, the usual site of a picket line will be on the sidewalks outside the entrance to the property.

The legal system in Canada recognizes picketing as a constitutionally protected freedom of expression. The courts recognize that the purpose of a picket line is not only to convey information to gain support for the strike, but also to put pressure on the employer. To increase pressure, the union may engage in mass pickets involving large numbers of picketers at the entrance to the workplace. The role of picketing in the legal system has been described as follows:

> When a union is on legal strike, Canadian collective bargaining law does not require the employer to stop production. Strikers have to force such a stoppage. One measure commonly used is the setting up of picket lines. These are walking billboards, advising would be workers and the general public that a legal strike is being conducted and that the strikers are seeking support for it.
>
> Picketing has two features: it supports immediate economic demands and it is also an educational exercise which seeks to broaden support for working class aims and aspirations. In large part, then, it is an exercise in free speech and freedom of association. At the same time, however, picketing often acts as a physical barrier to entry into the struck employer's operations.[46]

THE HISTORICAL DISTINCTION BETWEEN TYPES OF PICKETING

Until recently, the Canadian legal system made a distinction between different types of picketing based on the relationship of the picketers to the owner of the site being picketed. Traditionally, picketing was described as being one of three types:

---

45 D. Rapaport, *No Justice No Peace: The 1996 OPSEU Strike Against the Harris Government in Ontario* (Montreal and Kingston, ON: McGill-Queen's University Press, 1999), 119-20.

46 D. Drache and H. Glasbeek, "The Right To Strike: A Velvet Fist in an Iron Glove," in D. Drache, ed., *The Changing Workplace* (Toronto: Lorimer, 1992), 107-8.

- primary,

- allied, or

- secondary.

Primary picketing. When striking workers set up picket lines outside property owned, leased, or used by their employer, this was defined as primary picketing and would be generally permitted. It would be limited or prohibited only in circumstances where wrongful conduct occurred on the picket line.

Allied picketing. If the union could demonstrate that a third party had taken actions to directly assist the struck employer, this would be characterized as allied picketing. Allied picketing would be allowed as long as otherwise wrongful conduct did not occur.

Secondary picketing. The picketing of any third party—for example, suppliers or customers of the struck employer—was described as secondary picketing. This type of picketing was historically prohibited on the basis that the third parties who were being picketed could do nothing to resolve the dispute. Therefore, it was argued, they should be protected from any harm associated with picket lines.[47]

THE NEW APPROACH: PICKETING AS PROTECTED FREEDOM OF EXPRESSION

Under traditional rules, if a union wanted to picket at a supplier or customer of the employer, it would have to show that the customer or supplier had taken actions to make it an ally of the struck employer. The characterization of the picketing was crucial to the union's ability to picket at a location.

The Supreme Court of Canada recently abolished this requirement to characterize picketing. The court determined that picketing in a labour dispute was a protected freedom of expression under the *Charter of Rights and Freedoms* and could be limited only if it could be demonstrated that such a limit would be justifiable in a free and democratic society. The court ruled that a blanket prohibition against secondary picketing would violate this freedom under the Charter and could not be justified. Preventing the economic loss caused to third parties by secondary picketing, it concluded, would not be sufficient justification.

All picketing, then, is permitted unless it can be shown to be wrongful. The wrong caused by a picket line could be a civil wrong, called a tort, such as trespassing, nuisance, inducing breach of contract, or defamation. Or the wrong involved could be criminal, such as unlawful assembly or assault.

The Supreme Court made this change to the law in the *Pepsi-Cola* case. This case arose out of a strike at a Pepsi-Cola bottling plant. The picket lines set up at the struck plant were not sufficient to prevent production and distribution of the product. The employer hired replacement workers and continued production. The strikers then set up picket lines at the retail outlets to persuade store staff not to accept delivery of product from the struck plant. Strikers also picketed outside the hotels where the employer was housing the replacement workers. They also picketed outside the homes of management, where they chanted and yelled threats and

---

47 *Hersees of Woodstock Ltd. v. Goldstein* (1963), 38 DLR (2d) 449 (Ont. CA).

insults at the managers. Only the picketing and associated activities outside the homes of the management were stopped by order of the Supreme Court and that was because these activities amounted to nuisance and intimidation. Note that under the old rules, picketing at the hotel and retail stores would have been characterized as secondary picketing and stopped as well.[48]

The OLRB has the power to control picketing if the picket lines result in an unlawful strike. The board may limit picket lines at a work site to common entrances used by all the workers. It may order that specific entrances to the employer's premises that are not normally used by the striking workers not be subject to picket lines.[49]

Injunctions

An **injunction** is a court order to stop an activity entirely or to change the manner in which the activity is being conducted. The applicant for an injunction must show that the activity that he or she is complaining about is wrongful in some fashion. The injunction has been used by employers to control the actions of unionized workers and it is used particularly to limit picket lines.

There are two main types of injunctions: the interim injunction and the permanent or mandatory injunction. An interim injunction orders activities to stop pending a full investigation of the allegations made by the applicant. An interim injunction cannot last more than four days. A permanent injunction or mandatory order is issued after a full investigation. It is issued in cases where the court decides that the applicant has shown that the activity complained about should be stopped. The permanent injunction replaces an interim injunction. In order to get an interim injunction, the applicant must show the following:

1. There is a serious question to be tried.

2. The applicant will suffer irreparable harm if the immediate relief is not granted.

3. The balance of convenience favours the applicant—that is, the applicant will suffer greater harm if the injunction is not granted.

The Ontario Superior Court of Justice has the power to grant an injunction. To get an injunction, the applicant has to show that it made reasonable efforts to get the police to stop the activity it is complaining about and that the police were unable to control the activity. The applicant has to show that there are activities taking place that cause danger of damage to property; or danger of injury to people; or violence; and/or obstruction of lawful entry or exit from the property.

The employer or other applicant gets an injunction by making a motion to the Superior Court of Justice requesting an injunction. Under s. 102(8)(b) of the *Courts of Justice Act*, the applicant must give two days notice to the union that it has made such a motion, unless it can be shown that the two-day delay would result in

---

48 *RWDSU, Local 558 v. Pepsi-Cola Canada Beverages (West) Ltd.*, [2002] 1 SCR 156. Also note B. Adell, "Secondary Picketing After Pepsi-Cola: What's Clear, and What Isn't" (2003), vol. 10, no. 1 *Canadian Labour and Employment Law Journal* 135.

49 *Sarnia Construction Association*, [1982] OLRB Rep. June 922.

"irreparable damage or injury, a breach of the peace or an interruption in an essential public service."[50] The applicant then gives reasonable notice to the union by phone, fax, or other means. At the court hearing, the applicant has witnesses describe the events on the picket line, the attempts to get the problems stopped, the danger of imminent harm, and the means used to give the union reasonable notice of the motion. The applicant may also have videos or photos of the activities.

In the case of a motion with notice, the employer's lawyer prepares a factum in support of the motion. A factum is a document that outlines the facts and law that the employer is relying on in support of the injunction. The employer has a person who observed the illegal activity swear an affidavit outlining what he or she observed in support of the application.

An injunction is used in various situations. An employer could apply for an injunction to stop an illegal strike by its own employees. An injunction may also be used to limit the activities of picketers during a legal strike in cases where the picketers' activities extend beyond the peaceful and orderly distribution of information and there is violence or some other prohibited conduct on the picket line. An employer might also apply for an injunction to stop picketing by employees of another employer if the picket lines related to that job action cause the employer's own employees not to show up for work. In the event that picket lines cannot be controlled by the police and there is violence or destruction of property or blockading of entrances and exits, an employer or other party affected by the picket line can apply to the courts to have the union's right to picket limited.[51] The court has the power to order a union to stop picketing, or to limit pickets to a particular number, or to order the union to picket a certain distance from the work entrances. An example of another affected party would be an employer whose employees enter the workplace at the same location where the pickets are operating.

The use of the injunction can be demonstrated by an analysis of the cases of *Ogden Entertainment*,[52] *Ledcor Industries*,[53] and *Industrial Hardwood*.[54] These were all cases where the applicants were seeking to limit pickets that had been set up in support of a legal strike.

The striking workers in the *Ogden Entertainment* case were the cleaning staff in the Corel Centre in Ottawa. The Corel Centre is the arena where the Ottawa Senators of the NHL play. The striking workers were setting up large picket lines, or **mass pickets**, on the nights of hockey games when over 17,000 hockey fans, including people in more than 7,000 automobiles, arrived to see the game. Traffic jams resulted, causing traffic to back out onto the highway. Buses could not get into the parking lot. Motorists were parking on the side of the road. The fans entering the arena became irate and there were incidents between the fans and the picketing workers, which the judge described as road rage. He described the actions of the picketers as a nuisance because the only thing being accomplished by the picketers

---

50 RSO 1990, c. C.43.

51 *Courts of Justice Act*, ss. 101 and 102 and Ontario Rules of Practice, rule 40.

52 *Ogden Entertainment Services v. USWA, Local 440* (1998), 159 DLR (4th) 340; [1998] OJ no. 1769 (Gen. Div.), rev'd. in part (1998), 38 OR (3d) 448; [1998] OJ no. 1824 (CA).

53 *Ledcor Industries v. Sheet Metal Workers' Association*, 2004 ONSC 10148.

54 *Industrial Hardwood Products (1996) Ltd. v. International Wood and Allied Workers of Canada, Local 2693*, [2000] OJ no. 536 (Sup. Ct. J), var'd. (2001), 52 OR (3d) 694; [2001] OJ no. 28 (CA).

was the obstruction of vehicles. The judge also determined that efforts were made to obtain police assistance and that the police were unsuccessful. He also indicated that special rules may need to apply when large numbers of members of the entertainment-seeking public are inconvenienced. The judge granted an injunction ordering the picketers not to stop traffic entering the arena. This injunction significantly reduced the bargaining power of the union because they could no longer undermine the employer's largest revenue-generating activity.

The *Ledcor* case involved a picket line set up around a workplace that was undergoing substantial renovations and was essentially a construction site. The pickets blocked access to the site to construction workers who were not involved in the labour dispute. The judge decided that the decision of the Supreme Court in *Pepsi-Cola* would not support an outright ban on picketing in this situation. But to let the construction workers on the site, he did limit both the number and actions of the picketers in the following manner:

> Given the state of the law as I see it, on an interim interim basis I order as follows:
>
> 1. The Defendants or their servants or agents are restrained from obstructing or blocking places of entrances to or egress from the Applicant's business premises.
>
> 2. The Defendants or their servants or agents are restrained from threatening, harassing or intimidating or attempting to harass or intimidate any of the employees of the Applicant or any persons seeking to do business with the Applicant and/or any persons seeking to enter or leave the premises.
>
> 3. The Defendants or their servants or agents are restrained from informing employees and members of the public seeking entrance to or egress from the Applicant's business premises that an information line is in progress and that the line should be respected.
>
> 4. The Defendants or their servants or agents shall be restrained from blocking and/or impeding the vehicles having business with the Applicant or otherwise interfering in any manner whatsoever with the employees of the Applicant.
>
> 5. The Defendants or their servants or agents are permitted to offer the "Information Line Material" (exhibit No. 3) to all individuals seeking to access the Applicant's place of business, without comment on the contents of the document.
>
> 6. The Defendants or their servants or agents are restricted to having a maximum of 20 persons engaged in handing out "Information Line Material" at any one time while attending at the Applicant's business premises, and these individuals may wear or carry placards identifying themselves as representatives of the Defendants.
>
> 7. The Court Services Manager for the City of Ottawa shall be charged to ensure compliance with this order.

In the *Industrial Hardwood* case, the picketers were hindering the entrance of vans carrying replacement workers. They would delay the vans up to an hour and verbally abuse the replacement workers, shining flashlights in the window, damaging the vans, bouncing the vans, and pulling open the van doors. The police in this case stated that they had inadequate resources to deal with the picket lines. The judge concluded that the preconditions for an injunction were satisfied and made an order limiting the number of picketers to four at a time. He stated that no vehicle could be stopped, except for the purposes of presenting information and for no longer than five minutes, and ordered that the workers not attempt to induce a breach of contract by employees, customers or suppliers.

As these cases have shown, if the employer can obtain an injunction, it may successfully weaken the union's bargaining power.

Lost Days Statistics

One measure of the success of the labour relations system in the area of negotiations is whether the instances of strikes and lockouts are few. Recent data on lost days due to strike in Ontario are shown in table 4.1.

TABLE 4.1   Work Stoppages Under Ontario Jurisdiction, 1984 to June 2004

Year	Number of work stoppages	Number of employees involved	Number of employees per work stoppage	Number of person-days lost	Number of person-days lost per employee involved	Average duration of work stoppages (days out)	Person-days lost as % of estimated working time
1984	209	79,586	381	1,414,340	17.8	39	0.15
1985	302	72,723	241	1,232,170	16.9	31	0.12
1986	232	62,751	270	940,620	15.0	30	0.09
1987	246	64,339	262	1,108,870	17.2	27	0.10
1988	180	62,082	345	1,362,150	21.9	35	0.12
1989	190	45,679	240	868,630	19.0	35	0.08
1990	218	81,022	372	2,957,640	36.5	43	0.26
1991	153	25,448	166	453,520	17.8	43	0.04
1992	121	38,160	315	577,710	15.1	39	0.05
1993	81	15,620	193	371,150	23.8	42	0.03
1994	130	25,456	196	488,320	19.2	34	0.05
1995	136	57,318	421	476,960	8.3	39	0.04
1996	135	216,917	1,607	1,914,900	8.8	39	0.16
1997	113	176,029	1,558	1,904,210	10.8	50	0.16
1998	156	69,411	445	1,060,990	15.3	38	0.09
1999	143	44,980	315	651,100	14.5	39	0.05
2000	146	55,267	379	649,730	11.8	39	0.05
2001	144	34,652	241	671,990	19.4	35	0.05
2002	117	66,572	569	1,510,580	22.7	40	0.11
2003	94	23,807	253	494,880	20.8	38	0.04
2004 (Jan-Jun)*	56	13,515	241	254,940	18.9	27	0.04

* Preliminary

Source: Ontario, Ministry of Labour, Collective Bargaining Information Services (CBIS), Collective Bargaining Highlights—June 2004, table 8, http://www.gov.on.ca/LAB/english/lr/highlights/cbh2004-06_t8.html.

CHAPTER SUMMARY

Bargaining theories describe the process of negotiations and give guidelines for enhancing the likelihood of both negotiating success and the fostering of a healthy long-term relationship. One of the particular characteristics of labour negotiations is that they are part of a long-term interaction between labour and management and not a one-time-only agreement.

A typical bargaining process consists of many steps, including the selection of bargaining teams, the proposing of demands, advocating for the demands, communicating the progress of negotiations, and dealing with conflicts, including work stoppages. The employer, the union, and third parties all participate in the process.

The rules respecting the conduct of negotiations are intended to encourage the settlement of disputes without resort to industrial actions. Thus the law requires the parties to enter into good-faith negotiations with a mutual commitment to obtaining a settlement. The requirement of third-party assistance is also designed for this purpose.

The rules on industrial conflict are designed to minimize the impact on society of the parties' actions while still preserving the rights of the parties to exercise coercive techniques to force the opposing party to move closer to their position.

REVIEW QUESTIONS

1. Select a labour negotiation that is being reported on in the news media.

    a. Describe the actions that the parties take to enhance their bargaining power.

    b. Use the negotiations to illustrate the four subsystems of negotiations set out in Walton and McKersie's behavioural model of negotiations.

2. Use the Ministry of Labour's website to find the most recent monthly summary of labour settlements and answer the following questions:

    a. What is the CPI for the past quarter?

    b. What was the wage increase for that month?

    c. What were the major settlements during this period?

    d. What major negotiations are under way?

3. Distinguish between mediation and interest arbitration.

4. What is bad-faith bargaining? Give examples of conduct that could lead to a labour board finding that a union or employer engaged in bad-faith bargaining.

5. Describe how a mediator or conciliator acts to assist the parties in reaching an agreement.

6. What legal requirements must be met before a union can engage in a strike?

7. What options can an employer use to get workers on an illegal strike back to work? What is the preferable option?

8. How does an employer go about getting an injunction and what must the employer prove to get an injunction?

9. What must a union demonstrate to get the labour board to order a first-contract arbitration?

10. Describe three different types of picketing. Is there any legal significance to these distinctions?

11. What steps must be taken to engage in interest-based bargaining?

12. List and describe the alternatives to a strike that a union can use to force an employer to agree to the union's position in bargaining.

13. Contrast replacement workers and professional strike breakers. Why is one legal and the other illegal in Ontario?

14. Describe what is meant by a contract zone and a BATNA (best alternative to a negotiated agreement).

DISCUSSION QUESTIONS

1. "The right to strike should be abolished in all cases and replaced with interest arbitration." Discuss the pros and cons of such a proposal.

2. "The use of replacement workers is the cause of much of the violence and problems on picket lines and the use of these workers should be banned." Do you agree or disagree? State your position.

3. "Secondary picketing is not free speech—it is an unwarranted interference with the property rights of people who are not involved in the labour dispute and should be banned." Do you agree or disagree? Support your argument.

4. Do the rules with respect to negotiations, work stoppages, and picketing hit the right balance between the rights of workers and the rights of employees? Discuss.

5. Are the rules with respect to negotiations, work stoppages, and picketing consistent with the following purposes stated in s. 2 of the Ontario *Labour Relations Act, 1995*?

    1. To facilitate collective bargaining between employers and trade unions that are the freely-designated representatives of the employees.

    2. To recognize the importance of workplace parties adapting to change.

    3. To promote flexibility, productivity and employee involvement in the workplace.

    4. To encourage communication between employers and employees in the workplace.

    5. To recognize the importance of economic growth as the foundation for mutually beneficial relations amongst employers, employees and trade unions.

    6. To encourage co-operative participation of employers and trade unions in resolving workplace issues.

    7. To promote the expeditious resolution of workplace disputes.

CHAPTER 5

Administering a Collective Agreement

INTRODUCTION

In this chapter we will examine the process of administering a collective agreement. Once the collective agreement has been negotiated, much of its administration has to do with resolving disputes through the grievance process between the union and members of the bargaining unit on the one hand, and the employer on the other. The most common subjects of "rights" grievances will be discussed in some detail in this chapter. After examining the grievance process in the workplace, we will look at the arbitration process and its variations as the principal means of ultimately deciding grievances.

STRUCTURE AND PROVISIONS OF A COLLECTIVE AGREEMENT

Collective agreements are enforceable contracts. Their terms are largely a matter for the parties to work out based on issues and concerns in a particular workplace. But most collective agreements are similar in the issues they cover and in their structure. This is due to conventions and practices in the labour relations field that have developed over time. All agreements try to cover all workplace issues. Negotiators look at agreements in their own industry, and they look at the language and approach used in other agreements that have attempted to resolve similar workplace issues. In addition, some of the provisions of an agreement are prescribed by labour legislation and must be included in all agreements.

Legal Effect of a Collective Agreement

As noted, a collective agreement is a contract between the employer and a union. There are certain things that follow from this statement.

First, like all contracts, a collective agreement creates rights and obligations for both parties in the workplace. And because there are rights and obligations, there must also be remedies for breaches so that rights and obligations are legally enforceable.

Second, the parties to a contract are the only ones who can legally enforce it. The parties to a collective agreement are the employer and the union. Although many members of the bargaining unit do not realize it, they do not have individual rights to enforce the agreement when an alleged breach affects them. Though the contract gives a member a right to grieve when the member thinks his or her rights under the contract have been violated, it is up to the union to decide whether or not to proceed with the grievance. We will come back to this point when we discuss grievances.

Mandatory Requirements

As noted, most labour relations legislation in all jurisdictions in Canada require that certain provisions are to be included in every collective agreement. They set a floor below which the parties cannot bargain. The mandatory requirements for a collective agreement are as follows:

- There must be a provision that prohibits strikes and lockouts during the life of the agreement. This is designed to ensure employment stability while the agreement is in operation. The alternative is the use of strikes and lockouts to settle contract disputes during the life of the agreement. This is common in some parts of the world, but not in North America. When a bargaining unit resorts to a strike or walkout during the life of an agreement as a way of resolving a contract dispute, the strike, called a wildcat strike, is illegal (see chapter 4). The strike can be the subject of orders from the labour relations board that may result in fines for workers and union leaders.

- There must be a provision that provides access to binding and final arbitration of disputes arising under the agreement. Because strikes and lockouts cannot be used to settle contract disputes during the life of the agreement, this provision provides a necessary dispute-settling mechanism.

- There must be a provision that ensures that the agreement is in force for at least one year. This is to create some stability in the workplace.

- There must be a provision that recognizes the union as the exclusive bargaining agent for the employees in the bargaining unit. This means that all employees are bound by the agreement, and the employer cannot make individual deals on the side with workers, unless these side agreements are expressly permitted in the collective agreement.

- Six jurisdictions require a **mandatory dues check-off** if the union asks for it.

UP CLOSE

An Example of Legislated Mandatory Requirements for a Collective Agreement in Ontario

From the Ontario *Labour Relations Act, 1995*, SO 1995, c. 1, sched. A.

45(1) Every collective agreement shall be deemed to provide that the trade union that is a party thereto is recognized as the exclusive bargaining agent of the employees in the bargaining unit defined therein.

Recognition of accredited employers' organization

(2) Every collective agreement to which an accredited employers' organization is a party shall be deemed to provide that the accredited employers' organization is recognized as the exclusive bargaining agent of the employers in the unit of employers for whom the employers' organization has been accredited.

Provision against strikes and lock-outs

46. Every collective agreement shall be deemed to provide that there will be no strikes or lock-outs so long as the agreement continues to operate.

Deduction and remittance of union dues

47(1) Except in the construction industry and subject to section 52, where a trade union that is the bargaining agent for employees in a bargaining unit so requests, there shall be included in the collective agreement between the trade union and the employer of the employees a provision requiring the employer to deduct from the wages of each employee in the unit affected by the collective agreement, whether or not the employee is a member of the union, the amount of the regular union dues and to remit the amount to the trade union, forthwith. ...

Arbitration

48(1) Every collective agreement shall provide for the final and binding settlement by arbitration, without stoppage of work, of all differences between the parties arising from the interpretation, application, administration or alleged violation of the agreement, including any question as to whether a matter is arbitrable.

Same

(2) If a collective agreement does not contain a provision that is mentioned in subsection (1), it shall be deemed to contain a provision to the following effect:

Where a difference arises between the parties relating to the interpretation, application or administration of this agreement, including any question as to whether a matter is arbitrable, or where an allegation is made that this agreement has been violated, either of the parties may after exhausting any grievance procedure established by this agreement, notify the other party in writing of its desire to submit the difference or allegation to arbitration and the notice shall contain the name of the first party's appointee to an arbitration board. The recipient of the notice shall within five days inform the other party of the name of its appointee to the arbitration board. The two appointees so selected shall, within five days of the appointment of the second of them, appoint a third person who shall be the chair. If the recipient of the notice fails to appoint an arbitrator, or if the two appointees fail to agree upon a chair within the time limited, the appointment shall be made by the Minister of Labour for Ontario upon the request of either party. The arbitration board shall hear and determine the difference or allegation and shall issue a decision and the decision is final and binding upon the parties and upon any employee or employer affected by it. The decision of a majority is the decision of the arbitration board, but if there is no majority the decision of the chair governs.

Structure and Provisions of a Typical Collective Agreement

Set out below is a description of the provisions typically included in a collective agreement.

RECOGNITION AND DEFINITION OF BARGAINING UNIT

This provision, which is mandatory, identifies the union as the exclusive bargaining agent for the members of the bargaining unit. It then goes on to define who is in the bargaining unit.

Example

The union is recognized as the exclusive collective bargaining agency for all employees of the company except for those listed below:

a. foreman and all employees above the rank of foreman

b. all employees who work less than 10 hours per week

c. all employees who are members of the bargaining unit represented by the Consolidated Canadian Union.[1]

The provision may also define bargaining-unit work and determine whether those outside the bargaining unit may do bargaining-unit work, and if so, under

---

1 Examples of collective agreement clauses in this chapter have been adapted from *The Collective Agreement Between the Ontario Council of Regents for the Colleges of Applied Arts and Technology and Ontario Public Service Employees Union (for academic employees, September 1, 2001 to August 31, 2003)*. The full text of the current agreement is available online at http://www.thecouncil.on.ca/english/academic/academic.html.

what circumstances. For example, a foreman may be allowed to carry out certain tasks, such as maintaining machinery or checking inventory, but not be allowed to run the machines or move inventory in and out of storage.

STAFFING

Where there are part-time workers, this provision may give preference to assigning work to full-time workers, or set out the circumstances where part-time workers may be used. Where some part-time workers are members of the bargaining unit, their work may be differentiated from that of part-time workers who are excluded from the bargaining unit.

NO DISCRIMINATION

This provision may prohibit discrimination on the usual prohibited grounds by the employer and the union in the workplace and in connection with the administration of the collective agreement by either party to it. The provision may cover human rights issues such as gender, ethnicity, or religion. It may also prohibit discrimination (by either party to the agreement) against any employee for engaging in union activity, for a lack of union activity, or for exercising rights under the agreement, including grievance rights. For example, if a worker grieves, and subsequently is given a less desirable shift or workplace task, the worker may grieve that this is discrimination based on the exercise of rights under the collective agreement. A worker can technically grieve that the union has discriminated against him or her in not processing a grievance because of lack of previous union activity. However, because the union would control the grievance process in a grievance against itself in this case, a grievor is more likely to make a complaint to the labour board about the union failing in its duty of fair representation.

NO STRIKE AND NO LOCKOUT

This is a mandatory provision that stipulates that the employer will not lock out the employees, and the union will not strike while the agreement is in force. Labour relations legislation may also set out other requirements that must be met before a strike or lockout can occur after an agreement expires.

MANAGEMENT RIGHTS

This provision is usually very broadly drafted. It gives the employer the right to manage its operations and business, and to hire, fire, and discipline employees, provided that it exercises its management rights in a manner that is consistent with the agreement. For example, if there is a specific provision allowing an employee who is being laid off to **bump** another, less senior employee, the employer cannot simply lay off the employee without the employee being allowed to exercise **bumping rights**. Put another way, if the exercise of managerial authority does not violate a provision of the agreement, then it is a valid exercise of power. Many employees are chagrined to learn that stupidity and bad judgment by management are not necessarily violations of the employees' rights under the agreement.

UNION–EMPLOYER COMMITTEE

Many agreements will make provision for a joint union–employer committee. These committees provide a forum to discuss workplace problems that do not necessarily come under the agreement, and that cannot be settled by grievances or arbitration. For example, low-level supervisors may appoint friends to desirable jobs. The agreement may not cover this aspect of hiring or promotion, and the employer may have no policy or procedure in this area. If this is identified as an irritant by the union, the joint committee may agree that internal jobs should be subject to posting, application, and interview. In doing so, a workplace irritant may be quickly removed. The result for the workplace may be a new management policy that also has worker support.

The changes can also be more far-reaching. A change in management policy may effectively modify or extend what is in the written collective agreement. Over time, by custom and convention, the new policy may attain the status of **past practice**. It may become enforceable as if it were part of the written collective agreement, or at least become a tool for expanding the interpretation of general language in the agreement. Thus the union may argue, for example, that management must run competitions for low-level supervisory positions because it had agreed with the union in the union–employer committee to do this, had followed the practice over time, and by inference had incorporated the policy into the written agreement. The employer, however, may take a more formalized, strict constructionist approach and argue that the agreement may only be amended explicitly and not by inference, and that the policy to post positions is nothing more than the exercise of management's right to manage the company.

If the parties are willing, they may also incorporate a policy change developed in a joint committee into a local agreement for one workplace to supplement an existing agreement covering several workplaces. The local agreement would only cover the work site to which the parties intended it to apply. The policy change could also result in a formal amendment to a collective agreement. However, because most agreements do not extend beyond two or three years, it is more usual to apply the change informally, and leave its incorporation into the agreement to the next round of bargaining.

Example

A committee of 3 members appointed by management, and 3 members appointed by the union shall meet at a mutually agreeable time and place on seven days notice given by either party, in order to discuss matters including: the local application of this agreement, an internal complaint process for issues not covered by grievance procedures.

UNION BUSINESS

This clause may make provision for giving union officers time off work to deal with union duties during the workday—for example, processing grievances. In some cases, the union may have the right to purchase time off for some of its officers or stewards.

Example

It is agreed that up to 5 officers of the union local may be released from duty for sufficient time to engage in arbitration hearings, union committee meetings, and meetings with members, provided such release does not in the opinion of the plant manager interfere with the efficient operation of the plant. The union shall reimburse the employer for the salary portion, exclusive of benefits, for each officer so released. It is further agreed that up to 1 local steward in each worksite may be released from usual and regular work duties to provide services to members of the bargaining unit in that worksite.

UNION SECURITY

This provision may set out the requirement that all members of the bargaining unit must join the union as a condition of employment, an arrangement often called a union shop. Under some provisions, employees are not required to join the union, but once they do, they must maintain their membership. In the alternative, the clause may apply the **Rand Formula** to the workplace, requiring a mandatory deduction of dues from salary by the employer for all members of the bargaining unit, whether or not they have elected to join the union.

Example

There shall be an automatic deduction of an amount equivalent to the regular monthly membership dues from the salaries of all employees. The amount to be deducted shall be remitted to the Union Head Office, in the amount as determined from time to time by the union. ... The cheques shall be accompanied by a list of the names and work locations of employees from whom the deductions have been made.

Other provisions would include a requirement that the employee be a member of the union prior to being hired. In this situation, the union often operates a hiring hall and provides employees at the request of the employer. If the union operates a hiring hall, it is required under s. 75 of the OLRA to do so in a manner that is not arbitrary, discriminatory, or in bad faith.

WORKLOAD AND WORK PROCEDURES

These clauses vary widely. In some workplaces, procedures that might be contentious are defined. For example, the kind of work a foreman is allowed to do, or the kinds of tools he or she may carry, may be defined. The purpose is to avoid having a foreman take work from other employees while in a supervisory capacity. In other agreements, actual workload might be measured, particularly in jobs where the employee does not leave his or her work behind at the end of the workday. College teachers in Ontario, and CGEP teachers in Quebec, for example, have a workload formula that gives attributed hours of work for preparation and marking, activities that often take place outside the workplace.

In other workplaces, caseload may be categorized, measured, and capped to avoid workload inequity between employees and overload of individual employees. Once workload is defined to establish norms for a full-time employee, it becomes possible to define overtime. This contrasts with work measurement in collective agreements in more typical industrial settings, where the work is whatever is done during a prescribed workday at the direction of management, and no work is done outside of normal working hours. Here, overtime is defined by hours of work beyond the prescribed standard workday. Here, too, collective agreements might also have prescriptive clauses to prevent "speed-up," a situation where a production process is run at a faster pace than a prescribed standard allows.

SALARIES

The salary provision can vary tremendously from one agreement to another depending on the nature of the work, the job classifications, and the spread of salary levels within a classification. Often a salary schedule or grid for each classification will be an appendix to the salary clause of an agreement. In addition to the classification of the work done, the variables that determine salary may include an employee's

- probationary status (an employee on probation will be given a lower rate for several weeks or months, followed by an increase to the normal pay rate);

- satisfactory performance during the term of the contract or for some other period;

- years with the company (seniority);

- previous experience;

- relevant education; and

- acquisition of further skills or education.

In addition, there may be a **COLA** (cost of living) clause that during the life of an agreement allows for increases, usually on an annual basis, to cover increases in the cost of living due to inflation. COLA formulas are usually based on the federal government's consumer price index administered by Statistics Canada.[2]

VACATIONS AND LEAVES OF ABSENCE

The vacation provisions usually allow for a vacation after a year of service, with the amount of vacation increasing with seniority. The clause may also allow for premium payments for giving up a vacation period. It may also contain provisions allowing for the choice of vacation time to be based on seniority, subject to the discretion of the employer.

Example
A full-time employee who has completed one year of service shall be entitled to a vacation of two weeks to be scheduled at the discretion of the

---

2   There are several versions of the consumer price index; there are indexes for major cities, provinces, and regions, as well as a national index. The percentage rate of inflation can vary depending on which index is used. For more information, see Statistics Canada's website at http://www.statcan.ca.

employer. For each year of service, after the first year, the employee shall be entitled to an extra week for each year of service after the first year, to a maximum of 5 weeks of vacation.

The contract may also provide for leaves of absence for various purposes. Clauses that provide for several days per year with pay to look after family members who are ill are increasingly common, particularly in bargaining units with large numbers of women in them. Clauses may also provide for religious leave for employees, when days of religious observance do not coincide with statutory holidays, an important consideration for members of minority religious groups. An employer must take care where religious leave is discretionary not to violate provincial human rights codes by behaving in a discriminatory manner. Some contracts may also provide for other types of leave, including personal days, which are subject to the discretion of the employer and usually given without pay.

Example

Leave of absence for personal reasons, religious leave and special leave in extenuating personal circumstance may be granted at the discretion of the employer, without loss of regular salary. Where leave of absence for personal reasons is denied, reasons shall be given in writing to the applicant where requested.

SICK LEAVE

Many contracts have provisions for short-term sick leave as well as **long-term disability (LTD)**. For short-term sick leave, typically, an employee acquires a number of days of sick leave per year of service, which may be accumulated until needed. If the employee becomes ill, he or she can use accumulated sick leave, and continue to receive salary or wages. The clause may also require that the employee verify his or her illness by providing a doctor's note, if the employee is away for more than a day or two. If the employee runs out of days before long-term disability kicks in, he or she will draw no salary. In some contracts, accumulated sick days, if unused at the time of retirement or termination, can be cashed out within certain limits. In some cases, this may amount to half a year's salary. This was a common provision of public service contracts, when pay was much lower than it is now. The payout was seen as compensation for long service and a supplement to the pension. This provision is becoming increasingly rare, and has become a principal target for contract "take-aways" by management where it exists.

If the employee is injured on the job, the short-term sick leave plan may supplement the payment made under the *Workplace Safety and Insurance Act, 1997*[3] so that the employee receives what he or she would receive under the sick leave plan. Long-term disability plans kick in when the employee has been ill for a lengthy period of time and has exhausted the short-term sick leave plan or has completed the qualifying period to go on LTD.

Long-term disability is provided under a plan agreed to by the parties, and is usually operated by a private insurance company for the parties. The contract

---

3   SO 1997, c. 16, sched. A.

usually requires the employee to qualify for the plan by showing that he or she is chronically ill. In that case, depending on the plan, the employee will receive some portion of his or her former salary for as long as the disability continues up until retirement. The clause will also provide for apportionment of the insurance premium between the employer and the employees.

The cost of these plans has become contentious. It used to be the case that people who went on long-term disability were not on it for very long: they either recovered and returned to work, or died. Now it is more common to have employees become chronically ill, but stable. Thus, the length of stay on LTD has begun to lengthen, with costs rising accordingly. In some cases, the parties have also negotiated return-to-work programs in which individualized plans are developed to return employees to the workplace, at least on a part-time basis. A return-to-work plan can reduce the premiums for the LTD plan, sometimes dramatically.

MEDICAL INSURANCE

Although basic health care is covered by provincial health care plans, the parties may include provisions for drug, vision, hearing, and dental plans as well as for coverage of other uninsured health services. Depending on which party pays the premium, there may be a cap on the amount of annual coverage. The details of the coverage provided are usually set out in schedules to the agreement.

Example

The employer shall pay 100% of the billed premium of the Extended Health Care Plan for Employees covered thereby and subject to the eligibility requirements of the Plan. Effective October 1, Yr. 0, the Extended Health Plan shall be amended to provide for a combined maximum annual coverage for all covered paramedical services of $1,500.

MATERNAL AND PARENTAL LEAVE

With increased numbers of women in unionized workplaces, many contracts contain maternity or pregnancy leave provisions that go beyond the basic leave provisions of the federal *Employment Insurance Act*[4] and the *Employment Standards Act, 2000.*[5] Sometimes the provision will supplement the statutory minimums to bring an employee close to full wages or salary. Some contracts will go beyond maternity leave for a mother, and allow for parental leave for a father. To ensure that an employee is not using employment status to finance maternity leave, there are usually clauses to prevent this action. The clauses require that an employee work for the employer for a defined period of time before being granted leave, and continue in employment for a period of time after returning from leave. The provisions also give the employee the right to return to her previous position, or if there have been layoffs, provide that she be given rights she otherwise would have had under the layoff provisions.

---

4   SC 1996, c. 23.

5   SO 2000, c. 41.

SENIORITY AND JOB SECURITY

Most contracts set out criteria to discharge employees when there is not enough work to justify keeping all of the employees at work. This provision may also allow the employer to involuntarily transfer a worker to another work location or position, instead of laying the employee off. The usual method of determining who is to be laid off is to calculate seniority. Usually, an employee begins to acquire seniority after completing a probationary period, with credit for time back to the date of hire once the employee becomes permanent. Seniority is usually based on years of service with the employer. There are often detailed rules as to how an employee's seniority is to be calculated where he or she takes, for example, a leave of absence, or is on sick leave or maternity leave.

Seniority is sometimes used for the purpose of determining salary. But progression on a salary grid is rarely based simply on seniority, if it is based on seniority at all. It is usually based on merit alone or merit combined with years of service. In the latter case, the employee may progress on the salary grid annually, provided that performance is satisfactory.

When the employer plans to lay off or involuntarily transfer employees, most collective agreements require that the union be notified and be given the reason for transfer or layoff, along with the names of the affected employees. In a workplace with few job categories where skills are not a bar to transfer to other categories, straight seniority will prevail. That is, the person who has been there longest stays while more junior employees leave. Often an employer that is considering layoffs will just start at the bottom of the seniority list. Recall that a person slated for layoff has bumping rights and may name or "bump" a more junior employee, who in turn may bump one more junior still. However, if the job is skilled or requires training, most collective agreements will require the person being laid off to demonstrate that he or she has the necessary skills to do the job of the more junior employee he or she seeks to bump. The language used to describe the skill requirement may vary from agreement to agreement with important consequences for how the seniority provision works, as the following examples show.

Example

An employee shall be reassigned to displace another full-time employee in the same classification provided that the displacing employee *has the competence, skill and experience* to fulfill the requirements of the position concerned, and the employee being displaced has less seniority with the employer.

An employee shall be reassigned to displace another full-time employee in the same classification provided that the displacing employee *has greater competence, skill and experience* to fulfill the requirements of the position concerned, and the employee being displaced has less seniority with the employer.

In the first of the two clauses referred to above, the displacing employee needs to be as competent as the more junior employee. In the second, the displacing employee must be better at the job than the more junior employee. For those who are laid off, there is the possibility of being recalled or of accepting a severance payment determined by a formula based on years of service. Usually, if an employee elects severance, he or she is not entitled to be recalled.

Seniority as the basis for layoff has been criticized because it permits a less than stellar employee to keep his or her job, while an energetic and more productive employee is let go. The counterargument is that the system rewards loyalty to the company, expressed in years of service. It also imports an objective measurement rather than permit management to simply choose those who, for example, curry favour with their superiors.

HOURS OF WORK AND OVERTIME

This clause will set out the standard work week in number of hours per week and per day. On these caps will be based the definition of overtime, including the rate of pay for hourly rated employees, at time and a half, or double time, or whatever the parties agree to. For salaried employees, where there is no hourly rate, overtime may be based on a percentage of annual salary. This latter overtime provision is common in labour contracts involving professionals and white-collar workers. However, many salaried workers, even when unionized, do not have overtime provisions in their contracts.

PERSONNEL RECORDS

Because the employer is likely to conduct performance appraisals that will affect an employee's progression on the salary grid, what those appraisals say are important to both the employer and employee. The provision governing personnel research usually gives the employee a right to see the appraisal and to add his or her own comments.

> **Example**
> A performance appraisal, including written progress reports that are to be filed on the employee's record, shall be shown to the employee in advance. The employee may add the employee's views to such appraisal before it is filed. It is understood that an appraisal does not in itself constitute disciplinary action by the employer against the employee.

The clause will usually also provide that if the employee is disciplined, any written disciplinary notice will become part of the employee's record, with the corresponding right of the employee to examine the personnel file on reasonable notice to the employer. Some agreements may have a **sunset clause**, which requires the disciplinary notice to be removed from the personnel file after the passage of a prescribed time period, provided that there are no further disciplinary events. This is important in the context of **progressive discipline**, which assumes that increased penalties for repeated offences will deter the behaviour. If there are long time periods between offences, arguably there is no pattern of behaviour that would justify a more severe penalty for the latter offence.

This provision may also set out a protocol requiring a representative of the employer, usually the human resources (HR) director or the employee's immediate supervisor or both, to meet with the employee to issue a written or verbal reprimand. The employee should be given notice of the meeting and be entitled to have a union representative present.

Example

If the employer meets with an employee for the purpose of issuing a written disciplinary notice, including verbal reprimands, the employee shall be given reasonable notice of the meeting in order that the employee may arrange to have a union representative present if the employee so chooses.

GRIEVANCES

The grievance provision sets out the procedure that the parties to the agreement and the employees must follow in order to file grievances when contract provisions have been violated. The grievance procedure is usually a multistep process, starting with the employee and the immediate supervisor meeting informally, and then progressing to more formal meetings if the matter has not been resolved. Usually, the procedure sets out who may be present at each step, the time between each step, and the form of management's reply to the grievance. The provision may contain an arbitration clause, which is mandatory in any case, setting out who may sit as an arbitrator, how the arbitrator is to be chosen, and how the expenses of arbitration are to be shared. The provision may also allow for group grievances, union policy grievances, and grievances by management, each with slightly different grievance procedures. The grievance procedure is discussed in greater detail later in this chapter.

DURATION

The duration clause usually sets out the date on which the agreement comes into effect, and the length of time it will be in force. It will often allow the agreement to continue in the event that neither party opens up negotiations on the agreement's expiry date, and it may indicate how notice to negotiate a new agreement may be given.

Example

This agreement shall take effect commencing on the day it is signed by the parties. It shall have no retroactive effect or application. It shall continue automatically for annual periods of one year, unless either party notifies the other party in writing on January 1, [year] that it desires to amend the agreement.

Negotiations shall begin within 30 days following notification for amendment as provided in article [article number].

THE GRIEVANCE PROCESS

Because the collective agreement is a contract, it must have a means of enforcement if one party alleges a breach of the agreement by the other. Most contracts are enforced in court. In Canada, collective agreements constitute an early example of **alternative dispute resolution (ADR)**. Disputes arising under the collective agreement are resolved during the grievance process, where the parties meet to discuss the matter in dispute. If they cannot resolve it, it is referred to an arbitrator or board of arbitration for resolution. The parties are barred from taking breaches of the agreement to court and suing each other. Note also that although the union and the employer are the parties to the agreement, and can grieve, the employees may also grieve violations of the agreement, even though they are not direct parties to it.

Definition

A grievance is a complaint that one of the parties has violated a provision of the collective agreement. The person making the complaint is called the **grievor**, and when the grievor makes the complaint, he or she is said to have grieved the matter, or launched a grievance.

It is important to note that the grievance provision of the collective agreement presumes that the grievance is based on a violation of some part of the collective agreement, or arises from the interpretation or application of the collective agreement. Most agreements do not precisely define what a grievance is, though they may define what is not grievable. For example, many contracts do not permit a probationary employee to grieve dismissal.

As a matter of practice, an employee may grieve, through the various steps in the grievance process, something that is not a violation of the collective agreement. The employer may deny the grievance, claiming there is no provision of the collective agreement that the employee can point to that has been violated. But it cannot prevent the union or the employee from having access to the grievance procedure. If management is confident that there is no contract violation, then it can make a preliminary objection at the start of the arbitration hearing on this grievance, and ask the arbitrator to rule on whether he or she has jurisdiction. If the objection is accepted, the arbitrator will dismiss the grievance on the ground that the arbitrator has no jurisdiction to decide disputes arising outside of the collective agreement. Nevertheless, there can be benefits to this type of grievance for both sides: the issue or irritant is identified and discussed and may even be resolved.

As an alternative to this type of grievance, some agreements may provide for a union–management committee to meet to discuss grievances. The committee will try to resolve those workplace problems, issues, and irritants that cannot really be the subject of a valid grievance. For example, workers may have a supervisor whose management skills are plainly lacking, and who is causing morale to plummet. Management, under the management-rights clause of the agreement, has a right to manage, and that includes the right to manage badly through inept and incompetent supervisors. Because "bad management" is not a contract violation, there can be no valid grievance. But a union–management committee may provide a forum for employees to voice issues and concerns, and management may be prevailed upon to investigate the problem and take steps to resolve it.

Pros and Cons of the Grievance Procedure

There are advantages to both parties to have a grievance procedure in place, including the right to resort to arbitration. The advantages to an employee are set out below.

- The employee has a forum to use to address issues of unfair treatment.

- The employee has the union's support and assistance in proceeding with a workplace complaint.

- The employee does not have to bear the expense of being represented or of going to arbitration; the costs, including the use of legal counsel at arbitration, are paid for by the union.

- The employee has some expectation that the matter will be dealt with quickly because of enforceable response timelines in the grievance procedure.

Employees who are not covered by collective agreement and do not have the right to grieve are at a distinct disadvantage. A non-unionized employee in Nova Scotia or Quebec does have the right to have a work dispute arbitrated. So does a non-unionized employee in a federally regulated workplace under the *Canada Labour Code*. But a non-unionized employee may have only minimal rights to dispute adjudication procedures in other parts of Canada under employment standards legislation. An employee with a complaint about a supervisor, however, has no option except to resign. There is no internal process that will allow the non-unionized employee to pursue a complaint to the point where a neutral arbitrator will decide the issue.

Second, in framing and presenting an issue, an employee covered by a collective agreement has the assistance of union stewards and other union staff to help present the grievance right through to arbitration, at no financial cost to the grievor. A non-unionized employee who has an issue may get the assistance of an employee standards officer from the Ministry of Labour under employment standards legislation. However, the officer will intervene only in very limited areas, addressing issues such as vacation pay or overtime. Otherwise, the employee's remedies are limited to suing for wrongful dismissal on termination. And the employee has to hire and pay for his or her own lawyer, an expensive proposition that puts the remedy out of reach of the ordinary hourly-rated employee. Third, with time limits imposed in grievance procedures, the employee who has a right to grieve can theoretically have his or her issues addressed fairly quickly.

An employer at first glance sees the grievance procedure as an interference with the employer's unrestricted right to manage employees as it pleases. It may also see the grievance procedure as an expensive waste of time, with grievors and shop stewards taken away from their work for grievance meetings. On the other hand, progressive employers recognize the value of a process that allows the workforce a forum to air and resolve workplace complaints and irritants, which results in better workplace morale and a more positive and cooperative relationship between the employer and the employees.

THE "POLITICAL" USE OF THE GRIEVANCE PROCEDURE

Both the union and management may also use the grievance procedure to play politics. Management may argue that a low grievance rate indicates a happy and satisfied workforce. But it can also mean that the workers are intimidated or afraid to file grievances, or that management intransigence makes grieving too unpleasant for the employees and they avoid it altogether. Conversely, a union may encourage stewards to file grievances simply to demonstrate the union's effectiveness and diligence. Increasing grievance rates may also be used, even where the grievances are unsuccessful, to demonstrate the militancy or determination of the workforce—for example, when the parties are about to commence negotiations for a new contract. Using this approach to grievances and arbitrations, the union might say that even when you lose, you win.

THE IMPORTANCE OF THE GRIEVANCE PROCEDURE

Whatever the problems inherent in the grievance process, it does offer one clear advantage for both parties: production, work, and payment of salaries and benefits do not come to a halt when there is a workplace dispute. Before the institution of grievance processes, a workplace disagreement or dispute could lead to an illegal (wildcat) strike during the life of an agreement. For example, the firing of a union steward might produce a walkout and wildcat strike. To minimize and regulate conflict, this kind of dispute became the subject of a grievance rather than a walkout, with the right of the parties to have the dispute submitted to binding arbitration. Meanwhile, the employer's business continues to operate, and workers stay at their jobs. Put another way, the right of an employee to take disputes to an arbitrator is the price the employer pays for labour peace and stability during the collective agreement, with strikes and lockouts reserved as tactics to be used in the negotiation of a new agreement when the old one expires.

"DO IT AND GRIEVE"

One of the principles underlying the grievance process is that an aggrieved worker must continue to work and accept direction by management, with exceptions. In other words, the worker should work first and grieve later—that is, "do it and grieve." Even if the worker thinks the order or command violates the collective agreement, unless the order is illegal or violates a statute, the rule is to do it and grieve the matter. For example, if a worker is ordered to carry out a task normally done by a supervisor, the worker may state his or her objection, and indicate that he or she will grieve the order, but he or she still has to carry the order out. On the other hand, if a supervisor orders a worker to do something that is dangerous to others or that violates a statutory rule or the criminal law, then the worker may refuse to carry out the order. Note that under occupational health and safety legislation, instead of grieving an order to do work that is unsafe, the worker should follow legislated work-refusal procedures.[6]

THE RIGHT TO FILE GRIEVANCES

While employees whose collective agreement rights have been violated may file grievances, the union and management also have the right to file grievances.

The union's right to file grievances is limited to "policy" grievances—that is, a contract violation that no individual worker could grieve. Consider a clause in the collective agreement that limits the use of part-time workers to certain job categories. If management begins to hire part-time workers to do work usually done by full-time workers, no individual bargaining unit member's rights are violated, so there is no right of any individual member to grieve. But the union may still grieve. Many agreements say that if an individual has a right to grieve, then the individual must exercise that right. The union cannot do it for him or her. However, if the failure of the individual to grieve would set an unacceptable standard or practice that would harm other members of the bargaining unit, the union may grieve where an individual has not. There are a few situations where both the union and

---

6   See part V of the *Occupational Health and Safety Act*, RSO 1990, c. O.1, as amended.

an individual could grieve—for example, where management indicates that it is establishing a work assignment policy and begins to assign workers according to that policy. The individual could grieve the assignment, and if it is a policy potentially affecting many others in the bargaining unit, the union can grieve separately on the policy aspects.

Management also has the right to grieve, but it is very rarely exercised. When it is used, it may be used in response to an action, such as an unauthorized work stoppage. But even here, management may instead use its right to maintain order and discipline and simply discipline workers who stop work contrary to the employer's directions. Alternatively, management can file unfair-labour-practice charges under labour relations legislation with the labour board, if the union is behind the work stoppage.

DUTY OF FAIR REPRESENTATION: THE RIGHT TO PROCEED WITH A GRIEVANCE

Many members of the bargaining unit think they have an unfettered right to file a grievance and proceed to arbitration—that it is their case, and their decision. This is not so. The parties to the agreement are the union and the employer. It is the union, as a party with power to enforce the contract, that decides which grievances go on to arbitration. Most unions will assist members in filing grievances, and assist them by presenting the grievance at the various steps prior to arbitration. Even where the grievance is legally weak, the union will often carry it forward internally in the hope that some kind of resolution may be obtained. Management will often cooperate in this, in the interest of achieving workplace harmony. However, once the internal procedures have been exhausted, the union—not the grievor—has to decide whether or not the case should go on to arbitration. The union will be guided by the following questions:

• Does the complaint constitute a valid grievance?

• If it does, is there any likelihood of success?

• Would a dismissal of the grievance create an unfavourable precedent that would be bad for the bargaining unit or the union?

• Would the success of the grievance harm the interests of other members of the bargaining unit?

• Would the failure of the grievance confirm misconduct by the grievor that could be used against the grievor later?

• Does the gain to be made justify the financial cost of the fees of lawyers and arbitrators?

If the union concludes that proceeding to arbitration would not be productive, it can refuse to schedule the grievance for arbitration, in which case the grievance is deemed to be withdrawn. What the union may not do, however, is resort to improper considerations or act capriciously or arbitrarily in deciding not to go on to arbitration. For example, if the union's officers dislike the grievor, and regard him or her as a troublemaker for the union, that is not a valid reason to fail to proceed to arbitration. The union has to consider the grievance on its merits. If the union acts arbitrarily, the grievor may charge the union before the labour board with having breached its duty of fair representation.

The duty of fair representation requires the union to represent the interest of each member of the bargaining unit, whether he or she is a member of the union or not. The duty requires the union to rationally and objectively consider the pros and cons of proceeding with the grievance before it can refuse to grieve. Section 74 of the Ontario *Labour Relations Act, 1995* sets out the union's responsibility. Other provinces' legislation is similar.

> A trade union or council of trade unions, so long as it continues to be entitled to represent employees in a bargaining unit, shall not act in a manner that is arbitrary, discriminatory or in bad faith in the representation of any of the employees in the unit, whether or not members of the trade union or of any constituent union of the council of trade unions, as the case may be.

GRIEVANCES AND RETROACTIVE PAY

If a grievor is successful on a rate-of-pay grievance at arbitration, or at one of the pre-arbitration steps, then the date on which the new rate will take effect must be decided. Some contracts require the payment to be made from the time the right arose, regardless of when the grievance was filed. Others require that retroactive payments be made only from the time that the grievance was filed, regardless of the fact that the right to the payment arose much earlier. Others are silent on the issue. If the agreement is silent, management will argue that it should not be obliged to make a payment when it had no notice of a claim for payment or a right to payment. The union, on the other hand, will argue that if the right arose under the collective agreement, it should not be denied just because the grievor was unaware that his or her rights had been violated. Some agreements split the difference on these arguments by putting a time limit on retroactive payments and limiting them to a definite period—for example, six months prior to the filing of the grievance. Most agreements do not provide for interest on retroactive payments, although if the matter goes to arbitration, an arbitrator may award interest.

Steps in the Grievance Procedure

The typical grievance procedure is a multistep process. The number of steps is set out in the collective agreement and will vary depending on the size and complexity of the organization. As the grievor progresses through the steps in the procedure, the meetings become more formalized, and involve more senior management members and more senior union officers or grievance staff. At the first step in the process, the discussion is usually among the employee, the local area steward, and the local supervisor. Ideally, an informal and brief discussion will solve the problem. If the matter is not resolved, it progresses to the next step, where a more senior manager and the chief steward become involved. Because these individuals have more experience, and more authority, they may be able to resolve the problem. If they are not able to resolve the problem, the next step will involve senior HR personnel and more senior union representatives. These individuals often have more training and experience in what can be achieved or not achieved at arbitration. To ensure that the matter does not drag on indefinitely, becoming an ever larger workplace irritant, there are time limits for taking the next step that both parties must observe, and consequences if a time limit is missed. Usually, if the grievor misses a time limit, even inadvertently, the grievance is deemed to be abandoned. Once that occurs, it may be very difficult to restart the grievance process. Further, the right to grieve on an issue may be lost, unless management repeats the act that gave rise to the grievance. If management misses a time limit, there is no such penalty, but the grievor is entitled to move to the next step. The steps in the grievance procedure are discussed in more detail below.

UP CLOSE

A Typical Grievance Procedure

- oral complaint

- oral or written reply by supervisor

- step 1 written grievance

- step 1 meeting

- reply to step 1 grievance by management

- referral of grievance to step 2

- step 2 meeting

- step 2 reply

- referral to arbitration

- choosing of arbitrator and scheduling of arbitration

- arbitration

- arbitration decision

- implementation of the decision

COMPLAINT

This is the first step in an attempt to foster an informal and non-adversarial atmosphere conducive to solving the problem. The complaint is sometimes considered not to be part of the formal grievance procedure but is still seen as a prerequisite to starting the grievance. Failure to follow the complaint procedure may prevent the grievor from continuing with the grievance. An employee who has a complaint must raise it within a set time period after becoming aware of the problem. The complaint is usually made orally, usually after consultation with an area steward. The steward is an employee who is elected by other employees as the union representative in the local work area. Depending on the union, the steward receives some training in handling grievances for members. The steward often has "super-seniority" while serving as a steward, so that he or she is the last to be laid off, even though his or her actual seniority is much lower. This is so that the steward, who is often an activist, cannot be targeted for layoff because of union activity.

Often, following an informal discussion, the issue can be resolved by the supervisor and the employee. Before the supervisor makes a commitment, he or she should get advice from the HR staff to be sure that he or she is not about to make a decision that conflicts with existing HR or company policy. This is especially necessary where the complaint concerns a matter that is tied to a non-local issue or an issue administered by the HR department, such as accumulated sick leave or salary calculations. In this kind of complaint, the first meeting is often unproductive, because the supervisor is no more than a conduit for the decision made in the HR department. At later steps, a different and more senior manager may deliver the same message again, or the more senior manager may reconsider the application or interpretation of the contract. On the other hand, where the issue is a local workplace issue between the employee and the immediate supervisor, the informal and less adversarial complaint stage provides a valuable opportunity to solve a problem quickly, easily, and informally.

REPLY TO COMPLAINT

The immediate supervisor will often have a period of about a week to reply to the complaint. The reply may be in writing or it may be oral. If the reply is not made on time, the grievor can move immediately to the next step. If the reply is delivered on time, the grievor has a time period in which to decide whether he or she wishes to move to the next step. If the grievor misses his or her time period, the grievance is deemed to be abandoned, and cannot be revived. If the reply is satisfactory to the grievor, that is the end of the matter. If the grievor is not satisfied, the grievance must move to step 1.

STEP 1 GRIEVANCE AND MEETING

The grievor has a period of time, usually a week or two from the time he or she receives the reply to the complaint, to file a step 1 grievance. The step 1 grievance is made in writing and sets out the alleged contract violation and the remedy requested. Some unions use grievance forms; others use a memo format. Styles of presentation vary. Some cite articles of the collective agreement, while others describe the breach, as in the following example.

> Statement of grievance: My grievance is that the employer has failed to advance me to the next salary step on my anniversary date, though I had fulfilled the criteria for advancement to the next step.

> Remedy sought: That I be moved immediately to the next salary step, and that I receive all associated benefits and salary increases from my anniversary date, together with interest.

The grievor must sign the grievance and deliver it to the supervisor, who must schedule a grievance meeting within the time period provided for in the agreement. At that meeting, the grievor is usually accompanied by his area steward, and the supervisor is accompanied by a more senior manager. The grievor's steward presents the grievance and the parties discuss it. The matter may be resolved at the meeting, or the employer may indicate that the answer will be delivered in writing.

REPLY TO STEP 1 GRIEVANCE

Management has a time period in which to reply, failing which, the grievor may move the grievance on to step 2. The reply will note who was present at the meeting, what the union's position was, and what the management's response is to that position. An example of a step 1 reply is set out below.

Memo to: Grievor

From: H. Bloggs, Plant Manager

Re: Grievance dated March 3, Yr 0—salary step progression.

Present at the step 1 meeting were the grievor, the local steward, the local supervisor, and myself.

The union stated that the grievor, having satisfied all of the requirements, should have progressed a step on the salary grid from step 4 to step 5 on his anniversary date. The union described this as "automatic" provided that the employee's employment was continuous during the period. It is common ground between the parties that the grievor did not advance a step on the grid on his anniversary date.

It is the employer's position that to advance on the grid, the employee must work continuously through the period, but must also have a satisfactory performance review in accordance with article 16 of the collective agreement. The grievor's review noted that the quality of his work had deteriorated during the year, and that improvements were needed. Consequently it is the employer's view that the performance review was not satisfactory, and that the grievor was therefore not entitled to advance a step on the salary grid.

The grievance is therefore denied.

STEP 2 GRIEVANCE MEETING AND REPLY

If the grievor does not accept management's decision, he or she may move the grievance on to step 2 by stating in writing that management's reply at step 1 is unsatisfactory, and that the grievor requires that the grievance move to step 2. As before, there is a time period in which the grievor must move the grievance to step 2, or be presumed to have abandoned the grievance. Once management has received notice, a step 2 meeting must be called to discuss the grievance. At the step 2 meeting, more senior managers, often including the director of human resources, will attend for management. The union will usually send the chief steward or another senior union officer to represent the grievor. The idea here is that more senior people with more authority can override the less senior personnel who participated in step 1. Those attending at step 2 are felt to have a broader perspective and may be able to fashion a solution.

If they resolve the matter, the grievance ends. If they are unable to resolve the matter, management must give a formal reply in writing within the designated time period. If not, the grievor can refer the matter to arbitration. The reply will likely be similar in format to the reply at step 1. If the grievor does not accept the decision, again he or she may refer the matter to arbitration.

REFERRAL TO ARBITRATION

Steps 1 and 2 represent a process to settle contract disputes in the workplace. If the dispute cannot be settled, the grievor may refer the matter to arbitration, to have it decided by neutral, objective and external adjudicators. However, it is the union that usually makes the decision about which cases go to arbitration. As noted earlier, if the grievance is likely to be unsuccessful, the union may not wish to incur the costs of arbitration. Also, if a loss might be harmful to the bargaining unit by setting an unfavourable precedent, the union may refuse to take the matter forward on that ground.

If a matter is to go to arbitration, the parties will follow the procedure in the collective agreement to choose an arbitration board, and to schedule the matter for hearing. This usually means that the arbitration board will schedule a day for hearing usually within a month or two of the referral. However, if the arbitration takes more than a day, getting subsequent dates means finding clear days on which all the parties, lawyers, and arbitrators are available. With a popular and well-known arbitrator, this can be difficult. It is not uncommon for arbitrations involving five days of hearings to take two years to complete.

COMMONLY GRIEVED "RIGHTS" ISSUES

Rights issues are those that involve a worker's individual rights under an agreement. These contract rights are commonly the subject of grievances, and for that reason we examine them in more detail.

Seniority and Layoff

Almost every agreement contains a seniority clause. Under this clause, the parties agree to give preference to one employee over another based on length of service with the employer. Seniority can also be used to determine who has first call on particular jobs, shifts, promotions, and transfers. It also is used to determine the order in which employees are laid off, the most junior being laid off first and recalled last.

CRITICISMS OF THE SENIORITY PRINCIPLE

Seniority is an objective and equitable decision-making criterion. No subjective judgment is required to determine preferences based on seniority. All that management need do is count the employees' years of service. However, management will often argue that merit or ability also needs to be considered in promoting or laying off employees. The union will argue that merit invites often capricious and arbitrary preferences and distinctions, with "management pets" getting preferential treatment.

SENIORITY AND DECISION MAKING: A COMPROMISE

The result of the tensions between these two points of view is usually some kind of compromise where merit and seniority are joined in a clause that ranks employees for certain purposes. Clauses generally fall into one of the following categories governing promotion, transfer, job assignment, and layoff:

- Decisions are solely at the discretion of management; this is usually the case in non-unionized workplaces.

- Decisions are made on the basis of greater skill and ability.

- Decisions are made on the basis of equal skill and ability.

- Decisions are made on the basis of seniority, provided that the more senior worker has *greater* skill or ability than the more junior.

- Decisions are made on the basis of seniority, provided that the more senior worker has *equal* skill or ability to the more junior.

- Decisions are made on the basis of seniority, provided that the more senior worker has *some* skill or ability possessed by the more junior.

- Decisions are made on the basis of seniority, without any reference to comparative skill or ability.

The first and the last categories represent the most extreme positions, and are rare. Far more common are the categories that combine seniority tempered with some reference to skill or ability. Unions usually aim for the clause that gives preference to the more senior worker provided that the person has some competence. Management will incline toward a clause that requires the more senior worker to have greater skill and ability than the more junior.

Because ability and competence are subjective, applying seniority clauses can be difficult. How much greater does employee A's ability have to be than employee B's? What determines ability? Because of these uncertainties, a large number of seniority cases wind up in arbitration. From these arbitration cases, some guidelines for determining ability have emerged:

- Ability is often determined by looking at prior and current work experience, education, and credentials. In some cases, the results of proficiency tests are relevant.

- Where a worker has to show only "sufficient" or "some" ability to displace a more junior worker, management has the burden of showing that the more senior employee is unqualified.

- Where the ability of a worker is relatively evenly matched with that of a more junior worker, the burden is on management to show that the more senior one is unqualified. The burden is easier for management to discharge when the standard is "greater" ability rather than "sufficient" ability.

- Generally, minor differences in ability are not sufficient to discharge management's burden to show that the more senior worker is unqualified.

Because of the subjective element in determining a criterion like "ability" or "skill," it would be helpful to arbitrators to have the agreement set out guidelines for interpreting or weighing facts. However, guidelines are rarely found in agreements. This is largely because the parties usually have difficulty agreeing on how to balance seniority and merit and so may prefer to be purposely vague about how the balance should be achieved.

In assessing skill and ability, some agreements provide for a trial period for the employee to prove his or her skills and abilities. Some agreements go further and require the provision of limited training for those claiming another position. In some cases, there may be a jointly administered fund that will help workers targeted for layoff retrain to take vacant jobs or bump more junior employees.

BUMPING RIGHTS

Seniority becomes crucial when the employer wishes to lay off employees because there is not enough work. Where there is a seniority clause, the employer will begin by laying off the most junior employee. However, where a senior employee is targeted for layoff, he or she may bump a more junior employee, provided that the more senior employee has the required skill or ability to do the job done by the junior employee. That junior employee can then bump an employee who is even more junior, provided that he or she can do the job of the employee. The agreement may limit the number of bumps that take place as a result of a layoff.

The system works the same way but in reverse when workers are recalled to work. The most senior among those laid off are recalled first, and the more junior employees follow.

THE SENIORITY CLASS

When applying the seniority principle to rank employees for layoff, which employees should be included in the pool or class of employees to determine who may be displaced? The easy answer is that it should include all those in the bargaining unit governed by the collective agreement, ranked solely on the basis of seniority. In this case, managers simply to start with the most junior employee on the principle "last hired, first fired." But the situation is usually more complicated. Within the bargaining unit there may be several job classifications and categories. For example, an employee in one job category might be totally unsuited to performing the tasks of a more junior employee in another job category. However, he or she may be able to bump another more junior employee in still another job category.

Some typical seniority systems include the following kinds of arrangements:

- *Seniority class is restricted to occupants of certain a job classification or category.* All shop mechanics, for example, constitute a class. A senior mechanic can bump a more junior one, provided that the senior employee can do the job. But the senior mechanic cannot bump a more junior employee in another job category, even if he or she could do that junior employee's job.

- *Seniority class is two-staged.* An employee can bump a junior employee in his or her own job category, provided that the "bumper" can do the job of the "bumpee." If the senior employee cannot do the junior's job in his or her own job category, he or she can then name a more junior employee in another job category, who will be bumped if the senior employee can do the junior's job.

- *Skilled job groups with access to general labour class.* Here a more senior skilled employee can bump more junior employees in his or her own job category and in related categories that are grouped together for bumping purposes. If the senior employee is not successful in bumping in the skilled category, he or she can then bump into the general labour pool of unskilled workers.

- *Job progression links.* In some workplaces, jobs are ranked. A junior employee will start in an entry-level category and progress, with seniority, experience, and training, to more senior categories. If there are layoffs, a worker who has progressed up through the ranks is entitled to bump back down, displacing more junior employees.

- *Full-time to part-time.* Where there are part-time as well as full-time positions and a full-time worker is laid off, he or she may bump a more junior part-time worker or a contract worker.

It is important to recognize that when a senior employee bumps a more junior one, in many cases the senior gets no more than the junior had. For example, if a senior full-time employee bumps a junior part-time employee or one on contract, the senior employee gets part-time work, or contract work. When the contract ends, the senior employee's job is gone. If the senior employee is not recalled to his or her former job before the job disappears, all rights of employment for that employee are usually lost. Also, when a more senior employee can bump into other categories, and potentially could bump one of several more junior employees, the senior employee may be restricted to naming no more than two or three junior targets, and may be able to name only one prior to arbitration.

Some employees when laid off, particularly if they are junior, will often have the right to take a severance payment and leave the employer altogether, rather than attempt to bump someone else to preserve recall rights. Once an employee has elected severance, he or she loses the right to recall. Many agreements will set out severance amounts based on years of service, with payments made in a lump sum or over time. The amounts payable are usually more generous than the minimal severance rates prescribed by employment standards legislation.

Classification and Progression on a Salary Grid

In some collective agreements, a worker will start in a specific entry-level position and progress after a probationary period to a permanent job category. Thereafter, salary increases will depend on the outcome of contract negotiations. When the job classification system is this straightforward and simple, there are few job disputes.

But in job categories where there is a salary grid made up of many levels, and placement at the time of hire is based on experience and training, assessing the correct step at which to place a new employee can be difficult. Points may be awarded for each full year of relevant education and training, or for obtaining certain required degrees, diplomas, or certificates. Similarly, points may be awarded for relevant experience, with some attempt to control double counting of experience and training in the same year.

Assessing experience and education can be the source of dispute. How, for example, should a foreign degree or certificate be credited compared with a similar Canadian degree? How much of a person's previous work experience should be deemed to be relevant experience? If the person worked at a related but somewhat different occupation, should all of that experience count? Or should it be discounted by some percentage?

Usually, an employee is on probation when his or her initial placement on the salary grid is determined. Most agreements permit probationary employees to grieve on most issues, but usually prevent a probationary employee from grieving dismissal. The reason for this is that a probationary worker is being "tried out" before being made permanent. Management will argue that if the employee does not work out, it should be able to release the employee without being challenged by a grievance for dismissal without just cause. Consequently, a probationer who grieves his or her placement on the salary grid may be seen by management to be someone who "won't work out" and be released, without any right to grieve dismissal. For that reason, many unions advise a probationer who has issues about initial salary placement not to grieve during the probationary period. Instead, the grievance may be launched when the probationary period has been completed and the employee cannot be barred from launching a dismissal grievance if released.

However, choosing not to grieve during the probationary period creates other problems for the grievor. First, a grievor has a relatively short period of time to launch a grievance once he or she becomes aware of a potential contract violation. That time period usually expires long before the probationary period has ended. Consequently, the employer may argue that any grievance is barred by the expiry of the time period during which a grievance may be commenced. The union will counter with the argument that each time the employee is paid at the incorrect rate, the right to grieve arises afresh. If the union is successful with this argument, the grievor may have his or her salary adjusted retroactively but only from the date of the grievance, not from the date of hire.

Most entry-level placement assessments allow for a salary placement range from the lowest step to an entry maximum somewhere below the top step. Once an employee is placed on the salary grid, he or she then progresses toward the top of the grid annually based on satisfactory performance. This movement can take two forms: one where the employee progresses annually if he or she continues in the position, and the other where progression is annual but also dependent on a performance review. In the latter case, a review that is not wholly positive may result in failure to advance a step. Unions often argue that unless a worker has been disciplined for poor performance, employers should presume that performance was satisfactory and the employee should therefore be allowed to progress to the next salary step. If advancement is dependent on a performance review, unions will charge that this opens the door to arbitrariness, subjectivity, and favouritism. The employer, on the other hand, will argue that simply showing up for work should not be the basis for an increase, and that workers should get annual increases only on the basis of meritorious performance determined on a performance review. Where a positive performance review is required, unions will often try to work a provision into the agreement that employees can appeal an unfavourable review, and that the employee can also write his or her views about the comments in the report to point out any unfairness. Unions may also argue that failure to advance a step for "poor" performance is a form of progressive discipline, which in itself can be the subject of a separate discipline grievance.

Some collective agreements also contemplate post-hiring advancement on the salary grid on completion of further training or the acquisition of relevant qualifications. Usually the employee can move a step on the grid immediately on completion of the requirement, rather than on the anniversary of the date of hiring. Thus, the employee may move two steps within a year. For example, if an employee completes a training requirement in February, he or she would advance a step, and if the anniversary of the date of hire was in March, he or she would advance another step on that date.

Discipline

Discipline concerns the right of the employer to order and direct employees in the performance of their work, and in their conduct in the workplace, generally. It follows that if an employer can direct and order employees, it may also discipline them for failing to follow directions and carry out orders by imposing penalties, such as suspension without pay, transfer, or demotion to a lower position. An employee who thinks the discipline is unjustified or excessive may grieve that he or she has been disciplined without just cause.

INVESTIGATION OF A DISCIPLINARY OFFENCE

Because of the serious consequences that can flow from discipline for an employee, the employer who investigates an allegation leading to discipline must carry out a prompt, fair, and impartial investigation. Further, even if the collective agreement does not specify it, at any meetings with the employee to discuss the matter, the employer must advise the employee that he or she has the right to have a union representative present to advise and represent him or her.[7] The employee has the right to remain silent during an investigation, but a statement by an employee may be wise if it provides an explanation or provides information that may serve to reduce a penalty. In some circumstances, the employer may require a medical examination, but cannot compel the employee to see a doctor of the employer's choosing. Nor can the employer require the employee to undergo a lie detector test.[8]

---

7   *Sunworthy Wallcoverings*, [1986] OLRB Rep. Jan. 164.

8   S. Karshinsky and J. Sack, *Discharge and Discipline* (Toronto: Lancaster House, 1989), 1-4.

THE CONCEPT OF JUST CAUSE AND DETERMINATION OF PENALTIES

Just cause is the key concept used in arbitrations on discipline and dismissal. What this means is that an employer cannot discipline or discharge an employee on a whim or on an arbitrary or capricious basis. Instead, the employer must demonstrate at arbitration that there is just cause to use discipline. In non-disciplinary cases, usually the grievor has to present his or her evidence first and show that he or she has made out a case. But in a disciplinary case, the employer presents its case first. The employee has to respond only if the arbitrator decides that the employer has presented a case that, on its face, shows just cause. Only then does the grievor have to rebut the presumption of just cause. If there is just cause, the arbitrator then has to turn his or her attention to whether or not the penalty imposed by the employer is appropriate or whether it is too severe. Among the questions arbitrators consider are the following:

- The previous record of the employee: Does the employee have a clean discipline record? If there is a previous discipline history, is it recent or related to the current offence, or is it an isolated incident? A good record may result in a less severe penalty.

- What is the grievor's length of service? A long-serving employee with a good record should get a less severe penalty.

- Was there provocation, particularly by an agent of the employer, such as a foreman? Provocation may be seen as a mitigating factor that would reduce the severity of discipline.

- Was the offence due to impulsiveness? Was it a reaction to something or was it premeditated? Premeditation would support a more severe penalty.

- Does the penalty imposed create especially severe hardship for the employee? A penalty designed to have a specific negative impact may be too severe if the grievor's personal situation, particularly his or her economic situation, makes the impact more severe on the grievor than it would be for most employees.

- Have the employer's rules of conduct been made known to the employees, and were they enforced consistently when broken? A lack of posting and uniform enforcement may indicate discrimination and may void or reduce a penalty.

- Do the circumstances show that the employee did not intend to break a rule? For example, the grievor may have misunderstood an order or its significance. A lack of intention may reduce the penalty.

- How serious is the offence in terms of company policy or obligations? For example, harassment of other workers that might subject the employer to a human rights complaint, or a health and safety violation that might result in prosecution of the employer, might justify more severe penalties than in other cases.

- What other factors are relevant? For example, the employee may have been given an opportunity to apologize and did so, or may have otherwise shown remorse or contrition or acknowledged wrongdoing.[9]

Any one of these factors may cause an arbitrator to reduce the penalty imposed by the employer. The right of an arbitrator to substitute his or her authority for that of the employer was once a subject of considerable legal dispute but it is now confirmed by statute in most jurisdictions in Canada. Section 48(17) of the Ontario *Labour Relations Act, 1995* is an example of the legislative grant of this authority to arbitrators:

Substitution of penalty

Where an arbitrator or arbitration board determines that an employee has been discharged or otherwise disciplined by an employer for cause and the collective agreement does not contain a specific penalty for the infraction that is the subject-matter of the arbitration, the arbitrator or arbitration board may substitute such other penalty for the discharge or discipline as to the arbitrator or arbitration board seems just and reasonable in all the circumstances.

It is well known that arbitrators frequently reduce the severity of the penalty imposed by the employer. In this situation, it may well be the case that employers impose a more severe penalty than could be justified, in the expectation that it will be reduced at arbitration. In one case, in an unguarded moment, an employee relations manager apparently acknowledged this was the case to a grievor. The grievor had been reinstated by an arbitrator who had substituted a penalty of suspension without pay for the penalty of dismissal that had been imposed by the employer. The arbitrator, in the subsequent grievance that was held to implement the first arbitration award, noted the following:

The second grievance reply being unsatisfactory to the Grievor, he [the grievor] writes the Director of Employee Relations on February 10, 1997 advising that: "… I am requesting that this matter be referred to arbitration as expeditiously as possible." He gives as his reasons for the request:

At the Step II meeting, and in the presence of the others, you responded to my concerns about being treated unfairly, as a result of my having won my previous dismissal grievance, by indicating that the College had, in fact, only intended to obtain a long suspension rather than my dismissal. You indicated that the College had no reason to be malicious, at this time, in their treatment of me, because, and I quote:

You … don't understand how these things work. When the College wants to impose a lengthy suspension we know that Arbitration Boards rarely uphold a long suspension so we dismiss the employee, go through a long arbitration hearing, and when the employee is not compensated for lost wages, as in your … case, we got what we wanted in the first place.[10]

---

9 A.W. Craig and N. Solomon, *The System of Industrial Relations in Canada*, 5th ed. (Scarborough, ON: Prentice Hall, 1996), 346.

10 *Seneca College v. OPSEU*, [1998] OLAA no. 832, per MacLaren.

IS IT DISCIPLINE?

Not every action taken by employers to advise or direct an employee or to investigate an employee's conduct amounts to discipline. Consider the following examples:

- In a unionized retail store, a customer has written to the store manager to complain about discriminatory treatment by a sales clerk. On receiving the complaint, and having talked to the complainant, the manager suspends the employee with pay while she investigates the complaint. Although the suspension may make the employee think he has been disciplined, that is not the case. So far, the employer has not told the employee that he has done wrong. In fact, there is no finding of wrongdoing. And though the employee cannot come to work, he is still being paid. Further, the purpose of the suspension is to permit the employer to investigate the situation, not to punish the employee. No penalty has actually been imposed. If the investigation reveals no wrongdoing, the employee returns to work with a clear record.

- In another case, management investigates a situation, and decides that although the employee did not do the right thing, it was because the employee needed further training and instruction. If the employer orders the employee to undertake further training on company time, then that will not be seen by an arbitrator as being discipline.

PROGRESSIVE DISCIPLINE

For an employer's action to be considered disciplinary, the employee must be told clearly that certain conduct is wrong and unacceptable, and that the employee is being subjected to discipline, even if it is no more than a warning.

Generally, discipline is imposed on a progressive basis. This means that for a first offence, the penalty is relatively minor, but if the conduct is repeated, the penalty is more severe. If the conduct still continues, the employee is subjected to more severe penalties, up to and including the ultimate penalty, dismissal. However, when dismissing an employee on the basis of a long discipline history, the employer cannot simply review the employee's work record and then fire the employee; there must be a **culminating incident**. This is misconduct of the employee that becomes the cause for dismissal when considered with the total disciplinary history. The culminating incident may be relatively trivial—for example, being late for work. But when considered with, say, a history of lateness, it could be sufficient to justify dismissal.

Arbitrators sometimes consider factors that will lessen the severity of discipline. For example, if subsequent misconduct is unrelated to earlier misconduct, an arbitrator may not connect unrelated incidents to support an increasingly severe penalty. Also, if there is a long period of time between misconduct, arbitrators may reduce the penalty for the second offence. In these situations, the arbitrator may also not accept the incident as a culminating incident.

Progressive discipline normally proceeds along the following lines:

- A verbal warning describing the conduct complained of and, if not obvious, what must be done to correct it.

- A written warning with an indication that if there is a repetition of the conduct complained of, the worker may be subject to further discipline up to and including dismissal.

- A written notice and a suspension without pay, which may include loss of benefits or seniority or both.

- Further written notices and longer suspensions without pay, including loss of benefits and seniority.

- Dismissal.

The idea behind progressive discipline is that gradually increasing penalties will correct the behaviour of the employee. If the employee's behaviour does not improve, then dismissal is the last resort. However, if the employee's alleged misconduct is very serious, the employer may immediately dismiss the employee. For example, an employee who commits a serious assault on another employee or a supervisor, or who steals from or defrauds the employer, would likely be immediately dismissed. In cases such as these, the employee may also be charged with criminal offences. Of course, the employee has the right to grieve the dismissal or, in fact, any discipline. Most unions will advise an employee to do just that, either to clear his or her record or, in the case of dismissal, to obtain reinstatement.

If progressive discipline is to be effective and deter employees from misconduct, it must be imposed without delay. As well, if an accusation of misconduct is made, and the employee is not given timely notice of what is alleged, it may become difficult for an employee to defend against allegations made in the past. For this reason, delay may be fatal to any attempt to impose discipline.[11]

PROGRESSIVE DISCIPLINE AND THE MODERN WORKPLACE

Progressive discipline was developed for use in industrial workplaces where coordination of a large workforce required employees to obey all directions and orders without questioning them. In this environment, management style tended to be top down, using a chain of command, where employees were expected to follow orders, much like in the military. Employees were not expected to think critically, but simply follow orders to the letter. Any infraction could lead to dismissal.

Although progressive discipline was an improvement over dismissal for any infraction, some argue progressive discipline is no longer appropriate in modern workplaces. As the unionized workforce shifts from the industrial workplace to service and public sector workplaces, employees are often expected to exercise their judgment and act independently. This is particularly so for unionized professionals or highly skilled workers such as teachers or engineers, or for workplaces that have encouraged worker participation in decision making and that operate along more democratic and collaborative lines. In these cases, progressive discipline may no longer be appropriate.[12] Not every discretionary decision by an employee can objectively be determined to be misconduct, even when the results of the decision

---

11 See 57 LAC 4e 343, per Keller, and 2002 OLAA no. 165, per P. Picher.

12 G. Eden, "Progressive Discipline: An Oxymoron" (1992), vol. 47, no. 3 *Relationes Industrielles* 524. See also Craig and Solomon, *supra* note 9, at 338.

are negative. Professional judgments are often subjective applications of knowledge and experience. There may be a range of possible competent decisions that can produce results that the employer is not happy with. Nevertheless, there is little sign of progressive discipline being abandoned by arbitrators.

DISCRETIONARY VERSUS AUTOMATIC DISCIPLINE

So far we have described a disciplinary system where management assesses the nature of the infraction and its seriousness, and then chooses a penalty and imposes it. In some collective agreements, particularly in industrial workplaces, there may be a system where infractions are described with fixed penalties that are automatically imposed. Although this system is rigid, and may ignore what might otherwise be extenuating circumstances, it has the benefit of clarity. In theory, a worker will know what conduct constitutes a workplace offence, and what the penalty will be. In practice, it may not be that simple. Some conduct may not easily slot into an offence category, and in some cases an automatic penalty will be overly severe or lenient in the particular circumstances. But at least management's response will be both predictable and consistent. This approach, because of its rigidity, is increasingly out of favour in most workplaces, particularly where workers are expected to exercise discretion and judgment in the course of employment.

DISCIPLINE OR DISABILITY?

In some cases, what at first appears to be willful employee misconduct may actually be a manifestation of an illness or disability. For example, an employee who is an alcoholic with alcohol consumption under control may be subjected to unusual stress. This stress may touch off an alcoholic binge, resulting in the employee being intoxicated while at work. On its face this is misconduct of a serious nature, and worthy of discipline. But if excessive alcohol consumption is a symptom of an underlying mental or physical illness, should the worker be considered as having a health-related disability instead of being considered insubordinate or ungovernable? If the employee has a disability, the appropriate response might be for the employer to take steps to accommodate the employee's disability. This does not mean the employer has to permit the employee to be intoxicated while at work, but it may require the employer to provide or pay for counselling, sick leave, or other treatment rather than simply impose progressive discipline or, indeed, any discipline.

Whether inappropriate employee conduct will be seen as willful or the result of a disability depends on how the conduct and its cause are categorized by the arbitrator. This in turn may depend on how the employee has dealt with the problem. If an employee has sought medical assistance or counselling, it is easier to argue the case for a disability than if the employee had not sought help. Arbitrators are also fairly conservative about characterizing a pattern of conduct as a disability. For example, an employee who argued that his misconduct on the job was caused by an Internet addiction had his argument rejected. Although there was some support for the concept of addiction to the Internet among psychologists, the idea was novel, and had not specifically been accepted as a disability by most medical practitioners and psychiatrists.[13] There may also be a suspicion that some employees will use the idea of a disability as a smokescreen for willful misconduct.

UP CLOSE

Some Examples of Discharge and Discipline Grievances

Case 1: Abusive Language to a Supervisor

The grievor, a shipper-receiver with a disciplinary history of suspension for absenteeism, told the supervisor to "fuck off." He received a one-week suspension. The arbitrator ruled that the grievor was a good employee and was provoked by the supervisor, who started the confrontation. Although the grievor had an attendance problem at one time, he had long ago corrected it, so the previous disciplinary history was deemed irrelevant. The arbitrator revoked the suspension and awarded compensation to the employee.[14]

Case 2: Absence Without Leave

The grievor, a rock breaker with a mining company, had four years' seniority, and had previously been disciplined for absenteeism. The last time he was admonished, he had been warned that if there were further absences in the next 90 days, he would be dismissed. The grievor was absent, and was dismissed. The grievor's absenteeism stemmed from a severe domestic situation requiring travel from Elliot Lake to Quebec City. The grievor had asked for and been denied leave. The company ignored the grievor's domestic problems, and the absenteeism policy based on prescribed escalating penalties was judged to be too mechanical. A more understanding approach was required, along with warnings on absenteeism. Reinstatement was ordered, but only with partial compensation, because the grievor was considered to be partly responsible.[15]

Case 3: Loyalty to the Employer—Conflict of Interest

The grievor, a professional in the federal public service with 10 years' seniority, was discharged. Management had discovered his work phone number listed in an ad for a government liaison business run by his sister. He argued that he had provided his sister with information already in the public domain and that the inclusion of his phone number was an unintended printing error. The arbitrator found that the grievor's efforts to aid his sister did not violate conflict of interest guidelines. However, because the grievor failed to disclose his activity promptly when initially confronted by management, he was not blameless. He was reinstated but only with partial compensation.[16]

---

13 *OPSEU and Seneca College*, [2002] OLAA no. 415, per Carter.

14 Karshinsky and Sack, supra note 8, at 78; *Confederation Freezers*, LAN April 1983.

15 Ibid., at 27; *Denison Mines* 9 LAC (3d) 97.

16 Ibid., at 122; *Treasury Board, re: Sarin*, Public Service Employment Law, June 1987.

> ### Case 4: Work Performance
>
> The grievor, a firefighter with 13 years' seniority and a clear disciplinary record, was given a one-day suspension for driving a fire truck into the side of the fire hall while responding to an alarm. The arbitrator found that the grievor was careless, but that others had made similar mistakes without attracting this severe a penalty. Given the grievor's seniority and clear record, the arbitrator felt that the conduct was not wanton or reckless and that a note on the grievor's personnel file would be a sufficient penalty.[17]

ARBITRATION

When the union and the employer have not settled a contract dispute in the workplace at any of the various steps in the grievance process, the union may refer the grievance to arbitration. Arbitration is a dispute-settlement process used to settle grievance disputes that the parties have been unable to resolve themselves through the in-house grievance process. It is a form of alternative dispute resolution (ADR) that provides the parties, at least in theory, with a relatively inexpensive and speedy way to settle disputes without destroying the ongoing relationships among the employees, their union, and the employer.

In Canada, arbitration is the sole means of resolving contract disputes, and has been since the middle of the 20th century. Prior to that time, the parties could resort to the courts and sue for contract remedies. Some provinces (Ontario, for example) experimented with specialized labour courts in the 1940s but these were not particularly successful. Judges often did not understand the labour relations context in which the parties were operating, and unions argued that the courts were inherently biased against them. Today, federal and provincial labour relations statutes make an arbitration clause mandatory in all collective agreements, though the form that the arbitration process takes varies considerably from one collective agreement to another.

UP CLOSE

The Mandatory Arbitration Clause in the Ontario *Labour Relations Act, 1995*

48(1) Every collective agreement shall provide for the final and binding settlement by arbitration, without stoppage of work, of all differences between the parties arising from the interpretation, application, administration or alleged violation of the agreement, including any question as to whether a matter is arbitrable.

---

17 Ibid., at 222; *City of Scarborough*, Firefighters Employment Law, September 1986.

Same

(2) If a collective agreement does not contain a provision that is mentioned in subsection (1), it shall be deemed to contain a provision to the following effect:

> Where a difference arises between the parties relating to the interpretation, application or administration of this agreement, including any question as to whether a matter is arbitrable, or where an allegation is made that this agreement has been violated, either of the parties may after exhausting any grievance procedure established by this agreement, notify the other party in writing of its desire to submit the difference or allegation to arbitration and the notice shall contain the name of the first party's appointee to an arbitration board. The recipient of the notice shall within five days inform the other party of the name of its appointee to the arbitration board. The two appointees so selected shall, within five days of the appointment of the second of them, appoint a third person who shall be the chair. If the recipient of the notice fails to appoint an arbitrator, or if the two appointees fail to agree upon a chair within the time limited, the appointment shall be made by the Minister of Labour for Ontario upon the request of either party. The arbitration board shall hear and determine the difference or allegation and shall issue a decision and the decision is final and binding upon the parties and upon any employee or employer affected by it. The decision of a majority is the decision of the arbitration board, but if there is no majority the decision of the chair governs.

PRINCIPAL FEATURES OF THE ARBITRATION PROCESS IN CANADA

Under provincial and federal labour legislation, all arbitration procedures share the following characteristics:

- Arbitration usually follows attempts to settle disputes using in-house grievance settlement procedures.

- The arbitration decision is made by a sole arbitrator or by a board of arbitration, made up of a neutral chair and an equal number of union and management nominees.

- There is a procedure set out in the contract and, if not there, in labour relations legislation for choosing a neutral arbitrator.

- The arbitration decision is final and binding. There is no right of appeal to the courts except where the arbitrator has made a serious legal error. Even then, the court will only identify the error, then send the matter back to the arbitrator to exercise his or her jurisdiction properly. The court will not usually substitute its own decision on the merits of the dispute for that of the arbitrator.

- Arbitrators have sole and exclusive jurisdiction over all disputes arising under the collective agreement.

- Arbitrators have sole and exclusive jurisdiction over whether any dispute is arbitrable.

- Neither party may resort to work stoppages as an alternative to submitting disputes to binding arbitration.

Employer and Union Views of the Arbitration Process

Although both unions and employers have reached consensus on acceptance of the arbitration process, their views on the costs and benefits may differ.

UNIONS

Traditionally, unions have been reluctant to let outsiders settle their disputes. They have seen the threat to strike as a much more effective way of enforcing contract rights.[18] This view may stem from the rough ride unions had in the legal system, where initially they were seen as criminal conspiracies in restraint of trade, and where their activities were outlawed. Later, even when unions had been legitimized by legislation, unions did not place much faith in upper-middle-class professional judges and arbitrators. Today, most labour unions accept arbitration as part of the labour scene. In fact, in some situations unions see a benefit in having an issue heard by an outsider, even when the grievor loses, because management must appear in a neutral forum and justify what it has done. Few management witnesses in a court-like proceeding look forward to this experience.

But a union may have other concerns about the arbitration process. Unions are not always comfortable with the so-called neutral arbitrators, claiming that some simply do not understand the context of labour relations or the unionized work-place; and they see other arbitrators as less than neutral.[19]

Another issue concerns cost and delay. Arbitration as a form of alternative dispute resolution is often touted as being cheaper and quicker than a court proceeding. This is not necessarily the case; labour arbitration boards tend to be more formal and court-like than some administrative tribunals, which can make proceedings as slow as or slower than court proceedings. The length of the process and the use of lawyers, which is common at arbitration, also drive the costs up. If an arbitration takes more than one day, scheduling subsequent dates, where the members of an arbitration panel, counsel, and witnesses all have to be available at the same time, can be difficult. Thus, a grievance may have just a few days of

---

18 F. Kehoe and M. Archer, *Canadian Industrial Relations*, 10th ed. (Oakville, ON: Century Labour Publications, 2002), 169-70. This is the traditional view, dating back to the early 20th century, but it may be not reflect current realities. See also Craig and Solomon, supra note 9, at 338-39. A more complex view is presented here, which may better reflect the realities of labour relations at the beginning of the 21st century.

19 The Ontario Federation of Labour prepared a wall chart of arbitrators in Ontario indicating whether an individual arbitrator was pro- or anti-labour on various types of dispute. The chart may or may not have been accurate, but it demonstrates that labour assumed that some arbitrators were more receptive to the union's arguments than others.

hearings yet take months or years to complete,[20] with legal expenses for each party running between $50,000 and $100,000. Whatever benefits the process has, speed and economy are not among them.

MANAGEMENT

Prior to the establishment of a collective agreement, an employer has a great deal of freedom in managing its business and its employees. As noted earlier, an employee with a dispute can either accept management's position on the issue or resign. Management has often initially viewed the insertion of grievance rights into the process through a collective agreement as an interference with its authority to run a business. Similarly, it has resented the introduction of an arbitration process, where management can be told what to do in the management of employees. Nor do managers enjoy the process of giving evidence to justify their actions, or being cross-examined by the union's counsel. However, many employers whose authority is challenged by a grievance are quite happy with the considerable delays in the arbitration process, although some recognize that the prolonging of a workplace irritant may not be good for employee morale or make for a happy workplace.

The Evolution of the Arbitration Process

Arbitration as a process has evolved considerably since the mid-20th century. Initially, arbitrators came from various professions. Today, most arbitrators are lawyers, including law professors, who have a background in alternative dispute resolution. Many have also taken courses leading to certificates in labour relations arbitration, some offered by or through labour relations boards themselves. There is still a demand for more arbitrators with the relevant training and experience.

Beyond training and experience, employers and unions have sought to make arbitrators more representative of Canada's diverse population. Where unions and employers agree on the use of a pool or list of arbitrators, or **permanent umpires**, they may also agree to include arbitrators from designated groups such as women, aboriginal people, and visible minorities.

Today, the arbitration process is seen simply as the legal adjudication of disputes. Initially, however, it was seen by some practitioners as a clinical process, where the arbitrator attempted to delve into the dispute to try to deal with the underlying cause. The assumption was that workplace harmony could then be restored. In Canada and the United States today, the adjudicative model generally prevails. This means that the arbitrator defines a labour dispute as a legal dispute. The arbitrator interprets the language used in the collective agreement in accordance with conventional rules of interpretation of contract terms and looks at grammatical and syntactical rules to find the meaning of a contract term. The more adventurous and intellectually creative arbitrators will try to determine what the parties meant to do by considering the contract term in the context of the realities of the workplace, as revealed by the evidence.

---

20 One dismissal case had 12 days of hearings. From the date the grievance was filed, two and a half years passed before a decision was handed down.

Interest and Rights Disputes

Interest disputes are those that arise during the negotiation of a collective agreement. If the parties cannot agree on a provision, they may agree to submit that specific provision to binding arbitration and, having settled the issue in that way, move on with negotiations. Alternatively, they may agree to put the entire collective agreement to binding arbitration. In this situation, each party tries to persuade the arbitrator that its view of the matter is preferable.

Agreement to arbitration during negotiation is rare in Canada. Both unions and management generally prefer to fashion their own agreements and keep control of the process without more outside interference. Further, unions take the view that a workforce that could strike but asks for binding arbitration instead lacks the toughness and resolution required to get a good contract. Many feel that arbitrators share this perception and will have little respect for the arguments of the bargaining unit, given that it refused to use the strike remedy available to it.

Usually when interest arbitration does occur in Canada, it is because the legislature has imposed binding arbitration during a strike, usually in the public sector. Essential public sector workers may also be subjected to binding arbitration by a statute that denies them the right to strike. Police officers, ambulance workers, and firefighters, for example, will be compelled to use binding arbitration if their negotiations reach an impasse. In these cases, arbitrators know that the workers cannot strike, and they treat the union position with more respect than they would a union that asks for arbitration when it could strike. Indeed, in a number of settlements imposed under mandatory arbitration in the public sector, arbitrators have given generous awards. Some governments have responded by limiting the discretion of arbitrators and confining monetary awards to what is within set fiscal guidelines.

Interest arbitration can take several forms:

- The arbitrator may listen to the parties, and come up with his or her own position on each issue. This is the usual approach to interest arbitration.

- In final-offer selection, also called total-package selection, each side sets out its final offer, and the arbitrator selects one or the other, without changes or amendment.

- In final item-by-item selection, for each issue being negotiated, the arbitrator may select either management's or the union's proposal. At the end, the collective agreement may consist of both management and union positions.

Most unions and most employers dislike the all-or-nothing approach involved in final-offer or final item-by-item selection. Because these methods do not result in situations where the arbitrator takes a middle ground, the parties often feel they have had little impact. There are those, however, who argue that the gamble involved in these types of arbitration tempers the more outrageous or extreme positions that the parties might take. By being reasonable, each party will increase the likelihood that the arbitrator will choose its position.

Jurisdiction: The Issue of Arbitrability

Arbitrators determine not only the issue in dispute, but also whether they have the authority to hear it in the first place—that is, whether it is **arbitrable**. Note that even if management thinks a grievance is inarbitrable, it cannot prevent the matter from proceeding through the in-house process to arbitration. For example, consider the situation where a grievor grieves that a manager's decision is wrong. The employer argues that the matter is inarbitrable at all stages of the grievance and at arbitration. Management will say that because there is no provision in the collective agreement that requires a manager's decision to be right, no contract term has been broken, and there is no dispute about the contract for the arbitrator to resolve. Consequently, because managers otherwise have the power to manage the business, they may do so, and do so badly, without interference by the arbitrator. Usually the employer will raise arbitrability as a preliminary objection, and ask to have the issue determined first, without the parties presenting the case on the merits. If the arbitrator rules that the issue is inarbitrable because it is not covered by the collective agreement, then the grievance is dismissed without being heard on its merits. If the arbitrator states that the grievance is properly the subject of arbitration, then the case can begin. This should be distinguished from situations where the arbitrator finds that the matter is arbitrable but also finds on the facts that there has been no violation of the collective agreement. The key here is that whatever the nature of the complaint, it has to be based on the violation of a provision of the collective agreement, or be an issue in respect of the interpretation or administration of the agreement to be arbitrable. If the matter falls entirely outside the agreement, then the arbitrator has no jurisdiction to hear the matter.

Structure of the Arbitration Process

There are a number of different ways in which to structure the arbitration process. The most common way is to use a tripartite board. An alternative is to use a single arbitrator. This second approach addresses the concern of reducing cost and delay while ensuring that the procedure is fair.

TRIPARTITE BOARDS

The most common form of arbitration uses three-person boards of arbitration. In fact, many collective agreements and labour relations statutes require that this form be used. Section 48(2) of the OLRA states that a board must consist of an impartial chair, a union nominee, and a management nominee. The impartial chair is usually a lawyer or law professor with training as an arbitrator or with other ADR training. The management nominee, or management **sidesperson**, is often a lawyer or HR professional or consultant who reflects the management point of view. The labour sidesperson is often a lawyer or labour union consultant or a union officer from another union who reflects the worker viewpoint.

The parties will aim their presentation primarily at the neutral chair, because this is the person who needs to be persuaded. Usually the parties can assume that their own nominee will accept their argument without much persuasion. But it is the decision, ultimately, of the neutral chair that will prevail. Occasionally a decision will be unanimous, but usually if the decision favours one party, that party's nominee will endorse and agree with the chair's decision and the other party's nominee will file a dissent.

The decision-making process of a tripartite board is often a process of negotiation. The chair consults each nominee or circulates his or her view to the nominees for feedback. Some note that this consultative process often results in the arbitrator coming down in the middle, giving something to each side where possible. Arbitrators who try to build a consensus to obtain a unanimous decision may reinforce this type of result.

The negotiation process can also be used to mediate a grievance that has been referred to arbitration, which allows a compromise to be reached by negotiation. Here the chair can act as a mediator, and the labour and management representatives can shuttle back and forth between the parties, attempting to hammer out a deal. In this case, instead of the arbitrator giving his or her decision, the parties will sign a settlement agreement. Usually the arbitrator has only the power to make further orders to carry out the terms of this agreement.

There are disadvantages to this type of arbitration. First, it takes longer to choose and assemble a tripartite board than it does to appoint a single arbitrator. Second, because of the consultation process involved in decision making, it takes longer to get a decision, because the nominees each argue for and push for their side's view. Third, the whole process takes longer to complete because finding open dates where all three members are available is more difficult than if it were only the chair who needed to be available. Where the arbitration takes more than one day, the problem is compounded when open dates for subsequent days of hearing have to be booked.

SINGLE ARBITRATORS

In the interest of speeding up the arbitration process, some collective agreements permit the use of single arbitrators or permanent umpires. In this case, the arbitrator may be agreed upon as a permanent umpire during the life of the collective agreement, or be selected from a list of arbitrators appointed by agreement between the parties. Single arbitrators sit alone to hear arbitrations, which provides several advantages. They usually can be scheduled quickly, and hear a case more quickly than a tripartite board could. They also should be able to come to a decision more quickly because they do not have to consult or negotiate with sidespersons. The process should also be less expensive: there is no need to pay the fees of the two sidespersons.

Choosing an Arbitrator

Once a grievance has been referred to arbitration by the union, the collective agreement should set out a procedure for choosing an arbitrator. If it does not, the parties must follow the procedure set out in the relevant labour relations statute. In Ontario, s. 48(2) of the OLRA lays out the following procedure. Where it is a tripartite board, each party has to choose a sidesperson within a given period of time. The sidespersons then negotiate and agree on a neutral chair. In some agreements, the neutral chair may be a permanent umpire or come from a list of neutral chairs that the parties agreed to when the collective agreement was negotiated. In the case of a list, the chair will be chosen from it by lot, by availability, or in sequence.

Arbitration Procedure

The location for the arbitration is a hotel conference room or, in larger centres, hearing rooms in offices specifically set up for the purpose of hearing arbitrations. The arbitrator usually books the rooms. The fee is paid by the arbitrator and passed through to the parties in the arbitrator's fee.

The room is usually set up with the tables in a "U." The chair sits in the centre at the bottom of the "U," and the sidespersons on either side of him or her. The parties occupy each side of the "U." On the union side, counsel is close to the board, with the grievor next to him or her followed by the chief steward or other union officer. On the management side, next to counsel sits the senior HR manager, and the supervisor of the grievor.

Counsel are often lawyers, but management may use specialized labour relations employees with advocacy skills, or labour relations consultants. Unions, too, may use lawyers or labour consultants, their own grievance officers, or the union business agent. The proceeding is somewhat formal and structured, and generally follows the format of legal proceedings in a court, although the atmosphere is more informal and the rules of evidence somewhat more relaxed.

The grievor, usually the union on behalf of an individual, begins first. The union in this case has the **burden of proof**, usually on the **balance of probabilities**. It must show that it has a case that entitles it to a decision in favour of the grievor. If the union demonstrates through the presentation of its evidence, through witnesses, and through relevant documents that its version of events is more probable than not, the burden of proof shifts. Now, the employer has the task of rebutting the union's case by presenting its evidence, and showing that its version of events is more probable than not.

However, if the grievance involves unjust discipline, there is a reverse onus, and management must present its evidence first. In this case, the burden of proof is on management to show that discipline was justified. If management shows that it has a case, the burden shifts to the union to show that discipline was unjustified.

A hearing begins usually with the union filing a copy of the grievance, and providing a copy of the collective agreement. The parties usually provide each other with copies of relevant documents that they intend to rely on as part of their case at hearing, but the exchange of documents is usually done before the hearing. Either party may ask for specific and relevant documents in the possession of the other. If one side refuses to produce the documents, then the arbitrator may be asked to order that the documents be shown, or copies provided. Often, if there are many documents, the parties will put copies of them in binders and exchange sets of documents with each other.

Once these preliminaries are disposed of, union's counsel will give an overview of the case, summarizing the facts in a fairly neutral way. Counsel will then call the first witness, and conduct an **examination in chief** of that witness. Afterward, opposing counsel will conduct a **cross-examination** of that witness to try to counter the witness's testimony in his or her examination in chief. The same process will be repeated with the union's other witnesses.

Counsel for the employer will then open his or her case, summarizing what the employer's case is about, and proceed to call witnesses. These witnesses will be examined in chief by the employer's counsel and then cross-examined by union's counsel. When both sides have presented all the evidence, the union, followed by management, will give closing arguments. In the process, each may rely on and cite previous arbitration awards to support their views.

While witnesses are giving evidence, the arbitration board members will be taking notes of the evidence given. There is no court reporter taking down verbatim evidence, as is done in courts. Consequently, witnesses are often asked to go slowly, no faster, in fact, than the board members can write down the evidence. The formal rules of evidence used in court proceedings are generally followed in arbitration hearings, although they may be somewhat relaxed. Arbitrators will often accept **hearsay** evidence, which a court will not accept, although the evidence may not be given much weight or credibility.

At this point, the hearing is complete. Now the arbitrator must weigh the evidence of witnesses, consider the documents, and make findings of fact and interpret them in light of the relevant provisions of the collective agreement. However, in interpreting the contract, arbitrators may be persuaded by earlier decisions by other arbitration boards that dealt with similar cases. These **precedent cases** may be persuasive, particularly if they are decisions of well-respected labour arbitrators. Note, though, that no arbitration board is bound to follow a precedent in the way a lower court is expected to be bound by decisions of higher ones.

The labour and management sidespersons, in discussions with the chair, will try to persuade the chair to take their side's view of the matter and decide in favour of their side. When the chair has decided, he or she will hand down written reasons for the decision. The sidesperson who disagrees may write a dissenting opinion. Once the decision is made and communicated to the parties, it is final and binding, and not generally subject to appeal. Nor can the issues decided be litigated again before another board or court. The decision will then be reported through a number of published labour law reports, including online reporting services, so that other arbitrators may refer to it, and cite it as a precedent in their cases.

Underlying these procedures is the requirement that proceedings be fair. This requirement is sometimes referred to as the requirement of **natural justice** or procedural fairness. At a minimum, parties should have proper and timely notice of the date of hearing, and the right to attend, give evidence, cross-examine, and make submissions to the board. The failure of an arbitration board to meet these minimum standards of procedural fairness can result in a board's decision being overturned by a court.

Expedited Arbitration Procedure: Dealing with Delay

It has long been apparent that whatever the original intention, arbitration is slow and costly. This is of concern to both parties, who do not want to have labour disputes continuing to simmer and fester. It is of particular concern to the party that brings a grievance to arbitration. The person seeking a decision is usually interested in quick resolution. The other side against whom a decision is sought will often welcome delay. For example, if a grievor has been dismissed, he or she is likely to want to be quickly reinstalled rather than go months or years without an income. Because the party initiating an arbitration is usually the union, it is the union that is most interested in a speedy hearing process.

In some cases, the parties have sought to tackle the issue of delay by using a single arbitrator instead of a tripartite board, and by using an **expedited** process. The expedited process speeds things up by simplifying the process, reducing the use of oral argument and presentation in favour of written submissions, and imposing a timetable for completing each step. In an expedited arbitration procedure, the parties will agree to some or all of the following procedures and conditions:

- provision for notice that expedited arbitration has been selected in lieu of the regular procedure;

- use of a single arbitrator rather than a board;

- use of a permanent umpire or random selection from a list to be chosen within a specified time;

- determination of the number of hearing days required, or alternatively the scheduling of more than one day—the right to refuse days offered is to be limited;

- hearing to be completed within a specified time frame;

- notice of preliminary objections on arbitrability to be given at an early specified date; arguments to be made in writing prior to first hearing date;

- full disclosure of all relevant documents by each side to the other by a set date and prior to commencement of the hearing; and

- arbitrator to render a decision within a specified time frame.

Enforcement of Arbitration Awards

When an arbitrator has made a decision, the union and the employer usually obey the order. If the order requires the parties to take some further steps, such as calculating arrears of salary, the arbitrator will usually state that he or she "remains seized." This means that, although the arbitrator has decided the issue, he or she has retained jurisdiction to make further supplementary orders to implement the main decision. Otherwise, once that arbitrator has made a decision, he or she has no power to make further decisions on the issue before the board.

If the arbitrator has given a decision, what happens if one party or the other refuses to carry the order out? In this case, the order may be enforced as if it were a court order. This means that a court may specifically order a party to do something required by the arbitrator, and assess damages or make a contempt order for continued non-compliance with the arbitrator's original order. In order to initiate this process, the winning party will file the arbitration award at the office of the court.

Usually an order takes effect from the time it is made. However, many arbitrators take weeks if not months to render a written decision, often because they include detailed reasons for their decisions. This may mean a long wait, which can be difficult for a successful grievor who had been dismissed, and has no income. However, the arbitrator may award back salary to the date of dismissal, and also award interest on that amount.

In some circumstances, a party may refuse to carry out the order because the party believes that the order was illegal or so flawed that it should be set aside. In this case, the party must apply to the court for **judicial review** and ask the review court to **quash** the award.[21] The reviewing court is somewhat restricted in exercising this power. First, labour relations legislation often contains a **privative clause** that is intended to prevent the court from interfering with or judicially reviewing the decision of an administrative board. Notwithstanding this barrier to judicial review, courts have generally found ways to review the decision of a tribunal, such as an arbitration board, and will do so if it finds any of the following:

- The board's process was seriously unfair to one or the other of the parties, and denied a party natural justice. For example, a party may not have been permitted to fully present its case, or answer the case against it.

- The arbitrator exceeded his or her jurisdiction by deciding something that he or she had no right or power to decide, or failed to decide something that he or she should have decided. This might happen if the arbitrator fails to answer the question before the board, answers a question not before the board, or alters or amends the collective agreement.

- There was obvious bias by the arbitrator or fraud in the process.

- The arbitrator made an obvious error resulting in a misapplication of some rule or principle of law. However, the fact that the reviewing court does not agree with the outcome of the case is not in itself a ground to quash an award. This is particularly true when it comes to assessing the credibility of witnesses. A reviewing court does not hear or see the witnesses, so the members of the court cannot meaningfully substitute their judgment for that of the arbitration board, which observed the witnesses firsthand.

Note that if a court does quash an award, it does not substitute its decision for that of the board. Instead, it identifies the error and sends the case back to the arbitrator with directions to consider the matter properly.

Costs of Arbitration

The parties to the arbitration share the arbitrator's fee. The parties are charged for each day of hearing, for the writing of the decision, for the arbitrator's accommodation and travel expenses, and for the cost of the hearing room. Each side also pays the fees of its nominee, and pays for legal counsel if legal counsel was used. Unlike in civil court proceedings, the loser is not obliged to pay any part of the winner's costs.

---

21 The court procedure is quite different from an appeal of a court decision. See, for example, the *Judicial Review Procedure Act*, RSO 1990, c. J.1, as amended.

Arbitration and Charter of Rights Issues

The *Charter of Rights and Freedoms* was designed to protect individuals from legislative and administrative acts of governments at all levels. But the Charter does not protect individuals from the effects and actions of other private persons. So where does the arbitration process fit? At first glance, arbitrators are deciding a dispute between two parties to a private contract: a union and an employer. Even if the employer is a government, it can be argued that if a government institution is acting in the capacity of a private person—as a party to a private contract about employment—then the activity is not really "governmental," so the Charter would not apply.

But some argue that the Charter may apply in certain circumstances. The Charter, they note, applies to the interpretation of general legislation. Labour relations legislation, which provides a framework for arbitration, is general legislation. Therefore, the arbitration process may be subject to the application of the Charter. If so, the decisions of arbitration boards to date could be challenged if they violated rights such as the right to free speech or freedom of association. It is also likely that arbitrators themselves would have the task of applying the Charter, at least in the first instance. As an area of law, this is still developing.[22]

DISPUTE RESOLUTION OPTIONS

Although labour relations legislation sets out mandatory arbitration provisions for collective agreements, the parties are free to fashion alternative approaches or variations that suit their needs. Thus, not all disputes will necessarily go before a board of arbitration. The following are examples.

Health and Safety

Health and safety legislation, such as the *Occupational Health and Safety Act* in Ontario, takes many disputes about safety in the workplace outside of the collective agreement and the arbitration process. Whether the workplace is unionized or not, the legislation assumes that there is an internal responsibility system where workers and the employer share responsibility for ensuring workplace safety. A joint health and safety committee is established for this purpose. Committee members are entitled to training, to carry out inspections, and to bring issues to the committee for resolution. If the matter cannot be resolved internally by the committee, then the union or its members may call in inspectors from the Ministry of Labour. The inspectors may investigate and decide the issue, and lay charges for violations of the Act. Workers also have the right to refuse unsafe work without reprisal, provided that the refusal is made in good faith.[23]

---

22 See D.C. Carter, "Grievance Arbitration and the Charter: The Emerging Issues" (1989), vol. 44, no. 2 *Relations Industrielles* 338; and Craig and Solomon, supra note 9, at 352-54.

23 See the *Occupational Health and Safety Act*, supra note 6. For a useful and practical commentary on the Act, see N. Keith, *A Practical Guide to Occupational Health and Safety Compliance in Ontario* (Aurora, ON: Aurora Professional Press, 1995); see also S. McArthur and A. Vereschagin, *Occupational Health and Safety* (Scarborough, ON: Carswell, 1996).

Workplace Injuries

When a worker is injured on the job, the injury does not usually become the subject of a grievance. Rather, it is treated as a no-fault accident, where the worker and the employer are obliged to report the injury to a legislatively mandated insurance board. In Ontario, the board is called the Workplace Safety and Insurance Board and it is governed under the *Workplace Safety and Insurance Act.* If the worker is off work temporarily or permanently, or is partly or fully disabled, or is killed, pensions and benefits will be paid by the board, not the employer. The right to grieve against an employer in this situation or to sue the employer is very restricted.[24]

Human Rights

All workplaces, provincial and federal, are subject to human rights codes. If an employer violates the applicable code by discriminating against an employee on the prohibited grounds set out in the code, the employee may file a complaint with the Human Rights Commission. Many collective agreements also have no-discrimination and no-harassment provisions, of which the following is an example:

> The parties agree that in accordance with the provisions of the Ontario *Human Rights Code*, there shall be no discrimination or harassment against any employee by the Union or the Employer, by reason of race, ancestry, place of origin, colour, ethnic origin, citizenship, creed, sex, sexual orientation, age, record of offences, marital status, family status or handicap.
>
> It is understood that nothing in this section limits the right of an employee to grieve in accordance with the procedure as set forth in the article governing grievance procedures.

The effect of a provision like this is that an employee has the option to grieve rather than file a human rights complaint with the commission. There are advantages to grieving. The union will carry the grievance during the internal stages and at arbitration, providing assistance and covering the costs. This gives the grievor more control over the process than he or she would obtain with most human rights commissions. Generally the grievance process is quicker than proceeding at the commission. If the grievor's complaint is against the union, however, the complaint could go to the commission or the labour relations board. If the complaint is against another employee, the complainant should raise the issue with the employer.

In a modern workplace, employers recognize the importance of ensuring that the workplace is free from discrimination and harassment, and the employer has a responsibility to take action to stop discriminatory or harassing conduct. If the employer does not, then an employee may grieve the discriminatory or harassing treatment by another employee indirectly, by grieving the employer's failure to correct the situation. Many large employers will have their own office to deal with discrimination and harassment. This may also provide a forum for the resolution of such complaints, particularly when one employee is harassing another.

---

24 See the *Workplace Safety and Insurance Act, 1997,* supra note 3. For a useful discussion of how the Act works, see B. Shell, K. Coon, and S. Rashid, *Understanding the Workplace Safety and Insurance Act* (Aurora, ON: Canada Law Book, 1999).

Union–Employer Committees

Sometimes issues and disputes arise that cannot be resolved through the grievance process. Many collective agreements provide for the creation of a committee composed of senior union and management members who meet regularly to consider and resolve workplace irritants.

CHAPTER SUMMARY

This chapter examined a number of issues regarding the administration and enforcement of the collective agreement. In order to talk about enforcement of the agreement, the legal significance of a collective agreement as an enforceable contract was examined. This was followed by a discussion of common terms and provisions of collective agreements with examples of typical clauses, including those provisions that are mandated by legislation. The chapter then turned to a detailed examination of the grievance procedure as the principal contract enforcement instrument, examining the pros and cons of the process for both labour and management. Key principles surrounding the right to file grievances, the role of the union to fairly represent members' interests in the process, and the use of grievances rather than strikes to settle contract disputes were discussed. Actual grievance procedures were then discussed and described in detail up to the referral to arbitration. Following this discussion, there was an examination of some commonly grieved rights issues: seniority and layoff, progression on a salary grid, and discharge and discipline. The chapter then turned to a detailed examination of arbitration as the main means of settling disputes that the parties to the contract could not resolve through the grievance process. Next examined were the principal features of the arbitration process, including the structure of arbitration boards, their selection by the parties, how the parties see and use arbitration, and how arbitration orders are enforced. The distinction between interest and rights arbitrations was then made. This was followed by an overview of how an arbitration case unfolds. Finally, the chapter noted some areas where workplace disputes are resolved outside the collective agreement and the arbitration process: health and safety, workplace injuries, human rights, and union–employer committees.

REVIEW QUESTIONS

1. Are the provisions of collective agreements a matter for only the union and management to decide and to enforce? Explain your answer.

2. Identify the issues that are likely to be contentious with respect to the following provisions in a collective agreement:

    a. definition of the bargaining unit

    b. union business

    c. salary

    d. seniority.

3. Can a worker grieve any issue that he or she disagrees with management on?

4. What are the advantages of the grievance procedure for employees? For employers?

5. Who can file grievances?

6. What does a union have to do to fairly represent a grievor on a grievance?

7. What are the basic steps in a typical grievance process?

8. What are the differences between the employer and the union in their approach to seniority clauses?

9. If there is a salary grid, what factors are likely to affect progression?

10. If an employer wishes to fire an employee for misconduct, what protections does the employee likely have under the collective agreement?

11. How are arbitrators usually chosen?

12. What are the principal features of the arbitration process in Canada?

13. What is the difference between interest and rights disputes?

14. How are arbitration orders enforced?

DISCUSSION QUESTIONS

1. "Progressive discipline is no longer appropriate for the modern workplace." Do you agree or disagree? Support your answer.

2. What are the principal problems with the arbitration process in Canada today?

CASE STUDIES

Case Study 1: Mandy Milde

You are the chief steward for a local of a service workers union. You have been asked to report to the business agent on whether or not to proceed to arbitration on a number of grievances arising in the following situation. Your union's practice is to allow any member of the bargaining unit to file a grievance without necessarily consulting the union beforehand, but the union determines whether or not a grievance is sent to arbitration.

Your local represents salespersons in a chain of trendy clothing stores that cater mainly to adolescents and young adults, both male and female. The employer has a policy for dealing with customer and employee complaints, including complaints about discrimination or harassment by employees on any of the prohibited grounds of race, ethnicity, country of origin, family status, age, sex, sexual orientation, or disability.

A male customer entered the store, and asked a sales associate, Mandy, for assistance in choosing a pair of trousers. Mandy was a senior employee and an effective seller. She was also known to have a sharp tongue, and could be critical and short with customers and other employees. In this case, the customer was obese, and appeared to be in his late forties or early fifties. Mandy knew that the man did not fit the usual customer profile and was not part of the market targeted by the employer. In fact, Mandy doubted that she would be able to find a pair of pants that would fit this customer, let alone look stylish or becoming, in her view. She suggested that they probably would not find anything in the right size, and that he might find more choice and clothing more to his liking at BigBoy Clothing, on the other side of the mall.

The customer was incensed by Mandy's response, demanded to see the manager, and claimed that he was being discriminated against on the basis of age and disability (being obese). He made quite a scene, which was noticed by other customers and other employees in the store at the time. The manager advised him of the store's policy on harassment and discrimination, and asked if he wanted to file a formal complaint. He indicated that he did, and filed the complaint.

At the end of Mandy's shift, the manager suspended her with pay while the company's equity officer carried out an investigation. This took a couple of weeks while the officer interviewed the complainant, other customers who witnessed the event, the manager, and other employees who were present.

Mandy, meanwhile, had obtained some grievance forms and fired off a grievance that she had been unjustly disciplined by being suspended with pay. She claimed that the equity officer violated her rights, because she was not allowed to be present and sit in on all of the interviews conducted by the equity officer. She felt that she had a right to hear what was said about her and to respond, and to protect her interests. She also said that she was humiliated by the process because other employees knew she had been suspended.

Note, at this point, the following facts. The equity policy allows an employee to ask for a review of a decision if the employee feels that the findings are unjust. The collective agreement has no specific provision dealing with the equity procedures. There is a broad management-rights provision that indicates that management rights must be exercised in a manner consistent with the provisions of the collective agreement.

When the equity officer reported, he found that there had been no discrimination by Mandy. He noted that Mandy was correct in noting that there was, in fact, nothing in the customer's size. He noted further that her suggestion to try BigBoy Clothing was, objectively speaking, helpful, and could not, on any rational basis, be considered intentionally hurtful or discriminatory. However, he also noted employees' comments that Mandy could be short and curt with others. He recommended that Mandy be sent, at company expense, and with pay, to a sensitivity seminar, as part of further professional development or training. The manager confirmed that the company has a policy that employees should have opportunities for further on-the-job training and professional development, and that many employees avail themselves willingly of these opportunities. On receipt of the report, the manager told Mandy that she should return to work, and assigned her a shift for the coming week. She also told her that the job training mentioned in the report would be scheduled in the near future.

Mandy did not see it that way. She launched another grievance saying that the compulsory course was disciplinary in nature, and was unjust because it was based on innuendo and gossip that the equity officer heard from other employees and the manager.

You have discovered that Mandy and the manager have a history of low-level conflict, and neither likes the other. But Mandy has a clean disciplinary record, and good annual performance reviews. Mandy thinks the manager was out to get her, both on the suspension and in ordering her to go to a training program.

Write a report advising the business agent as to whether either of these grievances should proceed to arbitration. In doing so, review relevant facts and discuss the pros and cons of arbitration in this case.

Case Study 2: Del Smith

You are the supervisor of Del Smith in a unionized plant that produces rare gases used in the making of computer chips. Del is a highly competent and experienced technician who is in charge of the machinery that mixes the elements that are used to produce the gases. Some of these gases are very toxic, and if released, could create problems. Recently, Del seems to be distracted and inattentive at times, as if he had something on his mind. Last week, he came in with what smelled like alcohol on his breath. You noticed, and suggested that he take a sick day.

You recall that five years ago he got into an argument with another employee. They agreed to "have it out" in the parking lot, where they were found battling each other with fists. The fight was broken up by a security guard, and reported to management. Both Del and the other employee received verbal reprimands. There were no further incidents of that type.

Yesterday, Del said that he had a problem that he wanted to discuss with you. You didn't ask what the problem was, but indicated you were too busy to discuss it, and forgot about it. Today, Del was mixing gases. In the middle of the process, without being noticed by anyone, including you, he walked away from the control panel. He then went outside the building, sat down on a bench, and stared into space. While he was outside, the unattended machine that he was operating malfunctioned, causing a small amount of toxic gas to escape into the environment. This set off the alarms, which quickly identified the problem and caused a plant shutdown and evacuation. There is company policy on negligence in the operation of this type of machinery. Because of the risk, the policy says that an employee who is negligent in this situation may be summarily dismissed. What steps should you take with Del, and in particular should the policy be applied? What are the ramifications of applying or not applying the policy?

CHAPTER 6

Federal Labour Relations

INTRODUCTION

The federal government has some authority over labour relations in Canada, although it is limited to areas directly regulated by the federal government in the constitution. The provinces exercise the general power over labour relations. The general framework for federal labour relations is the same as the provincial structure, although there are some differences in specific rules. This chapter will outline the role of the federal government in labour relations, outline how the courts determine the boundaries between federal and provincial responsibilities, and describe some of the major differences between the federal rules and provincial rules.

SCOPE OF FEDERAL REGULATION

Labour relations are not a subject listed in any article of the *Constitution Act, 1867* (formerly called the *British North America Act*).[1] This is not surprising, because when the Act was written, the legal system still treated unions as a criminal conspiracy in restraint of trade. Thus, the regulation of unions was limited to criminal sanctions, a matter clearly given to the federal government under the constitution. The subsequent decriminalization of unions led to a series of federal laws on trade unions. The government continued to enact these laws until 1925, when the Privy Council of the United Kingdom (at that time the highest level of appeals for Canadian cases) decided, in the case of *Toronto Electric Commissioners v. Snider*,[2] that labour relations were generally a matter of "property and civil rights" under the *Constitution Act, 1867*. The matter of property and civil rights falls under the jurisdiction of the provinces. It includes the regulation of the property rights of the employer and civil rights in the sense of contracts, including contracts of employment. Thus, provincial statutes such as the Ontario *Labour Relations Act, 1995* (OLRA), and provincial labour boards such as the Ontario Labour Relations Board (OLRB), now set the web of labour relations rules for the majority of the Canadian workforce and Canadian workplaces.

However, this transfer of responsibility to the provinces did not eliminate the role of the federal government. The courts in subsequent cases decided that if the

---

1   *Constitution Act, 1867*, 30 & 31 Vict., c. 3 (UK).

2   [1925] AC 396; [1925] DLR 5 (PC).

constitution gave the federal government the power to regulate a particular workplace, then the federal government would continue to regulate labour relations at that workplace. In fact, if the federal government had authority over a workplace, then provincial regulations over labour laws and employment standards would not apply to that workplace, even if they did not conflict with federal laws. Thus, for example, provincial minimum-wage laws did not apply to a federally regulated workplace even when there was no federal minimum-wage law.[3] Workplaces that are regulated by the federal government are immune to provincial labour and employment laws, based on the rationale that labour relations are a vital part of the workplace and thus should be regulated by the federal government.[4] This result is referred to as **interjurisdictional immunity**.

As noted, the decision of the Privy Council in *Toronto Electric Commissioners* did not entirely eliminate federal power over labour relations matters. Instead, the federal government was limited to regulating those activities that are specifically within the legislative power of the federal government under the *Constitution Act, 1867*. The federal government has regular control over labour relations over certain industries and activities and may assume special control over more workplaces in cases of emergencies.

The areas of the workforce that remain under the regular control of the federal government are,

- first, those areas specifically listed in the *Constitution Act, 1867* as being under the regulation of the federal government;

- second, activities that have been declared to be in the general interest of Canada; and

- finally, areas that have been determined to be a matter of national interest; the courts have interpreted the federal government's residual power to legislate for "peace, order and good government" as authority that gives the federal government power over matters of national interest.

It must be noted that if a federally regulated company acquires ownership of a provincially regulated undertaking, labour relations at the new subsidiary are not thereby brought under federal regulation. Consider the example of an interprovincial railway company that acquires and operates a hotel. The federal government will continue to govern labour relations for the railway operation, but it will not take over regulation of the hotel, which will continue to be governed by the province.[5]

Workplaces Specifically Listed in Section 91 of the Constitution Act, 1867

The workplaces, industries, and positions specifically described in the constitution as being under federal regulation include

---

3   *Commission du salaire minimum v. Bell Telephone Company*, [1966] SCR 767.

4   P. Hogg, *Constitutional Law of Canada* (Toronto: Carswell, 1999), 371.

5   *Canadian Pacific Railway Co. v. Attorney-General for British Columbia*, [1950] AC 122.

- the federal civil service;

- Canada Post;

- the Canadian military;

- banks;

- marine hospitals;

- the fishing industry, both sea coast and inland;

- federal penitentiaries;

- judges of the superior courts, federal courts, and Supreme Court of Canada;

- interprovincial and international transportation, including ships, railways, canals, buses, trucking lines, and ferries; and

- telegraphs and any other works and undertakings connecting the province with any other or others of the provinces or extending beyond the limits of the province; these include telephone companies because their lines cross provincial boundaries.

In some cases these workplaces are governed by general legislation on labour relations. In the case of federal civil servants, they are covered by specific legislation, and in some cases, notably the military, the workers are excluded from collective bargaining.

Workplaces Declared To Be for the General Advantage of Canada

The federal government's power in this area is created as an exemption to the general power to regulate activities in a province. Under s. 92(10) of the *Constitution Act, 1867*, a province has the power to regulate activities that are entirely within the province except where

> [s]uch Works ... are ... declared by the Parliament of Canada to be for the general Advantage of Canada or for the Advantage of Two or more of the Provinces.

Works declared by the federal government to be for the general advantage of Canada or two or more provinces are under regular federal control. They include canals, bridges, dams, tunnels, harbours, wharves, telegraphs, hotels, restaurants, oil refineries, factories, theatres, mines, mills, and telephones. There have been over 400 such declarations by the government of Canada.[6]

The impact of a declaration that a work is for the general advantage of Canada has a profound effect on the labour relations regime faced by employers in that workplace. For example, the declaration contained in the *Atomic Energy Act* of 1946 that nuclear power plants were works for the general advantage of Canada meant that labour relations at power plants were governed by the *Canada Labour Code*,[7] a piece of federal legislation. This declaration has a significant impact on an

---

6 Hogg, *supra* note 4, at 535.

7 RSC 1985, c. L-2.

employer such as Ontario Power Generation, formerly part of Ontario Hydro. Ontario Power Generation generates electric power for the province of Ontario using coal-fired power plants, hydroelectric plants, and nuclear power plants. Labour relations at the coal-fired and hydroelectric plants are governed by the provincial labour legislation and labour relations at the nuclear plants are governed under federal rules.[8]

Workplaces Found To Be in the National Interest

Some workplaces have been determined to be of national interest and thus are under regular federal control as a consequence of the federal government's residual power to legislate to ensure peace, order, and good government. These workplaces include[9]

- air transport; and

- telecommunications, including radio, television, and telephone (although there are arguments that federal jurisdiction in this area is now determined by federal responsibility for interprovincial undertakings).

Emergency Powers

Finally, in cases of emergencies, the federal government can use the emergency part of its power to assume control over labour relations generally and govern both provincially regulated and federally regulated workplaces. The federal government may exercise this power in times of war and other national emergencies. For example, the Supreme Court of Canada held that the existence of significant levels of inflation could constitute an emergency. Thus, the federal government could use its emergency powers to override the wage provisions in all collective agreements across Canada and impose wage freezes or limit wage increases.[10]

DETERMINATION OF FEDERAL VERSUS PROVINCIAL JURISDICTION

Determining whether a business should come under federal or provincial regulations requires careful consideration. Does a taxicab company that does virtually all of its business in Windsor, Ontario become an international transport company and thus the subject of federal regulation if it takes one fare a year or one fare a month over to Detroit? What about a construction company building an airport, or a building company doing renovation work at a nuclear plant, or a catering company supplying meals to an airline? Are these businesses under federal or provincial regulation?

---

8 *Ontario Hydro v. Ontario (Labour Relations Board)*, [1993] 3 SCR 327.

9 See Hogg, supra note 4; T. Opie and L. Bates, *Canadian Master Labour Guide* (Toronto: CCH Canada, 1999); A.W.R. Carrothers, E.E. Palmer, and W.B. Rayner, *Collective Bargaining Law in Canada*, 2nd ed. (Toronto: Butterworths, 1986).

10 *Re Anti-Inflation Act*, [1976] 2 SCR 373.

To decide which level of government sets the rules for the business, the courts and the labour boards will look at factors such as

- whether the activity is a vital, integral, intimately connected part of a federally regulated operation; and

- the degree of consistency and regularity of the activity.

The courts and the labour board will consider whether an activity that is subject to federal regulation is a vital or integral part of the business. If an activity is vital or integral to the operation of a business, then labour relations for that business will be governed by federal rules. For example, pilots are an integral part of aeronautics because air travel is impossible without pilots. So an airline company is subject to federal regulation. But planes can be flown without supplying on-board meals, so a catering company is not subject to federal regulation.

The courts and the labour boards will also look at whether the activity is regular and ongoing, in addition to whether it is an integral part of a business. For example, an airport must be constructed before its operation, but the construction is not an integral part of the ongoing operation of the airport. Construction may be a precondition for operation, but that does not bring the construction activity under the control of the federal government. The construction work is not a continuous or permanent part of the airport's operation. Thus, provincial labour laws apply to construction workers putting up a project such as a new runway or hangar.[11] In contrast, workers who do ongoing maintenance on the facility are likely to be found to be regulated under the *Canada Labour Code*. The Supreme Court described the working of this test in the following terms:

> In order to determine the nature of the operation, one must look at the normal or habitual activities of the business as those of "a going concern" without regard for exceptional or casual factors; otherwise the constitution could not be applied with any degree of continuity and regularity.[12]

In the case of a transport company, the degree of interprovincial transit and the importance of this activity to the company will determine whether it is under federal or provincial control. If the interprovincial or international travel is regular or shows an identifiable pattern that is consistent and without interruption, then the transport company is likely to be regulated by the federal government.

The issue of which set of rules applies, federal or provincial, usually arises at the end of a union organization drive. If the union concludes that it has a better chance of being certified under the federal rules and believes that there is an argument that the federal rules apply, then the union may file its certification application with the federal board. The employer may respond by arguing that the federal board lacks jurisdiction over the matter and that the union should be required to refile its application with the provincial board.

---

11 Opie and Bates, supra note 9, at 12.

12 *Montcalm Construction Inc. v. Minimum Wage Commission*, [1979] 1 SCR 754.

CANADA LABOUR CODE

The general statute governing labour regulations under the federal government's responsibility is the *Canada Labour Code*. The Code is comprehensive and covers more than just labour relations, although it does not cover labour relations with federal public service employees. It is divided into three parts.

Part I covers labour relations, including certification of unions, negotiations, and arbitration.

Part II deals with occupational health and safety, including workplace health and safety committees, investigations of complaints, and enforcement.

Part III is the equivalent of provincial employment standards legislation and it covers minimum wage, hours of work, equal pay for equal work, vacations, holidays, parental and maternity leave, prohibition of sexual harassment, payment of wages, remedies for unjust dismissal, job protection during absence due to work-related illness and injury, sick leave, severance pay, permitted deductions from wages, notice requirements for termination, bereavement leave, and special rules for mass or group termination of employees.

CANADA INDUSTRIAL RELATIONS BOARD

The *Canada Labour Code* sets up an administrative tribunal called the **Canada Industrial Relations Board (CIRB)** to administer the labour relations portion of the Code and some parts of the health and safety part of the Code. The CIRB has 11 full-time and 2 part-time members. The offices of the board are located in Ottawa. The CIRB operates in much the same fashion and with many of the same powers as the Ontario Labour Relations Board. The CIRB describes its responsibilities in the following terms:

> The Canada Industrial Relations Board (CIRB) is an independent, representational, quasi-judicial tribunal whose aim is to contribute to, and promote, an effective industrial relations environment in any work, undertaking or business that falls within the authority of the Parliament of Canada. In this regard, the Board interprets and applies the relevant parts of the *Canada Labour Code* in a manner that supports and promotes free collective bargaining and the constructive settlement of disputes. It does this through such activities as certifying trade unions, investigating complaints of unfair labour practice, issuing cease and desist orders in cases of unlawful strikes and lockouts, rendering decisions on jurisdictional issues, and dealing with complex situations arising from corporate mergers or sales of businesses.[13]

Applications for certification in private sector workplaces regulated by the federal government are made to the CIRB. Also, the CIRB will determine allegations of unfair labour practices, unlawful strike or lockouts, and failure to bargain in good faith.

---

13 Canada Industrial Relations Board, *Report on Plans and Priorities for 2003/2004*, available online at http://www.cirb-ccri.gc.ca/down/report_plans_and_priorities_2003_2004_e.htm.

CONTRAST WITH ONTARIO LAW

As noted, the general framework for federal labour relations is similar to the provincial framework but the details may vary. These variations are highlighted below with respect to certification, negotiations, contract administration, and remedies for breaches of legislation.

Certification

The general scheme for certification under the federal model is similar to that under the Ontario model and includes the following features:

- the basic principle of the workers' ability to form and join the trade union of their choice applies;
- the union signs up members in the workplace;
- the union applies to a labour board—in the federal case, to the CIRB;
- the application must be made during an open period;
- the applicant must be a trade union;
- managers and confidential employees are excluded;
- membership evidence is confidential;
- the labour board determines the appropriate bargaining unit;
- the labour board decides whether the union has sufficient support;
- if necessary, there is a certification vote and the labour board will administer this vote to ensure adequate times and locations;
- if the union has sufficient support, the board certifies the union;
- it is an unfair labour practice to coerce or threaten workers to keep them out of the union; and
- employer control of unions is prohibited.

There are also some significant differences in the federal rules. These differences are outlined below.

1. ***Automatic certification***. Under s. 28 of the *Canada Labour Code*, if the union can demonstrate that it has the support of over 50 percent of the bargaining unit, then the CIRB will certify the union without holding a vote. If the union has between 35 percent and 50 percent, then the CIRB will order a vote and, if a majority of those voting support the union, then the CIRB will certify the union as long as at least 35 percent of the eligible voters in fact voted.

2. *Membership evidence.* Evidence of membership must include both a signed union card and a payment of at least $5 to the union.[14]

---

14 Canada Industrial Relations Board Regulations, SOR/2001-520, s. 33(1)(b).

3. *Geographic scope of bargaining units.* Under s. 34 of the Code, the CIRB has the power to create bargaining applicable to individual workplaces such as an individual bank, or it can create nationwide bargaining units, as with Canada Post. Finally, it can create specific geographically based units, as in all the long-shoring operations in British Columbia.

Negotiations

The general scheme for negotiations under the federal model is similar to that under the Ontario model and includes the following features:

- the duty to provide notice to bargain;
- the duty to bargain in good faith;
- the availability of a conciliation process before a strike;
- the requirement to give notice of a strike; and
- the requirement to hold a secret-ballot strike vote.

There are, however, some significant differences in the federal rules. These differences are outlined below.

1. *Notice period.* Section 49 of the Code states that the notice period is four months before the expiry of the collective agreement.

2. *First-contract arbitration.* The minister requesting the CIRB to investigate a dispute initiates first-contract arbitration. Under s. 80 of the Code, the CIRB has broad discretion to direct first-contract arbitration any time it considers that action either advisable or necessary.

3. *Technological change.* An employer is required to give the union both notice of **technological change** and information on the impact of the change. If the parties are in negotiations, then the technological change becomes part of the negotiation process. If there is a collective agreement in place when the notice is given, then the union has the option of reopening the agreement to negotiate provisions to deal with the technological change. Section 51 of the Code defines technological change as

> (a) the introduction by an employer into their work, undertaking or business of equipment or material of a different nature or kind than that previously utilized by the employer in the operation of the work, undertaking or business; and

> (b) a change in the manner in which the employer carries on the work, undertaking or business that is directly related to the introduction of that equipment or material.

The employer is required to give the union information on the technological change, such as

a. the reason and purpose for the technological change;

b. a detailed description of the nature of the technological change;

c. the date on which the employer proposes to effect the technological change;

d. the approximate number of employees, type of employees, and the names of the employees likely to be affected by the technological change; and

e. the effect that the technological change is likely to have on the terms and conditions or security of employment of the employees affected.

4. *Conciliation.* Sections 71 to 79 of the Code state that if the parties notify the minister of labour of the existence of a dispute, the minister has the option of doing nothing and allowing the parties to head to a strike or lockout. Alternatively, the minister may appoint a conciliation officer, conciliation commissioner, or conciliation board to resolve the dispute. Essentially, the conciliation commissioner is a one-person conciliation board. Both the board and the commissioner will submit a report to the minister with recommendations on how the dispute could be resolved if conciliation is unsuccessful. The conciliation board is an alternative to a conciliation officer, not a follow-up as it is in the provincial sector.

5. *Cooling-off period.* Under s. 89 of the Code, a cooling-off period of 21 days must be allowed before a strike or lockout becomes legal.

6. ***Essential services.*** Under s. 87.4(1) of the Code, during a strike or lockout there is a requirement to "continue the supply of services, operation of facilities or production of goods to the extent necessary to prevent an immediate and serious danger to the safety or health of the public." If the parties cannot agree on which operations are covered by this requirement, the CIRB will make the determination. Also, there is specific provision in the Code to require striking or locked-out employees to handle grain shipments.

7. *Limit on replacement workers.* Under s. 94(2.1) of the Code, an employer can use replacement workers to keep business going during a strike, but the employer will be ordered to stop if the CIRB determines that the purpose of the use of replacement workers is to undermine the union.

8. *Reinstatement of employees.* Under s. 87.6 of the Code, the employer is required to reinstate striking workers in preference to any replacement worker at the end of a strike. There is no time limit on this right.

Contract Administration

The general scheme for administering a contract under the federal model is similar to that under the Ontario model and includes the following features:

- no strike or lockout is permitted during the term of an agreement;

- arbitration for dispute resolution is required;

- a minimum one-year term for collective agreements is required;

- closed shops are permitted;

- a duty of fair referral is imposed on the union; and

- the Rand Formula must be given at the union's request.

Remedies

There are some remedies available to the CIRB for breaches of the *Canada Labour Code* that are not available to the OLRB for breaches of the OLRA. Perhaps the most significant additional remedy possessed by the CIRB is **remedial certification**, the ability of the CIRB to certify a union that cannot demonstrate enough support for certification. To qualify for this remedy, the union must show that management has engaged in unfair labour practices and that these practices have made it impossible to determine the true wishes of the employees.

CHAPTER SUMMARY

The labour relations authority of the federal government is limited but it is not insignificant. The regulation of such important matters as air transportation, nuclear energy production, and interprovincial transport is in the hands of the federal government. The rules employed by the federal government in labour matters are similar to the provincial rules and they share a common historical source. However, there are some significant areas of difference. Examples of significant differences include the right of the federal board to award certification without a vote in cases where the union has demonstrated sufficient support for certification or where the union can demonstrate that a vote result was tainted by the unfair labour practices of the employer.

REVIEW QUESTIONS

1. List the areas of federal responsibility for labour relations.

2. What are the significant differences between the federal rules and the provincial rules in the areas of

    a. certification?

    b. negotiations?

3. In what circumstances can the CIRB award automatic certification?

4. What is the effect of a federally regulated employer's decision to make a technological change?

5. What is the role of the CIRB in federal labour relations?

DISCUSSION QUESTIONS

1. Which legislative document's set of rules strikes a more appropriate balance between management and labour unions: the Ontario *Labour Relations Act, 1995* or the *Canada Labour Code*?

2. "Federal workplaces in a province should not be immune to the general labour and employment law rules that apply in that province." Do you agree or disagree? Support your answer.

3. "Labour relations are of such importance to Canada that they should be exclusively a provincial responsibility." Do you agree or disagree? Support your answer.

CASE STUDY

The Acme Cab Company is located in Windsor, Ontario. In the past, it has limited the area it serves to the city of Windsor. Recently, it adopted a policy that its drivers will be able to take fares to three sites in Detroit: a baseball stadium, a hockey arena, and the Renaissance Center. So far this service has not been requested.

The Union of Taxi Drivers is engaged in organizing the drivers and dispatchers of Acme Cab. It has only been able to sign up 51 members out of a total of 100 members in the appropriate bargaining unit. It blames its lack of success on the fact that its chief organizer was fired soon after the start of the organizing drive. The union claims that he was fired because he was an organizer for the union. Management claims that he was fired solely because there were discrepancies in his reports on the fares collected on some shifts. The union has filed a certification application with the CIRB. Management argues that the application should have been filed with the OLRB and has challenged the jurisdiction of the CIRB in this case.

1. What are the arguments in support of each side's positions?

2. Why have the two sides selected different jurisdictions?

CHAPTER 7

Public Sector Bargaining

INTRODUCTION

Collective bargaining in the public sector was made legal at a later time than collective bargaining for private sector workers. The rationale behind refusing to grant **public servants** the right to collective bargain was that a collective agreement would usurp Parliament's sovereign right to determine public policy issues such as the spending of tax revenues. Eventually the government abandoned this justification for denying basic rights to government employees. However, the right to negotiate terms and conditions of employment was sometimes limited, and the right to strike was often withheld.

Public sector bargaining is unique because the government is not only the employer but also the body that sets the rules for its interactions with its employees' unions. Governments have not hesitated to change the rules of the game to suit their needs, justifying their actions with a reference to the greater public interest. Governments have provided the right to strike to some public sector workers but then have sometimes legislated these workers back to work. Governments use their power to limit wage settlements or in some cases roll back settlements that they had previously agreed to. Public sector unions oppose these initiatives at the bargaining table, through strike action, both legal and illegal, and by engaging in political action. Their tactics include protests, lobbying, and acting to encourage the election of a political party more committed to free public sector labour relations.[1]

FEDERAL PUBLIC SECTOR

The regulation of employment rules for employees of the federal government is under the jurisdiction of the federal government. The *Public Service Staff Relations Act* governs collective bargaining for the federal public service.[2] The administrative tribunal charged with regulations in this area is the Public Service Staff Relations Board.

---

1   G. Swimmer and M. Thompson, *Public Sector Collective Bargaining in Canada* (Kingston, ON: IRC Press, 1995).

2   RSC 1985, c. P-35.

PROVINCIAL PUBLIC SECTOR

The provincial public sector is considered under two headings: those employees that directly work for the province and those employees that work in the broader public sector. In the broader public sector, the direct employer is not the provincial government. However, these employers deliver services that have a high degree of public control and funding and they are often governed by specific collective bargaining legislation.

Ontario Public Service

The legislation governing the Ontario public service is the *Crown Employees Collective Bargaining Act, 1993* (CECBA).[3] A Crown employee is defined under the *Public Service Act*[4] as a person "employed in the service of the Crown" or a person employed by an agency designated in the regulations to the *Public Service Act*.[5]

The CECBA mandates province-wide bargaining for employees of the provincial government on some terms and conditions of employment. Bargaining on other terms and conditions of employment takes place in six sectoral groups. The result of bargaining under the CECBA is one master agreement covering all the employees in the Ontario public service and six separate sector agreements covering the employees in each sector. The six sectoral groups are as follows:[6]

- Administrative

- Corrections

- Institutional and Health

- Office Administration

- Operations and Maintenance

- Technical.

The province-wide master agreement covers all the sectors and includes provisions covering items such as

- grievances and arbitrations;

- prohibitions against discrimination;

- employment security and mobility, including posting of vacancies, seniority, layoff, and recall;

---

3   SO 1993, c. 38.

4   RSO 1990, c. P.47.

5   The agencies referenced in the regulations to the Act are as follows: Algonquin Forestry Authority, Liquor Control Board of Ontario, McMichael Canadian Art Collection, Metropolitan Toronto Convention Centre Corporation, Niagara Parks Commission, Ontario Housing Corporation, Ontario Public Service Pension Board, Ottawa Congress Centre, Science North, Greater Toronto Transit Authority, Workplace Safety and Insurance Appeals Tribunal, Workplace Safety and Insurance Board, and Ontario Realty Corporation. Colleges of applied arts and technology are included but collective bargaining for colleges is governed under the CECBA.

6   D. Rapaport, *No Justice No Peace: The 1996 OPSEU Strike Against the Harris Government in Ontario* (Montreal and Kingston, ON: McGill-Queen's University Press, 1999).

- pensions;

- long-term disability insurance plans; and

- benefits to which all employees in the designated bargaining units are entitled.

The six sector agreements cover such items as:

- wages

- hours of work

- overtime

- standby and call-in pay.

Many of the provisions of the Ontario *Labour Relations Act, 1995* (OLRA) are applicable to the Ontario public service. An administrative tribunal called the Grievance Settlement Board (GSB) is created to deal with disputes, including rights arbitrations in this area. The CECBA states that the OLRA applies to the Ontario public service subject to these specific exemptions:

- non-application to managers, professionals such as lawyers and doctors, and public employees covered by other statutes;

- no provision for related-employer designations;

- non-application of construction industry provisions;

- no provision for common control declarations;

- non-application to certain employees covered specifically in the CECBA;

- non-application of Crown agencies/employees provisions;

- arbitration of disputes is dealt with by the GSB and there is no provision for sole arbitrators;

- no successor rights; and

- claims for damages for an unlawful strike or lockout go to the GSB.

Provincial government workers have the right to strike but before this right is exercised there must be agreements reached with the government to maintain essential services. Essential services are defined under s. 30 of the CECBA as services that are necessary to enable the Ontario government to prevent

(a) danger to life, health, or safety;
(b) the destruction or serious deterioration of machinery, equipment, or premises;
(c) serious environmental damage; or
(d) disruption of the administration of the courts or of legislative drafting.

The agreement between the union and the government must allow the employer to maintain essential services during a strike or lockout by using bargaining unit employees. The agreement must also allow for the use of additional employees in the case of emergencies.

The union and the government are required to agree on

- which services are essential,

- what level of those services must be maintained,

- what types of work must continue in order to provide essential services,

- how many employees performing the specified type of work must continue to work in order to maintain essential services, and

- which specific employees will have to keep working during the strike or lockout.

The negotiation of the essential-services agreement is often very difficult because the union will see a broad agreement as reducing the power of any strike and supporting management's bargaining position.

Broader Public Sector

Unions representing employees who are not direct employees of the government, but where the employer's decision making is either directly or indirectly controlled by the government, face a specific issue in negotiations. The employer may not be able to agree to contract improvements without the agreement of the government, but the government may not be represented at the bargaining table. The employer may not be able to deal with some of the union's major areas of concern without checking with the minister or the cabinet or perhaps the prime minister. The government "ghost at the table" problem is a special complication in these types of negotiations.

Some of the workers in these public sector areas are governed by part or all of the provisions of the OLRA while others have their own specific pieces of legislation. The following public sector employees are expressly excluded from the OLRA:

- firefighters

- members of a police force, including the Ontario Provincial Police (OPP)

- employees of community colleges

- teachers.

FIREFIGHTERS

Firefighters are excluded from the OLRA. Instead, the *Fire Protection and Prevention Act*[7] governs collective bargaining for firefighters. The Act deems firefighters working for a fire department to be an appropriate bargaining unit. The Act prohibits strikes by firefighters and mandates interest arbitration. In making his or her decision, the arbitrator must consider the following:

1. The employer's ability to pay in light of its fiscal situation.

2. The extent to which services may have to be reduced, in light of the decision, if current funding and taxation levels are not increased.

3. The economic situation in Ontario and in the municipality.

---

7 SO 1997, c. 4.

4. A comparison, as between the firefighters and other comparable employees in the public and private sectors, of the terms and conditions of employment and the nature of the work performed.

5. The employer's ability to attract and retain qualified firefighters.[8]

POLICE

Labour relations for members of municipal police forces are governed by part VIII of the *Police Services Act*.[9] Section 117 of this Act provides for collective bargaining between municipal police services boards, which represent as the employer, and police associations, which represent the employees. These associations must be independent and not affiliated with other unions.

The Act covers both uniformed officers and civilian employees of the police force. Under s. 118 of the Act, these two groups often bargain as separate bargaining units. Section 115 states that senior officers, defined as persons above the rank of inspector or persons in supervisory or confidential roles, are excluded from the association.

Section 119(3) of the Act specifies certain matters that may be negotiated, including remuneration, sick leave gratuity, pensions, and grievances. Section 126 also specifies that certain matters may not be negotiated, including police officers' duties, hiring criteria, the probationary period, the oath of office, the prohibition on political activity, the requirement to accommodate disabilities, the limit on outside employment, the civilian complaint procedure, special investigations, and the prohibition against paying officers' legal costs in cases of criminal charges. Section 119(6) provides that pension plan negotiations may be subject to control by the minister of municipal affairs if the pension is part of a general municipal pension plan. Section 120 of the Act specifies that the members of the bargaining team must be members of the police force. However, they are entitled to a lawyer as an adviser.

Section 122 of the Act provides that in the event that negotiation fails to produce an agreement, the solicitor general will appoint a conciliator. In the event that conciliation fails, the matter will go to arbitration. Conventional arbitration as well as mediation/arbitration, and mediation/final-offer selection, may be used.

If a matter is determined by interest arbitration, the arbitrator is required under s. 122(5) of the Act to consider the following criteria:

1. The employer's ability to pay in light of its fiscal situation.

2. The extent to which services may have to be reduced, in light of the decision or award, if current funding and taxation levels are not increased.

3. The economic situation in Ontario and in the municipality.

4. A comparison, as between the employees and other comparable employees in the public and private sectors, of the terms and conditions of employment and the nature of the work performed.

5. The employer's ability to attract and retain qualified employees.

---

8 *Fire Protection and Prevention Act*, s. 50.5(2).

9 RSO 1990, c. P.15.

6.   The interest and welfare of the community served by the police force.

7.   Any local factors affecting that community.

Under s. 123 of the Act, if there is a dispute during the term of the agreement, the matter will be referred to the solicitor general, who will appoint a conciliator. If conciliation fails, the matter will be referred to arbitration.

The Ontario Police Arbitration Commission is created under the Act. Sections 131 and 116 require that the commission consist of two representatives of police associations, two representatives of police services boards, and a neutral chair. The board exercises a number of functions under the Act, including

- determining whether a person is a senior officer;

- keeping a roster of arbitrators for both interest and rights arbitrations;

- appointing arbitrators if the parties cannot agree; and

- keeping a database of information.

Bargaining rights for members of the OPP are governed under part II of the *Public Service Act*. Part II prohibits strikes, and it mandates interest arbitration in the event of disputes.

EMPLOYEES OF COMMUNITY COLLEGES

Collective bargaining in the colleges of applied arts and technology is governed by the *Colleges Collective Bargaining Act*.[10] College employees are excluded from the operation of the OLRA and thus the *Colleges Collective Bargaining Act* is a complete code for labour relations in this sector. The Act sets up two province-wide bargaining units: one covering teachers, librarians, and counsellors, and the other covering support staff employees. Part-time workers are not included in these units and are thus excluded entirely from collective bargaining. The unions bargain with a Crown agency that is set up to act as the bargaining agent for the colleges. Each college is a separate employer but they are all governed by two province-wide collective agreements.

Prior to a strike or lockout, the parties will have to have engaged in bargaining. The employer's last offer must have been rejected by the bargaining unit members in a secret vote and a fact finder must have reported on the dispute. There is no requirement for conciliation. The appointment of fact finders, supervision of votes, and adjudication of disputes such as allegations of bad-faith bargaining are done by the College Relations Commission, which is a part of the Ontario Labour Relations Board (OLRB). In the event of a strike, the College Relations Commission will report to the minister of colleges and universities if the students' year is in jeopardy. In such a case, the minister is likely to introduce back-to-work legislation and impose interest arbitration on the striking employees.

TEACHERS

Collective bargaining for teachers is now governed by the OLRA, subject to modifications set out in part X.1 of the *Education Act*.[11]

---

10 SO 2008, c. H.14.

11 RSO 1990, c. E.2.

The province is divided into school boards. There are public school boards, Catholic school boards, and French-language school boards. The schools within a board are either elementary schools or secondary schools. The bargaining units are defined by the legislation. In each public school board, there are four bargaining units:

- secondary school occasional teachers

- secondary school teachers

- elementary school occasional teachers

- elementary school teachers.

Occasional teachers replace a teacher who is ill or absent. The board keeps the names of occasional teachers on a roster. Occasional teachers may belong to more than one bargaining unit if they are on several rosters at the same time.

The Act specifies not only the bargaining units but also the bargaining agents for teachers. In the past, other unions could and did represent occasional teachers, but they were decertified and replaced by these designated bargaining agents as a result of changes to the legislation governing teachers' collective bargaining. The unions that are entitled to represent teachers in the Act are as follows:

- Association des enseignantes et des enseignants franco-ontariens. Represents elementary and secondary school teachers at French school boards, both occasional and non-occasional.

- Elementary Teachers' Federation of Ontario. Represents public elementary teachers and both occasional and non-occasional teachers.

- Ontario English Catholic Teachers' Association. Represents Catholic elementary and secondary school teachers, both occasional and non-occasional teachers.

- Ontario Secondary School Teachers' Federation. Represents public secondary school teachers, both occasional and non-occasional.

Teachers have a right to strike and may be locked out in the event of an impasse in bargaining. A strike is defined as including

any action or activity by teachers in combination or in concert or in accordance with a common understanding that is designed or may reasonably be expected to have the effect of curtailing, restricting, limiting or interfering with,

(i) the normal activities of a board or its employees,

(ii) the operation or functioning of one or more of a board's schools or of one or more of the programs in one or more schools of a board, including but not limited to programs involving co-instructional activities, or

(iii) the performance of the duties of teachers set out in the Act or the regulations under it,

including any withdrawal of services or work to rule by teachers acting in combination or in concert or in accordance with a common understanding.[12]

---

12 SO 2001, c. 10.

This definition was specifically structured to make it more difficult for teachers to engage in activities involving work-to-rule and the collective refusal to provide after-school activities.

The *Education Act* also prescribes the start date and length of a collective agreement in this sector. All agreements ended on August 31, 2004 and subsequent agreements started on September 1, 2004 and run for three years.

HOSPITAL WORKERS

Labour relations for workers in hospitals are governed by the OLRA, except that the right to strike or lockout is eliminated and replaced by interest arbitration. The operation of the interest arbitration is governed by the *Hospitals Labour Disputes Arbitration Act.*[13] The Act provides that once a conciliation officer appointed under the OLRA has failed to get a settlement, the matters in dispute will be referred to arbitration. If the parties do not agree on the appointment of a sole arbitrator, then a three-person board decides the matters. If the parties cannot agree on an arbitrator, then the minister of labour can not only name the arbitrator but also select mediation/arbitration, mediation/final-offer selection, or conventional arbitration. The parties are given the opportunity to make submissions and present evidence supporting their positions. It is possible for several disputes to be referred to one board of arbitration for decision. The arbitrator is directed to consider all relevant factors, including the following:

1. The employer's ability to pay in light of its fiscal situation.

2. The extent to which services may have to be reduced, in light of the decision or award, if current funding and taxation levels are not increased.

3. The economic situation in Ontario and in the municipality where the hospital is located.

4. A comparison, as between the employees and other comparable employees in the public and private sectors, of the terms and conditions of employment and the nature of the work performed.

5. The employer's ability to attract and retain qualified employees.[14]

The decision of the arbitration board becomes the collective agreement between the hospital and its employees. Strikes and/or lockouts are prohibited and the OLRA has the power to deal with an application to stop the strike or lockout.

AMBULANCE WORKERS

The *Ambulance Services Collective Bargaining Act, 2001*[15] governs negotiations involving ambulance workers who do not work for hospitals or who do not work directly for the provincial government. Ambulance workers have the right to strike and they can be locked out. But before any strike takes place, an essential ambulance services agreement must be created. If the employer and the union cannot

13 Ibid., s. 1(1).

14 RSO 1990, c. C.15.

15 RSO 1990, c. E.2.

reach agreement on the provision of essential services, then the OLRB can impose an agreement. The agreement will specify which workers must continue to work during a strike or lockout in order to provide services such as

(a) ambulance services provided to,

(i) persons who have suffered a trauma or an acute onset of illness, either of which could endanger their life, limb or functioning, or

(ii) persons who have been judged by a physician or a physician's delegate to be in an unstable medical condition and to require, while being transported, both the care of a physician, a nurse, another health care provider, an emergency medical attendant or a paramedic and the use of a stretcher,

(b) call-taking and dispatching services required for the provision of ambulance services,

(c) if the employer provides integrated dispatching services, call-taking and dispatching services required for the provision of fire protection services or police services or both,

(d) work that is incidental to a service described in clause (a), (b) or (c),

(e) work that is performed on or in connection with an ambulance to protect health or safety, or

(f) the prescribed services.[16]

This is a broad list and covers many of the activities of an ambulance service. In fact, so many members of the bargaining unit may be working that it may render the strike or lockout ineffective. If a party believes this to be the case and more than 25 percent of the workforce are covered under the essential services agreement, then that party can apply to the OLRB for a declaration that the strike or lockout is ineffective and have the board order interest arbitration to resolve the dispute.

MUNICIPAL EMPLOYEES

Municipal employees are regulated under the OLRA and are governed by the same rules as private sector employees. Municipal workers have the right to strike.

UNIVERSITY EMPLOYEES

University employees are regulated under the OLRA and are governed by the same rules as private sector employees. University workers have the right to strike.

CHAPTER SUMMARY

The view that collective bargaining should not limit the government's power to decide on public policy led to a delay in the granting of unionization rights for public sector workers. Even though the workers eventually won that right, there continue to be limitations on public sector workers' ability to negotiate freely on their terms and conditions of employment. In some cases, their right to strike is limited or prohibited based on the need to maintain essential services for the

---

16 Ibid., s. 277.2(4).

public. Where the right to strike is removed, it is replaced by interest arbitration. The government has legislatively limited the traditional role of the interest arbitrator and directed the arbitrator to consider factors supportive of the government's position. Sometimes, certain terms and conditions of employment are removed from the scope of their negotiations and set by legislation and regulations as a part of public policy. In all cases, the government occupies a unique position as both employer and the maker of the rules of bargaining. The government has not hesitated to use this power to change the rules in order to generally enhance its bargaining position. It has also used this power to end disputes by removing the right to strike and imposing terms and conditions of employment on its employees.

REVIEW QUESTIONS

1. Define "essential services."

2. How have the powers of interest arbitrators been limited under legislation governing ambulances and firefighters in Ontario?

3. Why has the right to strike been limited for some public employees?

4. Why did collective bargaining rights extend to public employees later than they did to private sector employees?

5. List the sectors in the Ontario public service.

6. Describe the bargaining unit structure for teachers in Ontario.

DISCUSSION QUESTIONS

1. "Public servants should not be allowed to bargain collectively." Do you agree or disagree? Support your answer.

2. "The right to strike should not be extended to public servants because they are all essential to the public." Do you agree or disagree? Support your answer.

CHAPTER 8

Employment Standards

INTRODUCTION

Changes to the *Employment Standards Act, 2000* (ESA or "the Act")[1] made in 2001 both increased a union's obligation to enforce the Act through the grievance/arbitration system and clarified a union's ability to modify some of the standards to suit a particular workplace. This chapter will examine the general impact of employment standards legislation on the role of the union and set out the obligations of the union. It will then give an example of a case involving the enforcement of the obligations by the union. Finally, it will describe briefly the minimum standards that the union is charged with enforcing.

The ESA attempts to set a standard foundation of fair employment rules to cover all workplaces in Ontario, but it also tries to create sufficient flexibility in its rules to allow workplaces to respond to different workplace structures and methods of operation. The Act deals with workplaces that operate continuously, others that are open only during a 9-to-5 period, and others where the workers live at the work site. The resulting set of standards is often very complex and confusing. There is a long list of workplaces that are not subject to particular rules and there are complex qualifications for benefits under the Act, which were included to prevent abuse. The resulting piece of legislation is almost indecipherable.

EMPLOYMENT STANDARDS AND THE COLLECTIVE BARGAINING PROCESS: THEN AND NOW

Historically, the ESA both set a floor for collective bargaining and limited the scope of negotiations. A union could not negotiate a collective agreement that gave less than the legislated standards. For example, a union could not agree to a wage level that was lower than the minimum wage. In some circumstances, a union could not negotiate an equal alternative to the legislated standard and thus was constrained during negotiations.

A collective agreement cannot provide fewer public holidays than are listed in the Act, nor can alternate days be substituted for holidays listed in the Act. For example, the first Friday in July could not be substituted for July 1 as a holiday. In the case of holidays, the collective agreement would often include a copy of the list of holidays from the Act and add additional negotiated holidays. Or, the agreement would only make reference to the holidays in the Act and then list the additional negotiated holidays.

---

1   SO 2000, c. 41.

A collective agreement did not have to reference all the relevant sections in the ESA. If the agreement was silent on a matter covered by the Act, then the minimum standard set by the Act would apply and the Employment Standards Branch of the Ministry of Labour would enforce the Act's rules.

Recent changes to the Act tend to make the standards effectively part of the collective agreement and make the union responsible for enforcement of the Act through the grievance/arbitration process under the collective agreement even though the union may not have bargained on any of these issues. As part of this shift in policy, if a union fails in its duty to enforce the ESA it may be subject to duty of fair representation complaints brought by people in the bargaining unit.

Finally, amendments to the Act over time gave the union the ability to negotiate modifications to the standards, provided that the workers overall did not lose ground.

UNION OBLIGATION TO ENFORCE EMPLOYMENT STANDARDS

Section 99 of the Act provides that if there is a collective agreement in place between a union and an employer, or during any extension of the agreement or during the negotiations for a new collective agreement until the time when there is a legal right to strike or lockout, the union must enforce the obligations under the ESA as if they were part of the collective agreement. This means that allegations of a breach of the Act must be dealt with by the grievance/arbitration provisions of the collective agreement. In fact, s. 99(2) of the Act provides that these complaints are to be exclusively dealt with under the collective agreement.

An employee who is covered under a collective agreement and who has a complaint may want to file a grievance. However, the employee is bound by the decision of the union not to proceed with a grievance alleging a violation of an employment standard. The employee cannot launch a personal complaint. Under s. 99(5) of the ESA, if the employee disagrees with the action of the union, his or her remedy is to take the union to the Ontario Labour Relations Board (OLRB) and allege a violation of the duty of fair representation. To prove a complaint, the employee must show that the union acted in a manner that was arbitrary, discriminatory, or in bad faith. It would not be sufficient merely to show that there is a violation. Under s. 99(6) of the ESA, there is a residual power for the director of the Employment Standards Branch to order an employment standards officer to investigate an employee's complaint if the director considers holding such an investigation appropriate.

Sections 100 and 101 of the ESA provide that an arbitrator appointed under the collective agreement has the power to make any order that could be made under the Act, except for a notice of contravention. A notice of contravention involves a penalty being imposed for a failure to comply with the Act. A contravention of the Act could result in a fine of $250 for the first offence, $500 for the second offence within a three-year period, and $1,000 for the third offence within a three-year period. Directors of a company are protected from personal liability for orders that could be made under the ESA for a non-unionized corporation unless personal liability on directors is incorporated into the collective agreement. For example, directors may be made personally liable for unpaid wages under an order of an employment standards officer if the wages are not paid by the corporate employer or if the corporate employer is insolvent.

UNION AGREEMENTS ON MATTERS COVERED BY EMPLOYMENT STANDARDS

Section 5(1) of the ESA expressly prohibits a trade union from contracting out of any provisions of the Act: "[N]o employer or agent of an employer and no employee or agent of an employee shall contract out of or waive an employment standard and any such contracting out or waiver is void." However, s. 5(2) of the Act makes it clear that a union can negotiate greater rights than those in the Act:

> If one or more provisions in an employment contract ... that directly relate to the same subject matter as an employment standard provide a greater benefit to an employee than the employment standard, the provision or provisions in the contract ... apply and the employment standard does not apply.

It is not sufficient that the union believe that the negotiated agreement provides a greater benefit or that the members have voted to support the modification or that the employer agreed to the amendment. If an arbitrator decides that the provision or provisions in the agreement are not a greater benefit, then the arbitrator can refuse to enforce that part of the collective agreement.

The union is also expressly allowed to make agreements under the ESA with the employer on behalf of the employees. Section 7 of the Act provides that an "agreement or authorization that may lawfully be made or given by an employee under this Act may be made or given by his or her agent and is binding on the employee as if it had been made or given by the employee." An "agent" is defined under s. 1(1) of the Act to include "a trade union that represents an employee in collective bargaining." Thus, for example, an agreement made by the union to increase the hours in a workweek would be binding on the employees. If the employees wanted to challenge the actions of the union in making such an agreement, they would have to take the union to the OLRB and show that the union acted in a manner that was arbitrary, discriminatory, or in bad faith.

The interaction of the union's rights as the representative of the employees and the operation of the ESA is illustrated by the arbitrator's decision in the case of *Norampac*.[2]

In *Norampac* the employer and the union had entered into a practice of letting the workers work back-to-back 8-hour shifts so that they worked 16 hours in total. The employees would volunteer for double shifts and they would be paid premium pay for overtime. At the time of this case, s. 17(1) of the Act provided that an "employer shall give an employee a period of at least 11 hours free from performing work in each day." The word "continuous" was later added to the section. In any event, the arbitrator argued that the concept of a continuous break had to be read into the section. Otherwise, potentially constant work could be permitted as long as breaks were given that added up to 11 hours per 24-hour period (for example, a worker could work half an hour on, half an hour off indefinitely if the rest period

---

2   *Re Norampac and Independent Paperworkers of Canada* (Sept. 10, 2002), 73 CLAS (MacDowell).

could be broken up). The union argued that the double shifts provided a greater benefit to the employee than the employment standard in the Act because they both were voluntary and enabled the employee to earn premium pay. The union also argued that the 11-hour breaks could take place before the first 8-hour shift and then after the second 8-hour shift. That would be a schedule of 11 hours off, 16 hours on, 11 hours off.

The arbitrator rejected both arguments. The arbitrator held that the union could negotiate more of a rest break but not less, and that premium pay for work was separate from hours of work and thus would not be a greater benefit in the context of the section of the Act dealing with hours of work. The fact that the employees were not complaining about the shifts was also irrelevant. In this case, the employer wanted to get out of a practice it had agreed to for many years. The arbitrator also concluded that the 11-hours break had to be within the 24 hours that started when the employee started a work shift. It could not go beyond that 24-hour period as it would in the union's back-to-back shift schedule. Thus, the arbitrator ruled, the longest work shift that the union could possibly agree to would be 13 hours. In passing, the arbitrator noted that the 11-hour break did not have to occur within one calendar day. Otherwise, the traditional 9-to-5 work shift would not be legal, because the 24-hour calendar day would be split into a 9-hour break, followed by an 8-hour shift, and then a further 7-hour break. Instead, assuming that the 24-hour period starts when work starts means that the traditional 9-to-5 workday is 8 hours on and 16 hours off.

THE EMPLOYMENT STANDARDS

Some of the standards created under the ESA will be examined with a focus on the interaction of the standard with commonly negotiated collective agreement provisions.

Hours of Work

The Act attempts to control the number of hours that an employee will be required to work both on a daily basis and on a weekly basis. But it still allows some flexibility to suit the employer's scheduling needs and the employees' desire to compress their workweek. There are specific provisions in the Act to deal with the number of hours that an employee can work in a day and in a week and provisions for regular rest breaks.

DAILY HOURS

Section 17(1) of the Act says that an employee shall not be required to or permitted to work more than 8 hours a day unless the employer establishes a workday longer than 8 hours. This provision sets up a week of 8-hour workdays as the standard model. But it also permits other models, such as a compressed week of 10 hours per day for four days, provided that the employee or the employee's agent, the union, agrees.

Under s. 18 of the Act, the employee is to get at least 11 consecutive hours break from work each day unless the employee is on call. The employee must also get an 8-hour break between shifts unless the total time on the consecutive shifts is less than 13 hours and the employee agrees to the short turnaround time. Moreover, the employee must either get two days off each week or a four-day break every second week.

WEEKLY HOURS

Section 17(2) of the Act states that the workweek is to be a maximum of 48 hours long, unless the employee agrees in writing to work longer hours and the employee will not work more than 60 hours. If the employee and the employer want the workweek to exceed 60 hours, they must get permission from the director of the Employment Standards Branch of the Ministry of Labour.[3] The union may agree to such alternative arrangements through collective bargaining. An agreement to work longer hours can be revoked with two weeks' notice by the employee or reasonable notice by the employer.

EXCEPTIONAL CIRCUMSTANCES

Section 19 of the Act states that these limits on hours worked per week and per day can be exceeded if the longer hours are needed to deal with

- an emergency,
- urgent repair work needed on the plant,
- urgent repair work needed on the equipment,
- an unforeseen event that would disrupt the delivery of essential services,
- an unforeseen event that would interrupt continuous processes, or
- an unforeseen event that would interrupt seasonal operations.

Under s. 20 of the Act, the employee is entitled to an unpaid eating period of 30 minutes every five hours, unless the employee and the employer agree to break up the eating period into two eating periods during the five hours.

Overtime

Under s. 22 of the Act, the employer is required to pay a premium of one and a half times its regular hourly rate for all hours worked in excess of 44 hours per week, unless there is an averaging agreement (discussed below). An agreement also can be given to provide one and a half hours of paid time off for each overtime hour worked, instead of money. This is often called lieu time. Unions sometimes reach agreement with the employer that the overtime threshold will be less than 44 hours.

The Act allows the employer and the employee or the employee's agent, the union, to enter into an overtime averaging agreement. Work can be averaged over a four-week period for the purpose of determining overtime. Thus in a four-week

---

3 Exemptions, Special Rules and Establishment of Minimum Wage, O. Reg. 285/01, s. 31. If Bill 63 is passed, the employer will have to get permission from the director to exceed a 48-hour workweek.

period an employee could work 48 hours the first week, 40 hours the second week, 56 hours the third week, and 32 hours the fourth week and not be entitled to overtime because the average number of hours worked per week does not exceed 44. Averaging can take place over a longer time period if the director of the Employment Standards Branch agrees.

Public Holidays

Sections 24 and 1(1) of the Act require employers to provide a minimum set of paid public holidays. The holidays are

- New Year's Day,
- Good Friday,
- Victoria Day,
- Canada Day,
- Labour Day,
- Thanksgiving Day,
- Christmas Day,
- December 26, and
- any other day prescribed as a public holiday.

In general, to be eligible for pay for the public holiday, the employees must work their regular shift the day either before or after the holiday, unless they have a reasonable excuse for not showing up to work. The Act also allows for the operation of businesses on holidays, provided that the workers are given other paid days to replace the holiday that was worked. The employer must provide these paid days within three months of the holiday or a year of the holiday if there is an agreement to extend the time period.

Vacations

Section 33 of the Act provides that an employee is entitled to a two-week vacation period in each vacation year. The vacation year may be the 12-month period starting when the employee is hired or it may be some other 12-month period starting after the employee is hired. Under ss. 34 and 1(1), if the vacation period starts at a date after the employee is hired, it is referred to as an **alternative vacation entitlement year**. In that case, there will be a period of time between the start of employment and the start of the alternative vacation entitlement year that is called a **stub period**. An employee is entitled to vacation for the stub period on a proportional, or pro rata, basis. If the alternative vacation entitlement year starts six months after the employee is hired, the employee is entitled to a one-week vacation during the stub period.

The vacation must be taken no later than 10 months after the end of the vacation entitlement period, and it may be taken in periods as short as a day if the employer and the employee agree. If there is no agreement, it is either a two-week period or two one-week periods. In addition to vacation time, s. 35.2 of the Act states that the employee is entitled to **vacation pay** equal to 4 percent of the employee's wages earned during the period for which the vacation is given.

Pregnancy Leave and Parental Leave

Section 46 of the Act provides for a 17-week pregnancy leave, provided that the employee has worked for 13 weeks. It also provides for parental leaves for employees who have worked for 13 weeks. If a parental leave is combined with a pregnancy leave, then the parental leave lasts for 35 weeks. If a parental leave is not combined with a pregnancy leave, then the parental leave lasts for 37 weeks. If the employee taking leave has worked sufficient hours to qualify for employment insurance, then he or she will be able to collect benefits. Employment insurance provides for 15 weeks of benefits during a pregnancy leave, with a 2-week waiting period before the benefits start and then the ability to collect 35 weeks of benefits during a subsequent parental leave. These parental benefits can be split between parents. If no pregnancy leave is taken, but parental leave is, there is a 2-week waiting period for parental leave benefits.

There is no requirement to pay the employee during pregnancy or parental leaves, although some unions have negotiated additional money to be paid to these employees during their pregnancy or parental leaves. These top-up amounts must be set out in a **supplementary unemployment benefit plan (SUB plan)** and approved by the Canada Revenue Agency. The maximum top-up is 95 percent of salary.[4] If the SUB plan is approved, then these additional amounts will not be deducted from the employee's employment insurance benefits during the pregnancy or parental leaves.

Minimum Wage

The employer is required to pay employees at least the standard minimum wage (at time of writing, $7.15 per hour). There are, however some exceptions, including:[5]

- a student minimum wage (at time of writing, $6.70 per hour[6]),

- a liquor server's minimum wage (at time of writing, $6.20 per hour[7]),

- a homeworker's minimum wage (at time of writing, $7.87 per hour[8]), and

- a fishing and hunting guide's minimum wage (at time of writing, $35.75 for less than five hours in a day[9] and $71.50 for more than five hours[10]).

---

4 *Information Circular* 72-5R2, available online at http://www.cra-arc.gc.ca/E/pub/tp/ic72-5r2/README.html.

5 *Employment Standards Act*, s. 23 and Exemptions, Special Rules and Establishment of Minimum Wage, O. Reg. 285/01, s. 5.

6 Rising to $7.45 Feb. 1, 2005, then to $7.75 Feb. 1, 2006, then to $8.00 Feb. 1, 2007.

7 Rising to $6.50 Feb. 1, 2005, then to $6.75 Feb. 1, 2006, then to $6.95 Feb. 1, 2007.

8 Rising to $8.20 Feb. 1, 2005, then to $8.53 Feb. 1, 2006, then to $8.80 Feb. 1, 2007.

9 Rising to $37.25 Feb. 1, 2005, then to $38.75 Feb. 1, 2006, then to $40.00 Feb. 1, 2007.

10 Rising to $74.50 Feb. 1, 2005, then to $78.50 Feb. 1, 2006, then to $80.00 Feb. 1, 2007.

An amount for room and board can be deducted from the minimum wage if the employer is providing reasonable room and board to the employee. Some work is entirely exempted from minimum wage, including the work of janitors who live in the building that they maintain, and the work of students who are employed at summer camps for children.

Family Medical Leave

An employee is entitled to an 8-week unpaid medical leave to take care of a close relative who is seriously ill and at significant risk of dying.[11] The relative must be one of the following:

- the spouse of the employee;

- the parent, step-parent, or foster parent of the employee; or

- the child, stepchild, or foster child of the employee or of the employee's spouse.

A health practitioner must certify that the relative is at significant risk of dying within a 26-week period. In Ontario, a doctor will issue the certificate, but in other jurisdictions other health practitioners may issue the certificate. Leaves are for up to eight full 7-day periods starting Sunday and ending Saturday. Partial weeks cannot be taken. Only 8 weeks can be taken in total for one ill person, so the leave may be split between two parents of a sick child or a number of children of a dying parent. The employee returns from this leave after 8 weeks or after the last day of the week when the person dies, whichever is earlier. If the ailing relative dies, then the employee will be entitled to **bereavement leave**. If the ailing relative does not die, then, if a health practitioner issues a new certificate, another 8-week unpaid leave period may be taken.

Records

Under s. 15 of the ESA, the employer is required to collect and maintain certain records on the employees. These records include

- the employee's name and address;

- the employee's date of birth, if the employee is a student and under 18 years of age;

- the date on which the employee began his or her employment;

- the number of hours that the employee worked in each day and each week; and

- information about wage payments, deductions, vacation pay, and vacation time.

According to ss. 15.1(5) and 15(5) of the Act, most of these records have to be kept for at least three years.

---

11 *Employment Standards Amendment Act (Family Medical Leave), 2004*, SO 2004, c. 15.

Equal Pay for Equal Work

The employer is required to pay men and women equal pay in the following case: when they perform essentially the same work, when their working conditions are similar, and when substantially the same skill, effort, and responsibility are involved. There are exceptions for pay systems that determine pay not on the basis of sex but on the basis of seniority, merit, piecework, or other factors than sex. Under s. 42 of the Act, unions often negotiate pay grids, where earnings increase the longer an employee works and the more seniority he or she accumulates. Section 42(4) expressly forbids trade unions from negotiating pay systems based on sex.

Termination Pay

Section 56 of the Act provides minimum standards for the notice period if the employer terminates an employee without a good reason such as bad performance or improper conduct at work. If the employer has a good reason for termination, the employer can terminate the employee without notice. The employer may now choose to either give the notice period or pay the amount owed for that period as a lump sum instead of notice. The **termination pay** is to give the employee some resources to support himself or herself while searching for a new job. These are minimum levels. The union often negotiates a more generous package.

The minimum standards for termination pay are based on length of time employed. These standards are set out below:

- Less than three months: neither termination pay nor notice

- More than three months but less than one year: one week's pay or notice

- one year or more but less than three years: two weeks' pay or notice

- three years or more but less than four years: three weeks' pay or notice

- four years or more but less than five years: four weeks' pay or notice

- five years or more but less than six years: five weeks' pay or notice

- six years or more but less than seven years: six weeks' pay or notice

- seven years or more but less than eight years: seven weeks' pay or notice

- eight years or more: eight weeks' pay or notice.

Under s. 58 of the Act, if the employer terminates 50 or more employees in a four-week period, the employer has to give special notice to the Ministry of Labour and participate in adjustment measures to assist the employees in getting new jobs.

Unions often negotiate provisions in the collective agreement that provide for temporary layoffs based on reverse order of seniority when work is short, and employee recalls based on seniority when work picks up again. The employer should not have to pay the termination pay on a temporary work stoppage. However, an employer should not be able to avoid its obligations by calling a permanent layoff a temporary layoff.

Section 56(2) of the Act defines a temporary layoff as being any of the following:

- less than 13 weeks in any 20-week period;

- between 13 weeks and less than 35 weeks in any 52-week period if the employer continues to make payments to the employee, including payment to a SUB plan or benefits payments or payments to a pension plan; or

- a period longer than 35 weeks if the employee is represented by a union and the employer recalls the employee during the recall period of the collective agreement.

Also, s. 56(3.1) of the Act provides that if an employee's regular pay is cut back by at least half, that week will count as a week on layoff unless the employee's loss in pay was due to his or her being suspended, not showing up to work, or being on strike.

Severance Pay

Section 64 of the Act requires an employer to pay **severance pay** to employees if the employer is severing an employee who had worked for the employer for five years or more, and

a. there is a permanent stopping of all or part of the work being done at that particular location and more than 50 employees are severed over a six-month period, or

b. the employer has a payroll greater than $2.5 million.

Severance pay is essentially one week's pay for each year of work. An employee who worked 21 years and six months and is entitled to severance pay would receive 21.5 weeks worth of pay. The employer is entitled to deduct from the payment any SUB plan payments or any payments under the contract that are based on length of time working for the employer. Thus, under s. 65(8) of the Act, severance payments made under the collective agreement will be set off against any money that the employee is entitled to under the Act.

Under s. 63(1) of the Act, severing the employee includes terminating the employee, laying off the employee for more than 35 weeks in a 52-week period, or laying off the employee for an indefinite period.

Severance Payments, Termination Payments, and Recall Rights

An employee may be eligible for severance payments and/or termination payments based on a layoff of more than 35 weeks in a 52-week period, as discussed above. At the same time, the laid-off employee has the right to be recalled under the collective agreement. **Recall rights** may last for several years. The employee cannot both accept termination and severance payments and keep the recall rights. However, once the recall period expires, if the employee has not been recalled, he or she will cease to have any rights as an employee under the collective agreement.

An employee that has been severed has a choice: the employee can drop his or her recall rights and get immediate payment of the severance and/or termination pay, or the employee can elect to keep his or her recall rights. If the employee elects to maintain recall rights, the severance/termination payments are held in trust. This means that the money is held by an organization other than the employer and is protected if the employer later runs into financial difficulties. If the employee is recalled, the money in trust is paid back to the employer. If the employee's recall rights expire and the employee has not been recalled, then the money held in trust is paid to the employee, under s. 67 of the Act.

Lie Detectors

According to ss. 69 and 70 of the Act, an employee has the right to refuse to take a lie detector test. In fact, an employee should not even be asked to take such a test. An employer may be inclined to ask an employee to take a lie detector test as part of an investigation of theft at the workplace.

Leaves of Absence

If the employer regularly has more than 50 employees, those employees are entitled to 10 days of **emergency leave** without pay. Section 50 of the Act states that the employees may use these days to take care of personal injuries, illnesses, or medical emergencies, or the death, illness, injury, medical emergency, or urgent matter of a family member. Section 50(2) of the Act defines a family member as

- the employee's spouse;
- a parent, step-parent, or foster parent of the employee or of the employee's spouse;
- a child, stepchild, or foster child of the employee or of the employee's spouse;
- a grandparent, step-grandparent, grandchild, or step-grandchild of the employee or of the employee's spouse;
- the spouse of a child of the employee;
- the employee's brother or sister; or
- a relative of the employee who is dependent on the employee for care or assistance.

Many unions have negotiated provisions for paid **sick leaves** and bereavement leaves. Leaves under these provisions count toward the employer's obligations to provide emergency leaves.

CHAPTER SUMMARY

The *Employment Standards Act* is a complex piece of legislation and both the union and the employer need to be aware of its provisions and its potential impact on both their bargaining process and their contract administration process.

The Act allows the parties to contract for provisions that provide a greater benefit than the provisions under the Act. It does not allow the parties to trade off greater benefits in one area for lesser benefits in another area. It also allows for the union as bargaining agent to make agreements under the Act on behalf of its members. The union must do so in a manner that is not arbitrary, discriminatory, or in bad faith. In some cases, the union may not turn its attention to the employment standards implications of its actions during bargaining. Inadvertently, negotiations on hours of work may affect the provisions of the Act related to averaging of work.

Unions enforce the obligations under the ESA through the grievance/arbitration mechanism of the collective agreement when an employee has a complaint. However, unions have scarce resources to devote to arbitrations and they may decide not to expend these resources on an employment standards claim that may have some merit but limited application to the majority of the bargaining unit. As long as the actions of the union cannot be characterized as being arbitrary, discriminatory, or in bad faith, the aggrieved worker will not be able to personally pursue his or her claim.

The Act provides for minimum standards for treatment of workers in the following terms and conditions of employment:

- hours of work
- overtime
- public holidays
- vacations and vacation pay
- parental leave
- minimum wages
- emergency leave and family medical leave
- employer record keeping
- equal pay for equal work
- termination pay
- severance pay in certain circumstances
- use of lie detectors
- leaves of absence.

The union and management should be aware of the contents of these minimum rules before negotiations in order to assess the impact of their proposals relative to these minimum standards.

REVIEW QUESTIONS

1. Under what circumstances can a union negotiate a provision that is different from the provisions of the *Employment Standards Act, 2000*?

2. An employer intends to lay off 120 employees indefinitely. What costs will the employer incur in order to comply with the ESA?

3. What is the purpose of a SUB plan with respect to parental leave?

4. What are the emergency leave provisions under the Act?

5. How are employment standards enforced in a unionized workplace?

6. An employee in a unionized workplace is being laid off indefinitely. She has a 2-year recall period negotiated under the collective agreement at her workplace. She worked for 17 years before the layoff. How much is she entitled to in termination payments, and when should this money be paid to her if she maintains her recall rights and is never recalled?

7. Define a "temporary layoff." What is the importance of the characterization of a layoff as temporary?

8. June Jones has just found out that she is pregnant. She has been working at her present workplace for 2 years. What leave period is she entitled to from the workplace? If there is no provision for payments from her employer during that leave in her collective agreement, is she entitled to payment from the employer during the leave?

9. What records is an employer required to keep under the ESA?

10. There are several minimum wage levels under the ESA. Which groups under this Act have a separate minimum wage?

DISCUSSION QUESTIONS

1. Should the minimum standards in the *Employment Standards Act, 2000* be enforced as part of the grievance/arbitration system under the collective agreement? Should they instead be enforced through an application to the Ministry of Labour, as is the case in non-unionized workplaces?

2. Was shifting the enforcement of the ESA to the grievance/arbitration system simply intended to shift the costs of enforcing public policies onto private unions and employers?

3. The ESA sets minimum standards to prevent non-unionized workers with limited bargaining power from being improperly treated by employers. Unionization gives workers greater bargaining power. Should unionized workers, therefore, be free to negotiate any provision that varies from the ESA?

CASE STUDY

Acme Trucks and Cars employed Fred Jones for 31 years as a maintenance mechanic. Fred is represented by the United Truck Maintenance Workers Local 445. Because of a corporate reorganization, he and 67 other employees were laid off permanently. Because the entire maintenance department was eliminated, he could not exercise bumping rights under the collective agreement. The collective agreement contained no language on severance pay. The union and management made no agreements on the operation of these layoffs. Therefore, the company informed the affected employees by a letter dated January 1, 2004 that the employees had two compensation options. Option A permitted them to retire on an unreduced early pension. Option B provided a special retirement package. The package consisted of a lump-sum payment to employees who chose this option. The letter also contained the following unqualified representation about option A:

> The above provisions are inclusive of all amounts payable under any provincial legislation or otherwise, including notice, payment in lieu of notice, severance pay, and vacation pay. For your information, the above provisions exceed provincial requirements.

A financial analyst provided by the company advised Mr. Jones to take option A. It is clear that Mr. Jones relied upon the representation of his employer that option A exceeded what he was entitled to under provincial law. Unfortunately for Mr. Jones, the representation made by the company was inaccurate. Note that the union had not agreed to the financial analysis or the letter.

Subsequently, a group of former Acme employees who had accepted option A pursued a claim under the *Employment Standards Act, 2000* for severance pay in addition to the unreduced early pension. Mr. Jones read a newspaper report on March 23, 2004 concerning these employees and, upon making an inquiry, he was advised that a pending decision was expected to go in favour of the former employees. Mr. Jones took no further action at that time because he thought that he should await the result of the proceedings. On December 2, 2004, Mr. Jones read a further newspaper account that a decision had been rendered in favour of the employees. Mr. Jones then proceeded to consult a lawyer and on January 25, 2005, he was ready to initiate a similar claim under the Act.

1. What amounts was Mr. Jones entitled to for

    a. payment in lieu of notice?

    b. severance?

    c. vacation pay?

2. What actions should Mr. Jones take in order to obtain a remedy from the employer?

3. What problem does Mr. Jones face if the union agreed to these arrangements for the treatment of the employees facing the layoff?

CHAPTER 9

Emerging Trends in Labour Relations

INTRODUCTION

Until now in this text we have been concerned with how the current labour relations environment developed, and with how it actually works. In this chapter we will identify some of the changes in the workplace, and the world, that might affect the conduct of labour relations in the future. We will start with an overview of how the workplace has been changing since World War II, and then go on to a more detailed examination of some of the key factors that affect the workplace and future workplace trends that we are likely to see.

CHANGES IN THE WORKPLACE

The labour relations system that we are familiar with developed in large industrial settings that often involved primary resource extraction and processing, or large-scale manufacturing, with large workforces. Since the end of World War II, when the labour relations framework developed, this work environment has undergone tremendous changes. The changes have been driven to some extent by technological developments in communications, industrial production, and transportation. In addition, there have been political, economic, and social changes. Together these changes are transforming the workplace, and are presenting challenges to both labour and management that will transform labour relations in various ways. A good way to examine these changes is to begin with what the workplace looked like at the end of the World War II and to identify forces that are bringing about changes in the labour relations environment.

In 1945, at the end of World War II, Canada began a long period of economic growth. Workers, who were predominantly male, tended to start with and stay with one employer throughout their working career in full-time positions. Much of the workforce in resource extraction, transportation, and manufacturing was unionized. The service sector, then as now, tended to be unorganized. The public sector tended not to be unionized, though that changed in the 1960s and 1970s, as statutes were passed allowing for unionization in the public service. Wages, generally, were high, and inflation was low. The wage differential between skilled and unskilled workers was not as great as it was later to become, due in part to minimum wage legislation, and unionization among unskilled as well as skilled workers. High wages allowed many families to have a single wage earner who could support an at-home spouse with children. In fact, at the end of the war, to assure employment for returning soldiers, women were discouraged from continuing full-time employment. It was not until the 1970s that large numbers of married women began to enter or re-enter the workforce. Part of this trend was due to changes in the law and in social attitudes toward women in the workplace. And part of it was due, starting in the 1970s, to a desire to maintain family income and family consumption patterns by having both spouses working in a period of high inflation and falling real income.

Many full-time jobs carried benefit plans that covered items such as medical costs and insurance. Benefit plans also included pensions. In addition, starting in the 1940s the federal government began to create the "social safety net," beginning with the family allowance (or "baby bonus" as it was popularly known), and adding government-funded pensions, maternity leave, improved unemployment insurance, disability insurance, and universal health care. In the 1960s, educational opportunities also increased as the existing universities were expanded, new ones founded, and a system of community colleges established.

In general, it was still possible in the postwar period for unskilled and semi-skilled workers with a high school diploma or less to find secure, full-time, union-ized jobs with relatively high wages. These workers earned enough to provide a decent if not luxurious standard of living for their families.

Beginning in the 1970s this scenario began to change. The income gap between educated, skilled workers and unskilled workers widened. As well-paid unskilled and semi-skilled jobs became scarcer, such work was either exported to low-wage economies or kept in the local economy but increasingly given to part-time, casual, and contract workers. Job security in manufacturing, resource extraction, trans-portation, and communications became less common, as did lifetime service with a single employer. Recessions in the 1970s, '80s, and early '90s led to cost cutting and an effort to reduce labour costs based on the idea that technological change would reduce the need for full-time employees. The flipside of these changes was that workers became far less loyal to the employer, and more prone to change jobs and careers, because there was less to bind them to a particular employer.

We turn now to the factors in the external macro environment that are likely to underlie emerging trends in labour relations using a modified PEST (political, economic, social, and technological) analytic framework. Although a PEST analy-sis is usually used to examine the external environment affecting a particular business, we will apply the PEST analysis to the unionized environments. We will look at how political, economic, social, and technological factors help us predict the behaviour of players n the unionized environment.

POLITICAL CHANGES

The labour unrest during World War II brought about by labour shortages, com-bined with inflation and falling real wages, led to significant labour conflict. The government, seeking labour stability during the war, began to pass legislation that set up procedures to recognize unions as bargaining agents, and recognize and enforce collective agreements. Oversight of labour relations under statutes such as the Ontario *Labour Relations Act* in the late 1940s put unionized workplaces under provincial or federal labour boards. Under the Rand Formula, unions acquired rights to dues check-offs, where unions collected dues from members of the bargaining unit whether or not they were members of the union.

The stability achieved during this period has been challenged politically from two directions. Conservative, pro-business governments, such as the Ontario Progressive Conservative government in 1995, amended labour legislation in ways detrimental to unions or union members. The new legislation has expanded the categories of workers excluded from labour unions, permitted the use of outside workers during strikes, and attempted to take away the right to strike, to cite some examples.[1] Governments have also interfered readily in public sector strikes by using back-to-work legislation. Usually this kind of legislation refers outstanding matters to an arbitrator to decide. But arbitrators are often respectful of union demands made where the workers were prepared to strike but were legislated back to work. Consequently, in more recent back-to-work legislation, the government has imposed limits, caps, and restraints on arbitrators who determine the content of the new collective agreement. As public sector unions grow in size and strength, it is likely that legislative restraints will become common.

The *Canadian Charter of Rights and Freedoms*[2] has had a legal and political impact on the unionized environment. The Charter applies to the administrative acts of governments and to the content of legislation. Unions have attempted to use the Charter to challenge other legislation that has disadvantaged unions and their members. Challenges under the Charter generally involve the exercise of the right to freedom of association under s. 2(d). In hearing cases, courts take into account that Charter rights are subject to "reasonable limits prescribed by law as can be justified in a free and democratic society" under s. 1. Thus, the courts first determine whether there is a breach of a right. Then, if they conclude there has been a breach of a right, they must determine whether this breach is nevertheless justifiable under s. 1. Note that the test in s. 1 is subjective, inviting the court to import various political, economic and social values that a judge believes to be central to "a free and democratic society."

Not surprisingly, initial Charter decisions were not particularly consistent. Consider the challenges by unions and their members in the 1980s involving wage restraint and wage controls in the public sector. The unions argued that freedom of association under s. 2(d) of the Charter supported a right to strike and a right to engage in collective bargaining without interference in the process. However, most courts rejected these challenges to legislation by the unions on the following basis.[3] Generally, the legislation was seen as temporary or passed to cover exceptional circumstances, so the infringements on the rights of labour were regarded as justified under s. 1 of the Charter.

---

1   In 2004, at the time that this was written, the Ontario Liberal government had just introduced Bill 144, amending the *Labour Relations Act, 1995* to make it less pro-management.

2   *Canadian Charter of Rights and Freedoms*, part I of the *Constitution Act, 1982*, RSC 1985, app. II, no. 44.

3   J. Fichaud, "Analysis of the Charter and Its Applications to Labour Law," *Proceedings*, 20th Annual Meeting of the Canadian Industrial Relations Association, Vancouver, BC, vol. 11, at 599–600.

Some critics have argued that the courts have not recognized that these changes are part of a restructuring of government that may not be due to an emergency but may be permanent and long-term. Others have argued that with a focus on individual rights, a union's attempt to use the Charter to enforce collective and group rights is unlikely to succeed. However, in one case an individual did attack collective decision making and action by a union, and the court did uphold the union's right to act. In *Lavigne v. Ontario Public Service Employees Union*,[4] a member of the bargaining unit, Merv Lavigne, with the assistance of a conservative political group, the National Citizens Coalition, challenged the union's right to determine how dues are to be spent. The Supreme Court of Canada ruled that compulsory payment of union dues did not violate Lavigne's right to freedom of association. The court held that the union's right as an organization to determine how to spend dues was a legitimate infringement of Lavigne's rights under s. 1 of the Charter. It will clearly take a number of years to determine the extent to which collective and group rights advanced by unions will be upheld under the Charter.[5]

ECONOMIC CHANGES

Since the Great Depression of the 1930s, the world trading economy has gone through several transformations, all aimed at increasing world trade and reducing trade barriers. At the end of World War II, following the Bretton Woods conference, Canada was one of 44 nations that agreed to set up new international economic institutions. The three most important were the International Monetary Fund (IMF), the World Bank, and the General Agreement on Tariffs and Trade (GATT). The purpose of the IMF was to facilitate the expansion of international trade by managing and regulating international credit. The purpose of the World Bank was twofold: (1) to transfer funds through development loans from the leading industrial nations to rebuild war-damaged economies, and (2) to later encourage economic modernization in the Third World to promote foreign trade as a means of developing local economies. GATT was a multilateral trade treaty. GATT members agreed to grant "most favoured nation" status reciprocally to trading partners through bilateral trade treaties. This meant that Canada would give its trade treaty partner a trade deal as good as the best deal Canada had with any other trading partner.

The result of these postwar changes was that Canada largely abandoned its protective tariffs, which had sheltered domestic industries and those who worked in them from foreign competition. By liberalizing trade rules, Canada opened its borders to foreign imports, and in theory created more options for its exports. The trend in this direction continued over the 20th century, through a series of bilateral trade agreements, and sectoral agreements (such as the 1965 Auto Pact between Canada and the United States). Over time, international trade arrangements have

---

4   [1991] 2 SCR 211.

5   Although *Lavigne* established the principle that collective rights are not simply wiped out by the Charter's protection of individual rights, how this principle will be applied over time to other labour relations scenarios will require a number of subsequent case decisions that will fill in the details in the broad picture established by the *Lavigne* case.

evolved, from a series of bilateral trade agreements between Canada and other countries, toward worldwide free trade, a trend usually called **globalization**.

An important event in the globalization of the world economy occurred in 1995 when the World Trade Organization (WTO) replaced GATT. The WTO members agreed not only to liberalize trade in goods, but also to include protection for international trade in services and intellectual property. Members also agreed to adhere to all of the rules in a growing series of regional trade pacts. Under these pacts, extra-governmental bodies render binding decisions to settle disputes about trade rules. By April 2003, 146 nations had joined the WTO.

As a result of globalization, and even prior to the emergence of the WTO, Canada entered into the Canada–US free trade agreement in 1989. The even more expansive North American free trade agreement (NAFTA) involving Canada, the United States, and Mexico in turn superseded this, and came into effect in 1994. The current focus is on a free trade agreement of the Americas (FTAA), which is designed to integrate the economies of all of the countries in North and South America (except Cuba). It is expected that the FTAA will be in full operation by late 2005. The FTAA has had other features tacked on: strengthening democratic institutions, enhancing human rights, and addressing social and economic issues through hemispheric cooperation. Although the extension of a free trade zone to the whole of the Americas is easily understood as part of the general trend toward globalization, the political and human rights provisions of the FTAA are vague. What those provisions actually include and how those provisions will be applied and enforced are far from clear.

The effects of globalization in Canada so far, as a result of the FTA and NAFTA, are readily observable. The United States has long been Canada's main trading partner. By 2000, over 85 percent of Canada's exports went to the United States and over 74 percent of imports came from there. At the same time, US investment in Canada grew, as American companies such as Home Depot and Wal-Mart built big-box stores in Canada, dwarfing smaller Canadian chains and small businesses. Meanwhile, branch plants of manufacturers like GE and Westinghouse have closed Canadian operations, as the tariff advantages that existed prior to free trade were removed.

Unlike earlier trade agreements, NAFTA also affected government policies. Because rules forbid subsidies or payments to help producers with export products, conflicts have erupted in various industries. For example, environmental controls in the lumbering industry have come under attack and led to softwood lumber controversies between Canada and the United States. Also, supply management in the dairy and grain production businesses has been challenged. And environmental legislation designed for the welfare of Canadians was challenged when it interfered with an American chemical company's right to sell a gasoline additive in Canada that had been banned in the United States and in other parts of the world.[6]

The opposition to the WTO and to the implementation of NAFTA and the FTAA in Canada (and elsewhere) stems in large part from the perception by many that democratically elected governments may no longer be free to protect the interests of their citizens. The 1999 "Battle of Seattle" and the 2001 demonstrations

---

6   G. Monbiot, "Running on MMT: The Multilateral Agreement on Investments Will Force
    Governments To Poison Their Citizens," *The Guardian*, August 13, 1998.

in Quebec City were early manifestations of this opposition. They are unlikely to be the last. Among the concerns raised by opponents is the weakening of workers' rights. This issue will be addressed more specifically later in this chapter.

Along with worldwide trade rules has come the evolution of the **transnational corporation (TNC)**. Although these companies often have their head offices in North America, Europe, or Japan, their operations are everywhere, not just for the purpose of sales but also for production. By 1999, the 10 largest TNCs controlled assets representing three times the total income of the world's poorest 38 countries, which together had a population of over one billion people. Of the world's 100 largest economies, 29 are TNCs. While this kind of company is not new, its size and range have increased tremendously. The 1990s saw a number of mergers and takeovers that reduced the number of TNCs but increased the size of the remaining businesses. Also enhancing their operations is the trend to globalization, as a barrier-free, worldwide trade environment emerges that creates even greater economic freedom for these corporations. Indeed, this increasingly unrestricted environment allows them to operate with greater freedom than national companies do within the borders of their own countries.

SOCIAL CHANGES

Social changes since World War II have affected unions and unionized workplaces in significant ways and will continue to affect the workplace. Below, we examine changes in four areas: family structure, equity and equality, management–worker participation, and the aging workforce.

Family Structure

The idea that a woman after marriage left the workforce to raise a family and look after children while the husband went out to work is now gone. Well-to-do families provide the exception, where a husband's income is sufficient to maintain a family in this way. Starting in the 1960s, "second-wave feminism,"[7] stressing gender equality and gender equity, focused on creating options and opportunities for women to participate equally without sex discrimination in all societal institutions, including the workplace. Entering the workforce was seen as a liberating experience, a horizon of opportunity, and an alternative to staying home and raising children, which, many women felt, relegated them to an inferior and secondary role.

As feminism gained strength and social values shifted, more and more women entered the workplace. Between 1976 and 1999 the participation of women in the workplace in Canada rose from 37 percent of all women to 66 percent.[8] The increasing number of professionals, managers, and supervisors who are women reflects this movement.[9] For these women, raising a family is either delayed or does

---

7   First-wave feminism, occurring at the end of the 19th and beginning of the 20th centuries, was
    concerned with legal equality and focused on the right to vote.

8   K.L. Johnson et al., *Work-Life Compendium 2001: 150 Canadian Statistics on Work, Family and
    Well Being* (Guelph, ON: Centre for Families, Work and Well Being, University of Guelph, 2001),
    9.

9   Ibid., at 10.

not occur. And this is reflected both in a falling birth rate and in the relatively late age at which women have their first (and often only) child. In 1987, 20 percent of first-time mothers were over 30; in 2000, this had risen to 30 percent.[10] The older parents often find themselves working, raising children, and also looking after the needs of their own parents, creating the so-called sandwich generation.

However, women in higher-income families (often women who are well educated and in professional and managerial positions) usually have some choices: they may enter the workforce as a preferred alternative to staying home, or to earn income, or both. But for lower-income groups, including clerical and service workers, the fall in real wages since the 1970s has made two breadwinners in a family necessary to simply maintain a middle-class standard of living. Women in lower-income, single-parent families have even less choice.[11] Women in these groups experience some of the same pressures that their wealthier sisters do—balancing work and family responsibilities, especially child rearing. But having fewer economic resources makes the job more difficult for women and their spouses in the second group. For them, issues such as generous maternity and family leave, and inexpensive quality day care at the pre-school and school-age levels are central issues, even survival issues. Quebec's response in the 1990s of low-cost day care was a political recognition of some of the most obvious needs of this disadvantaged group.

Equity and Equality

Prior to World War II, discrimination on the basis of gender, ethnicity, and other social criteria was not uncommon. There were few legal remedies for inequitable treatment. But following the war, discrimination on the basis of race, ethnicity, and religion was no longer seen publicly as legitimate or appropriate behaviour. Human rights codes were passed that prohibited discrimination in basic services such as housing and employment. The types of prohibited discrimination gradually broadened to cover, for example, discrimination on the basis of sex, and discrimination on the basis of sexual orientation. The outlawing of discrimination has also expanded beyond basic needs to include private and public services of various types.

In addition to the banning of direct and intentional discrimination, there is also a move to redress indirect effects of discriminatory attitudes. One example that affects the workplace is the notion of "equal pay for work of equal value," otherwise known as pay equity. It has long been illegal to pay a woman doing the same job as a man lower wages because she is a woman. However, remedies for pay inequity did not touch what are sometimes referred to as "pink ghettos." These are workplaces that are predominantly staffed by women who perform what is traditionally thought of as women's work and who are paid less than men in traditionally "male" job categories, where the work is of equal value to the employer.

Evidence suggests that 70 percent of employed women are still employed in occupations that have been traditionally women's occupations,[12] so the pay equity issue continues to be important. The problem in assessing pay inequity is that, as

---

10 Ibid., at 17.

11 Statistics Canada, *Income in Canada*, 1998, catalogue no. 75-202XLE; Statistics Canada, *Women in Canada*, 2000, catalogue no. 89-503XPE.

12 Johnson et al., supra note 8, at 11.

one judge put it, "it is like comparing peaches to gerbils." Nevertheless, pay equity is the law under the *Canada Labour Code*, and it is the law in many provinces, usually in the public sector but often in the private sector, as well. Some large private employers in banking and communications have embraced it, even when not required to, simply because it is seen as "the right thing to do."

As society has been affected by legislation to control and prevent discrimination, so too have unions. Although unions perceive themselves to be politically progressive, and have supported laws aimed at preventing discrimination, workers have not always seen unions that way. Many unions, particularly in manufacturing, resource extraction, and the building trades, have been perceived as macho and not welcoming to women or ethnic minorities in the workplace or in the governance of the unions themselves. Labour federations such as the Canadian Labour Congress (CLC) and a number of unions have addressed these issues by making efforts to welcome minority workers both in the workplace and in the union.

New Approaches to Management–Worker Participation

Prior to World War II, the management in most workplaces was top down and used a chain of command. Managers gave orders, and workers carried them out. There was little in the formal structure of the workplace that encouraged collaboration or consultation between these parties. Unionization neither changed nor challenged the notion that management made decisions about how work was to be done. Instead, unions sought to advance the interests of their members and improve wages and benefits in the adversarial environment of the workplace. This is still the pattern for most unions.

But in the latter part of the 20th century there were a number of attempts to change the nature of the manager–worker relationship by introducing new models of management. These models invite worker involvement in one way or another. Two Canadian examples are discussed below: Algoma Steel, a private sector industrial employer, and Seneca College, a public sector service provider. We also examine a European experiment with worker involvement.

Algoma Steel. In 1990, Algoma Steel was in grave financial difficulties. It went to Ontario's then NDP government for financial assistance. The province agreed to give the company a loan guarantee, but with the requirement that Algoma's employees be given the opportunity to buy out company shares. Many took advantage of this opportunity and soon the workers had obtained 60 percent of the ownership of the company. This in turn led to workers sitting on the board of directors, and on all major company committees, with access to all corporate financial information. They were involved in development plans, the design of work, and production decision, and had veto power over major company decisions. The exercise of this kind of power required creative rewriting of the collective agreement between the company and its main union, the United Steelworkers. It also required workers to take responsibility for running the company as well as working on production. And it required workers in performing management functions to get expert help in order to act rationally and objectively. They also had to learn to think like managers, and figure out how to resolve the tension between workers and managers in day-to-day operations of the company. The result, at least initially, was a turnaround in the company's fortunes, with the generation of a profit, and an increase in the value of the price of shares. But worker involvement was no panacea. By 2000, the company was again in difficulty due to low prices, decreased demand, and dumping of cheap steel in Canada and the United States. The company sought protection from its creditors, from which it emerged in 2002. Production was scaled back, and there were significant job cuts in 2003. This experiment was not without its critics: public sector unions and the Canadian Auto Workers (CAW), which makes up the majority of workers included in the CLC, were and remain skeptical. The CAW has had some negative experiences in this area: representation by union members on the board at Chrysler in the 1980s brought no discernible benefit, in the view of CAW president Buzz Hargrove. Further, involvement in plant-floor management, and teamwork production in a joint Suzuki–GM–CAMI plant, resulted in a strike. The workers felt that the invitation to participate was more illusion than reality. They felt that management commitment to the cooperative values used in Japanese auto production was lacking and that managers had little interest in the workers' views on production. These problems were exacerbated by the fact that the CAW workers at the CAMI plant earned less than their counterparts at the Big Three auto plants, on the understanding that their product was competing with cheaper third-world products. The CAW's view is that this kind of worker participation is mere window dressing, and that the nature of the economic system virtually requires adversarialism if workers are to be protected. The tension between the Steelworkers' approach and the CAW's approach has not been resolved and a lively discussion continues within the union movement.[13]

Seneca College.   Unionized knowledge workers have presented special challenges in top-down work settings. Used to having control over the quality of the work in public sector work settings in particular, many of these workers often become frustrated when they lack control over what they do. At Seneca College an environment had developed where employees felt they had little input and little control with respect to their work. The board of directors initiated a strategic planning procedure that resulted in a participative decision-making model developed by outside consultants. The model focused on participation per se, rather than on process or results. The model required that the parties first identify the impediments to goals and then develop strategies to remove the impediments. Significantly, the model required the involvement of all those who were affected and concerned through action teams in local work units. This in turn required training in consensus building. Within four years it was clear that the system would not work. Unlike the Algoma case, but like the CAMI case, there was no systemwide acceptance. Key senior managers did not embrace the plan and employees complained that no structural changes had been made to ensure their participation in decision making. Further, there was insufficient focus on process and training, so the norms, values, and managerial culture in the institution did not change. The result of this failed participative management initiative was enhanced skepticism and cynicism for employees, in effect making matters worse than they would have been had

13 T. Pritchard, "CAMI's Striking Experiment," *Globe and Mail*, October 13, 1992, B18; J. Steed, "Algoma's Man of Steel," *Ottawa Citizen*, June 9, 1994, C8.

the effort never been made. A renewed attempt at strategic planning in 2003-4 with involvement by the same managers was with the same skepticism and cynicism from union officials and employees, who have not forgotten the previous experience.[14]

The European experiment. The Europeans, though militant trade unionists, have had a much stronger tradition of worker participation in management of businesses. German unions, for example, have long engaged in worker–management cooperation schemes, with emphasis on worker input into the creation of work practices, and training, particularly for skilled work. In the 1980s, structural changes in the provision of services in the public sector, particularly where private sector business models were introduced, produced a search for greater involvement by workers. Workers were encouraged to participate more in the operations of the enterprise, and a more participative approach to work organization was also emphasized. For example, the Irish airport management authority, Aer Rianta, pursued a policy of participatory management. Under amendments to its legislation, Aer Rianta in the 1990s was committed to the pursuit of its economic and commercial opportunities. With structural support from legislation governing worker participation, Aer Rianta was able to set up discussion groups in 1991 with its unions, with state officials, and with senior managers to identify challenges and ways of solving them. From these informal discussions, the structures for participative management were developed under a Compact for Constructive Participation in 1994. With an agreed-to participatory culture developed over four years, the parties went on to develop working groups, formed around various Aer Rianta operations, to deal with labour, finance, and other operations issues.[15] There was also a central group staffed by stakeholders overseeing the efforts of the working groups and Aer Rianta's operations as a whole, much as was the case for Algoma. But the Aer Rianta approach has gone further: it has tried to develop not only structural changes but also cultural changes, which takes a considerable amount of time. And unlike the Seneca College approach, considerable resources were expended on training, process definition and measurement of results.

Aging Workforce

Absent high levels of immigration, as a society with low birth rates, Canada faces a problem in some sectors, particularly for skilled workers, where there may not be enough young workers to replace retiring baby boomers (those born in the "baby boom" following World War II, from the mid-1940s to the mid-1960s). This problem is compounded by the fact that the retiring baby boomers form a large age cohort compared with the age cohort of the younger workers replacing them. This will have some ramifications in both the workplace and with the Canada Pension Plan and private pensions.

The workplace problem is simply: where do we find new workers to replace those who retire? One answer seems to be fine-tuning immigration policy to entice workers who possess the skills in demand to immigrate to Canada. Another is to

---

14 L. Olivo, "Participative Management … How Not To Do It," in C. Dibelius, ed., *New Forms of Work Organisation: Innovation, Competitiveness and Employment (Report on the Sixth European Ecology of Work Conference)* (Dublin, Ireland: Fondation Européenne, 1999), 66-68.

15 B. Browne and G. O'Connor, "Constructive Participation at Aer Rianta," ibid., 12-13.

abolish mandatory retirement at age 65. This latter option is favoured by some provincial political parties, who define it as a "freedom to work" issue, and point out that it takes the strain off the Canada Pension Plan and private pensions plans. Many pension plans depend on the contributions of those currently working to fund the payments to those who have retired. If there are too few of the former earning too little, it could create an unfunded liability. However, if pensions were collected at a later age, perhaps at 67 or 70, this could take pressure off the pension plans. And it may make some sense for those in service or clerical positions, where, in particular, older workers are still able to carry out their duties effectively.

Another solution to the problem of an aging workforce is a policy for industrial education and training. Although there is federal and provincial money for job retraining where someone is unemployed, there is very little support for many apprenticeship programs, which facilitate entry to the workforce. In Germany, by contrast, such apprenticeship programs are a feature of the workworld. There, students may choose to apprentice in a variety of skills and trades starting in high school. This system creates a coherent link between educational institutions and employers, where employers take responsibility for part of the training, including the cost. Here in Canada, apprenticeship programs are narrower in focus, and not closely connected to a coherent and organized program for skills-based training across a large variety of job categories. Rather, the job is left to community colleges, some employers, and some unions in the traditional skilled trades.

TECHNOLOGICAL CHANGE

Rapid technological change in the last two decades has resulted in decreased employment opportunities in some sectors, particularly for unskilled and semi-skilled workers. Among the changes that have had a major impact on the workplace are CAD-CAM manufacturing techniques, the "paperless" office, and telecommuting:

Computer-assisted design and manufacturing techniques (CAD-CAM). This system, together with the use of robotics, in theory could result in a workerless assembly line. For example, a paint shop on an auto assembly line formerly staffed by a number of workers could be "staffed" by paint-spraying robots commanded by computer software, with one or two workers to oversee the machinery and the process. Skilled knowledge workers, therefore, are finding new employment opportunities involved in managing new technologies. Many of these workers are well paid for their skills, adding to the disparity in income between skilled workers and unskilled casual workers in industry. Displaced lower-skilled workers increasingly are marginalized to service sector jobs at or close to minimum wage (often called survival jobs or "McJobs," referring to the casual, low-paid positions in fast food businesses such as McDonald's). Usually, these lower-paid positions provide incomes that are insufficient to support a family.

The paperless office. The proliferation of office computers and voice mail has made written and oral communication easier, and by doing so, has increased the volume and frequency of those communications. As the means of communications expand, the workers involved may increase in this case rather than decrease, as new ways of using the new technology are devised. For example, computerized phone systems, and cheap long distance rates have made it much easier to expand telemarketing as a marketing tool. However, this creates a service industry allowing for the use of casual, part-time, and low-paid employees. And it raises labour issues involving health and safety. In particular, repetitive strain injuries and keyboard-related injuries have become common. There have also been concerns expressed about low-level radiation from computer monitors. Workplace injuries are now far more likely than formerly to be associated with office work.

Telecommuting. E-mail, cellphones, teleconferencing, and the ease with which large amounts of data can be moved electronically all have given rise to the argument that workers no longer need to speak to each other face to face in the course of the workday. In theory, this means that workers can telecommute—that is, stay at home and work from home, communicating by fax, phone, and e-mail with co-workers. This raises a number of labour issues, particularly for unionized workers. How should such workers be supervised? How will their work be monitored? What privacy issues are involved? What compensation should be paid, if any, for the use of an employee's home or personal resources? Who is responsible if an employee is injured "on the job"?

The Consequences of Technology: Labour Utilization Trends and Stressful Workplaces

As employers shed employees in the 1980s and '90s, there were also attempts to reduce labour costs by using fewer full-time workers, in favour of part-time, casual, and non-permanent contract workers. "Just-in-time" delivery of inventory was matched by "just-in-time" delivery of labour, allowing for labour costs to be fine-tuned by treating labour like an input in the production process, to be used when needed.

By 2000, the results of these changes were well documented: 20 percent of Canadian workers were in part-time jobs. Fifteen years earlier, only 15 percent were in such positions, and twenty-five years earlier, only 10 percent of the workforce was part-time. This use of fewer full-time workers allowed employers much greater flexibility in scheduling and arranging work. But the real savings came from the fact that part-time workers and temporary, contract workers usually were not given benefits. This could reduce labour costs significantly, as benefits typically amount to 20 percent of the cost of employing an individual worker. Figure 9.1 shows the annual averages of full-time and part-time employment in Canada over the 1976-2002 period.

The trend toward an impermanent workforce also led to an increase in self-employment, which accounted for two-thirds of the jobs created in the 1990s. It is likely that many of the self-employed are, in reality, short-term contract workers. By 2000, self-employed workers accounted for 16 percent of the workforce. Of these workers, only 17 percent had benefits, according to Statistics Canada.

The clearest example of the use of just-in-time workers is in the service sector. Between 1976 and 1996, employment in the service sector increased from 67 percent to 75 percent of the workforce, primarily in consumer services and business services. In 2000, for every industrial job created, 10 others were created in the service sector.[16]

16 S. Cote and A. Heisz, "Are Jobs Less Stable in the Services Sector?" (1998), vol. 11, no. 5 *Canadian Economic Observer* 3.

FIGURE 9.1   Full-Time/Part-Time Employment in Canada, Annual Averages, 1976-2002

Year	Full-time employed % of total employed	Part-time employed % of total employed	Voluntary part-time % of part-time employed	Involuntary part-time % of part-time employed
1976	87.4	12.6	89.4	10.6
1986	83.0	17.0	74.2	25.8
1996	80.1	18.9	65.1	34.9
2002	81.3	18.7	72.9	27.1

Source: Statistics Canada, Labour Statistics Division, Labour Force Survey.

FIGURE 9.2   Employment by Sectors, Canada, 1961 and 2002

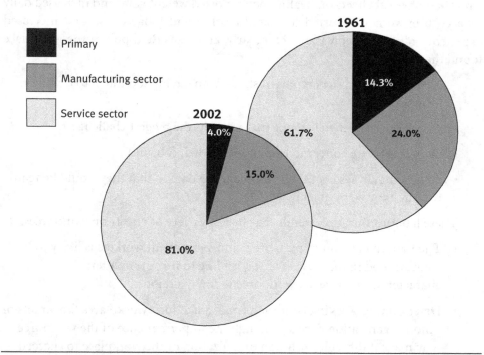

Source: Statistics Canada, Labour Statistics Division.

Of the service sector jobs, 77 percent were full-time in 1997, compared with 92 percent in the manufacturing sector. Today, 9 out of 10 part-time workers are in the service sector. Many of these part-time workers will be engaged in shift work. And 32 percent of all workers experience shift work, both full- and part-time.[17] Figure 9.2 shows the change in employment by sectors in Canada between 1961 and 2002.

Workers who are in full-time positions appear to be working longer and harder than previously. A labour force survey by Statistics Canada conducted in 1998 showed

17 K. Johnson, *Shiftwork from a Work and Family Perspective* (Ottawa: HRDC, Applied Research Branch, 1997); S. Compton and M. Vickers, "One Hundred Years of Labour Force" (2000), 57 *Canadian Social Trends* 2.

that one in five full-time employees worked overtime, averaging almost nine additional hours of work per week or the equivalent of an extra day—and all this despite technological changes designed to reduce the size of the workforce while reducing workloads. The case may be that, although technological change allows the reduction in size of the workforce, the remaining full-time employees using new technology are given greater responsibilities and more work than they previously had. Many take on this work unwillingly because of a lack of job security, or out of economic need, but there is some evidence that so-called workaholics become addicted to long hours. Often these are highly paid individuals who work long hours in paid employment and who have children under the age of 18.[18]

It should not be surprising, then, given the impact of technology on employees, that many workers find their workplaces unstable and stressful. Sixty percent of workers surveyed in 1991 indicated that the technological complexity of their work had increased.[19] The surveyors also found that long hours and workplace stress had physical effects on health: men reported weight gain, and increased daily tobacco use; women reported increased alcohol and tobacco use, and increased experience of major depression.[20] Similarly, an Angus Reid poll of the workplace found that

- 55 percent of workers reported stress from having too much to do in too little time;

- 46 percent described keeping up to date as the biggest challenge;

- 20 percent were concerned about losing their job; and

- 40 percent always kept their résumé up to date so that they would be ready to search for work quickly.[21]

These labour utilization trends may have a variety of effects on workforces:

- The marginalization of part-time, non-permanent workers is likely to be concentrated in the service sector, leading to turnover patterns characteristic of a casual workforce in low-paid jobs.

- Deteriorating working conditions may make such workplaces the targets of union organization drives, although the impermanence of the workforce may make it difficult for union organization of the workplace to succeed.

- Where unions are in the workplace, hours, shift premiums, and access to full-time, permanent positions will be major negotiation and contract-administration issues, often coupled to seniority or some other objective basis of employee selection.

---

18 A. Kemmeny, "Driven To Excel: A Portrait of Canada's Workaholics," in Statistics Canada, *Canadian Social Trends*, Spring 2000, catalogue no. 11-008.

19 A surprising finding, considering that technology is often introduced to simplify work processes. See S. Gera and P. Masse, *Employment Performance in the Knowledge Based Economy* (Ottawa: HRDC, Applied Research Branch, 1996) and see *The Evolving Workplace: Findings from the Pilot Workplace and Employee Survey* (Ottawa: Statistics Canada and HRDC, Ministry of Industry, 1998). Catalogue no. 71-583-XPE.

20 See M. Shields, "Long Working Hours and Health" (1999), vol. 11, no. 2 *Health Reports* 33.

21 Angus Reid Group, *Workplace 2000: Working Toward the Millennium*, 1997.

EFFECTS OF WORKPLACE CHANGES ON UNIONS

Now that we have identified some of the domestic and international political, economic, social, and technological forces that have changed the workplace, we can try to anticipate how those forces are likely to affect unions and the unionized work environment. In this context, we will look at changes in the size and structure of unions, the potential effect on bargaining, and the effect on unions' political and social action programs.

Union Organization and Structure

The changes in the economy and in the nature of employment in the last 20 years have had a big impact on unions. With the removal of tariff protection from domestic manufacturing that came with free trade, many manufacturers have closed Canadian plants, so there are fewer unionized industrial workers than formerly. At the same time, public sector unions such as the Canadian Union of Public Employees, and professional unions such as teachers' and nurses' unions, now have some of the largest union memberships in the country. Service workers, mostly unorganized to start with, continue that way.

The private service sector tends to use casual, contract, and part-time labour, particularly in retail operations. Even where an organizing drive is successful, unions often are decertified later because of employee turnover. Those who were involved in bringing in the union leave, and new workers coming in may lack the commitment or the time to participate in a union. Long-term, permanent employees appear to be essential for maintaining a union. They provide a stable base of union activists necessary to build relationships with the members, and maintain a stable and active union organization. The various attempts to organize workers in the fast food business provides ample evidence of how difficult unionization is in this sector.

That unionization is difficult does not mean that it will not be attempted. Most unions recognize that there is strength in numbers, and that there is a need to continue to organize new locals, and to unionize workplaces. From a union's point of view, organizing the unorganized is always a goal based on basic principles of trade unionism: organizing is one of the things unions do. There is also a practical aspect: a union that is losing members is also losing the union dues paid by members. And it cannot function long without a dues base. So as a matter of institutional survival, in a volatile work world, unions have to organize or die. Because the largely unorganized service sector is growing, and because pay and working conditions are often less than ideal in the service sector, this is where union organization efforts will be going. The Canadian Auto Workers, for example, although an industrial union with a strong base in the automobile manufacturing industry, has focused organizing activities on the largely unorganized private service sector. At times it has organized directly, or used affiliates such as the Canadian Service Workers Union (CSWU), although some of its successes have been at the expense of older service sector unions, such as the Service Employees International Union (SEIU).

For example, in 2002, the full-time and summer casual groundskeepers at the Mount Pleasant Group of Cemeteries in Toronto opted in favour of representation of the CSWU at the end of their SEIU contract with the employer. To some extent, there may be intra-union competition over who represents already unionized workforces in the service sector.

In the end, the numbers tell the story: according to Statistics Canada, about 39 percent of the workforce was unionized at the beginning of the 1990s. The shrinkage of unionized workers in industry and manufacturing had been balanced by the growth in membership in public sector unions. This contrasts with the United States, where unionized workers comprise about 15 percent of the workforce. But by 2003, even with growth in the unionized public sector and organizing efforts in the service sector, the percentage of unionized employees in the total workforce had declined to about 32 percent. In 2002, the CLC began to develop strategies and put more of its resources and that of its member union into organizing in the services sector. The sector's low pay, poor working conditions, shift work, and lack of job security have all made it an attractive target. Even highly paid knowledge workers, such as software developers, long thought to be immune to organizational efforts, have become more likely prospects in the face of job security issues and long working hours.[22]

UNION CONSOLIDATION

Historically, unions in Canada have tended to be fragmented. Many unions developed around specific skilled trades, or job categories, or industries. Some were regionally organized. Although a small number of large unions by size account for the bulk of unionized workers, there are many small, independent unions. This trend toward proliferation of unions continues; but, at the same time, labour has recognized a need for consolidation. Consolidation has advantages. Larger unions are more effective at collective bargaining. Small unions have neither the money nor the staff to provide research, handle grievances, or engage in worker education; nor are they as effective in lobbying or organizing.

Much of the consolidation occurred during the 1990s. Among the more notable examples was the consolidation of the Canadian Paperworkers Union, the Communications Workers of Canada, and the Energy and Chemical Workers Union into one union: the Communications, Energy and Paperworkers Union of Canada.[23] The Canadian Auto Workers provides another example. Originally part of the international United Auto Workers (UAW), the Canadian locals seceded from the UAW to form the CAW in 1984. Based on its ability to negotiate good collective agreements for its auto sector workers, the CAW has established a reputation as a strong union. It has gone on to enter merger agreements with other private sector unions from a wide variety of workplaces to become the largest private sector union. It has also been aggressive in organizing new workplaces, and in raiding other unions, often international ones.

Labour boards that see mergers as a key to more orderly and effective labour relations have encouraged the merger movement, and in cases ordered it. For example, in 1988, the Letter Carriers Union of Canada was by order of the Canada

---

22 V. Galt, "Union Covering Fewer of Canada's Workers," *Globe and Mail*, October 13, 2003.

23 Also, in 1994, NABET and the Southern Ontario Newspaper Guild joined, bringing membership up to 150,000—a large private sector union by Canadian standards.

Labour Relations Board (CLRB) merged into the Canadian Union of Postal Workers (CUPW). The result was one merged union, called CUPW, and a lot of friction between members of the formerly separate bargaining units, including a raid by the International Brotherhood of Electrical Workers encouraged by dissidents in CUPW. The CLRB was not deterred from pursuing merger policies, and went on in 1992 to order the merger of a number of railway unions. Again, many of the unions involved opposed the merger, but it went ahead anyway. It is not unlikely that mergers will continue for the foreseeable future. Some will occur because the members of two or more unions see an advantage, and some will occur because a labour board has seen the need for more rational, orderly labour relations in a particular industry or sector.

THE FUTURE OF INTERNATIONAL UNIONS

International unions, with members in the United States and Canada, for the most part began as American unions, which organized Canadian workers in the same industry. This was not a matter of altruism. Because of Canadian trade policy from the end of the 19th century to the end of World War II, Canada had a system of high tariffs to protect local industry. American multinational or transnational corporations leapt the tariff wall to tap the Canadian market by establishing local branch plants. They also came to Canada to take advantage of a lower-wage economy. With lower costs (compared with the United States) a transnational could produce goods more cheaply than the company's US plants could. This Canadian competition by transnationals (and by domestic Canadian businesses) had the potential to erode union bargaining power in the United States.

Partly to address this problem, a number of unions sought to unionize workforces at transnational companies operating in Canada and in the United States. The United Steelworkers International Union, the Service Employees International Union, the International Brotherhood of Electrical Workers, and the United Auto Workers (prior to its loss of its Canadian arm) are examples of international unions with members and locals in both countries. This trend was so pronounced that, by 1975, nearly half of the unions in the Canadian Labour Congress were international unions, also affiliated with the American AFL-CIO labour federation.[24]

Over the years, these unions have worked for wage parity for their members on both sides of the border. This has generally resulted in gains for Canadian workers. But those gains in turn have reduced the competitive position of the branch plants, leading to closures in Canada. With the advent of the hemispheric trade pacts and globalization, the original rationale for international unions has become weaker, as both Canada and the United States are left open to competition by cheap labour in the third world.

There are other forces at work affecting international unions. In the automobile industry, Canadian plants were often newer and more efficient than American plants, and labour costs were often lower in Canada because publicly funded health care reduced the cost of employee benefit packages, and because of the lower Canadian dollar. In these circumstances, Canadian locals of an international union, like the UAW, may have perceived that they could bargain better terms for their members on their own, given the profitability and efficiency of Canadian plants.

24 "Union Membership by Congress Affiliation, 1942-75," in Statistics Canada, Series E178-189.

That was one reason for the mostly amicable exit of the Canadian members of the UAW to form the CAW.

But this was not the only reason for the formation of the CAW. An enhanced sense of Canadian nationalism since the 1960s, popular on the left in Canada, encouraged the idea of nationally based unions. This was reinforced by the growth of public sector unions such as the Canadian Union of Public Employees (CUPE), and their impact on the labour movement and the CLC. The public sector, by its very nature, is national or provincial in scope, and has little reason to fuel an interest in international unionism.

But, although the international unions seem to be losing ground to Canadian-based unions, is their disappearance certain? Perhaps not, First, many internationals have moved to restructure so that Canadian locals and Canadian divisions have more autonomy locally, and more of a voice in head office affairs. For example, the United Food and Commercial Workers International Union has two distinct Canadian sections that now enjoy meaningful autonomy and can develop distinct Canadian policies. Second, it is arguable that with the collapse of the border as a trade barrier under globalization, the old concerns about parity between US and Canadian workers will become increasingly irrelevant and there will be increasing concern about developing an interest in parity among a transnational corporation's many employees around the world. It is too early to tell how this might unfold. The anti-globalization initiatives are more likely to come from national labour federations than from individual unions because the federations have the perspective and the resources to take up these issues. For example, it might be expected that federations will take initiatives for improving the position of the lowest-paid workers in low-wage economies, working with and encouraging labour federations in those countries, mirroring the earliest efforts of international unions in Canada in the 20th century. This does not mean that international unions as we know them will persist or become directly involved in organizing and representing workers across national boundaries, as they did in the United States and Canada. Rather, stronger links may result between national unions, or national union federations, as they cooperate internationally in dealing with transnational corporations and globalization. Time will tell.

CHANGES IN PUBLIC SECTOR UNIONS

When discussing trends in public sector unions, it is best to distinguish between federal and provincial sectors. The federal government provides relatively few services directly to the public. In the current political environment, the federal government acts like a giant cheque-writing machine, providing funding for programs carried out by provinces. Or, it makes direct payments to individuals, such as under the Canada Pension Plan. This means that many federal government employees perform clerical or regulatory functions. A large number of these employees are represented by the Public Service Alliance of Canada (PSAC). Many of these workers are clerical workers and not highly paid, but tend to enjoy good benefits and pensions. One former attraction, job security, has become more tenuous with the deficit cutting and job reductions in the public service. At first this seems paradoxical, as public sector employment has actually grown. But the growth, where it has occurred, is often in part-time and temporary contract positions. In addition to the PSAC units, there are a number of smaller unions representing workers in the technology and science areas.

Most of the unions in the federal public sector have the right to strike, and when they exercise it, it can be readily felt as services grind to a halt, particularly services involving transfer payments to individuals. However, federal workers who provide direct services, for example, in the corrections area, may be classed as essential and not have the right to strike.

When the right to strike was granted in the 1960s, it allowed federal workers to improve their salary position compared with the private sector because the government usually tried to avoid the negative publicity a strike would bring. The threat of public service strikes has had two effects beyond improving contracts for federal workers. First, because the strikes have much more impact on the public than a strike in the private sector, the right to strike is under political attack. Second, it is argued that public sector settlements have a whipsawing effect in that private sector workers then use recent public sector settlements as a benchmark for contract improvements.

There is one other factor that will affect salaries in the public sector, and that is the long battle between PSAC and other unions and the federal government over pay equity. With a large number of women in clerical positions, what was a $600 million claim when it was launched in the late 1980s is now a claim for several billion dollars in retroactive pay. The decision on pay equity for federal workers will also have the effect of raising the pay levels for many government clerical positions where most of the employees are women.

The provincial public sector presents a different profile. Notwithstanding cutbacks in the provincial public sector in staff and services, the actual job numbers have remained strong, although many of the new positions are part-time or temporary contract positions. Statistics Canada reports that, despite widely publicized downsizing of the civil service in Ontario starting in 1995, by 2003 the number of provincial employees was nearly back to where it was before the cuts. In 2002 alone, the number of provincial employees increased by 3.7 percent, or about 15,000 employees.[25] Provincial employees in unions such as the Ontario Public Service Employees Union (OPSEU) and CUPE provide clerical services like their federal counterparts. However, they are more likely to offer essential services, and many of the workers who provide them are highly visible to the public—ambulance drivers, highway workers, prison guards.

Many of these employees work directly for the government, but others work for public agencies funded by the government in the broader public sector, such as health care workers of various kinds, college faculty, and mental health and community workers. The right to strike was given to some but not all provincial employees, and those that have that right have exercised it, particularly when confronted by governments that are bent on reducing government services and expenditures. Public service strikes such as the OPSEU strikes against the Ontario government in the 1990s were often bitter confrontations where the union did not gain much, and where the parties became even more polarized.

One of the big changes in the public sector is that professionals such as nurses, other medical professionals, teachers, accountants, and even lawyers have joined unions or are members of professional associations that increasingly have come to

25 S. Tuch, "Number of Public Servants Up Since '02," *Globe and Mail*, October 4, 2003.

act like unions.[26] In some cases, these workers are members of professional associations that have come to be virtually indistinguishable from unions in their negotiation of labour contracts. The Ontario Nurses' Association is one example of a professional association that acts quite consciously like a union for its members, almost all of whom are now public employees, thanks to government funding of health care and, in particular, hospitals. The Ontario Medical Association performs a similar function by negotiating fee schedules for doctors.

Traditionally, members of these professional groups would have seen themselves as having little in common with unions. They often see themselves in terms of their own traditions as autonomous, self-governing professionals who determine how they do their work. They are often unfamiliar with the culture of Canadian unionism and seem uncomfortable with it: the idea of doctors singing "Solidarity Forever" on a picket line still takes a lot of imagination. But as the reality of governmental control over their income, hours, and working conditions sinks in, some of these workers may become more positive about unionism, and begin to participate in mainstream labour organizations. For example, Ontario teachers' unions that long held aloof from labour federations have now joined the Ontario Federation of Labour. It may well be the case that other professional workers will follow suit.

As in service industries in the private sector, there is a similar emphasis on union organizing in the public sector. Downsizing and privatization have led to reduction in public service union memberships, although public sector unions are still stronger than those in the private sector. In this volatile situation, public service unions try to reorganize their former members, who are now privatized workers. They may also compete to represent workers who have been privatized who were previously represented by other unions. For example, when the Harris government began its downsizing activities in the mid-1990s, the civil service shed jobs, and the Ontario Public Service Employees Union found itself shedding members, as many employees were terminated or were transferred to privatized corporations or quasi-public corporations in the broader public sector. OPSEU's reaction was to put more resources into organizing drives to reorganize workers it had lost to private and newly created government corporations. For example, OPSEU succeeded in reorganizing property tax assessors, who had formerly been part of the civil service, and forming new locals from their ranks.

It is likely that public sector organizing will be more successful than private sector organizing. Many of those who are the focus of the organizing drives were previously union members, and were long-term employees. Many may resent what they see as deterioration in their wages, hours, and working conditions in the quasi-public organizations now employing them. These workers may be relatively open to organizing.

Private sector organizers may face a more difficult task. They are often focused on workplaces, often small ones, that have no history of union memberships, and where the workforce has often been casual and part-time: few people, after all, aspire to careers flipping hamburgers in fast food businesses, or selling T-shirts in retail clothing corporations. If they are just "passing through," they may not be

---

26 In the 1990s lawyers employed by the Ontario government formed an association of Crown attorneys and another organization for other government lawyers, the Association of Law Officers of the Crown.

interested enough in improving their own salary and working conditions to participate in a unionization drive. As well, unions have, up till now, focused on full-time employees. Few collective agreements have much in them that benefits part-time or seasonal employees. Unions will have to change their approach and address these issues if they are to reach the hearts and minds of these employees.

THE IMPACT OF WOMEN IN AND ON UNIONS

As has been noted, since the 1970s the percentage of women in the workforce, particularly women 25 years old or older, has risen dramatically. The number of women in unionized jobs has increased dramatically as well, not just because of workforce participation rates generally, but also because of the unionization of jobs in the public service and broader public sector. Today, clerical, teaching, and nursing jobs are all overwhelmingly "women's occupations." Between 1966 and 1992 there has been a fivefold increase in the number of women in unions. Now 31 percent of employed women are in unions, compared with 33 percent for employed men. Women now comprise 46 percent of union members; they were only 20 percent in the 1960s. But because of the concentration of women in clerical, teaching, and nursing occupations, women now comprise about half of the unionized workers in the public sector.[27] If the next target for unionization is jobs in the service sector, the number of women involved in unions can be expected to rise even more.

The increased involvement of women in unions will likely increase pressure for negotiating demands that might not otherwise come to the table. The most obvious demands will be more generous maternity-leave benefits, four-day workweeks, flexible hours, and leave arrangements to care for family members.

Canadian Collective Agreements in 2000 Reflect Family-Related Concerns

- 52 percent had access to some paid maternity leave above the EI minimum

- 52 could percent keep seniority, or could accrue further seniority, during maternity or family leave

- 42 percent had access to paternity leave for fathers

- 33 percent could refuse overtime

- 23 percent had access to a compressed workweek

- 21 percent had access to flextime options

- 6 percent had access to day care in or through the workplace.

Many of these provisions were, in many agreements, subject to the discretion of management.

Source: *Work and Family Provisions in Canadian Collective Agreements*, February 2001, HRDC, Canada Labour Programs.

---

27 Statistics Canada, *Perspectives on Labour and Income: Fact Sheet on Unionization 2002*, vol. 14, no. 4, at 4-7.

Within unions themselves, women have long been underrepresented in executive positions within both local unions and labour federations such as the CLC. The macho culture of many unions, particularly industrial unions, is not attractive to or encouraging for many women. The use of racist or sexist language, unfamiliar rules or procedures, the favoured treatment of male protégés, and meetings in inappropriate places or at inconvenient times may tend to discourage women who might otherwise become involved with their unions or be receptive to a unionization drive.[28] This is not just an equity issue for unions. How attractive a unionized environment is for women and how welcoming unions are will have a major impact on future organizing drives in the service sector with its large number of female employees.

By the mid-1980s, unions in Canada had begun to recognize the need to welcome women, and began to actively recruit and promote women within the union movement. In public sector unions in particular, women have begun to play major roles, and occupy executive positions.[29] The CLC has taken some steps to actively promote women within its executive. Many unions have created equity agencies within their own organizations to encourage and promote women and minority members. It is likely that unions will increasingly attempt to raise the participation rate of women within unions and labour federations, and will in turn become increasingly involved in government lobbying on social issues, such as health and education issues, and on matters relating to support for families.

VISIBLE MINORITIES AND UNIONS

The same observations about women's involvement in unions may also be made about ethnic minorities. Workplaces that have large numbers of workers who are members of visible or ethnic minorities are unlikely to be positively disposed to unions if these members are continuously underrepresented on the union executive, or if they do not feel welcomed. Unions in the public sector, with a relatively long involvement with equity hiring, began to respond to these issues earlier and in depth by recognizing minority issues, creating offices or agencies within the union, and recognizing minority caucuses within the union organization. The challenge will continue to be greater for unions in the service sector, where the next big organizing drives are likely to occur.

Union Political and Social Action

Union activists have long distinguished between conservative trade unionism, also called business unionism, which focuses primarily on negotiation of and administration of a collective agreement, and political unionism. Political unionism similarly focuses on the collective agreement, but also engages in social activism and politics as an element of trade union activity.

The more conservative approach has been characteristic of the older craft unions, such as the International Brotherhood of Electrical Workers, whose primary interest was in controlling wages, hours, and working conditions for the

---

28 V. Galt, "Unions Urged To Promote Women," *Globe and Mail*, February 8, 1993, quoting an ILO study.

29 Judy Darcy, president of CUPE, and Leah Casselman, president of OPSEU, are two prominent examples.

skilled workers who are its members. These unions had little interest in and spent few resources on political or social issues.

Vertically organized industrial unions such as the CAW, and the public sector unions with a much broader and often lower-paid membership, have often been more active than conservative unions in pursuing a social and political agenda. This activity includes joining umbrella groups to promote such programs as medicare or opposing trends such as globalization, and affiliating with and supporting the New Democratic Party.

For the social activists, labour federations such as the Ontario Federation of Labour or the Canadian Labour Congress often provide a platform for this activity. But many unions will become directly involved in political activity. And it is possible that some of this activity may find its way to the bargaining table. For example, some unions try to ensure that the employer is not using products or inventory made through forced labour or child labour, and that companies engage in ethical sourcing of materials.

The focus of political activism may shift with the times. In the 1970s much effort was expended on opposing wage and price controls. At present, many unions will involve themselves in anti-globalization initiatives, and resistance to privatization of public services. There is some evidence that both unions and some elements of the NDP are re-examining the nature of the union–party relationship. It is possible that in the future labour will have less direct involvement in party affairs, in part so that unions can seek support for policies from whoever is in power. As well, some party members would like to see the party making a more direct appeal to individual voters and members, without being seen as the party of labour.

For public sector unions, union–party relations may be even more complex. In 2002, for example, the OPSEU executive voted to make a $200,000 contribution to one candidate in the federal NDP leadership race. But in 2003, OPSEU advised its members to vote for the candidates in the upcoming provincial election who could best defeat the Conservatives—whether that candidate was NDP or Liberal. This approach is referred to as strategic voting and more colloquially within the union movement as the "CAW solution," because the CAW has been a proponent of this approach, and a critic of automatic union support for the NDP. Public sector unions, in particular, always have the problem of possibly supporting or trying to defeat whoever will be sitting opposite them at the bargaining table. This can lead to a kind of political schizophrenia, as when OPSEU had to deal with an NDP government that cut their salaries. Many members found it difficult to support the party that was reducing the size of their paycheques. A decoupling of labour unions from the NDP is no longer the forbidden subject among union members it once was.

The Effects of Globalization on Labour Standards

As we noted earlier, the FTA, NAFTA, and the FTAA all offer great opportunities for businesses. But do these trade agreements include any guarantee of basic labour standards? It appears not. Any participating state would be quite free to scrap its legislation governing labour relations, health and safety, or employment standards. Without these protections, labour may come under attack in two ways. First, where such legislation exists, many businesses may move their operations to states where wages are low and labour standards weak or non-existent. Second, as jurisdictions compete with each other to attract transnational corporations, labour standards are likely to be further eroded as part of that competition. This move by businesses to low-wage jurisdictions has been referred to as "social dumping," and it has been attacked not only by organized labour but also by others, including right-wing populists in the United States such as Pat Robertson and Ross Perot. Perot, when he made his run for the presidency in the 1990s, spoke of this trend. He voiced his opposition to US involvement in hemispheric free trade, saying Americans would hear a "giant sucking sound" as jobs left the United States for Mexico.

Some models have emerged, such as that of the European Union, that would prevent the problems that labour anticipates as a result of free trade pacts. The European Union (EU) began as an iron and coal trade treaty in Europe at the end of the World War II, and then became a regional free trade zone known as the European Economic Community. By the 1980s it had evolved into a political union as well, where national governments did not just cede rights to those who wished to trade, but ceded some governing rights to the European Union government to protect basic individual rights. And it is the creation of a supranational pan-European jurisdiction that has made the difference for labour. The EU has created a basic common set of enforceable labour standards that all member states must obey. Under its own governing machinery, the EU can, on the basis of the complaint of a member state or on its own, order a member state to enact national labour legislation that meets the EU minimum standard. If the member state fails to do so, then legal proceedings may be commenced in the European Court of Justice. As well, individual citizens of member states may bring a complaint to the court if they can show that they have been directly affected by a member state's non-compliance with the EU standard.

But the EU model remains the exception. In fact, because of the political reaction to the lack of protection of labour standards, this matter was considered by the WTO. It was determined at the WTO meeting in Singapore in 1996 that core labour standards would not form any part of the WTO rules. Instead, the WTO members indicated that labour standards were to be left to the International Labour Organization (ILO). This organization, made up of representatives of business, labour, and governments, is affiliated with the UN. Prior to World War II it was affiliated with the now defunct League of Nations. Although the ILO tries to promote workers' rights, its powers are limited. It can investigate, publicize, and report violations of basic standards, but it has no practical means of enforcing those standards except by moral suasion. It did impose sanctions on Myanmar over the issue of forced labour, but there is no indication that the sanctions had much effect or were enforced. Labour legislation in Ontario was also subject to review by the ILO when the Harris government in 1998 denied the rights of school vice-principals and principals to organize, bargain collectively, and strike. On the basis of an interim report, Ontario changed its legislation to allow these individuals the right to organize, bargain, and strike.

Within the WTO there is a clear division of opinion on whether labour standards should be protected. Industrialized nations, such as Canada, have pushed for comprehensive protections. These nations have argued that the enforcement of labour standards allowing collective bargaining, freedom of association, freedom from workplace abuse (including forced labour and some forms of child labour), and the elimination of discrimination in the workplace should be enforced by the

WTO member states. They argue that this policy would establish minimum standards that would encourage member states to improve workplace conditions.

But the developing states, and some developed states, argue that the inclusion of labour standards is another form of protectionism, and that it would undermine the advantage that lower-wage states would have in competing in world trade. They argue a version of supply-side economics where "a rising tide lifts all boats." If there is economic growth unfettered by core labour standards, they assert, conditions will improve over time, and labour rights will then develop.

In the case of NAFTA, the parties included a side deal, the North American Agreement on Labor Cooperation (NAALC). The agreement, which came into effect in 1994, recognizes the right of each country to set its own labour legislation as part of its domestic law. NAALC does not establish minimum standards all must adhere to, nor does it harmonize labour law standards. But it is able to review a country's enforcement of its own labour laws by carrying out investigations. If the matter is not resolved, then a member state may take the dispute before a panel of arbitrators. The panel may make findings of fact and recommend action, including fines or suspension of some NAFTA trading rights, but it cannot compel a member state to adopt even minimal labour standards, or to enforce the ones it has.

Selected Articles from the North American Agreement on Labor Cooperation

Article 1: Objectives

The objectives of this Agreement are to:

1. improve working conditions and living standards in each Party's territory; ...

3. encourage cooperation to promote innovation and rising levels of productivity and quality;

4. encourage publication and exchange of information, data development and coordination, and joint studies to enhance mutually beneficial understanding of the laws and institutions governing labor in each Party's territory;

5. pursue cooperative labor-related activities on the basis of mutual benefit;

6. promote compliance with, and effective enforcement by each Party of, its labor law; ...

Article 2: Levels of Protection

Affirming full respect for each Party's constitution, and recognizing the right of each Party to establish its own domestic labor standards, and to adopt or modify accordingly its labor laws and regulations, each Party shall ensure that its labor laws and regulations provide for high labor standards, consistent with high quality and productivity workplaces, and shall continue to strive to improve those standards in that light.

The lack of clear minimal labour standards and the lack of real enforcement powers indicate that the NAALC is unlikely to have any substantial effect on improving workers' rights anywhere, anytime soon. And the FTAA that is currently in the works also appears to include no guarantee that core labour standards will receive any protection.

Case: Violating NAALC Principles

Echlin Case, US NAO (National Administration Office) Case No. 9703

Facts

In 1996, workers in an auto-parts factory in Ciudad de los Reyes, Mexico State, then owned by the US-based Echlin company, were concerned about unhealthy and unsafe working conditions in the plant. As well as handling asbestos, workers were exposed to other toxic materials in poorly ventilated conditions. Wages were low, and workers endured sexual harassment and abuse from supervisors. The workers were represented by the CTM, a union associated with the ruling political party in Mexico, the Institutional Revolutionary Party (PRI). At the time, the PRI had governed Mexico continually since the 1920s. Its unions were perceived as ineffective and more attuned to the employers' interests than to the interests of its members.

When the workers tried to change their union representation from the CTM, company managers intimidated them, using such tactics as surveillance and heavier workloads for supporters.

Voting procedures for the new union were marked by irregularities, such as threats from management, and an open—not secret—ballot. The result was that the CTM won the election.

In December 1997, the petitioners, the Echlin Workers Alliance (made up of a group of US and Canadian unions, as well as human rights organizations and several non-governmental organizations), filed a complaint under the NAALC before a US panel. The petitioners alleged that the Mexican government was permitting violations of NAALC principles in respect of freedom of association, the right to organize into a trade union of one's choice, and the right to bargain collectively. There were also allegations of a failure to take basic steps to prevent occupational injuries and diseases, and against the Mexican government, for failing to maintain fair and impartial labour tribunals.

Issues

Were workers' rights to freedom of association and to collective bargaining interfered with by the employer or by the Mexican government? Did the Mexican government fail to enforce health and safety regulations in the plant?

Decision

The US panel held a public hearing on the case in March 1998 and published a report four months later. It confirmed that the workers faced threats of physical attack and dismissal, and that pro-PRI union thugs intimidated workers during union voting. Authorities turned a blind eye toward these abuses, and labour tribunals aided and approved the outcome of these flawed processes. As well, health and safety regulations were not enforced at the plant, largely due to what was described as a seriously flawed inspection system.

The outcome of these findings was that in May 2000, Mexico and the United States arrived at a ministerial agreement to hold several public seminars. The US and Mexican governments agreed jointly to discuss health and safety techniques. With respect to interference by PRI in the union organizing process, an action plan included overall goals for the Mexican government to pursue, without detailing how these were to be achieved. The plan stated:

> The Mexican Department of Labor and Social Welfare will continue promoting the registry of collective bargaining contracts in conformity with established labor legislation. At the same time, efforts will be made to promote that workers be provided information pertaining to collective bargaining agreements existing in their place of employment and to promote the use of eligible voter lists and secret ballot elections in disputes over the right to hold the collective bargaining contract.

A substantially similar case was filed at the same time in Canada (Canadian NAO case no. 98-1).

THE IMPACT ON BARGAINING: AN OVERVIEW

It is important to recognize that the changed work environment may bring about a changed emphasis in bargaining and negotiating positions for both employers and unions. Expect to see some of the following:

- Employers may press to bargain for "take-aways" on working conditions, overtime, and hours of work because of competition from low-wage work environments like Mexico. This is most likely to occur with manufacturing and product finishing as Mexican **macquiladoras** compete head-to-head with Canadian manufacturers.

- Employers may seek to ease layoff restrictions, increase the use of part-time workers without increasing their wages or benefits, contract work out to third parties, introduce new technology, make job classifications more flexible, and make it easier to move workers from one job classification to another to meet production demands. In general the employer goal is to make the workforce more flexible: just-in-time inventory may be followed by just-in-time employees. Unions can be expected to resist these initiatives, and aim for job guarantees, guarantees against plant closures, and job security in general.

- Some unions may bring some of their social concerns to the bargaining table, looking, for example, for restrictions on the use of products in the workplace that have been produced by non-union labour, or by child or slave labour. Unions may also seek restrictions on inventory that has not been **fair traded**, and may bargain for **ethical sourcing** controls.

- Unions are likely to take an increased interest in representing part-time and short-term contract workers, and in improving their benefits, working conditions, and wages. Alternatively, unions may seek to restrict the use of such workers, particularly if they are not part of an existing local bargaining unit.

- Unions will continue to bargain for mandatory retirement in order to make room for new workers, even though mandatory retirement is likely to disappear on two grounds. First, it may amount to unjustified age discrimination and violate the *Charter of Rights and Freedoms*. Second, demographic projections into the early 21st century indicate that a continued low birth rate in Canada will result in labour shortages. More important, projections show that there will not be enough young workers paying into the Canada Pension Plan, and private pension plans, to fund the pensions of older workers.

  The union movement is not of one mind on the issue of mandatory retirement: in some areas, there is support for its end, but most unionists do favour it, particularly where the worker has an adequate pension plan. As well, unions in the industrial sector, where members engage in physical labour, argue that by age 65, the normal retirement age, their members are physically worn out and should not have to work longer than they are comfortably able to. Employers may also be interested in mandatory retirement because the wage levels of senior employees are usually much higher than those of junior employees.

- There is likely to be continued growth in public sector unions, if only because these jobs are not easily exported to the Third World.

- As professionals are drawn into the public sector, either directly or because of public funding, professional autonomy is likely to decrease, and these highly educated and highly paid workers may turn to unions as a vehicle to control their work environment.

- Increased numbers of women will enter the workplace and join unions and union activism will change both the workplace and the unions themselves. Work issues such as maternity leave, flextime work scheduling, daycare support, permanent part-time work, and pay equity are all likely to be increasingly emphasized in collective agreements. At the same time, women will increasingly become involved in unions themselves and this will likely affect union positions on various political issues, including such matters as sexual equality, sexual discrimination, and pay and employment equity.

CHAPTER SUMMARY

This chapter examined some likely future trends affecting unions, their members, and unionized workplaces. The chapter began with an overview of changes in the external environment, changes in the nature of work, and changes in the workplace since World War II. It then noted specific political, economic, social, and technological factors that underlie emerging trends in the workplace. Political factors include the impact of the *Canadian Charter of Rights and Freedoms* on the rights of both unions and their members. Economic factors of importance centre on the move to globalization, and its effect on jobs and the unionized workforce in the face of changing patterns of labour utilization. Social factors include the effect of increased numbers of women in the workforce, family structure, the increasing importance of equity issues, and new management styles. The chapter then considered the impact of technology on the nature of work, and job generation and loss. Having set out key macro-environmental factors, the chapter examined changes to union organization and structure, the evolution of international unions, changes in public sector unions, the impact of women and minorities on unions, union political and social action initiatives, and the effect of globalization on labour standards. The chapter concluded with an examination of how bargaining issues are likely to change as a result of a changing work environment.

REVIEW QUESTIONS

1. Describe five ways in which the workplace has changed since 1945 that will affect the way labour relations are conducted in future.

2. What three changes in labour relations would you expect to see as a result of some of the changes described in question 1?

3. How has globalization affected labour standards?

4. What is the approach taken by unions that focus on business unionism?

5. What problems have public sector unions faced in today's labour environment?

6. In which sector(s) would you expect to find union organizing drives occurring in the future?

7. How does the EU differ from NAFTA in how it deals with labour standards?

8. How has the increase of married women in the workforce changed the unionized workplace?

DISCUSSION QUESTIONS

1. You are the HR manager for Sportball Ltd., a company that is in the business of manufacturing sports equipment, including baseball bats, hockey sticks, footballs, soccer balls, and baseballs. Although business is steady, and your market share is now stable, you recently lost part of your

market share to competitors who are producing baseballs and soccer balls at lower cost in Haiti and in macquiladoras in Mexico. Your production-line workers are unionized, but the office staff and sales staff are not. It is April 15, Yr. 0. The collective agreement expires in five months, on September 15, Yr. 0. Nobody really wants a strike, and both sides would like to conclude a new agreement.

   a. What demands is the employer likely to bring to the table when negotiating for a new collective agreement?

   b. How can the employer's demands be presented in a way that the union could find acceptable?

   c. What demands is the union likely to bring to the table?

   d. How can the union's demands be presented in a way that the employer could find acceptable?

2. Debate the following proposition: "RESOLVED, that minimum labour standards will not be part of free trade rules."

Case Study: Negotiating a Collective Agreement

INTRODUCTION

The material in this appendix may be used to conduct a mock negotiation or as the basis for discussion on the process of labour negotiations. If mock negotiations are to be conducted, the participants should first read the Background, Data, and Collective Agreement sections below. Participants will then be assigned to either a union team or a management team and allocated specific roles for their team. The teams should then refer to the Procedure section below, and prepare detailed proposals and costing based on the Collective Agreement and on the information provided in the Background and Data sections. Participants will need to refer to the specific, relevant provisions in the Collective Agreement provided in order to prepare their demands.

BACKGROUND

The union and management at Joe's Furniture Corporation are preparing to negotiate the renewal of a collective agreement. The relevant text of the agreement is found at pages 268-289 of this appendix.

The union has held a demand-setting meeting and has adopted the following demands:

- increase salary to a level at least as high as that of comparative manufacturing plants,

- increase vacation entitlement by one week for each group,

- increase shift premium to 75 cents per hour,

- restore a cost-of-living allowance that had been removed in the last round of negotiations,

- increase the amount for prescription safety glasses, and

- expand the list of relatives to whom bereavement leave applies.

In response to a series of failed arbitration awards and membership demands, the union will also propose that

- promotion language be changed to provide that if an employee has sufficient ability to do the job, then seniority will prevail; and

- in the event of technological change, the employer shall reopen the agreement and negotiate the impact with the union.

Management has held meetings at which it decided that its agenda would include

- more flexibility on the hours of work so that it could average work over a number of weeks and so that there would be no overtime if work averaged 40 hours over a period of time;

- a change from a three-person arbitration board to a sole arbitrator; and

- the removal of the limits on contracting out work.

The management bargaining team will include, at least,

- the Human Resources Manager

- the Production Manager

- the Production Supervisor(s)

- the Accounting Manager

- the Legal Adviser.

The union bargaining team includes:

- the Staff Negotiator

- the Local President

- the Shop Steward(s)

- the Local Representative elected at a meeting of the entire membership (at least one from each of the three areas)

DATA

The parties will need the following additional information.

1. For salary calculations, the parties will need to know the number of employees at each salary level:

Job Rate	Number of Employees
40	4
39	7
37	10
36	12
35	7
34	11
32	9
20	8
9	15

Job Rate	Number of Employees
8	32
7	47
6	21
5	25
4	37
3	21
2	19
1	5

2. For vacation calculations, the parties will need to know the following service times for employees:

Service Times	Number of Employees
Less than 1 year	17
1 year to less than 4 years	38
4 years to less than 8 years	42
8 years to less than 13 years	55
13 years to less than 20 years	80
20 years plus	58

3. For shift-premium calculations, the parties will need to know the number of instances of shift premiums. The average is that each employee works 30 shifts per year to which a shift premium applies.

4. Financial data for the employer. Because this is a private corporation, the data will only be available to the management side. It is for management to decide whether to reveal all or part of the information.

PROCEDURE

1. The class will be divided into two teams for this exercise. One team will represent the management of Joe's Furniture Corporation. The other team will represent the union. The selection and composition of the teams will be determined by the instructor.

2. In preparation, the teams should do the following:

   a. Use the Ontario Ministry of Labour website to develop salary demands and responses. Go to http://www.gov.on.ca/LAB/english/lr/ pubs_type.html.

   b. Develop a set of proposals and priorities and prepare costing for these proposals.

3. Present and articulate these proposals to the other team.

4. Attempt to negotiate an agreement or reach a position where the best alternative is to engage in either a strike or a lockout. The number and duration of meetings will be determined by the instructor.

COLLECTIVE AGREEMENT

BETWEEN

JOE'S FURNITURE CORPORATION
(hereinafter referred to as "the Company")
– and –
UNITED FURNITURE WORKERS OF AMERICA,
AFL-CIO-CLC, through its Agent, Local 510
(hereinafter referred to as "the Union")

TERM OF AGREEMENT:

September 1st, 2004 to August 31, 2005

INDEX

Article

1	Purpose of Agreement	21	Leave of Absence
2	Recognition	22	Jury Duty
3	Management Rights	23	Bereavement
4	Union Activity	24	Tools and Supplies
5	Union–Company Cooperation	25	Wage Rates
6	No Discrimination	26	Vacations with Pay
7	Strikes and Lockouts	27	Transfers
8	Representation	28	Union Security
9	Grievance Procedure	29	Job Evaluation
10	Arbitration	30	Pay on Day of Injury
11	Discipline and Discharge Cases	31	Health and Welfare
12	Hours of Work	32	Pension Plan
13	Seniority	33	Overtime—Saturday and Sunday Work
14	Job Posting	34	Pay Day
15	Reporting Pay	35	Shift Premium
16	Standby Pay	36	Canada Savings Bonds
17	Rest Periods	37	Automation and Technological Changes
18	Bulletin Boards	38	Time-Study Observations
19	Safety and Health	39	Duration of Agreement
20	Paid Holidays		

Schedule "A": Job Classification and Wage Rates

Schedule "B": Enrollment in and Administration of the Benefit Plan

THIS AGREEMENT made and entered into this 20th day of September, 2004.

ARTICLE 1: PURPOSE OF AGREEMENT

1.01 The parties are agreed that the purpose of this Agreement is to provide orderly collective bargaining relations between the Company and the Union, to secure prompt and equitable disposition of grievances, and to eliminate interruption of work and interference with the proper operation of the Company's business.

ARTICLE 2: RECOGNITION

2.01 The Company recognizes the Union as the collective bargaining agent for all of its employees at its Furniture Division in Peterborough, save and except supervisors, persons above the rank of supervisor, office staff, sales staff, and persons employed by the Company exclusively to perform the work of security guards.

2.02 The word "employee" or "employees" whenever used in this Agreement shall mean any or all employees, male or female, in the bargaining unit as defined above.

ARTICLE 3: MANAGEMENT RIGHTS

3.01 The Union recognizes the right of the Company to hire, promote, or transfer employees and to suspend, demote, discharge, or otherwise discipline any employee for just cause subject to the terms of this Agreement.

3.02 The Union further recognizes the responsibility of the Company to operate its business in all respects in accordance with its commitments and responsibilities. The location of equipment, the products to be manufactured, the number of employees, the schedules of production, the methods, processes, and means of manufacturing are exclusively the responsibility of the Company.

3.03 It is agreed that the above Management's rights shall not be exercised in a manner that violates any of the provisions of this Agreement.

ARTICLE 4: UNION ACTIVITY

4.01 The Union agrees that there will be no Union activity of any kind on the Company's premises during working hours, except that which is necessary in connection with the handling of grievances and the enforcement of this Agreement, and that there will be no collective Union activity on the Company's premises unless specific permission is granted by the Company in writing.

ARTICLE 5:   UNION–COMPANY COOPERATION

5.01 The Union and the Company agree to cooperate in order to maintain quality of production.

ARTICLE 6: NO DISCRIMINATION

6.01 There shall be no discrimination, intimidation, or coercion by the Company or the Union or its members against any employee.

ARTICLE 7: STRIKES AND LOCKOUTS

7.01 The Company agrees that it will not lock out the employees.

7.02 The Union agrees that it will not call, authorize, encourage, or support any strike, stoppage of work, or slowdown, partial or complete.

7.03 No employee or employees shall instigate or participate in any unlawful strike, stoppage of work, or slowdown that would be detrimental to the production of the Company.

ARTICLE 8: REPRESENTATION

8.01 The Union shall appoint a Union Shop Committee consisting of a number of Stewards, each of whom must have been in the employ of the Company for a minimum period of six (6) months before their appointment.

8.02 The Union agrees to furnish the Company and to maintain from time to time a complete, up-to-date list of its Stewards.

8.03 One Steward shall be appointed and shall represent each one of the departments or zones that are established by the parties at the time of the signing of this Agreement. It is understood that the Company may effect changes in the makeup of zones or departments for the purposes of Steward representation, provided, however, that the numerical representation of employees by Stewards shall be retained. The Company shall advise the Union of any changes which it effects in the makeup of departments or zones and it is understood that the right of the Company to make such changes shall not be of a recurring nature so as to continually disrupt the consistency of the Union Shop Committee.

8.04 It is understood that Stewards have regular duties to perform in connection with their employment. Before leaving regular duties to function as a Steward, an employee must first obtain permission from a supervisor to do so. Such consent from the supervisor will not be unreasonably withheld. If duties as a Steward make it essential for the employee to leave their own department or go to another department, they must first report to the supervisor of that department, before contacting any employee. The Company agrees that it shall make every reasonable arrangement without undue delay to assure that its supervisors will take necessary steps to arrange for the attendance of Union Stewards in any particular department in order to carry out legitimate Union business without interference.

8.05 The Company will pay for time spent by Stewards not working on incentive, during working hours, for discussions of grievances in the plant or with the Company at basic hourly rates. Stewards working on incentive shall, during the period they are engaged directly on grievances, be paid an amount equal to their average hourly earnings calculated over the previous four (4) weeks worked, not to exceed the previous six (6) weeks, for time involved on such grievances. There shall be no abuse of these privileges. The allowances shall not in any case be in excess of a total of six (6) hours per month for each steward and a total of thirty-five (35) hours per month for the Chief Shop Steward.

8.06 Whenever a Union representative or Union Staff Representative visits the factory to discuss matters with employees, they shall, upon entering the premises of the Company, identify themselves, and make known to a representative of the Company the names of any employees they wish to see so that necessary arrangements may be made in a manner not to unnecessarily disrupt production. Such a Union representative or Union Staff Representative may have access to the workers at reasonable times.

ARTICLE 9: GRIEVANCE PROCEDURE

9.01 It is the mutual desire of the parties hereto that all claims of an alleged violation of this Collective Agreement shall be adjusted as quickly as possible. It is understood that an employee has no grievance until they have personally processed it in accordance with the following steps of the Grievance Procedure.

STEP 1

The employee shall present a grievance in writing to their supervisor, or in the alternative, the written grievance of the employee may be presented to the supervisor of the employee concerned by the Union Steward. The supervisor shall render a decision in writing not later than two (2) working days following receipt of the grievance.

STEP 2

In the event that the grievance is not settled under Step 1, the employee or the Steward of the employee concerned may present the grievance within two (2) working days after the written answer of the supervisor has been received to the Production Manager, who shall render a written decision on the grievance not later than three (3) working days after receipt thereof.

STEP 3

In the event that the grievance has not been settled, any member of the Union Shop Committee may present the written grievance to the Human Resources Manager within three (3) working days after the written answer of the Production Manager has been received. When the grievance is discussed at this Step, the authorized officer, or a representative of the Union, may attend at the request of either party. The Human Resources Manager shall render a written decision on the grievance not later than five (5) working days after the grievance meeting. The Local President should be present in all Third Step Grievances. The Local Union shall pick up the cost.

9.02 The Union shall have the right to submit a policy grievance in writing to the Company. For the purpose of this clause, a policy grievance is one which directly affects one or more employees on a matter of interpretation, administration, or alleged violation of this Agreement, but shall not relate to matters of administration or discipline through discharge, suspension, warning, reprimand, or demotion. A policy grievance under this clause shall be submitted to the Company at a meeting between the representatives of the Company and the Union called together for this purpose which meeting may be called by either party on five (5) days notice. In the event that any such policy grievance presented by the Union is not settled within four (4) days after presentation, it will be subject to arbitration in the same manner as other forms of grievances.

9.03 At any stage of the Grievance Procedure, including arbitration, the conferring parties may have the assistance of the employee, or employees concerned, and any necessary witnesses, and all reasonable arrangements will be made to permit all conferring parties to have access to the plant to view disputed operations and to confer with the necessary witnesses.

9.04 Any and all time limits set forth in this Article and Article 10 may, at any time, be extended by mutual agreement between the parties hereto.

9.05 A grievance of any kind shall not be considered if nine (9) working days have elapsed from the time when the matter in dispute occurred up to the time of the presentation of the grievance. Only under unusual circumstances will any grievance be considered by the Company when presented after this nine (9) working day period. For this purpose, unusual circumstances are defined to be restricted to plant shutdown, vacation period, absence from work due to leave of absence, personal illness, or personal illness of the supervisor to whom certain grievances must be presented. When any of such unusual circumstances exist, the grievances must be presented no later than twenty-one (21) working days after the occurrence of the matter in dispute.

9.06 All decisions, which shall be rendered in writing at each level, arrived at between the Company and the Union representatives shall be final and binding upon the Company, the Union, and the employee or employees concerned.

9.07 During all periods of the Grievance Procedure and Arbitration, the employees shall carry on with their allotted work.

9.08 The Company has the right to present a grievance against the Union, its officers, its members in the bargaining unit, or other representatives for failure to comply with the terms of this Agreement. Any grievance presented by the Company shall be in writing to the Union Staff Representative of the Union for the plant, and in the event that any grievance presented by Management is not settled within four (4) working days after presentation, it will be subject to arbitration in the same manner as a grievance presented by an employee, a group of employees, or the Union.

ARTICLE 10: ARBITRATION

10.01 Failing settlement under the Grievance Procedure of any difference concerning the interpretation or alleged violation of this Agreement, the matter in dispute may be taken to arbitration, provided that if no written request for arbitration is received within ten (10) working days after the final decision is given under the Grievance Procedure, it shall be deemed to have been settled or abandoned.

10.02 When either party requests arbitration as hereinafter provided, it shall make such request in writing, addressed to the other party to this Agreement, and at such time, name their arbitrator. Within five (5) days the other party shall appoint an arbitrator; the two arbitrators shall meet immediately, and if within three (3) full working days they fail to settle the grievance, they shall attempt to select by agreement a Chair of the Arbitration Board.

10.03 If they are unable to agree upon such a Chair within the further period of twenty-four (24) hours, either may then request the Minister of Labour for the Province of Ontario to assist them in selecting an impartial Chair.

10.04 No person may be appointed arbitrator who has been involved in an attempt to negotiate or settle the grievance.

10.05 No matter may be submitted to arbitration that has not been properly carried through all steps of the Grievance Procedure.

10.06 The Arbitration Board shall not be authorized to make any decision inconsistent with the provisions of the Agreement, nor to alter, modify, or amend any part of this Agreement. The Company and the Union agree that the use of a Sole Arbitrator will be considered on a case-by-case basis subject to the agreement of both parties.

10.07 The proceedings of the Arbitration Board will be expedited by the parties hereto, and the decision of the majority of such Board shall be final and binding upon the parties hereto.

10.08 Each of the parties hereto shall bear the expense of the arbitrator appointed by it and the parties shall jointly bear the expense, if any, of the Chair of the Arbitration Board.

10.09 In the event that either party fails to appoint a person to act as its nominee on the Arbitration Board, and accordingly such appointment is made by the Minister of Labour for the Province of Ontario, such person appointed by the Minister of Labour will be considered for all purposes as the appointee of the party who originally failed to appoint and accordingly such person will be paid by that party.

10.10 In the event that there is no majority decision of the Board of Arbitration, the decision of the Chair shall be final and binding upon the parties hereto.

10.11 In the event that there is a dispute involving work standards, any chair appointed or selected for a Board of Arbitration shall be a person who is technically qualified to deal with the matters in dispute.

10.12 The authority of any Arbitration Board in dealing with a dispute following discharge, suspension, or other discipline of an employee shall be limited, whereby in the event of a grievor's claim arising from unjust discharge, unjust suspension, or unjust disciplinary action be successful, the compensation which may be granted to the grievor by the Arbitration Board shall be confined to actual net loss of wage earnings as a result of the discharge, suspension, or other discipline.

ARTICLE 11: DISCIPLINE AND DISCHARGE CASES

11.01 A claim by a permanent employee that he or she has been discharged, suspended, or otherwise disciplined without just cause shall be treated as a grievance, provided a written statement of such grievance signed by the discharged, suspended, or disciplined employee is lodged with the Company within nine (9) working days after the employee ceased to work for the Company or was suspended or otherwise disciplined by the Company.

11.02 Such grievance shall be settled by confirming the Company's action in dismissing, suspending, or otherwise disciplining the employee or by reinstating the employee with or without compensation for time lost with full retention of seniority subject to the terms of Article 9 above.

11.03 When a derogatory notation is placed against the record of an employee, notice of such notation shall be given to the employee and the Steward in the employee's department.

11.04 In the event that a period of twelve (12) calendar months has elapsed since a derogatory notation was placed upon an employee's personnel record and no further derogatory notation has been placed upon such employee's personnel record during the twelve (12) calendar month period, such derogatory notation shall be removed from the employee's personnel record.

11.05 The Company shall notify the Chief Shop Steward or the Local President, the Departmental Steward or the Union Staff Representative of the Union of any discharge or suspension within two (2) hours thereafter but if none of the aforesaid persons are available within the period of two (2) hours, then such notification shall be given by the Company as soon as possible after the discharge or suspension. Notification given under this Article shall be in writing and shall state the reason or reasons for discharge or suspension.

11.06 A Union Steward shall be in attendance at any meeting between an employee and a representative of the Company held for the purpose of determining whether a derogatory notation may be placed upon the employee's personnel record or whether a more severe form of disciplinary action may be taken against the employee. A Union Steward will attend at any meeting between an employee and a representative of the Company held for the purpose of discussing a pay rate.

11.07 An employee to whom a suspension of two (2) or more working days is issued shall be required to serve the suspension on consecutive working days.

ARTICLE 12: HOURS OF WORK

12.01 The standard and normal workweek shall consist of forty (40) hours of work performed Monday to Friday, eight (8) hours per day. The normal starting time each day shall be 7:30 a.m. and the employees shall have a one-half (½) hour lunch period. The schedule of forty (40) hours shall not be construed to mean a guarantee of hours of work per day or per week.

12.02 Hours of work shall be calculated on a quarter (¼) hour basis so that employees who are only required to work a portion of any quarter (¼) hour period past normal starting time shall be paid for the full quarter (¼) hour in which such work was performed.

12.03 It is agreed that the normal daily working hours for any employee may be altered when necessary, provided, however, that the Company shall notify the Union in writing, giving reasons, in advance of making any contemplated changes in working hours, so that the matters may be discussed by the parties.

12.04 An employee who is sent home due to lack of work prior to the end of the employee's regular scheduled shift shall be given two (2) hours notice or be paid two (2) hours pay in lieu of notice at the employee's base rate.

ARTICLE 13 SENIORITY

13.01 An employee shall be considered on probation until after he or she has worked a total of thirty-five (35) days for the Company. His or her name shall be placed on the seniority list and his or her seniority date shall commence from the date of last hiring. There shall be two (2) types of seniority, being departmental and plant-wide seniority.

13.02 One main plant-wide seniority list and one departmental seniority list shall be prepared to cover all employees who have completed their probationary period.

13.03 In the event of a layoff or recall for a period which extends beyond the remainder of a working day or a working shift, an employee may exercise departmental seniority. In the event of a layoff or recall for a term in excess of five (5) working days, an employee may exercise plant-wide seniority. The seniority right for an employee may be exercised provided they have the skill, ability, experience, and qualifications to perform the required work. In determining the skill, ability, experience, and qualifications of an employee under this Article, the Company agrees that it will not act in an arbitrary manner.

13.04 Permanent transfers will be based primarily on the skill, ability, experience, and qualifications of the employee concerned, but as between two persons of approximately equal standing based on the above factors, seniority shall govern. The Company shall not discriminate or act in an arbitrary manner and any employee who claims that he or she has been discriminated against in this regard is entitled to invoke the Grievance Procedure. The filling of supervisory positions shall not be subject to the provisions of this Agreement. This Article shall not apply to transfers brought about due to layoff or because of a demotion.

13.05 An employee transferred out of the bargaining unit shall lose all seniority rights and, if returned to the bargaining unit, shall re-enter as a new employee.

13.06 An employee shall not lose any seniority because of absence due to sickness or injury provided that he or she furnishes the company with a satisfactory medical certificate specifying the type of illness or injury suffered during his or her absence and that he or she will be able to return to work on a regular basis to perform the required work. If such employee has not returned to work within two (2) years, his or her employment may be terminated.

13.07 It is agreed that the Company will furnish the Union with a list of all employees who are eligible to be placed on the seniority list and this list will contain the name and hiring date of every employee who qualifies, and such seniority list will be revised and posted in convenient locations in the plant every six (6) months. The Union shall be provided with twenty (20) copies of the seniority lists. At the Union's request, the Company will provide a job title list, separate from the seniority list.

13.08 Laid-off employees shall be called back to work in the inverse order to that in which they were laid off, subject to the skill, ability, experience, and qualifications of any employee to perform the required work. Should any employee dispute a decision of the Company in this regard, he or she may present a written grievance.

13.09 In the event of any layoff or recall, the Union President, Union Stewards, and the most senior safety committee representative shall enjoy top plant-wide seniority, subject, however, to the fact that in order to exercise such seniority the Union President, any Union Steward, or the safety committee representative must have the skill, ability, experience, and qualifications to perform the required work. The most senior safety committee representative shall be the person with the greatest length of continuous service with the Company.

13.10 Whenever there are employees on short-term or long-term layoff and the Company finds it necessary to hire additional employees for new or unfilled classifications, the employees who are on layoff shall be granted preference by the Company before hiring new employees.

13.11 An employee shall lose his or her seniority rights and his or her employment shall be deemed to be terminated for any one of the following reasons:

(a) the employee is discharged for proper cause;

(b) the employee voluntarily quits or leaves employment with the Company;

(c) the employee is absent without leave for a period greater than three (3) working days without providing an explanation satisfactory to the Company;

(d) after layoff, the employee fails to report to work for seven (7) days after recall, unless satisfactory explanation is given;

(e) the employee has been laid off for a period of twelve (12) consecutive months; or

(f) being granted leave of absence by the Company, the employee accepts employment elsewhere during the term of leave of absence.

13.12 The Company will not hire students when regular employees who are willing to return or qualified are on layoff or reduced hours.

ARTICLE 14: JOB POSTING

14.01 When any of the jobs in the bargaining unit become vacant the Company will post a notice of the vacancy for the period of two (2) working days in the department where the vacancy exists and on the main plant bulletin board. The notice will specify the nature of the job, the shift, the qualifications required, and the rate of pay. An employee who wishes to be considered for the position so posted shall signify a desire by making formal application to the Personnel Department. All transfers shall be completed within two (2) weeks of the selection of a successful applicant except where the posting is cancelled, a replacement is not available, or when the employee is receiving a Company convenience payment.

14.02 In filling any posted vacancy under this Article, the Company will consider the requirements of operations and the skill, ability, experience, and qualifications of the individual to perform the normal required work and where these are, in the opinion of the Company, equal, seniority shall govern. If the job is not filled as a result of the posting or if no suitable applications are received, the Company reserves the right to hire.

14.03 Except for a vacancy occasioned by the placing of the successful applicant in the position so posted, any further vacancy may be filled by the Company without posting.

14.04 Should any employee selected for a day work job prove unsatisfactory within five (5) working days, he or she may apply to or may be required to be returned to his or her former job when another suitable employee can be found to fill the position. Should any employee selected for an incentive job prove unsatisfactory, he or she shall be dealt with in accordance with paragraph 6 of Schedule "A" upon completion of any training period fixed by the Company. In the event that an employee selected proves unsatisfactory, the vacancy thereby occasioned may be filled without further posting.

14.05 An employee who has successfully bid under this Article shall not be entitled to bid on a posted job for six (6) months from the date of a successful bid, except by the mutual agreement of the Company and the Union.

14.06 Any job which is vacant because of illness, accident, vacation, leave of absence, temporary transfer, or a temporary promotion or any other temporary vacancy shall not be deemed to be vacant for the purposes of this Article. This Article shall not apply in the event of layoff or recall from layoff.

ARTICLE 15: REPORTING PAY

15.01 The Company agrees that any notice to any employee or employees not to report to work at a particular time will be given by posting a notice on the bulletin board in the department of employees affected and, provided such notice is posted before normal quitting time, such posting will be accepted as constituting full notice to all employees concerned. Should the Company fail to give notice in the manner referred to above, then a telephone call or a telegram to the employee shall constitute proper notice. Any employee who has not been notified as outlined herein and who reports for work and finds that the Company has not sufficient work to occupy him or her for a period of four (4) hours shall receive

    (a) normal earnings for the time actually worked; or

    (b) base rate for any time not actually worked during the first four (4) hour period after reporting for work.

Whenever the Company intends to give notice in written form under the terms of this article, it shall also attempt wherever possible to give verbal notice to employees affected. The Company must post notices of layoff within the department.

    15.02 It is understood that the Company shall not be responsible to pay the worker for the said four (4) hours in any case where it is not the fault of the Company that work is not available, such as breakdown of machinery or part of the necessary employees not reporting to work, which would make it impossible for the other employees to work, or when an employee has been suspended or discharged for just cause during the four (4) hour period.

ARTICLE 16: STANDBY PAY

    16.01 The Company reserves the right to send employees home if there is no available work up to the end of the day or up to noon hour, whichever comes first, due to machine breakdown, and in this event the seniority provisions on layoff shall not prevail. In the event there is any undue delay in affecting necessary repairs to rectify any defect in machinery, the Company shall do whatever is reasonably possible to provide extra or alternative work for the employee affected to be paid for at his or her regular rate.

    16.02 The Company will take all reasonable and available steps to relocate employees on other work in the event that there is a machine breakdown or heating failure.

ARTICLE 17: REST PERIODS

    17.01 The Company agrees to continue rest periods of ten (10) minutes each in the morning and afternoon. The Company also agrees to give the employee an allowance for cleaning up immediately before noon and at the end of the working day. This allowance is to be three (3) minutes.

ARTICLE 18: BULLETIN BOARDS

    18.01 The Company agrees that it shall provide adequate bulletin board facilities for the exclusive use of the Union, provided that no notices shall be posted thereon which contain any material detrimental to the interests of the Company or to any of the products of the Company, and provided that such notices shall pertain to meetings, social activities, and the Union business.

ARTICLE 19: SAFETY AND HEALTH

    19.01 The Company, the Union, and the employees will cooperate in the prevention of accidents and the enforcement of safety rules in the plant.

    19.02 It is agreed between the parties that no employee shall be penalized by reason of his or her refusal to operate a faulty machine, provided, however, that any employee working on a machine found to be faulty by him or her will notify

Management immediately of such fault, and in the event that Management does not attempt to rectify such fault when so informed, the earnings of the employee will not be affected during the period of neglect by the Company.

19.03 The Company will post the *Occupational Health and Safety Act* in prominent places throughout the plant.

19.04 Effective May 1st, 1990, the Company will pay the cost of prescription safety eyeglasses, to a maximum of one hundred ($100.00) dollars per year.

ARTICLE 20: PAID HOLIDAYS

20.01 The Company agrees to pay for holidays as follows: New Year's Day, Good Friday, Easter Monday, Victoria Day, Canada Day, Civic Holiday, Labour Day, Thanksgiving Day, Christmas Day, Boxing Day, December 31st.

20.02 Pay for such holidays for all employees in the bargaining unit shall be eight (8) hours pay at the applicable rate (including bonuses).

20.03 It is agreed that an employee shall only be entitled to be paid for any of the aforesaid holidays provided he or she (a) has completed his or her probationary period, and (b) works the last scheduled shift immediately before and the first scheduled shift immediately following the holiday. Absence from work on either of these two qualifying days because of personal illness, layoff, or death in the immediate family (as defined in Article 23) shall not deprive any employee from receiving holiday pay, provided that the employee would otherwise have been eligible to receive holiday pay and the absence from work commenced not more than six (6) working days (including the qualifying day) prior to the holiday or six (6) working days (including the qualifying day) after the holiday. An employee shall not be deemed to have been absent on a qualifying day as provided for herein by reason only of being late for work on such day, provided that the employee reports for work within one (1) hour of the regular scheduled starting time and gives a reasonable and proper excuse acceptable to the Company for such lateness. An employee who does not qualify for holiday pay under this Article but who also has not commenced receiving sick-pay benefits for which they are qualified will be paid for the holiday.

20.04 If any of the above holidays fall on a Saturday or a Sunday, such holidays shall be observed on the following Monday or on the previous Friday. No two holidays shall be observed on the same day. In the event that any of the above-mentioned holidays fall within the period of the annual vacation of any employee, such employee will be granted an extra paid day of vacation in accordance with Article 20.02 and 20.03. The extra day, whenever so granted, shall be deemed an extra day of vacation for all purposes of this Agreement.

20.05 It is agreed that any employee in the bargaining unit who works on a holiday or day observed as such as provided for in this Article shall receive normal earnings plus his or her full base rate for the hours worked together with normal holiday pay, provided they are otherwise qualified to receive same under the terms of this Agreement.

ARTICLE 21: LEAVE OF ABSENCE

21.01 An employee may, except for the purposes of obtaining employment elsewhere, obtain a written leave of absence without loss of seniority at any time at the Company's option, but if during his or her term of leave of absence so granted an employee accepts employment elsewhere, he or she shall lose all seniority rights.

21.02 The Company shall grant a leave of absence without loss of seniority to not more than five (5) employees at any one time who require such leave of absence to attend a Union Conference or Convention, provided the Company is given at least fourteen (14) days prior notice and thirty (30) days prior notice whenever possible, or any shorter period of notice as may be mutually agreed by the Company and the Union.

21.03 The Company shall grant a leave of absence without loss of seniority to not more than two (2) employees elected or appointed to a full-time Union position. Such employees shall continue to accumulate seniority for the former job classification held to each anniversary date of the leave of absence during the term of such leave of absence.

ARTICLE 22: JURY DUTY

22.01 Employees who must attend to serve for jury duty shall be compensated for any loss of total daily base rate earnings because of such compulsory attendance up to a maximum of five (5) working days, provided that any employees so affected who are called for jury duty but not required to attend the Court for any half shift will report to work for such shift.

ARTICLE 23: BEREAVEMENT

23.01 Employees who suffer bereavement within the immediate family circle will be granted three (3) consecutive days leave of absence with pay. Immediate family in such circumstances means wife or husband, son or daughter, sister or brother, mother or father, mother-in-law or father-in-law. Employees will be granted one (1) day's leave of absence with pay in the event of the death of the employee's grandparent, sister-in-law, or brother-in law.

ARTICLE 24 TOOLS AND SUPPLIES

24.01 The Company shall supply soap and paper towels to all employees in the bargaining unit.

24.02 The Company shall supply at its cost the first issue of the following items when same are required for normal work:

   (a) scissors
   (b) screwdrivers
   (c) tack hammers
   (d) adjustable wrenches
   (e) upholstery regulators
   (f) pliers
   (g) woodworking protractors
   (h) upholstery aprons
   (i) claw hammers
   (j) all-purpose brushes
   (k) tape measures
   (l) trimming knives.

The Company shall replace these items when replacement is required through normal use. Employees will be required to replace any item if it is lost or damaged through negligent use.

24.03 The Company shall supply at its cost the first issue of non-prescription safety glasses, gloves, safety hats, and ear protectors for those employees who are designated by the Company as requiring same for safety purposes, and these shall be replaced by the Company when replacement is required through normal wear.

ARTICLE 25: WAGE RATES

25.01 Attached hereto and forming part of this Agreement are the following schedules:

(a) Wage Rates

(b) Conditions relating to Enrollment in and Administration of the Benefit Plan.

ARTICLE 26: VACATIONS WITH PAY

26.01 The Company will shut down the plant for a period of two (2) weeks for the annual vacation. The Company agrees to give to employees covered by this Agreement who have the necessary service as of the 1st day of May in any vacation year, and who are in the employ of the Company at the date of shutdown, a vacation pay based on the following schedule:

(a) any employee with less than one (1) year's service with the Company shall receive a vacation pay equal to four (4%) percent of his or her total wages earned for the twelve (12) month period immediately prior to the first pay day following May 1st in any vacation year;

(b) any employee who has been in the service of the Company for one (1) year or more shall receive an amount of vacation pay equal to four (4%) percent of his or her total wages earned during the period of twelve (12) months prior to the first pay day following May 1st in any vacation year;

(c) any employee who has been in the service of the Company for four (4) years or more shall receive an amount of vacation pay equal to five (5%) percent of his or her total wages earned during the period of twelve (12) months prior to the first pay day following May 1st in any vacation year;

(d) any employee who has been in the service of the Company for eight (8) years or more shall be given a vacation of three (3) weeks and receive vacation pay equal to six (6%) percent of his or her total wages earned during the period of twelve (12) months prior to the first pay day following May 1st in any vacation year;

(e) any employee who has been in the service of the Company for thirteen (13) years or more shall be given a vacation of four (4) weeks and receive vacation pay equal to eight (8%) percent of his or her total wages earned during the period of twelve (12) months prior to the first pay day following May 1st in any vacation year; and

(f) any employee who has been in the service of the Company for twenty (20) years or more shall be given a vacation of five (5) weeks and receive vacation pay equal to ten (10%) percent of his or her total wages earned during the period of twelve (12) months prior to the first pay day following May 1st in any vacation year.

26.02 It is the intention of the Company to have the vacation period during the two (2) week period immediately preceding the first Monday in August.

26.03 Whenever possible an employee who is entitled to a vacation of three (3) weeks shall be permitted to take his or her vacation in consecutive weeks. However, this arrangement is subject to the normal production requirements of the Company.

ARTICLE 27: TRANSFERS

27.01 All earnings on transfers shall be paid according to an agreement between the Union and the Company.

ARTICLE 28: UNION SECURITY

28.01 It is understood and agreed that all employees who are members of the Union within the scope of this Agreement shall maintain membership in good standing for the duration of this Agreement as a condition of continued employment.

28.02 It is further understood and agreed that any employee within the scope of the Agreement who is not presently a member of the Union shall, as a condition of his or her continued employment, apply for membership in the Union. All such employees shall remain members in good standing for the duration of this Agreement as a condition of continued employment.

28.03 It is further understood and agreed that all new employees admitted into membership shall continue to be members of the Union in good standing for the duration of this Agreement as a condition of continued employment.

28.04 The Company shall forthwith, upon receiving written notice thereof from the Union, discharge an employee whose application for membership in the Union has been denied or who has been suspended or expelled from the Union, provided that such denial of membership in or suspension or expulsion from the Union was not imposed in bad faith nor was discriminatory nor arose from membership in any other trade union nor resulted from refusal by the employee concerned to act contrary to this Agreement or contrary to law and provided that the denial of membership in or suspension or expulsion from the Union was effected in accordance with the Constitution and By-laws of the Union.

28.05 The written notice from the Union of action taken against any employee denying or terminating his or her membership in the Union shall contain or be accompanied by a statement of the reasons for such action being taken and of the steps and procedures followed by the Union prior to such action being taken.

28.06 Should the reason or reasons for denying or terminating Union membership be other than the failure or refusal of an employee to tender the regular, periodic dues, fees, or assessments properly authorized and uniformly demanded from all Union members, the Company may delay the discharge of the employee, but in such case, it shall, within five (5) days of the receipt by it of the said notice from the Union, nominate an arbitrator, and a Board of Arbitration shall be constituted as provided for in Article 10 of this Agreement. The Board of Arbitration shall have jurisdiction to determine whether or not the denial of membership in or suspension or expulsion from the Union met the requirements contained in the foregoing sections of this Article. If the Arbitration Board finds that it did not, the Company shall not be required to discharge the employee affected, and the employee affected shall either be accepted into membership in the Union in the normal manner or be recognized as a member in good standing in the Union, depending on whether the arbitration arose by reason of the employee being refused membership or suspended or expelled from the Union. Following such arbitration award, the employee affected shall also be bound by the terms of this Agreement to maintain his or her membership in the Union in good standing as a condition of continued employment. If the Board finds that action by the Union met such requirements, the Company shall discharge the employee affected not later than five (5) working days after the award has been delivered to the parties.

28.07 The Company agrees to deduct from each pay due weekly to each employee the amount from time to time fixed by the Constitution and By-laws of the Union for initiation fees, assessments and weekly dues and to remit the same no later than the 15th day of the same month to the Union, together with a list of all employees from whom deductions have been made.

28.08 The Company agrees to supply a list at the end of every month of all names and clock numbers and reasons for leaving of employees who have left the employment of the Company during the month.

28.09 The Company will not contract out work for the term of the Collective Agreement (other than that which is already contracted out) except in cases of lack of available materials or qualified employees, cost competitiveness within reasonable limits, productivity, and emergencies beyond the company's control, etc. In such cases, work will not be contracted out without the Union's agreement, which agreement shall not unreasonably be withheld. The Company will provide the Union with all relevant information and data in its possession.

ARTICLE 29: JOB EVALUATION

29.01 The Company and the Union recognize that the current form and administration of the existing job evaluation system shall be continued during the term of this Agreement.

ARTICLE 30: PAY ON DAY OF INJURY

30.01 Any employee injured on the job shall be paid for the balance of his or her shift on which the injury occurred at the premium rate (Average Hourly Earnings) if, as a result of such injury, the employee is sent home by the doctor or Company nurse or is hospitalized.

ARTICLE 31: HEALTH AND WELFARE

31.01 The Company shall pay the monthly premium costs of the following benefits for the duration of the term of this Agreement:

(a) Group Life Insurance: $35,000.

(b) Accidental Death and Dismemberment: $35,000.

(c) Extended Health Care for employees and their dependants as outlined in the Master Contract.

(d) Ontario Health Insurance Plan (OHIP).

(e) Standard Benefit Dental Plan: employees will be eligible for enrollment in the Plan upon completion of twelve (12) months of employment with the Company. Payments will be based on the Ontario Dental Association schedule of fees for the previous calendar year.

31.02 All employees shall receive a booklet which outlines the full benefit program provided by the above and it is understood that payment of any benefit shall be made in accordance with the terms of any Group Policy as underwritten.

31.03 It is understood that the obligation on the part of the Company to pay the monthly premium cost for any benefit for any employee or his or her dependants shall not apply in the event that the employee or his or her dependants are covered for any one or more benefits under a policy or plan which is provided for and paid for by the employer of the husband or wife of any employee.

31.04 It is further understood that the payments made by the Company as outlined above shall constitute the total and full responsibility of the Company during the term of this Agreement toward the cost of health and welfare program.

31.05 Benefit plan documents and policies, including the Pension Plan document, shall be provided to the Union Staff Representative.

ARTICLE 32: PENSION PLAN

32.01 Benefits under the Pension Plan are as follows in accordance with the provisions of the Pension Plan.

32.02 Effective March 1, 1996, an employee with at least 30 years of service with the Company may retire with an unreduced pension at age 60 (sixty) years.

32.03 The particulars of the Pension Plan shall be as more particularly described in the Pension Plan document.

ARTICLE 33: OVERTIME—SATURDAY AND SUNDAY WORK

33.01 Overtime work shall be performed on a voluntary basis and all authorized overtime work performed shall be paid at the rate of one and a half (1½) times base rate. For the purposes of this Article, authorized overtime work shall be considered to include only the following:

(a) working hours performed before an employee's normal starting time at the request of the Company; and

(b) working hours performed after an employee's normal quitting time, provided the employee has either worked a full normal eight (8) hour shift or commenced to work after the normal starting time at the request of the Company.

33.02 It is agreed by the parties that employees engaged as plant maintenance worker, janitors, or engineers may be scheduled to work in a manner so that Saturday forms part of their regular work week and these normal Saturday hours are not subject to payment at overtime rates.

33.03 Whenever possible it is agreed that no overtime work will be performed on the regular Local Union monthly meeting night. The Company undertakes to provide the Union with a list of employees who have been required to work on Union meeting evenings.

33.04 Whenever an employee is required to work on Sundays, he or she shall be paid his or her earnings plus his or her full base rate.

33.05 Overtime required to be performed from Monday to Friday inclusive shall be requested from employees in the following order of preference:

(a) to the employee who is performing the particular work that will still be in progress in overtime hours; and

(b) according to departmental seniority, to those employees who are willing and able to perform the overtime work assignments.

33.06 Overtime required to be performed on Saturday, Sunday, or a holiday (excluding any regular shift which commenced on or ends on one of these days) shall be requested from employees in order of departmental seniority, provided that the employees are willing and able to perform the overtime work assignments. Notification of overtime work assignments shall be given to all employees affected as early as possible.

ARTICLE 34: PAY DAY

34.01 The Company agrees that employees will receive their pay on every Thursday morning so long as this procedure is not made impossible due to sickness or emergencies beyond the Company's control.

ARTICLE 35: SHIFT PREMIUM

35.01 A shift premium of forty (40¢) cents per hour shall be paid for each hour worked on any shift which is scheduled by the Company and commenced on any day after 11:30 a.m.

ARTICLE 36: CANADA SAVINGS BONDS

36.01 The Company agrees that it shall, upon receiving written authorization from an employee, deduct and remit payments in regard to purchase of Canada Savings Bonds and those deductions will continue as specified in the written authorization form signed by the employee until terminated by the employee.

ARTICLE 37: AUTOMATION AND TECHNOLOGICAL CHANGES

37.01 The Company agrees that it shall take every reasonable step to retrain and relocate any employees who have lost their jobs due to automation or technological changes. Employees will be given as much prior notice as is possible in the event that it is contemplated that they are likely to lose their jobs under this Article so that the system of retraining can be instituted at an early date. The Union, and the employees about to lose their jobs, shall be notified in writing at least two (2) weeks prior to the termination of their job.

ARTICLE 38: TIME-STUDY OBSERVATIONS

38.01 The Company agrees that whenever time-study observations are taken, the following conditions shall prevail:

(a) The Company shall notify Department Stewards or the Shop Chair prior to the taking of a time study.

(b) The operator shall have knowledge that the observation is being made.

(c) Employees who are to be studied for the purpose of incentive rates shall be average, experienced employees working on the particular operation.

(d) Time studies shall be taken under normal working conditions when using stock and material which the operator can normally expect to receive. All information pertinent to the work performed and being studied shall be recorded in detail showing all the elements into which the operation has been broken down, the element and points, the sequence of elements, the methods, the motion pattern, and a sketch showing the location of tools, equipment, and stock.

(e) Whenever a time study is made of any task or operation, the time-study person shall, before leaving the particular work site, furnish in writing to the Union official involved the following information:

(i) the duration of the time study;

(ii) the number of units produced during that time; and

(iii) the level at which the employee's performance rated.

The final tabulation, expressed in minutes, will be provided within two (2) working days.

(f) All incentive standards in effect at the signing of this Agreement shall not be changed for other than one or more of the following reasons:

(i) a change in tools or equipment, layout, materials, design, methods (but not the employee's coordination and proficiency), sequence of operations; or

(ii) other factors which have an effect equal to at least five (5%) percent of the existing standard for the operation. Variations of less than five (5%) percent may be accrued and an adjustment rate made when the accrued changes amount to five (5%) percent of the existing standard. It is understood that where such job changes have occurred, the changes in the incentive rate will be limited to those parts of the job changed. It is further understood that a change in name or style number to correct obvious errors or omissions does not constitute a change.

(g) The Department Steward of an employee may, in his or her discretion, check to confirm that the above conditions have been complied with.

(h) The Company will provide time-study data (as opposed to predetermined times) to the Union Staff Representative or Chief Steward.

ARTICLE 39: DURATION OF AGREEMENT

39.01 This Agreement shall be binding and remain in effect from the 1st day of September, 2004, until the 31st day of August, 2005, and shall continue in force from year to year thereafter unless either party shall furnish the other with written notice of termination or proposed revision at least thirty (30) days prior to the 31st day of August, 2005 or at least thirty (30) days prior to the expiration date of any anniversary thereafter.

DATED AT Peterborough, this 20th day of September, 2004

FOR THE COMPANY: **FOR THE UNION:**

_____   _____

_____   _____

_____   _____

_____   _____

SCHEDULE "A"

Classifications: There are three classifications of jobs.
   Maintenance
   Product Design and Engineering
   Production

Job Titles: Within each classification there are job titles. Each job title has an assigned job rate.

Maintenance

Job Rate	Job Title
40	Industrial Electrician
39	Journeyman other trades
37	Fabric Cutters
36	Maintenance III
35	Bundlers
34	Maintenance II
32	Maintenance I

Product Design and Engineering

Job Rate	Job Title
20	Leather Cutters

Production

Job Rate	Job Title
9	Fabric Inspectors
9	Workshop Expeditors
9	Senior Repairperson
9	Truck Driver
9	Utility Worker
8	Woodworking Machine Operators
7	Upholsterers
7	Spray Painters
7	Woodworking Inspectors
7	Lift Truck Operators
7	Material Handlers
6	Trimmers
6	Wrappers
6	Foam and Felt Cutters
6	Frame and Arm Assemblers
6	Springers
6	Shippers
5	Cushion Fillers
5	Janitors

4	Sewers
3	Panel Makers
2	Machine Setup
1	Training Rate all jobs

Hourly Wage Rates Effective from September 1, 2004, to August 31, 2005

Job Rate	Hourly Wage Rate
40	$32.50
39	$29.50
37	$28.40
36	$27.50
35	$26.50
34	$25.00
32	$24.50
20	$24.25
9	$24.00
8	$23.80
7	$23.60
6	$23.20
5	$22.60
4	$22.20
3	$21.60
2	$21.20
1	$19.20

CONDITIONS APPLICABLE TO SCHEDULE "A"

1. Whenever any new job classifications have been determined, the Company shall institute new job rates for any or all such classifications within one (1) month.

2. All employees, after the signing of this Agreement, shall have their earnings based solely on the base rate set forth in Schedule "A," or at such new base rates as are established from time to time as a result of the job evaluation program. Employees whose base rates are higher than those set forth in Schedule "A" shall not have their base rates reduced during the term of the Collective Agreement unless permanently transferred to a lower base rate job as an alternative to layoff.

3. All incentive rates shall enable the average worker working the normal incentive pace to make between twenty (20%) percent and thirty (30%) percent above base rate while working on incentive.

4. Incentive workers on new jobs such as new styles or new methods will receive one hundred and twenty-five (125%) percent for the first two runs or until incentive rates are set.

5. The starting rate for all new employees will be the rate set out in Group 1 of Schedule "A." New employees on day work jobs will have their rate adjusted to the job rate upon completion of the probationary period. New employees on incentive will be paid at the job rate after they have earned standard or better for three (3) consecutive weeks.

6. Employees who are working on incentive jobs shall receive full base rate for a period of up to three (3) consecutive weeks during which they do not meet the set standards for their job. However, by granting this form of wage guarantee, the Company specifically reserves the right to terminate the employment of any employee affected whose performance below standard continues beyond the period of three (3) weeks or to take disciplinary action against any employee who fails to maintain standard.

7. Any award of an Arbitration Board or the terms of any settlement under the Grievance Procedure shall be limited to compensation of wages lost up to a maximum of three (3) months on any dispute on calculation of pay.

SCHEDULE "B": ENROLLMENT IN AND ADMINISTRATION OF THE WELFARE PLAN

DISCHARGE, RESIGNATION, AND RETIREMENT All benefits cease on the day on which the employee terminates his or her employment with the Company.

LAYOFF Coverage will remain in effect until the end of the month following the month in which the layoff occurred.

SICKNESS AND WORKERS' COMPENSATION Coverage will remain in effect until the end of the twelfth (12th) month following the month in which the disability occurred. Arrangements can be made at the employee's request to provide for continuation of coverage at the employee's cost.

LEAVE OF ABSENCE Coverage will remain in effect until the last day of the month. An employee can assure continuation of coverage by applying in writing and paying for coverage in advance for the duration of the leave of absence.

NEW EMPLOYEES All new employees will have a three (3) month waiting period.

RECALLED AND REHIRED EMPLOYEES Employees when rehired or recalled within six (6) months can be reinsured without any waiting period, providing they were covered prior to their termination. Employees who have been away for a period greater than six (6) months will be considered as new employees.

MATERNITY LEAVE Coverage will remain in effect until the end of the fourth (4th) month following the month in which the absence commenced.

WEEKLY INDEMNITY PLAN The Weekly Indemnity Plan provides that an employee, following completion of the three (3) month waiting period, is entitled to a maximum of fifteen (15) weeks of sick benefits supplemented by a further maximum of fifteen (15) weeks of sick benefits pursuant to the *Employment Insurance Act.*

Benefits under the plan are payable to an employee who is unable to work on a full-time basis due to an off-the-job injury or illness and who is under the regular care and personal attendance of a licensed physician.

Benefits under the Plan are payable commencing on the 1st day of hospitalization or disability due to accident or on the eighth (8th) day of disability due to sickness. No benefits are payable as a result of absence due to pregnancy or any pregnancy-related condition.

(a) Benefits are payable under the Plan in the amount of two-thirds (⅔) of an employee's average weekly earnings up to a maximum of $275.00 per week.

(b) Effective March 1, 1996, benefits are payable under the Plan in the amount of two-thirds (⅔) of an employee's average weekly earnings up to a maximum of $300.00 per week.

The above is a summary of the provisions of the Weekly Indemnity Plan. For more complete details concerning the extent of coverage and benefits, contact the Company Personnel Office. Detailed terms on the application of this Schedule are outlined in the Master Contract.

Glossary

age cohort describes the characteristics of the members of an age grouping in the general population such as adolescents aged 13-19, often to distinguish it from other age groupings on the basis of various characteristics of one cohort that differentiate or distinguish it from other cohorts

allied picketing picketing a workplace that is not the employer of the striking workers but a workplace where work has been reorganized to directly assist the employer of the striking workers

alternative dispute resolution (ADR) techniques such as arbitration and mediation that are used to settle disputes instead of going to court

alternative vacation entitlement year a period used in calculating the entitlement to vacation that does not start with the employee's hiring date or the anniversary of the hiring date

anti-union animus ill will; where an employer takes an action in order to defeat the employees' right to join a union of their choice

arbitrable whether or not an issue in dispute is one which the arbitrator has jurisdiction to hear

automatic certification certification that is granted without a vote if a union demonstrates that more than 50 percent of the employees in the bargaining unit have joined the union

bad-faith bargaining the practice of engaging in bargaining with no intention of making an agreement with the other party

balance of probabilities the standard of proof in civil lawsuits and most arbitrations; requires that a party prove that its version of the facts is more probable than that of its opponent

bargaining unit a grouping of employees at a workplace that the labour board decides it would certify if a union signs up sufficient members

bereavement leave permission not to come in to work in order to take part in activities related to the funeral of a relative

bump; bumping rights the rights of more senior employees to claim the jobs of more junior ones, when the senior employee has been slated for layoff

burden of proof the task of the party to prove its case according to the standard of proof required, such as on the **balance of probabilities**

business unionism describes unions that do not express a political preference, that see themselves as politically neutral or apolitical, and that focus almost entirely on the immediate needs of their members in the negotiating and enforcing of collective agreements

Canada Industrial Relations Board (CIRB) an administrative tribunal set up to administer the labour relations portion of the *Canada Labour Code* and some parts of the health and safety part of the Code

certification the process where a union shows it has sufficient support among the employees for the labour board to give the union the legal right to act as the exclusive bargaining agent for those employees

COLA cost of living adjustment; usually an annual percentage increase in salary during the life of an agreement to cover inflationary increases in the cost of living

company unions unions that were not worker organized or controlled, where there was connivance between union leaders and the employers

conciliation a process where a third party attempts to assist the parties in reaching a negotiated agreement; conciliation is a prerequisite to a legal strike

confidential a worker who regularly has access to information that is normally kept from the union and who would be in a conflict of interest if he or she were included in the bargaining unit

contract zone the area between the positions of the parties where settlement is possible

cost of living clauses clauses in collective agreements that give increases in wages during the life of an agreement based on increases in the cost of living due to inflation; also called **escalator clauses**

craft unions   unions that organize on the basis of membership in a particular craft or trade, such as electrical or cabinet making, and ignore unskilled workers or members of other trades or crafts; also called **horizontal unions**

cross-examination   a form of questioning where opposing counsel asks questions that can elicit yes or no answers; cross-examination permits counsel to probe the credibility of the witness

culminating incident   the last incident of employee misconduct in a long history of misconduct; used to support dismissal

decertification   the legal process by which a group of unionized employees remove the union at their workplace

dependent variable   a factor that changes as a result of the effects on it of an independent variable

dual unionism   one union organizes several trades or crafts, rather than just one

effective recommendations   workers who do not make the final decisions to hire, fire, demote, or promote and employee but whose recommendations are virtually always followed by their superiors are said to make effective recommendations

emergency leave   permission to be absent from work for 10 days per year in order to deal with the needs of family

employee   a worker whose decisions do not affect the economic lives of other workers and whose relationship to the employer is such that he or she is integral to the operation of the organization and whose work is often directed by the employer

escalator clauses   clauses in collective agreements that give increases in wages during the life of an agreement based on increases in the cost of living due to inflation; also called **cost of living clauses**

essential services   services that must be maintained during a strike or lockout; employees involved in delivering essential services will not have the right to strike

ethical sourcing   the notion that TNCs should not buy products or raw materials produced by abusive labour practices, such as child or forced labour

examination in chief   a form of questioning where counsel examines his or her witness, using open-ended questions that allow the witness to give evidence without constraint

exclusive jurisdiction   one union is recognized as having a monopoly over the organization of a particular trade or industry

expedited   speeded up, accelerated

fair traded   refers to the prices paid to raw material producers being fair and equitable, to provide enough for a producer to live on without being reduced to penury; the term is used in the coffee industry, where fair-traded coffee beans are purchased by processors at a fair price that will keep the grower above mere subsistence, notwithstanding actual market prices, which might be very low

final item-by-item selection   a form of interest arbitration in which the arbitrator accepts either the union of management's position in full on a particular bargaining issue

final-offer selection   a process where an interest arbitrator selects either management's proposal or the union's proposal; the arbitrator is not allowed to split the difference

final-offer vote   a process where management can legally require the union to take its last settlement proposal to the members of the bargaining unit for a vote

globalization   a trend toward an international, unrestricted market in goods and services in which control or intervention by national governments is restricted and limited

grievor   the person who starts a grievance

hearsay   oral evidence given by a witness who does not have direct, personal knowledge about the evidence given, where the witness was told the information by someone else who had direct, personal knowledge

horizontal unions   unions that organize workers in a particular craft or trade; also called **craft unions**

hot cargo clause   a provision in a collective agreement stating that the employees have the right to refuse work if it involves goods or materials produced in a workplace that is subject to a strike

impacted costs   an expense to the employer that is not directly increased in bargaining but will increase because of other provisions negotiated in bargaining

independent variable   a factor or phenomenon that causes changes to dependent variables

industrial unions   unions that organize all the workers in an industry, whether skilled or unskilled; also called **vertical unions**

injunction   an order by a court for a person or union to stop or limit an activity, such as picketing

interest arbitration   a process where a third party imposes an agreement on the parties

interjurisdictional immunity   the provincial government cannot make rules that affect vital parts of a federally regulated operation; in other words, workplaces that are regulated by the federal government are immune to provincial labour and employment laws

judicial review   a process whereby the decision of an administrative board can be reviewed for legal correctness

labour relations officer   an employee of the labour relations board who has duties including investigating and mediating disputes between unions and management

lead hands   employees who direct the work of other employees but who are not managers because they do not hire, fire, or do other managerial functions

lockout   a refusal by management to let the employees conduct their work in order to further a collective bargaining purpose

long-term disability   a plan to pay employees who have a chronic or long-term illness

macquiladoras   factories set up in a free trade area, close to the US border in Mexico; at these locations, non-Mexican companies set up assembly and finishing plants, moving raw materials and inventory freely across the border, while using low-wage Mexican labour

manager   a worker whose decisions affect the economic livelihoods of other workers by actions such as hiring or firing other workers

mandatory dues check-off   see **Rand Formula**

mass pickets   Bringing in large numbers of picketers to make crossing the picket lines and going to work more difficult

mediation   a process where a third party assists the parties to reach an agreement; mediation is voluntary and can occur at any time in the process

memorandum of settlement/tentative agreement/ memorandum of understanding   the agreement between the parties that is the result of negotiations or that is imposed by arbitration

mitigation of damages   the rule that persons claiming damages must take action to minimize the harm they suffer

natural justice   a basic procedural principle and requirement that a party has the right to an impartial and unbiased tribunal, the right to adequate notice of the proceeding, and the right to present its case and answer the case of an opponent

no-board report   a decision by the minister of labour not to appoint a conciliation board to investigate a labour dispute; a no-board report starts the clock running for a legal strike

open period   the period during which a trade union may apply to the labour board for certification

organizing drive   activity where a union engages in a concerted effort to sign up members at a workplace in order that it will either be certified by the labour board or be granted voluntary recognition by the employer

past practice   if the parties have agreed to and followed a particular procedure that affects or adds to the meaning of a clause in the collective agreement, either party may argue that because both parties have accepted the interpretation over time, custom and usage require that the parties be entitled to rely on the practice as if it were part of the agreement

pattern bargaining   a practice where a settlement at another workplace becomes a template for the settlement at other workplaces

permanent umpires   neutral arbitrators (or arbitrator) named by the parties to hear all arbitrations during the life of a collective agreement

political unionism   union activity that goes beyond negotiation and enforcement of a collective agreement to embrace broader political issues of importance to workers

precedent case   a case that is similar to the case currently before a board in the facts it presents and the issues it raises

primary picketing   picketing the employer of the striking workers at the work site of the employees on strike

privative clause   a clause that prohibits the court from reviewing the decision of an administrative tribunal

progressive discipline   if there are repeated infractions, the penalties are increased on the assumption that increased penalties will act as a deterrent

public servant   an employee of the government or government agencies

quash   to nullify or set aside an order of a lower court

Rand Formula   a formula for resolving labour disputes, developed by Ivan Rand, a Supreme Court of Canada justice; it provides that the employer shall deduct union dues from the salaries of all employees in the bargaining unit, and remit the deduction to the union, whether the member has joined the union or not; this is also known as a **mandatory dues check-off**

ratification   the process where the union's and management's negotiating teams get a tentative agreement approved by the membership and management

recall right   the right of an employee who is laid off from work to be called back to work before the employer can hire a new person

remedial certification   if the union demonstrates that it has some support for certification and the unfair labour practices of the employer make it impossible to determine the true wishes of the employees in a vote, then the union will be certified without a vote

reverse onus   normally, the party alleging a violation of the Ontario *Labour Relations Act, 1995* has to raise evidence to support its point; in a reverse-onus situation, the party merely has to make an allegation and it is up to the other party to bring evidence to show the allegation is not supported

right-to-work laws   laws that make it harder for unions to organize workers and become certified, usually by providing for the right of individual workers not to join or be made to join a union as a condition of employment

secondary picketing   picketing at a supplier or customer of the employer or another party who is not involved directly in the dispute

severance pay   payments to employees with more than five years service who are terminated when the employer closes all or part of the operations at a workplace

sick leave   an excused absence from work because of illness

sidesperson   a nominee by either labour or management to a board of arbitration

sleeping on its rights   a union that does not try to get a collective agreement after certification is said to be sleeping on its rights and for that reason may be decertified

strike   the concerted actions of employees to reduce production in a unionized workplace

stub period   the period of time between the employee's hiring date or the anniversary of the hiring date and the start of the employee's alternative vacation entitlement year

sunset clause   a clause that requires removal of disciplinary notices from an employee's personnel file after passage of a prescribed period of time, provided that there are no further infractions

supplementary unemployment benefits plan (SUB plan)   a plan in which the employer makes an additional payment to a worker who is collecting employment insurance benefits; plan benefits are not deducted from employment insurance benefits if they are registered with Canada Revenue Agency and are for the purposes of and according to the limits set out by the agency

surface bargaining   going through the motions of meeting with the other party but with no real attempt to reach an agreement

sweetheart deal   a contract in which the union leaders engage in collusion with the employer and sacrifice the workers' interest in exchange for payoffs from the employer

technological change   introduction of new machinery and equipment that changes the way in which work is done at a workplace

termination pay   payment to an employee who has been terminated because of lack of work

trade union   an organization of employees that has as one of its objectives engaging in collective bargaining

transnational corporation (TNC)   a business that conducts its operations in more than one country; also called a multinational corporation

vacation pay   a minimum of 4 percent of pay per year for workers

vertical unions   unions that organize workers in a particular industry or who work for a large employer, regardless of their skill level or occupation; also called **industrial unions**

voluntary recognition   management may agree to accept a union in the workplace without requiring the union to get a certificate from the labour board; this is legitimate if the union has membership support, but it is not legitimate if management is simply trying to avoid a more militant union

wildcat strike   an unauthorized or illegal strike

Index

A

age cohorts   53
All-Canadian Congress of Labour (ACCL)   7, 16
allied picketing   142
alternative dispute resolution (ADR)   161
alternative vacation entitlement year   226
Amalgamated Society of Carpenters and Joiners   10
Amalgamated Society of Engineers   10
Ambulance Services Collective Bargaining Act, 2001   218
ambulance workers   218-19
American Federation of Labor (AFL)   5, 6, 7, 11, 14, 17
arbitration
    arbitrability of dispute   187
    awards, enforcement of   191-92
    Charter issues, and   193
    choice of arbitrator   188
    clause, mandatory inclusion   182-83
    cost of   192
    evolution of process   185
    features of   183-84
    interest disputes   186
    management view of process   185
    procedure   189-90
        expedited   190-91
    structure of process
        single arbitrator   188
        tripartite board   187-88
    union view of process   184
Asbestos Strike   6, 17
attitudinal structuring   107
automatic certification   205

B

bad-faith bargaining   119-21
Bakke, E.W.   29
balance of probabilities   189
bargaining
    bad-faith bargaining   119-21
    committees, selection of   110-11

conciliation   121-22, 123
conciliation board, use of   124
demands, determination of   111
fact finding   124
federal public sector   211
final-offer vote   116-17
good-faith bargaining   118
human resources managers, role of   108-9
industrial action resulting from
    boycott   135
    legality of   134-35
    lockouts   133-34
    lost days statistics   146
    notice to job applicants   136
    sit-down strike   135-36
    strikes   132-33, 136-46
    work-to-rule   135
mediation   122, 123
meeting requirements   114-15
notice to bargain   109
procedure   115-16
proposals, costing of   113-14
provincial public sector
    ambulance workers   218-19
    community college employees   216
    firefighters   214-15
    hospital workers   218
    municipal employees   219
    Ontario civil servants   212-14
    police   215-16
    teachers   216-18
    university employees   219
ratification   117-18
research needs   111-12
    inflation statistics   113
    sample contract clauses   113
    settlement information   112-13
settlement stages   131
structure of negotiations   109-10
tactics   116

bargaining (cont.)
  theoretical approaches
    bargaining power models 105-6
    behavioural models 106-7
    contract zone model 104-5
    economic model 103-4
    prescriptive models 107-8
    strategic models 108
  third-party assistance 121
    compulsory interest arbitration 125
    first-contract arbitration 125-29
    interest arbitration practice 129
    interest arbitration problems 129-31
    modified interest arbitration 131
    voluntary interest arbitration 124-25
  union negotiating teams, role of 108-9
  workplace changes, effect on 261-62
bargaining power model 105-6
bargaining unit
  craft unions 84
  defined, OLRA 82
  determination by OLRB 82-84
  eligible members 74
  professional engineers 85
  provision, collective agreement 152
  security guard exclusion 85
behavioural models of bargaining 106-7
bereavement leave 228
boycott 135
bumping rights 153
burden of proof 189
business cycle, stages of 52
business unionism 3, 24

C

Canada Labour Code
  application of 61-61, 204
  Canada Industrial Relations Board and 204
  certification provisions 205-6
  negotiations under 206-7
  remedies 208
Canadian Association of University Teachers (CAUT) 113
Canadian Auto Workers (CAW) 4, 5, 18, 25, 109-10, 252, 257
Canadian Catholic Confederation of Labour (CCCL) 9, 17

Canadian Charter of Rights and Freedoms
  collective bargaining and 60
  equality provision and certification 93
  freedom not to associate and 60-61
  freedom to associate 75
  grievance arbitration and 59-60
  labour relations, effect on 58-59
  right to strike, and 60
Canadian Congress of Labour (CCL) 7, 15, 16, 17
Canadian Federation of Labour (CFL) 7, 18
Canadian Industrial Relations Board (CIRB) 204
Canadian Labour Congress (CLC) 2, 6, 8, 18, 31, 32, 33, 37, 38-40, 242, 250, 252, 257
Canadian Service Workers Union (CSWU) 249
Canadian Union of Postal Workers (CUPW) 19, 251
Canadian Union of Public Employees (CUPE) 4, 110, 253
certification, *see also* decertification
  applications for 86
    certification package 87-88
    documents filed 88
    employer response 89-90
    information provided 88
  bars to 93
  federally regulated workplaces 205-6
  OLRB, and 92
  open periods 86-87
  post-voting procedures 91-92
  pre-voting procedures 90
  voluntary recognition 92
  voting procedures 90-91
COLA clause 156
collective agreement
  administration 149-95
  arbitration, *see* arbitration
  bargaining, *see* bargaining
  case study 265-89
  Charter of Rights and Freedoms, and 60
  grievance procedure, *see* grievance procedure
  legal effect of 149-50
  mandatory requirements 150-52
  mechanism, union amalgamation 23
  negotiating, *see* bargaining
  provisions
    arbitration 182-83
    bargaining unit, definition of 152-53
    duration of agreement 161
    grievances 161
    hours of work 160

job security   159-60

leaves of absence   157

management rights   153

maternal and parental leave   158

medical insurance   158

no discrimination   153

no strike/lockout   153

overtime   160

personnel records   160-61

salaries   156

seniority   159-60

sick leave   157

staffing   153

union business   154-55

union–employer committee   154

union security   155

vacations   156

work procedures   155-56

workload   155-56

Colleges Collective Bargaining Act   216

Committee for Industrial Organizations (CIO)   5, 8, 14, 16, 17

Commons, John   26-27

Communications, Energy and Paperworkers Union of Canada   250

community college employees   216

company unions   12

conciliation   121-22, 123

Conciliation Act   13

conciliation board   124

Confederation of Democratic Unions (CDU)   9, 19

Confederation of National Trade Unions (CNTU)   9, 10, 17, 19

confidential, defined, OLRA   73

Constitution Act, 1867   56-58, 61, 199

Constitution Act, 1982   58

consumer price index (CPI)   113

contract zone   104

contract zone model of bargaining   104-5

Co-operative Commonwealth Federation (CCF)   4, 16

cost of living clause   52

craft unions   4, 5, 84-85

Craig, Alton   45-56

Craig model, labour relations system

actors

employers   47

third parties   47

unions   47

components   45-46

external inputs

economic factors   51-52

political factors   50-51

social factors   52-53

technological factors   54

illustration   46

inputs to outputs, conversion of   55-56

internal inputs   48-49

Criminal Law Amendment Act, 1872   9

cross-examination   189

Crown Employees Collective Bargaining Act, 1993   63, 212

culminating incident   178

D

decertification   94-96

demographics   52-53

dependent contractors   76

disability, discipline and   180

discipline

disability and   180

discretionary versus automatic   180

investigation of offence   175

grievances arising from   181

just cause concept   176

penalties, determination of   176-77

progressive discipline   178-79

distributive bargaining   106

dual unionism   6

Dunlop, John   29, 44-45

E

economic growth rate   52

Education Act   216-18

education levels   53

effective recommendations   73

emergency leave   231

employee, determination whether, union organization   71-72

Employment Standards Act, 2000

agreements covering provisions under   223-24

application   63, 221

collective bargaining process, and   221-22

employee records   228

equal pay for equal work   229

family medical leave   228

Employment Standards Act, 2000 (cont.)
   hours of work   224
      daily hours   224-25
      exceptional circumstances   225
      weekly hours   225
   leaves of absence   231
   lie detectors   231
   minimum wage   227-28
   overtime   225-26
   parental leave   227
   pregnancy leave   227
   public holidays   226
   recall rights   230-31
   severance pay   230
   termination pay   229-30
   union obligation to enforce   222-23
   vacations   226
equal pay for equal work   229
escalator clause   52
essential service   207
ethical sourcing   262
examination in chief   189
exclusive jurisdiction   6
expedited process   191

F

fact finding   124
fair trading   262
family medical leave   228
federally regulated workplaces
   Canada Industrial Relations Board   204
   Canada Labour Code governance   204
   constitutionally designated   200-1
   declared general advantage to Canada   201-2
   emergency powers and   202
   federal versus provincial, determination of   202-3
   in national interest   202
   Ontario law, contrasted to
      certification   205-6
      contract administration   207
      negotiations   206-7
      remedies   208
final-offer vote   116
firefighters   214-15
first-contract arbitration
   grounds for   126-27
   procedure   127-29
Fisher, Roger   107

fraud, union termination and   94
friendly unionism   25

G

globalization
   defined   239
   labour standards, effect on   257-61
good-faith bargaining   118
grievance procedure
   collective agreement provisions   161
   commonly grieved issues
      bumping rights   172
      disability accommodation   180
      disciplinary offence investigation   175
      discretionary versus automatic discipline   180
      just cause   176
      penalty determination   176-77
      progressive discipline   178-80
      salary grid classification   173-75
      seniority class   172-73
      seniority principle   170-72
   definition   162
   "do it and grieve"   164
   duty of fair representation   165-66
   importance   164
   political use of   163
   pros and cons   162-66
   retroactive pay and   166
   right to file grievance   164-65
   steps   166-70
grievor, defined   162
guerrilla unionism   25

H

Harbison, Frederick   29
hearsay evidence   190
hold-up unionism   26
hospital workers   218
Hospitals Labour Disputes Arbitration Act   218
hot-cargo clause   133
hours of work
   collective agreement provision   160
   employment standards provision   224
Hoxie, Robert   24-26
Human Rights Code
   certification, bars to   93
   dispute resolution under   194

I

impacted costs   113

industrial actions, *see also* lockouts; strikes

    boycott   135

    legality of   134-35

    lockouts   133-34

    lost days statistics   146

    notice to job applicants   136

    sit-down strike   135-36

    strikes   132-33, 136-46

    work-to-rule   135

Industrial Disputes Investigation Act   13, 14, 57

industrial unions   4, 5

inflation rate   51

injunctions   143

integrative bargaining   106

interest arbitration

    compulsory interest arbitration   125

    distinguished from rights arbitration   124

    first-contract arbitration   125-29

    modifications   131

    problems associated with   129-31

    procedure   129

    voluntary interest arbitration   124

interim injunction   143

interjurisdictional immunity   200

International Brotherhood of Electrical Workers (IBEW)   4, 5, 18

International Labour Organization (ILO)   30, 258

International Workers of the World (IWW)   5, 8, 12

intra-organizational bargaining   107

J

job security provision   159

judicial review   192

K

Katz, H.C.   30

Kerr, Clark   29

Kochan, T.A.   30

Knights of Labor   10-11

L

labour costs   51

labour federations, listing of   7-8, 9

labour movement

    Canadian trade unionism   2-6

    Canadian unions, historical development   8-19

    historical development   1

    labour organizations, overview   7-8

    theories and philosophies   20-31

    trade unions, structure and function   31-40

Labour Relations Act (OLRA)

    amendments to   98

    application   62-63, 74-76

    bar to certification, provision for   93

    bargaining unit, defined   82-85

    certification procedures   86-92

    certification, termination of   94-96

    conciliation, application for   121-22

    conciliation board, provision for   124

    employees, eligibility   71-74

    final-offer vote   116

    first-contract arbitration   125-29

    grievance, union's responsibility to proceed   166

    mandatory requirements, collective agreements   151

    meeting requirements, bargaining   114-15, 119

    notice to bargain   109

    Ontario public service and   213

    ratification of contract   117-18

    related employers, determination   97

    rights and responsibilities during organization   77

    strike, provisions for   132-33, 134, 136-40

    unfair labour practices, determination   77-80

    union succession rights   96

    voluntary interest arbitration   124

    voluntary recognition, provision for   92

    workplaces not covered under   74-76

labour relations officer   81

Labour Relations Statute Law Amendment Act, 2004   98

labour relations system

    classic theories

        Craig   45-56

        Dunlop   44-45

    constitutional legislation affecting   56-61

    economic changes   238-40

    federal legislation affecting   61-62

    political changes   236-38

    provincial legislation affecting   62-64

    relationship of inputs to outputs   43

    social changes

        aging workforce   244-45

        equity and equality   241-42

        family structure   240-41

        management–worker participation   242-44

labour relations system (cont.)
  systems theory, basis for   43
  technological change   245-48
  workplace, emerging changes   235-36
    effects on unions   249-57
lead hand   73
leaves of absence
  collective agreement provision   156
  employment standards provision   231
legal enactment process   23
Lenin, V.I.   21
lie detectors   231
lockouts, *see also* industrial actions; strikes
  defined   133-34
  legality of   134-35
  remedies, illegal lockout   138
long-term disability   157

M

macquiladoras   261
management rights provision   153
manager, defined, OLRA   72-73
mandatory dues check-off   150, 155, 237, 238
Marx, Karl   20-21
Marxism   20-21
Marxist-Leninist theory   20-21
mass picket   144
maternal leave
  collective agreement provision   158
  employment standards provision   227
McKersie, R.B.   30, 106
mediation   122, 123
medical insurance provision   158
memorandum of settlement   117
memorandum of understanding   117
minimum wage   227
mitigation of damages   81
municipal employees   219
mutual insurance mechanism   23
Myers, Charles   29

N

National Union of Public and General Workers   18
natural justice   190
New Democratic Party (NDP)   3, 4, 18
no-board report   122
North American Agreement on Labor Cooperation   259-61

O

Occupational Health and Safety Act
  application   63-64
  dispute resolution under   193
One Big Union (OBU)   5, 8, 12
Ontario Labour Relations Board (OLRB)
  application to unionize   67
  appropriate bargaining unit, determination of   82-86
    new unions   69
  certification vote procedure   90-91
  employees, determination of   71, 76
  related employers, determination of   97
  terminating bargaining relationship   94-95
  unfair labour practices, determination of   77, 80-82
  votes, supervision of   86, 90-91, 96
Ontario Public Service Employees Union (OPSEU)   25, 110, 253, 257
organizing drive, *see also* workplace organizing
  employer actions to avoid   80
  goal   71
  initiation of   69
overtime
  collective agreement provision   160
  employment standards provision   225

P

parental leave
  collective agreement provision   158
  employment standards provision   227
past practice   154
pattern bargaining   109
Perlman, Selig   27-28
permanent injunction   143
permanent umpires   185
personnel records
  collective agreement provision   160
  employment standards provision   228
PEST analysis   50, 236
police   215-16
political unionism   3
precedent cases   190
predatory unionism   25
prescriptive models of bargaining   107
primary picketing   142
privative clause   192
professional, defined, OLRA   73
professional engineers   85
progressive discipline   160, 178-79

public holidays   226
Public Service Act   212
Public Service Alliance of Canada (PSAC)   252
public service employees   212-14
Public Service Staff Relations Act   62

Q

quash award   192
Quebec Federation of Labour (QFL)   9, 17, 19
Quiet Revolution   17

R

raiding   96
Railway Disputes Act   13
Rand Formula   16, 36, 155, 237
Rand, Ivan   16
ratification   117
recall rights   230
remedial certification   208
replacement workers   137-38
Rerum Novarum   6
reverse onus   81
revolutionary unionism   25
right-to-work laws   50, 245

S

salary grid   173-75
salary provision, collective agreement   156
scab   138
secondary picketing   142
security guards   85
seniority provision   159
Service Employees International Union (SEIU)   4, 249
severance pay   230
sick leave
    collective agreement provision   157
    employment standards provision   231
sidesperson   187
sit-down strike   135-36
sleep on its rights   94
strategic models of bargaining   108
strike breakers   137
strikes, *see also* industrial actions
    defined   132
    duration   136-37
    injunctions, use of   143-46
    legality of   134

lost days   146
picketing   140
    as freedom of expression   142-43
    purpose and limits   141
    types, historical distinction   141-42
professional strike breakers   137
remedies, illegal strike   138-40
replacement workers   137-38
sit-down   135-36
stub period   226
SUB plan   227
sunset clause   160
supplementary unemployment benefit (SUB) plan   227
surface bargaining   120

T

Taft-Hartley Act (US)   17
Tannenbaum, F.   28-29
teachers   216-18
Teamsters   25, 26
technology
    change
        impact on workplace   245-48
        notice of   206
    effect on labour relations system   54
tentative agreement   117
termination pay   229
Thompson, Mark   31
Toronto Trades Assembly (TTA)   9
trade unionism   2-6
trade unions, *see also* unions
    defined, OLRA   68
Trades and Labor Congress (TLC)   8, 11, 15, 17
Trades Union Act   9, 57
transnational corporation   240

U

unemployment rate   51
unfair labour practices
    anti-union animus   78
    firing   79
    illegal contractual provisions   79
    interference, union formation   78
    intimidation by union   77
    refusal to employee   79
    remedies   80-82
    statutory freeze to combat   79-80
    threats and coercion   78-79

union business provision   154
union–employer committee
   dispute resolution mechanism   195
   provision in collective agreement   154
union security provision   155
unions
   certification, *see* certification
   decertification   94-95
   international branches   37-38
   locals   33-36
   national federations   38-40
   organization of, *see* workplace organizing
   provincial labour federations   37
   regional and district councils   36-37
   structural components
      international union   33
      national union   32
   succession rights   96-97
   workplace changes, effects on
      union organization and structure   249-56
      union political and social action   256-57
United Auto Workers (UAW)   14, 18, 109, 250
United Steel Workers of America (USWA)   4
university employees   219
uplift unionism   25
Ury, William   107

V

vacation
   collective agreement provision   156
   employment standards provision   226
vacation pay   227
Verma, Anil   31
vertical unions   14
voluntary recognition   92

W

Wagner Act (US)   13, 14, 15
Walton, R.   106
Webb, Beatrice   22-23

Webb, Sidney   22-23
Winnipeg General Strike   12, 36
Wisconsin School   26
work procedures provision   155
work stoppages   146
work-to-rule   135
workload provision   155
workplace organizing
   bargaining unit, determination of   82-84
      professional engineers   85
      security guards   85
      skill and craft unions   84
   certification   71
      bars to   93
      employment status issues after   76
      procedures   86-92
      related employers, OLRB determination of   97
      succession rights   96
      termination of   94-96
   employee rights during   77
   employee wishes, determination of   86
   employees, defined   71-72
   employer actions to avoid   80
   excluded workers   72-74
   goal, organizing drive   71
   organizing drive   69-70
   rationale for   67-68
   trade union qualifications   68-69
   unfair labour practices during
      avoiding complaints   80
      by employer   78-80
      by union   77
      procedures and remedies   80-82
   union rights during   77
   voluntary recognition   92-93
   workplaces not under OLRA   74-76
Workplace Safety and Insurance Act, 1997
   application   64
   dispute resolution under   194
   collective agreement disability provision and   157